CW00820092

Texts in Philosophy
Volume 24

Karl Popper

A Centenary Assessment

Volume I

Life and Times, and Values in a World of Facts

Texts in Philosophy Series Editors
Vincent F. Hendriks   vincent@hum.ku.dk
John Symons   jsymons@utep.edu
Dov Gabbay   dov.gabbay@kcl.ac.uk

Karl Popper

A Centenary Assessment
Volume I
Life and Times, and Values in a World of Facts

Edited by

Ian Jarvie
Karl Milford
and
David Miller

This edition is a reprint of the Ashgate edition of 2006.

ISBN 978-1-84890-190-2

College Publications
Scientific Director: Dov Gabbay
Managing Director: Jane Spurr

http://www.collegepublications.co.uk

Original cover design by Laraine Welch

Printed by Lightning Source, Milton Keynes, UK

Contents

Part 2   Values in a World of Facts

List of Figures

Preface

For five warm summer days (3-7 July 2002), more than 300 people from more than 50 countries attended KARL POPPER 2002, a congress held in Vienna to commemorate the 100th anniversary of Popper's birth (28 July 1902). The principal activity at the meetings held in the main building of the University of Vienna, his alma mater, was, in keeping with Popper's outlook, critical engagement with his intellectual achievement in the many fields to which he contributed. Besides the investigation, development, and critical assessment of Popper's ideas, participants were able to enjoy a walking tour of Vienna sites relevant to Popper's early career, a recital of his organ fugue at the church of St Michael in Heiligenstadt, an exhibition at the Palais Palffy of his life and work, the unveiling of a bronze bust in the *Arkadenhof* in the University main building, and the opening ceremony at the City Hall (*Rathaus*) at which the Honorary President of the Congress, Professor Dr Hans Albert, gave the Inaugural Address. There was also an excursion after the congress to the University at Klagenfurt, where Popper's working library is housed.

The three volumes are a selection from more than 200 invited lectures and contributed papers presented at Vienna. The cull was made as follows. Chairs of sessions and members of the programme committee made an initial selection based upon what they had heard and read. Contributions planned for publication elsewhere were excluded. Every selected paper was sent to two referees. Authors made their final revisions in the light of the referees' reports. We are grateful to those who shortened their papers on request.

In addition to Albert's lecture (in both English and German) and the Closing Address given by Professor Marcello Pera, Volume I contains papers on Popper's life and influence, and on democracy and the open society. Volumes II and III are devoted respectively to papers on Popper's metaphysics and epistemology, and to papers on the various sciences to which he contributed.

The notes on the contributors and editors have been revised for this edition. The text of the volume is otherwise identical with that of the Ashgate edition of 2006, except for the correction of a few typographical and linguistic errors, some amendments to the index, and some inconsequential formatting changes.

KARL POPPER 2002 was more than six years in the planning. Many were involved in its organization, but it would not have taken place without the heroic efforts of Heidi König in Vienna. The editors should like to thank, in addition, the speakers, chairs, and referees, and Mrs Melitta Mew and the Karl Popper Charitable Trust. All royalties earned by these three volumes will go to the Trust.

Ian Jarvie
Karl Milford
David Miller

Notes on the Contributors

(*revised 2016*)

Hans Albert, formerly Professor of Sociology and Philosophy of Science at the University of Mannheim, is the author of numerous books on critical rationalist themes. He is academic advisor to the SERIES IN THE PHILOSOPHY OF KARL R. POPPER AND CRITICAL RATIONALISM (Rodopi, Brill), and to the Austrian College, Alpbach.

John T. Blackmore is a historian with interests in science and philosophy. Most of his publications have been on Ernst Mach and Ludwig Boltzmann. They include two books on Boltzmann (both 1995) and one on Mach (2001). He and his colleagues Ryoichi Itagaki and Setsuko Tanaka have published more recently several further books on Mach, including *Ernst Mach's Science: Its Character and Influence on Einstein and Others* (Tokai University Press 2006) and *Mach's Philosophy: Pro and Con* (Sentinel Open Press 2009).

Bruce Caldwell is a Research Professor of Economics and Director of the Center for the History of Political Economy at Duke University. He is the author of *Hayek's Challenge: An Intellectual History of F. A. Hayek* (University of Chicago Press, 2004), and since 2002 has served as the General Editor of the book series, *The Collected Works of F. A. Hayek*. E-mail: `bruce.caldwell@duke.edu`

Hans-Joachim Dahms worked in a number of projects at the Vienna Circle Institute in Vienna until his retirement in 2011 (mainly about the history of the philosophy of science). He lives now in Berlin (Germany) and continues to publish about the history and philosophy of the social sciences as well as Austrian and German university history. E-mail: `dahmsh6@univie.ac.at`

Malachi Haim Hacohen (PhD, Columbia) is the Fred W. Shaffer Associate Professor of History, Political Science, and Religion at Duke University. His *Karl Popper – The Formative Years, 1902-1945*, CUP 2000, has won several prizes. His book *Jacob and Esau Between Nation and Empire: A Jewish European History* is in preparation. E-mail: `mhacohen@duke.edu`

Troels Eggers Hansen was Librarian at Copenhagen University Library from 1963 to 1999. Author of 'Confrontation and Objectivity', *Danish Yearbook of Philosophy*, 1970. Editor of 'Bibliography of the writings of Karl Popper', included in *The Philosophy of Karl Popper*, Open Court 1974; Karl Popper, *Die beiden Grundprobleme der Erkenntnistheorie* (1930–1933), Mohr Siebeck 1979, 1994; and Karl Popper, *Frühe Schriften* (1925–1936), *Gesammelte Werke I*, Mohr Siebeck 2006. E-mail: `troels.eggers.hansen@mail.dk`

Michel ter Hark is Professor of the Philosophy of Language and Cognition at the Faculty of Humanities of VU University Amsterdam. He has published on Popper's early psychology. His book *Popper, Otto Selz and the Rise of Evolutionary Epistemology*, CUP 2004, is a close study of the relation between Popper's early psychology and his epistemology. E-mail: `m.r.m.ter.hark@vu.nl`

Rachael Knight, following five years of German studies, including research and study in Germany, worked for the New Zealand Embassy in Berlin. She later obtained a degree in law at the University of London and currently works for New Zealand's Immigration and Protection Tribunal. E-mail: `rachaelknight@sunbourg.com`

Heidi König has been a research worker in projects on linguistics and translation, philosophy of science, and Vienna Circle philosophy (Institute for Philosophy of Science/Institute Vienna Circle/Institute for Contemporary History, Vienna). She has co-edited Volume 5 of the Moritz Schlick Edition and has published on the history of philosophy of science, science in translation (General Relativity in the English speaking world), and political philosophy. E-mail: `heidi.koenig@univie.ac.at`

Nicholas Maxwell is Emeritus Reader at University College London. He has published eight books arguing for a revolution in academic inquiry, including: *What's Wrong With Science?*, Bran's Head Books 1976, *From Knowledge to Wisdom*, Blackwell 1984, *The Comprehensibility of the Universe*, OUP 1998, *Is Science Neurotic?*, Imperial College 2004, and *How Universities Can Help Create a Wiser World: The Urgent Need for an Academic Revolution*, Imprint Academic 2014. Web site: `www.ucl.ac.uk/from-knowledge-to-wisdom`. E-mail: `nicholas.maxwell@ucl.ac.uk`

Ali Paya is an Adjunct Professor of Philosophy at the National Research Institute for Science Policy in Iran, a Senior Visiting Research Fellow at the Centre for the Study of Democracy, University of Westminster, and a Professor of Philosophy at the Islamic College in London. Among his publications, *Analytic Philosophy: Problems and Prospects* received the award for the best philosophical book of 2003 in Iran. His recent publications include *The Misty Land of Ideas and the Light of Dialogue: An Anthology of Comparative Philosophy: Western and Islamic* (editor, 2014), *A Critical Pathology of the Social Sciences and Humanities in Iran* (co-author, 2015), *Analytic Philosophy from a Critical Rationalist Point of View* (2016), E-mail: `A.Paya1@westminster.ac.uk`; `alipaya@hotmail.com`

Marcello Pera has taught philosophy at the University of Catania and philosophy of science at the University of Pisa. He has been Visiting Fellow at the Pittsburgh Center for Philosophy of Science, the Van Leer Jerusalem Foundation, MIT, and the LSE. He is the author of many publications, including *The Ambiguous Frog. The Galvani-Volta Controversy on Animal Electricity*, Princeton 1992, and *The Discourses of Science*, Chicago 1994. He was a member of the Italian Senate from 1996 until 2013, and from May 2001 to May 2006 served as its President. E-mail: `marcellopera@yahoo.it`

Raphael Sassower is Professor and Chair of Philosophy at the University of Colorado, Colorado Springs. His latest publications include *Confronting Disaster: An Existential Response to Technoscience*, Rowman & Littlefield 2004, and (with Louis Cicotello) *Political Blind Spots: Reading the Ideology of Images*, Rowman & Littlefield 2006. His *Popper's Legacy* was published by Acumen in 2006. E-mail: `rsassower@gmail.com`

Ulrich Steinvorth is Professor of Philosophy at the University of Hamburg. Main areas of interest: ethics, political philosophy, and metaphysics. Recent publications: *Gleiche Freiheit*, Akademie Verlag 1999; *Was ist Vernunft?: Eine philosophische Einführung*, Beck 2002; *Docklosigkeit oder zur Metaphysik der Moderne*, Mentis 2006. E-mail: `ulrich.steinvorth@uni-hamburg.de`

Harald Stelzer is Professor of Political Philosophy at the University of Graz. He has been a research assistant at the University of Minnesota and a Fulbright scholar at the University of Washington. He has also worked as project scientist at the Institute for Advanced Sustainability Studies in Potsdam. His latest book on the moral philosophy of communitarianism has been published as Volume XXI in the SERIES IN THE PHILOSOPHY OF KARL R. POPPER AND CRITICAL RATIONALISM. E-mail: `harald.stelzer@uni-graz.at`

Geoffrey Stokes is Deputy Pro Vice-Chancellor (Research) in the College of Business at RMIT University. He works in the areas of social and political theory and democratic theory. He is the author of *Popper: Philosophy, Politics and Scientific Method*, Polity 1998 and, with Jeremy Shearmur, is the co-editor, of *The Cambridge Companion to Popper*, 2016. E-mail: `geoffrey.stokes@rmit.edu.au`

Kiichi Tachibana is Professor at Akita University. He was President of the Japan Popper Society between 2002 and 2006. His chief papers written in English are 'Moral Decision in Popper's Critical Rationalism' and 'Tolerant Rationalism', both in the *Annals of the Japan Association for Philosophy of Science*. He has also published Japanese translations of Magee's *Popper* and Agassi's *The Continuing Revolution*. E-mail: `tachiba@ed.akita-u.ac.jp`

Andrew Vincent is Professor Emeritus at the University of Sheffield and Distinguished Honorary Professor of Political Philosophy at the University of Cardiff. He is author of several books, most recently *The Politics of Human Rights*, OUP 2010, *British Idealism: A Guide for the Perplexed*, Continuum 2012, and *Comparative Political Thought* (edited with Michael Freeden), Routledge 2013. E-mail: `andrew.vincent@sheffield.ac.uk;` `vincentaw1@cardiff.ac.uk`

John Wettersten is Adjunct Professor at the University of Mannheim. He has published over seventy articles. His books are *Learning from Error*, Open Court 1984 (with William Berkson); *The Roots of Critical Rationalism*, Rodopi 1993; *Whewell's Critics: Have They Prevented Him from Doing*

Good?, Rodopi 2005; and *How Do Institutions Steer Events?*, Ashgate 2006. E-mail: `wettersten@t-online.de`

Renate Wustinger studied romance languages and music at the University of Vienna. She has been a grammar school teacher, lecturer at the Institute of Romance Languages at the University of Vienna, and a teacher trainer at numerous in-service training courses. In 1993 she obtained a diploma as a professional supervisor. Since 2000 she has been a member of the Board at the Sir Karl Popper School in Vienna, a pilot project for the highly gifted. She retired in 2012. E-mail: `wustinger@chello.at`

Notes on the Editors

(*revised 2016*)

Ian Jarvie (editor in chief) is Distinguished Research Professor in Philosophy (Emeritus) at York University, Toronto, and Managing Editor of the journal *Philosophy of the Social Sciences*. His books include *The Revolution in Anthropology*, Routledge 1964; *Philosophy of the Film*, Routledge 1987; and *The Republic of Science*, Rodopi 2001. E-mail: `jarvie@yorku.ca`

Karl Milford is Associate Professor of Economics at the University of Vienna. He has written extensively on the epistemological views of Carl Menger, for example in *Zu den Lösungsversuchen des Induktions und Abgrenzungsproblems bei Carl Menger*, Verlag der Österreichischen Akademie der Wissenschaften 1989. E-mail: `karl.milford@univie.ac.at`

David Miller is Emeritus Reader in Philosophy at the University of Warwick, where he taught logic (and some other things) from 1969 until 2007. He is the editor of *Popper Selections*, Princeton 1985, and author of *Critical Rationalism. A Restatement and Defence*, Open Court 1994, and of *Out of Error. Further Essays on Critical Rationalism*, Ashgate 2006. Web site: `http://www.warwick.ac.uk/go/dwmiller`; E-mail: `dwmiller57@yahoo.com`

Introduction

Karl Popper and Philosophy in the Twentieth Century[*]

Hans Albert

Without doubt Karl Popper is one of the most important thinkers of the twentieth century. He was born here in Vienna one hundred years ago, in July 1902. He first developed his philosophical views in Vienna, taking issue with ideas he encountered here, first of all with the ideas of the 'Vienna Circle' — he was nicknamed the 'official opposition' — and also with the various kinds of Kantianism he found here, as well as Marxism, Psychoanalysis, and Individual Psychology.

That we shall be trying to discuss his views critically is in accordance with his outlook, for in his philosophy — which he named 'critical rationalism' — he gave central importance to criticism. He was convinced that one honours a view exactly by taking great pains to analyse it critically.

Popper's ideas have influenced above all the development of the philosophy of science and of social philosophy, but also the development of many sciences and the public discussion of political problems. As to the influence of his philosophical thinking on other areas of cultural life, there are two other philosophers who have a greater influence: namely Ludwig Wittgenstein and Martin Heidegger, whose ideas were strongly opposed to Popper's. In my view, these thinkers both had a completely different significance from Popper's for rationalism and for thinking in the tradition of the Enlightenment. In order to show this it may be useful to consider briefly the philosophical situation at the beginning of the last century.

At this time there were in Europe — apart from various versions of Kantianism — two great philosophical reform movements: the analytic movement inspired by Bertrand Russell and the phenomenological movement founded by Edmund Husserl. Both movements were anchored in the tradition of European rationalism and realism and took a positive attitude towards science. Whereas the analytic movement belonged to empiricism, the phenomenological movement was a new version of apriorism. Only the first movement is associated with developments in modern logic, but the second movement also proceeded from logical investigations. For the first of these movements Ludwig Wittgenstein played a role similar to that played by Martin Heidegger for the second.

[*]I am very grateful to Gretl Albert and to the editors for help with the translation.

Already in his first book, *Tractatus Logico-Philosophicus* (1921/1922),
Wittgenstein had dealt with the linguistic constitution of the world and
thereby given analytic thinking a turn that led away from Russell's realism.
Later he moved in his analysis of concrete language games into a kind of
pragmatism — which had the consequence that not only metaphysical investigations but also epistemological ones would be obsolete. In phenomenological
thinking already its founder himself, Edmund Husserl, went over to transcendental analysis. His pupil and critic Heidegger then initiated with his main work
Sein und Zeit (1927) a hermeneutic turn in this approach which was also connected with the claim to have overcome metaphysics and epistemology. In
both cases the critical impulse that had inspired these movements got lost.
Their former rationalism gave way to a kind of thinking that was incompatible
with scientific thinking and with a world view shaped by the sciences.

With the first of these philosophers, namely Wittgenstein, Popper took
issue already in his first book.[1] The contrast between their views shows
very well in the famous confrontation that took place in 1946 at the Cambridge Moral Sciences Club, reported by several persons in quite different
ways.[2] As is well known, Wittgenstein had always rejected the claim that
there are genuine philosophical problems. When Popper gave him examples
of such problems Wittgenstein denied their philosophical character. Wittgenstein had already developed the ideas about language games that were published posthumously as his later philosophy. Therewith he made his departure
from philosophical thinking. His influence was not diminished by this.[3]

Popper never himself discussed the views of the other of the two thinkers I
have mentioned, namely Martin Heidegger. He did mention him occasionally,
characterizing him as a representative of irrationalism. Heidegger attacked
modern culture in so radical a way that he tried to escape from rational
thinking altogether and to call into question both logic and the descriptive
function of language together with the idea of truth connected to both.[4] The
question of the meaning of being, which he formulated in his book *Sein und
Zeit*, was answered neither in this book nor later, or even clarified. Nevertheless, he tried in this book to treat problems that, at least in his opinion,
arose out of the philosophical situation of his time. Later he more and more
abandoned the cognitive enterprise of the search for truth and came to rest
in a word music that is demanding and not only for the normal reader.

His most influential pupil, Hans-Georg Gadamer, who is today considered
a classic hermeneutical thinker, did not follow Heidegger into this blind alley. But he continued the antirationalism of Heidegger.[5] In any case, the
hermeneutic turn, which goes back to Heidegger and Gadamer, had consequences that strengthened those problematic traits of the German tradition

---

[1]Cp. Popper (1930-1933), *passim*; cp. also his (1945), Chapter 11, note 51, where Popper deals with the *Tractatus Logico-Philosophicus*.

[2]Popper (1974/1976) § 26; Watkins (1999); Edmonds & Eidinow (2001).

[3]Recently his influence has been deemed less than was usual earlier; cp. Grayling (1988).

[4]Cp. the analysis in Albert (1994), pp. 1-35.

[5]Ibidem, footnote 4, pp. 36-77, and my (2002).

that are opposed to the Enlightenment. There are attempts today to reconcile this philosophical approach with that of Karl Popper.[6] But they seem to be based on glaring misunderstandings.[7]

I myself became acquainted with the thought of Karl Popper only in the fifties of the last century, that is, shortly after the Second World War, after a long journey through philosophical thinking that began with the philosophy of history of Oswald Spengler and led me finally to the philosophy of the Vienna Circle. At that time it seemed to me that Popper's views belonged to Logical Positivism. Then I met Popper in 1958 at the 'European Forum Alpbach'[8] and found out that this was an error, though an error in which I was not at all alone and that is still with us.

The first thing I learnt was that the Vienna Circle's criticism of metaphysics was untenable because there are logical relationships between particular metaphysical propositions and propositions of the empirical sciences,[9] so that the well-known thesis that metaphysical sentences are meaningless is invalid. Later I had even to accept that the views of the Vienna Circle have themselves a partially metaphysical character[10] and that it might be difficult to avoid metaphysical propositions totally. That, of course, may be a thesis on which it is not possible to reach consensus.[11]

Since, as it were, I have now let the cat out of the bag, I should like to say briefly how I understand the critical rationalism that I defend. As central components of this view I am used to listing critical realism, consistent fallibilism, and methodological criticism or revisionism, and I believe this list to be in agreement with the views of Karl Popper. But that is, of course, only a rough answer that would need much elaboration for which there is no time here.[12] As is well known, the devil lurks in the details.

As to Popper's realism, it stands in contrast to the antirealist views that have spread even into analytical philosophy. Fallibilism, the thesis of the fallibility of reason, a view that Popper defended against classical justificationism, seems to be increasingly popular, but with respect to this one often finds appeals to Charles Sanders Peirce without acknowledgement of the problems connected with this appeal.[13] Popper's methodological revisionism, which

---

[6]Cp. Grondin (1999a), p. 336. Grondin refers to the rehabilitation of prejudice in Gadamer's thought and to the treatment of this problem by Popper.

[7]The same is true for Grondin's hints about deficits in Popper's thought. Cp. Grondin (1999b) in Kanitscheider & Wetz (1999), and the criticisms in my (1999b).

[8]This international organization was founded in August 1945 by Otto Molden, a leading member of the Austrian resistance against Hitler, together with Simon Moser, a *Dozent* of the University of Innsbruck. It has been very important for the diffusion of Popper's ideas in the German speaking lands. Otto Molden, who died in June 2002, was inspired by the vision of a unified Europe. Cp. his (1981).

[9]There are for instance logical relationships between the metaphysical general causal principle, causal laws, and singular causal propositions; cp. Watkins (1958).

[10]Cp. Bergmann (1954).

[11]As far as I can see, some representatives of empiricism are even today not prepared to accept this thesis; cp. the discussion in: Böhm, Holweg, & Hoock (2002), p. 117-125.

[12]Cp. my (1987).

[13]Cp. for a critical analysis Schantz (1998).

arose from his emphasis on the falsifiability of theoretical statements and the demand for serious attempts at refutation, was later developed into a methodology for general problem solving not only in the realm of knowledge but also in other realms of human praxis.[14]

If critical rationalism is characterized in this way it can easily be seen that it involves metaphysical views, especially views that have a close connection with the cognitive praxis of the factual sciences. These views are, of course, following Popper, not to be treated as dogmas but as hypotheses. Popper has tried to show how metaphysical propositions can be rationally discussed and he himself has made contributions to this kind of discussion. But many of his followers who are prepared to accept this in principle have partly questioned the solutions that he has proposed to some central problems. This is true above all for his proposed solution to the body–mind problem, which goes back to his three-world view, and for his theory of propensities. In addition, his proposals for the solution of problems of the social sciences have been criticized, because in them he seems to have abandoned his general methodological views. That he has solved totally or at least partly the problem of induction is usually accepted by the representatives of critical rationalism. But there is a controversy about the question how his solution is to be interpreted. Here is not the place to consider this matter.

As far as I can see, there are three great controversies in which Karl Popper's thought has played a central role. One of them is the discussion with the representatives of Logical Positivism that I have mentioned above, in which he for the first time publicly offered his views for discussion. As is well known, he developed them into a voluminous manuscript with the title *Die beiden Grundprobleme der Erkenntnistheorie*, which at that time could not be published because of its size.[15] A radically shortened version was published as *Logik der Forschung*[16] and became a classic of modern philosophy of science. It contains his criticism of the central theses of Logical Positivism and of the conventionalism of Hugo Dingler in connection with an attempt to solve the two problems that he deemed to be the central problems of epistemology, namely the problem of demarcation and the problem of induction. The first problem, which he traced back to Kant, is the problem of the demarcation of science from metaphysical and other systems of propositions; the second is the question, already treated by David Hume, how far experience can legitimately be used to predict events in the future, a question that, as is well known, was negatively answered by Hume.

At that time Popper tried to solve both problems simultaneously by using the methodology developed in this book, which is usually discussed under the rubric 'falsificationism'. The rules he formulated had the aim of guiding the

---

[14]In factual science it can be used as a rational heuristic for the guidance of cognitive praxis; cp. my essay (1984) and Gadenne (1996). For its applicability in politics cp. Magee (1999).

[15]Later it was published in an incomplete version. Cp. Popper (1930-1933).

[16]Popper (1935).

cognitive praxis of the factual sciences. Since, as has justly been claimed,[17] Popper from the outset took into account the social dimension of this praxis, one can speak with a certain authority of an 'institutional turn in the philosophy of science'. For his primary concern was not the logical analysis of certain propositions, but the institutionalization of adequate norms of scientific research.[18] As far as necessary he did, of course, use logical analysis as an instrument for this purpose. The emphasis was on the strict testing of theories designed to lead to their refutation. Their corroboration would be the result of the failure of such attempts at refutation.

The relationship of Popper to the Vienna Circle is often represented as if he had exaggerated the differences between his views and the views of members of the Circle. Their dispute with Popper at the time seems then to be between different variants of positivism. But that conceals a principal contrast that Popper stressed. He had, for instance, never participated in the linguistic turn characteristic of the Vienna Circle, namely the aim to eliminate metaphysics, something that led their philosophical thinking into a blind alley.[19]

In later work Popper further developed his methodology against the background of metaphysical realism and connected it with an evolutionary epistemology,[20] which refers to Darwinian ideas. As is well known, another Viennese, namely Popper's friend Konrad Lorenz, developed in the forties of the last century a Kantian evolutionary epistemology.[21] Already in Popper's first book we can find the central idea of this doctrine.[22]

Many thinkers closely connected with critical rationalism confine themselves to Popper's methodology and regard other components of his philosophy with scepticism. Among the generality of philosophers of science Popper's claim to have solved within his methodology the problem of induction is controversial to this day. Above all that is the case with the so-called pragmatic problem of induction.[23]

The second of the controversies mentioned above began in the 1960s after the publication of Thomas Kuhn's *The Structure of Scientific Revolutions*.[24] It is usual to refer to this as the 'challenge of the history of science' to logical empiricism, associated with the names of Norwood Russell Hanson, Thomas Kuhn, Paul Feyerabend and Imre Lakatos. Popper's views have been included in this attack in spite of the fact that Popper had anticipated many of the objections to neoclassical empiricism. He had for instance rejected the positivistic two-language thesis, and stressed the theory-ladenness of observational statements. He had brought the historical dimension into philosophy of

---

[17]Cp. Jarvie (2001).

[18]Cp. for this problem the above mentioned book by Jarvie, and also Max Albert (2002).

[19]Cp. for this, Hacohen (2000), pp. 208-213, where the 'positivistic legend' is refuted.

[20]Cp. Popper (1972).

[21]Cp. Lorenz (1941) and Lorenz (1973).

[22]Cp. Popper (1930-1933), § 11, p. 88.

[23]Cp. Böhm, Holweg, & Hoock (2002).

[24]Cp. Kuhn (1962).

science.[25] Meanwhile I think it has transpired that the arguments put forward against Popper's methodology during the 1960s are not valid.[26] Much of what he objected to in the dominant views of that time is taken as obviously wrong today. Often enough, mentioning his name in this connection is conveniently forgotten.

The third controversy began in Germany, likewise in the sixties, in connection with a lecture given by Popper at a conference of sociologists at Tübingen in 1961. It was the so-called 'Positivist Dispute', in which the critical rationalism of Popper was attacked as a version of positivism by representatives of the Frankfurt School.[27] This controversy, in which Popper himself scarcely participated, began with grotesque misunderstandings on the side of the critics, misunderstandings that only slowly disappeared. Not only Popper's methodology of the social sciences was discussed, but also the social philosophy offered in his book *The Open Society and Its Enemies* (1945), to which I shall come back later.

Some of Popper's critics advanced against his views a transcendental epistemology in which an instrumentalistic interpretation of the natural sciences and an interpretation of the cultural and social sciences based on Gadamer's hermeneutics were combined with a criticism of ideology that went back to Marx and Freud. This epistemology also included a consensus theory of truth. Other critics of Popper, the Erlanger School, combined an epistemology going back to Dingler's idea of an ultimate foundation with the philosophy of Martin Heidegger. With these latter critics the reproach of positivism was changed to the reproach of scientism. They took aim at the fact that Popper had proposed a uniform methodology for all the factual sciences, for instance also for the cultural and social sciences. Strictly speaking, this criticism did not so much affect Popper himself, who with his conception of understanding had modified his former position in this respect, but rather the representatives of critical rationalism who had maintained his original methodological views. They are to be found above all in the social sciences.[28]

For Popper had originally accepted the search for causal laws and causal explanation as part of the aim of the social sciences. This aim seemed to him to be important for practical reasons, because nomological statements are in principle useful for social technology. Whoever thinks that social reforms are necessary is obviously dependent on the application of relevant technological insights. Popper thought that these were valuable for changing the institutional structure of society by adequate legislation. At the same time such insights make possible a criticism of utopian projects for social planning which are deemed necessary by some social philosophers. It has been said in criticism that Popper later abandoned his original views of the social sciences

---

[25]The methodological views of Imre Lakatos have also been influenced by Popper's ideas in this respect. Theoretical pluralism too is compatible with Popper's methodology; cp. my (1985) and my (1987).

[26]Cp. in defence of Popper, Andersson (1994); Musgrave (1999); Miller (1994).

[27]Cp. Adorno et. al. (1976).

[28]Cp. Vanberg (1975); Michael Schmid (1994); and also Meyer (2002).

and replaced the search for laws by the proposal to apply a problematic principle of rationality.[29] This replacement has also been criticized because it calls into question the possibility of a rational reform politics, although such politics had been an essential part of his original conception.

With that I come back to Popper's contribution to social philosophy and to his conception of an open society, which played an important role in public discussion in the last century. That century was marked by two world wars and by the rise and fall of two totalitarian systems. One of them began in the first of those wars and lasted about seventy years. The second of them brought us to the second of the wars and perished in it after twelve years. In his book *The Open Society and Its Enemies*[30] Karl Popper attempted to clarify the intellectual foundations of these systems and to analyse their character. He characterized them as closed societies and contrasted that to his idea of an open society.

As to Popper's analysis of the intellectual foundations of totalitarianism, it was soon criticized. Most of all, his critiques of Plato and Hegel were claimed by many to be defective,[31] but so was his critique of Karl Marx, whose work he had treated with great sympathy. Here is not the place to consider such matters. By contrast, Popper's conception of an open society scarcely played any role in Anglo-Saxon discussions in the second half of the twentieth century, except for some shortly after the end of the war. The centre of Anglo-Saxon discussions of the last part of the century was the theory of justice of John Rawls and views offered as alternatives to his. In Continental Europe, where the population had been directly confronted with the consequences of totalitarian systems, Popper's conception played a great role.[32] It has even had practical consequences that could hardly have been foreseen by Popper.[33]

It is one of the peculiarities of Popper's social philosophy that it is closely connected with his epistemology.[34] The fallibilism, the realism, and the critical approach of his epistemology are also the basis of his conception of social philosophy. The open society as it has been characterized by Popper is a society whose members have the possibility to decide freely about how to lead their lives and to participate in decisions about their common affairs. By the institutionalization of competition and criticism in all social realms such societies are in a condition to find new solutions for problems of all kinds, to analyse and to discuss these solutions, and to come to reforms. That is, they can practise the kind of problem-solving behaviour that has been deemed appropriate by Popper.[35] In this way the methodological criticism

---

[29] Cp. the works mentioned in footnote 28 above.

[30] Cp. Popper (1945).

[31] Cp. Hacohen (2000), pp. 438f., where the author tries to show that Popper's criticism of Hegel does not comply with the requirements that he himself has stated for serious criticism.

[32] Cp. Jarvie & Pralong (1999a), pp. 7ff.

[33] Above all I think here of the activity of George Soros and the significance of his Open Society Institutes and of the Central European University founded by him.

[34] Cp. above all, Jarvie (2001).

[35] Cp. Magee (1999), where the author tries to show that this kind of behaviour in politics is not at all usual.

and revisionism of Popper's epistemology can be anchored in the institutional arrangements and in the traditions of a society. With respect to politics this means that power has been tamed by law. Therefore the rule of law — the constitutional state — is the centrepiece of a social order of this kind.[36]

The basic value of Popper's idea of the open society is, as he himself once pointed out, human freedom.[37] But it was clear to him that this freedom has to be protected by the state and that on the other hand only a state that is controlled by free citizens can protect their freedom. His idea of an open society is an attempt to transform the European idea of freedom into a sociological construction that can be seen as an ideal type in the sense of Max Weber.[38] Three remarks are perhaps appropriate here. First: the idea of such a society is an ideal, so that a concrete society can approximate it more or less. Second: this ideal can be used as a standard for criticizing the existing social order and also as a guide for attempts to reform them. And third: attempts to approximate this ideal can lead to very different constitutions, for in the endeavour to achieve it one has to take into account the different historical conditions in each case.

Karl Popper embedded the construction of his model of the open society into a historical, sociological, and anthropological framework which has inspired many critical examinations.[39] For its assessment it is therefore reasonable to distinguish between his normative project and the theoretical hypotheses and historical analyses connected with it, which have turned out to be more or less questionable. As to the question whether science as an institutional structure can be seen as a paradigm of an open society as Popper has sometimes insinuated, it is also a question whose answer presupposes an analysis of the respective facts.

With respect to this there is one point that seems to me to be important and should be emphasized. It is the close connection that in Popper's view exists between institutional support for freedom of thought and of communication characteristic of an open society, and the possibility of the growth of knowledge.[40] Without the assumption of a connection of this kind it would be difficult to understand the significance of the rules that he has proposed in his methodology, as far as their social dimension is concerned.

With this we come back to the second of the above mentioned controversies in which critical rationalism played a central role. In this controversy there emerged Kuhn's paradigm thesis, a view that has been criticized by Popper as 'the myth of the framework'.[41] He later devoted to it a careful examination in which he considered an important aspect of the problem of rationality that is

---

[36] Cp. Popper (1992, Volume I, pp. IX-XIV).

[37] Cp. Popper & Lorenz (1985), p. 136.

[38] Cp. Jarvie (1999).

[39] Cp. for instance Jarvie (1999) and Hall (1999).

[40] Already in Popper's main work of social philosophy this connection is to be found; cp. for instance note 13 of Chapter 13 in (1945), where he refers to a possible sociological law of this kind.

[41] Cp. Popper (1970).

also relevant for the problems discussed in the third controversy.[42] The view criticized by Popper is that a rational and fruitful discussion is impossible if the participants do not have a common framework of fundamental assumptions or at least accept them for purposes of discussion.[43] Popper attacks this view and contrasts it with the thesis that the very confrontation of different frameworks of this kind — as well as cultural differences — can lead to fruitful discussion and in fact has led to them. He further claims that to be fruitful a discussion of this kind need not lead to a consensus. Therefore a consensus is necessary neither initially nor as the outcome of such a discussion.

The myth of the framework amounts to the thesis that a rational discussion of principles is impossible: *De principiis non disputandum est.* If that were the case then so-called ultimate presuppositions would be immune from any criticism. But this thesis has turned out to be untenable.[44] By the way, it has fatal consequences for any cognitive practice. That is to say it has the consequence that one dogmatically asserts one's own principles as true or one accepts a relativism with respect to truth by which the truth of propositions is relativized to the preferred frame of presuppositions.[45] This is the dilemma between foundationalism and relativism described as insurmountable by Leszek Kolakowski.[46]

I encountered this 'myth of the framework' very early when I became an adherent of Oswald Spengler's philosophy of history. He defended the view that there is no meaning between cultures. Only within the frame of one of the high cultures he described were there meaning and the possibility of understanding. Of course, the relativity of truth he was proposing was not applied to his own conception.

The theory of science of the German pragmatist Hugo Dingler, whose views Popper analysed in his first book, likewise perpetuated the 'myth of the framework' though without relativistic consequences. In Dingler's view the only frameworks that had to be taken into account for scientific research were Aristotelian logic, Euclidean geometry, and Newtonian physics.

In recent decades in Europe and the Anglo-Saxon world antirealistic tendencies have spread. These come out of a common pragmatic-hermeneutic turn in which the 'myth of the framework' is more or less accepted, sometimes with relativistic consequences, sometimes with the claim of an ultimate foundation. In Germany this includes the universal hermeneutics of Hans-Georg Gadamer mentioned above and the other versions of transcendental hermeneutics developed by Karl Otto Apel and by Jürgen Habermas out of the ideas of Gadamer, Horkheimer, and Scheler, as well as the constructivism of the Erlanger School of Paul Lorenzen, which combines ideas of Dingler and Heidegger. In Anglo Saxon countries it includes so-called 'internal realism', which is Hilary Putnam's version of pragmatism, and other versions which I cannot consider in

---

[42] Cp. his essay 'The Myth of the Framework' in his (1994), pp. 33-64.

[43] Ibidem, pp. 34f.

[44] For a criticism of this thesis cp. ibidem, pp. 59-61, and my (1985) pp. 45-47.

[45] Cp. my (1996).

[46] Cp. Kolakowski (1977), p. 96.

more detail here.[47] The consensus theories of truth connected with them I
only mention, without considering them more closely.[48]

With that I come back to what I have said about the philosophical situation at the beginning of the last century. I have hinted at the two reform
movements that developed at that time in the frame of epistemological realism
and rationalism: namely the analytic and phenomenological movements. The
versions of Kantianism of that time I have not considered. But also within
Kantianism there was a kind of realism, namely the transcendental realism
of Oswald Külpe, which can be seen as a precursor of Popper's philosophy.
His critical examination of Kantian philosophy and his comparative analysis
of the epistemological conceptions of his time led Külpe to the view that a
hypothetical realism has to be preferred to all alternatives. In Külpe Kant's
transcendental realism is replaced by a conception that treats the question
of the conditions of the possibility of knowledge in the frame of a realistic
research programme. In his view also the classical idea of foundation is abandoned and replaced by the assumption that a useful problem solution can be
attained only by a comparative analysis of possible solutions on the basis of
certain criteria that make possible a decision between them.[49]

In contrast to this, modern forms of antirealism that have developed above
all under the influence of the ideas of Heidegger and Wittgenstein, are nothing else than new versions of transcendental idealism in which language as
the constitutive factor has replaced the mental capacity for knowledge. They
do differ from the Kantian view in one essential point. Already with Kant a
central role is played by the idea of a categorical framework that is not only
a necessary condition of knowledge but moreover shapes its objects. But in
modern antirealism this framework loses its uniqueness. It becomes culturally
and historically variable and in spite of this remains immune to any criticism. That means that this antirealism takes over an essential component of
classical rationalism, that is, the idea of the immunity of so-called ultimate
presuppositions from any criticism. But it combines this idea with the highly
variable results of cognitive practice. By that means truth is relativized to the
framework that is accepted in each case. But this framework is valid only for
a community in which a consensus about its validity obtains. The idealism
of the Kantian theory of constitution is connected to the relativism of the
modern theory of consensus. The idea of objective truth as a regulative idea
of cognitive practice is sacrificed more or less openly to the idea of consensus.
The aim is not the adequate representation of facts but the fabrication of
systems of propositions that for some reason are able to find the agreement
of a community. With that, pragmatism has been victorious over realism.

The critical rationalism of Karl Popper is in any case incompatible with all
these views. It connects, as I have already related, a realistic metaphysics and

---

[47]For a criticism cp. Gadenne (1998).

[48]But cp. Musgrave (1993), pp. 247-273, for a criticism of these views.

[49]Popper also arrived at this outcome; cp. his (1972), Chapter 2, § 5, and later also Devitt
(1991), p. 61.

epistemology with a consistent fallibilism and a methodological revisionism and therefore is not compatible with ultimate justifications nor with any kind of relativism with respect to truth. It rejects the 'myth of the framework', and substitutes for the search for certainty, and for the demand for consensus at any cost, the search for truth, which is not restricted to any framework. With that it continues under modern conditions the tradition of the Enlightenment, as much as regards the search for knowledge as with respect to its moral and political consequences.

With this I come finally to a question that I have not so far treated, namely the question of whether Popper's critical rationalism can answer ethical problems. As is well known Popper himself declared that ethics is not a science but that science has an ethical basis. That, of course, does not mean that one cannot treat ethical problems rationally for his methodology of criticism applies not only to scientific problems but to problems of all kinds. He has drawn attention to the possibility that in the realm of ethics as much as in the area of scientific knowledge we learn from our errors without having at our disposal a criterion of absolute moral rightness.[50] We are for instance able to use scientific knowledge in order to criticize ethical views with the help of adequate bridge principles such as 'ought implies can'.[51] With respect to ethics a relapse into relativism can be avoided also if one practises Popper's criticist methodology, which admits the revisability of standards in this realm also.[52]

It is also well known that Popper explicitly recommended certain answers to ethical questions. For instance he recommended an ethics of tolerance that is congruent with his fallibilist epistemology. This epistemology is compatible not only with a pluralism of theoretical traditions but also with a pluralism of values. It is against the demand for a comprehensive consensus,[53] a characteristic feature of, for example, the views of thinkers who stick to the idea of a community of faith. A community of this kind has in any case nothing to do with Popper's ideal of an open society.[54]

With that I come back to the attempts mentioned above to harmonize Popper's critical rationalism with the versions of hermeneutical pragmatism that are to be found, above all, in contemporary European thought. I think that we render poor service to the tradition of the Enlightenment as represented by Popper if we take pains to blur the differences between philosophical views with the aim of reconciling the disputing parties. An illusionary consensus such as could be attained in this way is in any case incompatible with

---

[50] Cp. Popper (1945/1962), Addendum to Volume II, 'Facts, Standards, and Truth: A Further Criticism of Relativism' (1961), pp. 369-396. Cp. also Pralong (1999), and 'Abschnitt 6: Erkenntnis, Moral und soziale Ordnung', in my (2000), pp. 76-91.

[51] Cp. my (1985), Chapter III, 'Knowledge and Decision'.

[52] With respect to the revisability of standards cp. Nilsson (2000).

[53] Above all we find this demand in the work of Jürgen Habermas, for the central idea of his philosophical conception is 'undistorted communication' ('die Idee der unverkürzten Verständigung'). This conception is a variant of the hermeneutics of Gadamer.

[54] For a criticism of the ideal of consensus cp. for instance also Rescher (1993); Engländer (2000), (2002); and Steinhoff (2001).

the striving after truth and clarity that is characteristic of the tradition of the Enlightenment. A fruitful discussion may, as Popper justly stressed, conclude with the outcome that the disputing parties have not attained a consensus but they have attained more clarity about the alternatives that are open to them.

Bibliography

Adorno, T. W., Albert, H., Dahrendorf, R., Habermas, J. & Popper, K. R. (1976). *The Positivist Dispute in German Sociology*. London: Heinemann.

Albert, H. (1984). 'Transcendental Realism and Rational Heuristics. Critical Rationalism and the Problem of Method'. In G. Andersson, editor (1984), pp. 29-46. *Rationality in Science and Politics*. Dordrecht: D. Reidel Publishing Company. Reprinted as Chapter II of Albert (1999a).

———— (1985). *Treatise on Critical Reason*. Princeton NJ: Princeton University Press.

———— (1987). *Kritik der reinen Erkenntnislehre*. Tübingen: J. C. B. Mohr (Paul Siebeck).

———— (1994). *Kritik der reinen Hermeneutik. Der Antirealismus und das Problem des Verstehens*. Tübingen: J. C. B. Mohr (Paul Siebeck).

———— (1996). 'Der Mythos des Rahmens. Zur Kritik des idealistischen Rückfalls im modernen Denken'. In Gadenne & Wendel (1996), pp. 9-28.

———— (1999a). *Between Social Science, Religion and Politics. Essays on Critical Rationalism*. Amsterdam & Atlanta: Editions Rodopi B.V.

———— (1999b). 'Der Naturalismus und das Problem des Verstehens'. In Kanitscheider & Wetz (1999), pp. 3-20.

———— (2000). *Kritischer Rationalismus. Vier Kapitel zur Kritik illusionären Denkens*. Tübingen: J. C. B. Mohr (Paul Siebeck).

———— (2002). 'Critical Rationalism and Universal Hermeneutics'. In J. Malpas, U. Arnswald, & J. Kertscher, editors (2002), pp. 15-24. *Gadamer's Century. Essays in Honour of Hans-Georg Gadamer*. Cambridge MA: MIT Press.

Albert M. (2002). 'Kritischer Rationalismus und die Verfassung der Wissenschaft'. In Böhm, Holweg, & Hoock (2002), pp. 231-241.

Andersson, G. (1994). *Criticism and the History of Science. Kuhn's, Lakatos's and Feyerabend's Criticisms of Critical Rationalism*. Leiden: Brill.

Bergmann, G. (1954). *The Metaphysics of Logical Positivism*. New York: Longmans, Green.

Böhm, J. M., Holweg, H., & Hoock, C., editors (2002). *Karl Poppers kritischer Rationalismus heute*. Tübingen: Mohr Siebeck.

Devitt M. (1991). *Realism and Truth*. 2nd edition. Oxford: Basil Blackwell.

Edmonds, D. & Eidinow, J. (2001). *Wittgenstein's Poker*. London: Faber & Faber.

Engländer, A. (2000). 'The Illusions of Discourse Theory'. *Associations* **4**, pp. 223-251.

———— (2002). *Diskurs als Rechtsquelle? Zur Kritik der Diskurstheorie des Rechts*. Tübingen: Mohr Siebeck.

Gadenne, V. (1996). 'Rationale Heuristik und Falsifikation'. In Gadenne & Wendel (1996), pp. 57-78.

———, editor (1998). *Kritischer Rationalismus und Pragmatismus*. Amsterdam & Atlanta: Editions Rodopi B.V.

Gadenne, V. & Wendel, H. J., editors (1996). *Rationalität und Kritik*. Tübingen: J. C. B. Mohr (Paul Siebeck).

Grayling, A. C. (1988). *Wittgenstein*. Oxford: Oxford University Press.

Grondin, J. (1999a). *Hans-Georg Gadamer – eine Biographie*. Tübingen: J. C. B. Mohr (Paul Siebeck) 1999.

——— (1999b). 'Die Hermeneutik als Konsequenz des kritischen Rationalismus'. In Kanitscheider & Wetz (1999), pp. 38-46.

Hacohen, M. H. (2000). *Karl Popper – The Formative Years, 1902-1945. Politics and Philosophy in Interwar Vienna*. New York: Cambridge University Press.

Hall, J. A. (1999). 'The Sociological Deficit of *The Open Society*, Analyzed and Remedied'. In Jarvie & Pralong (1999b), pp. 83-96.

Heidegger M. (1927). *Sein und Zeit*.

Jarvie, I. C. (1999). 'Popper's Ideal Types: Open and Closed, Abstract and Concrete societies'. In Jarvie & Pralong (1999b), pp. 71-82.

——— (2001). *The Republic of Science. The Emergence of Popper's Social View of Science 1935-1945*. Amsterdam & Atlanta: Editions Rodopi B.V.

Jarvie, I. C. & Pralong, S. (1999a). 'Introduction'. In Jarvie & Pralong (1999b), pp. 3-16.

———, editors (1999b). *Popper's Open Society after Fifty Years. The Continuing Relevance of Karl Popper*. London: Routledge.

Kanitscheider, B. & Wetz, F. J., editors (1999). *Hermeneutik und Naturalismus*. Tübingen: J. C. B. Mohr (Paul Siebeck).

Kolakowski, L. (1977). *Die Suche nach der verlorenen Gewißheit. Denk-Wege mit Edmund Husserl*. Stuttgart: Kohlhammer.

Kuhn, T. S. (1962). *The Structure of Scientific Revolutions*. Chicago: University of Chicago Press. 2nd edition 1970.

Lorenz, K. (1941). 'Kants Lehre vom Apriorischen im Lichte gegenwärtiger Biologie'. In K. Lorenz (1978), pp. 82-109. *Das Wirkungsgefüge der Natur und das Schicksal des Menschen*. Munich & Zurich: R. Piper.

——— (1973). *Die Rückseite des Spiegels. Versuch einer Naturgeschichte der menschlichen Erkenntnis*. Munich & Zurich: R. Piper.

Magee B. (1999). 'What Use is Popper to a Practical Politician?' In Jarvie & Pralong (1999b), pp. 146-158.

Meyer, W. (2000). *Grundlagen des ökonomischen Denkens*. Tübingen: Mohr Siebeck.

Miller, D. W. (1994). *Critical Rationalism. A Restatement and Defence*. Chicago & La Salle IL: Open Court Publishing Company.

Molden, O. (1981). *Der andere Zauberberg*. Vienna: F. Molden.

Musgrave, A. E. (1993). *Common Sense, Science and Scepticism. A Historical Introduction to the Theory of Knowledge*. Cambridge: Cambridge University Press.

——— (1999). *Essays in Realism and Rationalism*. Amsterdam & Atlanta: Editions Rodopi B.V.

Nilsson, J. (2000). *Rationality in Inquiry. On the Revisability of Cognitive Standards*. Umeå: Department of Philosophy and Linguistics, Umeå University.

Popper, K. R. (1930-1933). *Die beiden Grundprobleme der Erkenntnistheorie.* First published 1979. Tübingen: J. C. B. Mohr (Paul Siebeck). 2nd edition 1994.

———— (1935). *Logik der Forschung. Zur Erkenntnistheorie der modernen Naturwissenschaft.* Wien: Julius Springer Verlag. English translation 1959. *The Logic of Scientific Discovery*. London: Hutchinson & Co.

———— (1945). *The Open Society and Its Enemies*. London: George Routledge & Sons. 4th edition 1962. 5th edition 1966. London: Routledge & Kegan Paul.

———— (1970). 'Normal Science and Its Dangers'. In I. Lakatos & A. E. Musgrave, editors (1970), pp. 51-58. *Criticism and the Growth of Knowledge*. Cambridge: Cambridge University Press.

———— (1972). *Objective Knowledge*. Oxford: Clarendon Press. 2nd edition 1979.

———— (1974). 'Intellectual Autobiography'. In P. A. Schilpp, editor (1974), pp. 1-181. *The Philosophy of Karl Popper*. La Salle IL: Open Court. Reprinted as *Unended Quest* (1976). London & Glasgow: Fontana/Collins.

———— (1992). *Die offene Gesellschaft und ihre Feinde*. 7th edition of the German translation of Popper (1945). Tübingen: J. C. B. Mohr (Paul Siebeck).

———— (1994). *The Myth of the Framework. In Defence of Science and Rationality*. London: Routledge.

Popper, K. R. & Lorenz, K. (1985). *Die Zukunft ist offen. Das Altenberger Gespräch*. Munich & Zurich: R. Piper.

Pralong, S. (1999). '*Minima Moralia*. Is There an Ethics of the Open Society?'y In Jarvie & Pralong (1999b), pp. 128-145.

Rescher, N. (1993). *Pluralism. Against the Demand for Consensus*. Oxford: Clarendon Press.

Schantz, R. (1998). 'Verifikationismus und Realismus in der Philosophie des Pragmatismus. Eine Studie zu Peirce und James'. *Zeitschrift für philosophische Forschung* **52**, pp. 363-382.

Schmid, M. (1994). *Rationalität und Theoriebildung. Studien zu Karl Poppers Methodologie der Sozialwissenschaften*. Amsterdam & Atlanta: Editions Rodopi B.V.

Steinhoff, U. (2001). *Kritik der kommunikativen Rationalität*. Norderstedt: BoD GmbH 2001.

Vanberg, V. (1975). *Die zwei Soziologien. Individualismus und Kollektivismus in der Sozialtheorie*. Tübingen: J. C. B. Mohr (Paul Siebeck).

Watkins, J. W. N. (1958). 'Confirmable and Influential Metaphysics'. *Mind* **67**, pp. 344-365.

———— (1999). 'The Truth Will Out'. *The Philosophers' Magazine*, Spring 1999, p. 11.

Wittgenstein, L. J. J. (1921). 'Logisch-philosophische Abhandlung'. *Annalen der Naturphilosophie* **44**, pp. 185-262. English translation 1922. *Tractatus Logico-Philosophicus*. London: Routledge & Kegan Paul.

Einleitung

Karl Popper und die Philosophie im 20. Jahrhundert

Hans Albert

Karl Popper war ohne Zweifel einer der bedeutendsten Denker des 20. Jahrhunderts. Er wurde im Juli 1902, also vor 100 Jahren, hier in Wien geboren und hat seine philosophische Auffassung zunächst in Wien entwickelt, in Auseinandersetzung mit Ideen denen er hier begegnet ist, vor allem mit den Ideen des „Wiener Kreises", als dessen offizielle Opposition er angesehen wurde, mit den Versionen des Kantianismus, mit denen er in Berührung kam, und mit dem Marxismus, der Psychoanalyse und der Individualpsychologie.

Dass man ihr eine kritische Auseinandersetzung widmet, ist ganz in seinem Sinne, denn er hat in seiner Philosophie, die er den „kritischen Rationalismus" genannt hat, der Kritik zentrale Bedeutung eingeräumt. Und er war der Ansicht, dass man eine Auffassung gerade dadurch ehrt, dass man sich die Mühe macht, sich kritisch mit ihr auseinanderzusetzen.

Poppers Denken hat vor allem die Entwicklung der Wissenschaftslehre und der Sozialphilosophie beeinflusst, aber auch die vieler wissenschaftlicher Disziplinen und die öffentliche Diskussion über politische Probleme. Was aber den Einfluss des philosophischen Denkens auf andere Bereiche des kulturellen Lebens angeht, so scheinen mir zwei andere Philosophen stärker gewirkt zu haben, deren Denken in scharfem Gegensatz zu dem Karl Poppers stand: nämlich Ludwig Wittgenstein und Martin Heidegger. Beide hatten, wie ich meine, für den der Aufklärung verpflichteten Rationalismus eine gänzlich andere Bedeutung als Popper. Um das zu zeigen, ist es vielleicht zweckmäßig, kurz auf die philosophische Situation zu Anfang des vorigen Jahrhunderts einzugehen.

Damals gab es in Europa abgesehen von verschiedenen Versionen des Kantianismus zwei große philosophische Reformbewegungen, nämlich die von Bertrand Russell inspirierte analytische und die durch Edmund Husserl begründete phänomenologische Bewegung. Beide Bewegungen waren in der Tradition des europäischen Rationalismus und Realismus verwurzelt und nahmen eine positive Haltung zur Wissenschaft ein. Während die analytische Bewegung dem Empirismus zuzurechnen war, repräsentierte die phänomenologische Bewegung eine neue Version des Apriorismus. Nur die erste der beiden war mit der Entwicklung der modernen Logik verbunden, aber auch die zweite ging von logischen Untersuchungen aus. Um nun auf die beiden oben erwähnten Denker zurückzukommen: Für die erste der beiden Bewegungen spielte Ludwig Wittgenstein eine ähnliche Rolle wie für die zweite Martin Heidegger.

Schon in seinem ersten Buch *Tractatus-Logico-Philosophicus* (1921) hatte sich Wittgenstein mit der sprachlichen Konstitution der Welt befasst und damit dem analytischen Denken eine Wendung gegeben, die vom Russellschen Realismus wegführte. Später ging er dann mit seiner Analyse konkreter Sprachspiele zu einer Art Pragmatismus über, der die Konsequenz hatte, dass nicht nur metaphysische, sondern auch erkenntnistheoretische Untersuchungen überholt seien. Im phänomenologischen Denken vollzog schon sein Begründer selbst, nämlich Husserl, den Übergang zur transzendentalen Fragestellung. Sein Schüler und Kritiker Heidegger leitete dann mit seinem Hauptwerk *Sein und Zeit* (1927) eine hermeneutische Wende in diesem Denken ein, die ebenfalls mit dem Anspruch verbunden war, Metaphysik und Erkenntnistheorie überwunden zu haben. In beiden Fällen ging der kritische Impuls, der diese Bewegung anfangs belebt hatte, verloren, und der Rationalismus, der mit ihnen verbunden war, machte einer Denkweise Platz, die mit dem wissenschaftlichen Denken und einer durch die Wissenschaften geprägten Weltauffassung unvereinbar ist.

Mit dem einen der beiden Philosophen, nämlich Ludwig Wittgenstein hat sich Popper selbst auseinandergesetzt, und zwar schon in seinem ersten Buch.[1] Der Gegensatz ihrer Auffassungen kommt sehr gut in der bekannten Szene zum Ausdruck, die sich im Jahre 1946 im Moral Sciences Club in Cambridge abgespielt hat und über die dann verschiedene Leute ganz unterschiedlich berichtet haben.[2] Damals hat Wittgenstein bekanntlich die These zurückgewiesen, dass es echte philosophische Probleme gibt, worauf Popper ihm Beispiele für solche Probleme gab, deren philosophischer Charakter aber von Wittgenstein bestritten wurde. Wittgenstein hatte schon seine Ideen über Sprachspiele entwickelt, die dann als seine Spätphilosophie posthum veröffentlicht wurden und hatte damit seinen Ausstieg aus dem philosophischen Denken vollzogen. Sein Einfluss ist davon unberührt geblieben.[3]

Mit dem anderen der beiden Denker, nämlich Martin Heidegger, hat sich Popper nicht selbst auseinandergesetzt, obwohl er ihn gelegentlich erwähnt und als Vertreter des Irrationalismus apostrophiert hat. Dieser Philosoph hat insofern die moderne Kultur in radikaler Weise attackiert, als er versucht hat, aus dem gegenständlichen Denken überhaupt auszusteigen und mit der Logik zugleich die objektivierende Sprache und die mit ihr verbundene Wahrheitsidee infrage zustellen.[4] Die Frage nach dem Sinn von Sein, die er in seinem Buch *Sein und Zeit* gestellt hat, hat er weder in diesem Buch noch

---

[1]Vgl. dazu Popper (1930-1933), passim; vgl. auch sein (1945), Kap. 11, Anmerkung 51, sowie Popper (1957), Bd. II., Kap. 1, Anmerkung 51, wo sich Popper mit dem *Tractatus Logico-Philosophicus* beschäftigt.

[2]Vgl. dazu Popper (1979), pp. 175-178, Watkins (1999), Edmonds und Eidinow (2001).

[3]Neuerdings wird dieser Einfluss aber als geringer eingeschätzt, als das bisher üblich war. Vgl. dazu Grayling (1999).

[4]Vgl. dazu meine Analyse in (1994), pp. 1-35.

später beantwortet oder auch nur geklärt. Immerhin hatte er in diesem Buch noch den Versuch unternommen, Probleme zu behandeln, die sich für ihn aus der damaligen philosophischen Situation ergeben hatten. Später ist er dann immer mehr aus dem Unternehmen der Erkenntnis, der Suche nach Wahrheit, ausgestiegen und bei einer Wortmusik gelandet, die nicht nur für normale Leser eine Zumutung ist.

Zwar ist ihm Hans-Georg Gadamer, sein einflussreichster Schüler, der heute als Klassiker des hermeneutischen Denkens gilt, nicht in diese Sackgasse gefolgt, aber er hat mit seiner universalen Hermeneutik dennoch den Heideggerschen Antirationalismus fortgeführt.[5] Die hermeneutische Wende, die auf Heidegger und Gadamer zurückzuführen ist, hat jedenfalls zu Konsequenzen geführt, durch die die problematischen Züge der deutschen Tradition verstärkt werden, die im Gegensatz zur Aufklärung stehen. Es gibt heute Versuche, diese philosophische Richtung mit dem Denken Karl Poppers in Einklang zu bringen,[6] aber sie scheinen mir auf offenkundigen Missverständnissen zu beruhen.[7]

Ich selbst bin erst in den 50er Jahren des vorigen Jahrhunderts, also kurz nach dem zweiten Weltkrieg, mit den Gedanken Karl Poppers bekannt geworden, nach einem längeren Weg durch das philosophische Denken, der mit der Geschichtsphilosophie Oswald Spenglers begann und mich gerade zur Philosophie des „Wiener Kreises" geführt hatte. Damals rechnete ich die Poppersche Auffassung dem logischen Positivismus zu, der in diesem Kreis vertreten wurde. Dann lernte ich Karl Popper 1958 auf dem „Europäischen Forum Alpbach" kennen[8] und musste feststellen, dass das ein Irrtum war, ein Irrtum allerdings, mit dem ich keineswegs allein war und der sich bei einigen Leuten bis heute gehalten hat.

Das erste, was ich lernte, war, dass die Metaphysik-Kritik des „Wiener Kreises" unhaltbar war und zwar schon deshalb, weil es logische Beziehungen zwischen bestimmten metaphysischen Aussagen und den Aussagen der Realwissenschaften gibt,[9] sodass die bekannte Sinnlosigkeitsthese ungültig ist. Später wurde mir deutlich, dass die Auffassungen der Vertreter des „Wiener Kreises" teilweise selbst metaphysischen Charakter haben[10] und dass

---

[5]Vgl. dazu Albert (1994), pp. 36-77, und mein (2002), pp. 15-24.

[6]Vgl. dazu zum Beispiel Grondin (1999a), p. 336; dabei geht es um die Rehabilitierung des Vorurteils bei Gadamer und um die Behandlung dieses Problems durch Popper.

[7]Das gleiche gilt für Grondins Hinweise auf die Defizite des Popperschen Denkens. Vgl. dazu Grondin (1999b) in Kanitscheider & Wetz (1999), pp. 38-46, und meine Kritik in meinem Beitrag (1999b) im gleichen Band, pp. 3-20.

[8]Diese internationale Veranstaltung war von Otto Molden, einem führenden Mitglied des österreichischen Widerstandes gegen Hitler, zusammen mit dem Dozenten Simon Moser schon im August 1945 ins Leben gerufen worden. Sie hatte für die Verbreitung Popperscher Ideen im deutschen Sprachbereich große Bedeutung. Dem Wirken Otto Moldens, der im Juni 2002 gestorben ist, lag die Vision eines vereinten Europa zugrunde. Vgl. dazu Molden (1981).

[9]Es gibt zum Beispiel logische Beziehungen zwischen dem metaphysischen allgemeinen Kausalprinzip, Kausalgesetzen und singulären Kausalaussagen. Vgl. Watkins (1958), pp. 344-365.

[10]Vgl. dazu Bergmann (1954).

es überhaupt schwer sein dürfte, metaphysische Aussagen ganz zu vermeiden. Damit bin ich allerdings bei einer These angelangt, über die vermutlich kein Konsens erzielt werden kann.[11]

Da ich nun gewissermaßen die Katze aus dem Sack gelassen habe, möchte ich in aller Kürze noch skizzieren, wie ich den kritischen Rationalismus verstehe, den ich vertrete. Als zentrale Komponente dieser Auffassung pflege ich den kritischen Realismus, den konsequenten Fallibilismus und den methodologischen Kritizismus oder Revisionismus anzuführen, und ich glaube mich mit dieser Feststellung in Übereinstimmung mit den Auffassungen Karl Poppers zu befinden. Aber das ist natürlich nur eine sehr grobe Antwort, die genauer Erläuterung bedürfte, wozu hier keine Zeit ist.[12] Der Teufel steckt bekanntlich im Detail.

Was den Popperschen Realismus angeht, so steht er im Gegensatz zu den antirealistischen Auffassungen, die sich auch im Bereich des analytischen Denkens teilweise ausgebreitet haben. Der Fallibilismus, die These der Fehlbarkeit der Vernunft, die Popper seinerzeit gegen das klassische Begründungsdenken verteidigt hat, erfreut sich zwar zunehmender Beliebtheit, aber man beruft sich in dieser Hinsicht vielfach lieber auf Charles Sanders Peirce, allerdings ohne die Probleme zu beachten, die man sich damit einhandelt.[13] Den methodologischen Revisionismus, der aus der Akzentuierung der Falsifizierbarkeit theoretischer Aussagen und der Forderung nach strengen Widerlegungsversuchen hervorgegangen ist, hat Popper später zu einer Methodologie der Lösung von Problemen weiterentwickelt, die sich nicht nur im Bereich der Erkenntnis, sondern in allen Bereichen der menschlichen Praxis anwenden lässt.[14]

Wenn der kritische Rationalismus so charakterisiert wird, wie ich das getan habe, ist leicht zu erkennen, dass er metaphysische Auffassungen involviert, und zwar solche, die einen engen Zusammenhang mit der Erkenntnispraxis der Realwissenschaften haben. Diese Auffassungen sind allerdings im Sinne Poppers nicht als Dogmen zu behandeln, sondern als Hypothesen. Popper hat ja zu zeigen versucht, dass man auch Aussagen dieser Art rational diskutieren kann, und er hat selbst Beiträge zu einer solchen Diskussion geliefert. Viele seiner Anhänger, die bereit sind, das grundsätzlich zu akzeptieren, haben allerdings die von ihm vorgeschlagenen Problemlösungen teilweise in Frage gestellt. Das gilt vor allem für seine Vorschläge zur Lösung des Leib-Seele-Problems, die auf die von ihm entwickelte Drei-Welten-Lehre zurückgehen, und seine Theorie der Propensitäten. Auch seine Vorschläge zur Lösung sozial-

---

[11]Manche Vertreter des Empirismus können sich, soweit ich sehe, noch heute nicht zur Anerkennung dieser These durchringen. Vgl. dazu die Diskussion in Böhm, Holweg, & Hoock (2002).

[12]Vgl. dazu mein (1987).

[13]Vgl. dazu Schantz (1998), pp. 363-382.

[14]In der Wissenschaft kann sie als eine rationale Heuristik zur Anleitung der Erkenntnispraxis dienen. Vgl. dazu Albert (1984) in Albert (1999a), sowie Gadenne (1996) in Gadenne & Wendel (1996), pp. 57-78. Für ihre Verwendbarkeit im politischen Bereich vgl. Magee (1999) in Jarvie & Pralong (1999b), pp. 146-158.

wissenschaftlicher Probleme sind auf Kritik gestoßen, weil er in ihnen seine allgemeinen methodologischen Auffassungen aufgegeben zu haben scheint. Dass er das Induktionsproblem ganz oder zumindest teilweise gelöst hat, pflegt von den Vertretern des kritischen Rationalismus akzeptiert zu werden. Allerdings gibt es eine Kontroverse darüber, wie seine Lösung aufzufassen ist. Aber es ist hier nicht der Platz darauf einzugehen.

Es gibt soweit ich sehe, drei große Kontroversen, in denen das Denken Karl Poppers eine zentrale Rolle gespielt hat. Die eine ist die oben schon erwähnte Auseinandersetzung mit den Vertretern des logischen Positivismus, in der er zum ersten Mal seine Auffassungen öffentlich zur Diskussion gestellt hat. Er hat sie bekanntlich in einem umfangreichen Manuskript mit dem Titel *Die beiden Grundprobleme der Erkenntnistheorie* entwickelt, das damals wegen seines Umfanges nicht publizierbar war.[15] Eine radikal gekürzte Fassung wurde als *Logik der Forschung*[16] veröffentlicht und wurde zu einem Klassiker der modernen Wissenschaftslehre. Sie enthält seine Kritik an zentralen Thesen des logischen Positivismus und am Konventionalismus Hugo Dinglers im Zusammenhang mit einem Versuch der Lösung der beiden Probleme, die er als Grundprobleme der Erkenntnistheorie ansah, nämlich des Abgrenzungs- und des Induktionsproblems. Beim ersten dieser Probleme, das er auf Kant zurückführte, geht es um die Abgrenzung der Wissenschaft gegen metaphysische und andere Aussagensysteme, beim zweiten um die schon seinerzeit von Hume behandelte Frage, inwieweit man bisherige Erfahrungen legitimerweise benutzen kann, um zukünftige Ereignisse vorherzusagen, die von Hume bekanntlich negativ beantwortet wurde.

Beide Probleme hat Popper damals gleichzeitig mit Hilfe seiner in diesem Buch entwickelten Methodologie zu lösen versucht, die unter der Bezeichnung „Falsifikationismus" diskutiert zu werden pflegt. Die Regeln die er dabei formuliert hat, waren dazu gedacht, die Erkenntnispraxis in den Realwissenschaften anzuleiten. Da er dabei, wie mit Recht festgestellt wurde,[17] von vornherein die soziale Dimension dieser Praxis berücksichtigt hat, kann man mit einem gewissen Recht von einer „institutionellen Wende" in der Wissenschaftslehre sprechen. Denn es ging ihm primär nicht um die logische Analyse bestimmter Aussagen, sondern um die Institutionalisierung adäquater Normen der wissenschaftlichen Forschung,[18] wobei die logische Analyse natürlich, soweit nötig, als Hilfsmittel verwendet wurde. Der Akzent lag dabei auf der strengen Prüfung von Theorien, die geeignet ist, zu ihrer Widerlegung zu führen. Ihre Bewährung war an das Scheitern solcher Widerlegungsversuche gebunden.

Vielfach wird das Verhältnis Poppers zum „Wiener Kreis" so dargestellt, als ob er den Unterschied seiner Auffassungen zu denen der Mitglieder dieses Kreises übertrieben hätte. Die damalige Kontroverse zwischen Popper und

---

[15]Es ist dann später in unvollständiger Fassung erschienen. Vgl. dazu Popper (1930-1933).

[16]Popper (1935).

[17]Jarvie (2001).

[18]Vgl. zu diesem Problem Jarvie (2001) und Max Albert (2002) in Böhm, Holweg, & Hoock (2002), pp. 231-241.

ihnen sieht dann wie eine Diskussion zwischen verschiedenen Varianten des
Positivismus aus. Aber das läuft auf eine Verschleierung eines prinzipiellen
Gegensatzes hinaus, den Popper selbst mit Recht betont hat. Er hat zum
Beispiel nie die für den „Wiener Kreis" charakteristische linguistische Wende
mitgemacht, die auf die Beseitigung der Metaphysik abzielte und das philo-
sophische Denken in eine Sackgasse geführt hat.[19]

Später hat Popper seine Methodologie auf dem Hintergrund des metaphysischen Realismus weiterentwickelt und hat damit eine evolutionäre Erkenntnislehre[20] verbunden, die an Darwinische Ideen anknüpft. Bekanntlich hat ein
anderer Wiener, nämlich der mit Popper befreundete Konrad Lorenz, in den
40er Jahren im Anschluss an Kants Ideen eine evolutionäre Erkenntnistheorie
entwickelt.[21] Aber schon in Poppers erstem Buch ist die Grundidee dieser
Lehre enthalten.[22]

Viele Theoretiker, die dem kritischen Rationalismus nahe stehen, be-
schränken sich darauf, die Poppersche Methodologie zu akzeptieren, während
sie die anderen Komponenten seiner Philosophie mit Skepsis betrachten. Aber
auch der Anspruch Poppers, durch seine Methodologie das Problem der Induktion gelöst zu haben, ist, wie ich schon erwähnt habe, bis heute kontrovers
geblieben. Dabei geht es vor allem um das so genannte pragmatische Induktionsproblem.[23]

Die zweite der von mir erwähnten Kontroversen begann in den 60er Jahren
nach der Publikation des Buches von Thomas Kuhn *Die Struktur wissenschaftlicher Revolutionen*.[24] Dabei ging es um die so genannte wissenschaftshis-
torische Herausforderung des logischen Empirismus durch Norwood Russell
Hanson, Thomas Kuhn, Paul Feyerabend und Imre Lakatos. In sie wurden
die Popperschen Auffassungen einbezogen, obwohl Popper selbst vieles vor-
weggenommen hatte, was dabei gegen den neoklassischen Empirismus vorgebracht wurde. Er hatte zum Beispiel die positivistische Zwei-Sprachen-These
zurückgewiesen und die Theoriegeladenheit von Beobachtungsaussagen betont. Er hatte die Bedeutung von Erkenntnisprogrammen und damit gleichzeitig die Bedeutung metaphysischer Ideen für die Entwicklung der Realwissenschaften herausgearbeitet. Und er hatte auf diese Weise die historische
Dimension in die Wissenschaftslehre eingebracht.[25] Inzwischen hat sich wohl
herausgestellt, dass die Argumente, die gegen die Poppersche Methodologie
damals vorgebracht wurden, nicht stichhaltig sind.[26] Vieles, was er damals
gegen herrschende Auffassungen vorgebracht hat, wird heute für selbstver-

---

[19]Vgl. dazu Hacohen (2000), pp. 208-213, wo die „positivistische Legende" ad absurdum
geführt wird.

[20]Popper (1973).

[21]Lorenz (1941); (1978); (1973).

[22]Popper (1930-1933), Abschnitt 11, p. 88.

[23]Vgl. dazu Böhm, Holweg, & Hoock (2002).

[24]Kuhn (1967).

[25]Die methodologischen Auffassungen von Imre Lakatos waren auch in dieser Hinsicht
durch Poppersche Ideen geprägt. Auch der theoretische Pluralismus ist mit der Popperschen
Methodologie vereinbar. Vgl. dazu Albert (1968) und Albert (1987).

[26]Vgl. dazu Andersson (1988), Musgrave (1999), Miller (1994).

ständlich gehalten. Und nicht selten wird vergessen, in diesem Zusammenhang seinen Namen zu erwähnen.

Die dritte Kontroverse begann im deutschen Sprachbereich, ebenfalls in den 60er Jahren, und zwar im Anschluss an einen Vortrag Poppers auf einem Soziologentag in Tübingen 1961. Es war der so genannte Positivismusstreit, in dem der kritische Rationalismus von Vertretern der „Frankfurter Schule" als eine Version des Positivismus attackiert wurde.[27] Diese Kontroverse, an der sich Popper selbst kaum beteiligte, begann mit grotesken Missverständnissen auf Seiten der Kritiker, die nur langsam verschwanden. In ihr ging es nicht nur um die Methodologie der Soziawissenschaften, sondern auch um die Sozialphilosophie Karl Poppers, die er in seinem Buch *Die offene Gesellschaft und ihre Feinde* (1957-1958) vorgelegt hatte und auf die ich noch zurückkommen werde.

Ein Teil seiner Kritiker setzte ihm eine transzendentale Erkenntnislehre entgegen, in der eine instrumentalistische Deutung der Naturwissenschaften und eine an die Gadamersche Hermeneutik anknüpfende Deutung der Kultur- und Sozialwissenschaften mit einer auf Marx und Freud zurückgehenden Ideologiekritik verbunden war und die eine Konsenstheorie der Wahrheit enthielt. Ein anderer Teil, die Erlanger Schule, verband eine auf Dingler und seine Idee der Letztbegründung zurückgehende Wissenschaftslehre mit der Philosophie Martin Heideggers. Der Positivismus vorwurf dieser Kritiker verwandelte sich in den Vorwurf des Szientismus, mit dem man darauf zielte, dass Popper eine einheitliche Methodologie für alle Realwissenschaften vorgeschlagen hatte, also zum Beispiel auch für die Kultur- oder Geisteswissenschaften. Genau genommen traf diese Kritik nicht so sehr Popper selbst, der ja mit seiner Konzeption des Verstehens seine frühere Position in dieser Hinsicht modifiziert hatte, als die Vertreter des kritischen Rationalismus, die seine ursprüngliche Methodenauffassung beibehalten hatten. Man findet sie vor allem in den Sozialwissenschaften.[28]

Popper hatte nämlich ursprünglich die Suche nach Kausalgesetzen und kausalen Erklärungen auch als Zielsetzung der Forschung in den Sozialwissenschaften akzeptiert. Diese Zielsetzung schien ihm auch aus praktischen Gründen wichtig zu sein, weil sich nomologische Aussagen prinzipiell sozialtechnologisch verwerten lassen. Wer soziale Reformen für notwendig hält, ist offenbar auf die Anwendung entsprechender sozialtechnologischer Einsichten angewiesen. Das gilt vor allem auch für die Beeinflussung des institutionellen Gefüges einer Gesellschaft durch eine entsprechende Gesetzgebung, wie er sie befürwortete. Gleichzeitig ermöglichen solche Einsichten die Kritik an utopischen Entwürfen sozialer Planung, wie sie von manchen Sozialphilosophen für notwendig gehalten werden. Dass Popper später für die Sozialwissenschaften von seiner ursprünglichen Auffassung abging und die Suche nach Gesetzmäßigkeiten durch den Vorschlag der Anwendung eines problematischen Ra-

---

[27]Vgl. Adorno u.a. (1969).
[28]Vgl. zum Beispiel Vanberg (1975), Schmid (1994), sowie Meyer (2002).

tionalitätsprinzips ersetzte, ist auf Kritik gestoßen,[29] und zwar auch deshalb, weil damit die Möglichkeit einer rationalen Reformpolitik in Frage gestellt wurde, die ein wesentlicher Bestandteil seiner Konzeption war.

Damit komme ich zurück auf Poppers Beitrag zur Sozialphilosophie und damit auf seine Konzeption der offenen Gesellschaft, die in der öffentlichen Diskussion des vorigen Jahrhunderts eine bedeutende Rolle gespielt hat. Dieses Jahrhundert war bekanntlich durch die beiden Weltkriege und durch die Entstehung und den Untergang von zwei totalitären Systemen geprägt. Das eine von ihnen begann im ersten dieser Kriege und hielt sich etwa siebzig Jahre, das zweite brachte uns den zweiten dieser Kriege und ging in ihm nach zwölfjähriger Dauer unter. Karl Popper hat in seinem Buch *Die offene Gesellschaft und ihre Feinde*[30] den Versuch unternommen, die geistigen Grundlagen dieser Systeme zu klären und ihren Charakter zu enthüllen. Er hat sie als geschlossene Gesellschaft gekennzeichnet und ihnen seine Idee der offenen Gesellschaft entgegengesetzt.

Was seine Analyse ihrer geistigen Grundlagen angeht, so ist sie schon früh auf Kritik gestoßen. Vor allem seine Platon- und seine Hegel-Kritik wurde von vielen beanstandet,[31] aber auch seine Kritik an Karl Marx, dessen Werk er mit großer Sympathie behandelt hatte. Es ist hier nicht der Platz, darauf einzugehen. Seine Konzeption der offenen Gesellschaft hat dagegen in der angelsächsischen Diskussion der zweiten Hälfte des 20. Jahrhunderts kaum eine Rolle gespielt, wenn man einmal von der Diskussion in England kurz nach Ende des Krieges absieht. In derem Zentrum standen in den letzten Jahrzehnten die Rawlssche Theorie der Gerechtigkeit und Auffassungen, die sich als Alternativen zu dieser Theorie anboten. Nur in Europa, dessen Bevölkerung unmittelbar mit den Konsequenzen totalitärer Systeme für das alltägliche Leben konfrontiert war, spielte die Popperschen Konzeption eine größere Rolle.[32] Hier hat sie sogar praktische Konsequenzen gehabt, die Popper selbst kaum vorhersehen konnte.[33]

Es gehört zu den Eigenheiten der Popperschen Sozialphilosophie, dass sie in engem Zusammenhang steht mit der von ihm entworfenen Erkenntnislehre.[34] Der Fallibilismus, der Realismus und der Kritizismus seiner Erkenntnislehre ist auch die Grundlage seiner sozialphilosophischen Konzeption. Die offene Gesellschaft, wie sie Popper charakterisiert hat, ist eine Gesellschaft, deren Mitglieder die Möglichkeit haben, frei über ihre Lebensführung zu entscheiden und an den Entscheidungen über gemeinsame Angelegenheiten mitzuwirken. Durch die Institutionalisierung von Konkurrenz und Kritik

[29]Vgl. die in Anmerkung 28 erwähnte Literatur.

[30]Popper (1945), (1957-1958).

[31]Vgl. dazu Hacohen (2000), pp. 438f., wo der Autor zu zeigen versucht, dass Poppers Hegelkritik nicht den Anforderungen entspricht, die dieser selbst an eine ernsthafte Kritik zu stellen pflegte.

[32]Vgl. dazu Jarvie & Pralong (1999a), pp. 7f.

[33]Ich denke hier vor allem an das Wirken von George Soros und die Bedeutung seiner Open-Society-Institute und der von ihm gegründeten mitteleuropäischen Universität.

[34]Vgl. vor allem Jarvie (2001).

in allen sozialen Bereichen sind in ihr die Bedingungen gegeben, neue Lösungen für Probleme aller Art zu finden, zu analysieren und zu diskutieren und entsprechende Reformen herbeizuführen, also die Art des Problemlösungsverhaltens zu praktizieren, die Popper für angemessen hielt.[35] Der methodologische Kritizismus und Revisionismus der Popperschen Erkenntnislehre kann auf diese Weise in den institutionellen Arrangements und in den Traditionen einer Gesellschaft verankert werden. In politischer Hinsicht bedeutet das offenbar, dass in ihr die Zähmung der Herrschaft durch das Recht gelungen ist. Der Rechtsstaat ist daher ein Kernstück einer solchen Ordnung.[36]

Der Grundwert der Popperschen Idee der offenen Gesellschaft, ist, wie er selbst einmal festgestellt hat, die menschliche Freiheit.[37] Aber ihm war klar, dass diese Freiheit durch den Staat gesichert werden musste und dass andererseits nur ein durch freie Bürger kontrollierter Staat ihnen Sicherheit verschaffen könnte. Bei seiner Idee der offenen Gesellschaft handelt es sich um einen Versuch, die europäische Freiheitsidee in eine soziologische Konstruktion zu transformieren, die man als im Max Weberschen Sinne idealtypisch ansehen kann.[38] Dazu ist dreierlei zu sagen: Erstens ist die Idee einer solchen Gesellschaft ein Ideal, dem sich eine konkrete Gesellschaft mehr oder weniger annähern kann. Zweitens kann dieses Ideal als Maßstab der Kritik für bestehende soziale Ordnungen verwendet werden und damit auch als Leitlinie für Versuche sie zu reformieren. Und drittens können Versuche der Annäherung an dieses Ideal zu ganz verschiedenen Verfassungen führen, da in ihnen die jeweils unterschiedlichen historischen Bedingungen berücksichtigt werden müssen.

Karl Popper hat die Formulierung seines Modells der offenen Gesellschaft in eine historische, soziologische und anthropologische Analyse eingebettet, die viele kritische Untersuchungen auf sich gezogen hat.[39] Für die Beurteilung seiner Darstellung ist es daher zweckmäßig, zwischen seinem normativen Entwurf und den betreffenden theoretischen Hypothesen und historischen Analysen zu unterscheiden, die mit diesem Entwurf verbunden sind und die sich teilweise als mehr oder weniger problematisch erwiesen haben. Was die Frage angeht, ob die Wissenschaft als institutionelles Gebilde als Musterbeispiel einer offenen Gesellschaft gelten kann, wie das von Popper teilweise unterstellt wurde, so ist auch sie eine Frage, deren Beantwortung diesbezügliche Faktenanalysen voraussetzt.

In dieser Beziehung ist ein Punkt hervorzuheben, der mir wichtig zu sein scheint. Es ist die enge Beziehung, die nach der Popperschen Auffassung zwischen der institutionellen Stützung der Freiheit des Denkens und der Kommunikation, wie sie für eine offene Gesellschaft charakteristisch ist, und der

---

[35] Vgl. dazu Magee (1999), wo darauf hingewiesen wird, dass diese Art des Verhaltens im politischen Bereich keineswegs selbstverständlich ist.

[36] Vgl. dazu Popper (1992), Bd. I., pp. IX-XIV.

[37] Vgl. dazu Popper & Lorenz (1985), p. 136.

[38] Vgl. Jarvie (1999).

[39] Vgl. zum Beispiel Jarvie (1999) und Hall (1999).

Möglichkeit des Erkenntnisfortschritts besteht.[40] Ohne die Annahme einer
Beziehung dieser Art wäre der Sinn der Regeln schwer zu verstehen, die er in
seiner Methodologie vorgeschlagen hat, jedenfalls, soweit ihre soziale Dimension in Frage kommt.

Damit kommen wir zurück auf die zweite der erwähnten Kontroversen, in
denen der kritischer Rationalismus eine zentrale Rolle gespielt hat. In dieser
Kontroverse tauchte mit der Kuhnschen Paradigmathese eine Auffassung auf,
die von Popper als „Mythos des Rahmens" kritisiert wurde.[41] Er hat ihr später
eine gründliche Untersuchung gewidmet, in der er auf einen wichtigen Aspekt
des Rationalitätsproblems eingeht, der auch für die in der dritten Kontroverse
diskutierten Problematik relevant ist.[42] Diese Auffassung besteht darin, dass
eine rationale und fruchtbare Diskussion unmöglich ist, wenn ihre Teilnehmer
nicht einen gemeinsamen Rahmen von Grundannahmen haben oder zumindest
für den Zweck der Diskussion akzeptieren.[43] Popper, der diese Auffassung
attackiert, stellt ihr die These entgegen, dass gerade das Aufeinandertreffen
verschiedener solcher Rahmen — und damit auch kultureller Unterschiede —
zu fruchtbaren Diskussionen führen kann und tatsächlich geführt hat. Und
er stellt weiter fest, dass eine fruchtbare Diskussion dieser Art keineswegs zu
einem Konsens führen müsse. Weder als Ausgangsbasis, noch als Ergebnis
einer solchen Diskussion ist demnach also ein Konsens notwendig.

Der „Mythos des Rahmens" läuft auf die These hinaus, dass eine rationale
Diskussion von Prinzipien unmöglich ist: *De principiis non disputandum est.*
Wenn das so wäre, dann wären so genannte letzte Voraussetzungen immun
gegen jede Kritik. Diese These hat sich aber als unhaltbar erwiesen.[44] Sie hat
übrigens fatale Konsequenzen für jede Erkenntnispraxis. Sie führt nämlich
dazu, dass entweder die eigenen Prinzipien dogmatisch als wahr erklärt werden oder ein Wahrheitsrelativismus akzeptiert wird, der die Wahrheit von
Aussagen auf den jeweils bevorzugten Rahmen von Voraussetzungen relativiert.[45] Damit führt sie zu einem Dilemma zwischen Fundamentalismus
und Relativismus, wie es zum Beispiel Leszek Kolakowski als unüberwindbar
hingestellt hat.[46]

Ich bin diesem „Mythos des Rahmens" schon sehr früh begegnet, nämlich
als ich Mitte der 30er Jahre Anhänger der Geschichtsphilosophie Oswald
Spenglers wurde, der die Auffassung vertrat, es gebe keinen Sinn zwischen
den Kulturen. Nur im Rahmen einer der von ihm dargestellten Hochkul-
turen gab es seiner Auffassung nach Sinnzusammenhänge und die Möglichkeit
des Verstehens. Den Wahrheitsrelativismus, den er damit verband, konnte er

---

[40]Schon in seinem sozialphilosophischen Hauptwerk ist diese Beziehung angedeutet. Vgl.
zum Beispiel Popper (1992), Bd. II., Kap. 13, Anmerkung 13, wo er auf ein mögliches
soziologisches Gesetz dieser Art hinweist.
[41]Vgl. Popper (1970).
[42]Vgl. dazu seinen Aufsatz „The Myth of the Framework" in seinem (1994), pp. 33-64.
[43]Ibidem, pp. 34f.
[44]Zur Kritik dieser These vgl. ibidem, pp. 59-61, und mein (1968), pp. 41-43.
[45]Vgl. mein (1996).
[46]Vgl. dazu Kolakowski (1977), p. 96.

natürlich für seine eigenen Thesen nicht gelten lassen.

Die Wissenschaftslehre des deutschen Pragmatisten Hugo Dingler, mit der sich Karl Popper in seinem ersten Buch auseinandergesetzt hat, enthielt ebenfalls diesen „Mythos des Rahmens", allerdings ohne relativistische Konsequenzen. Für Dingler kamen als Rahmen der wissenschaftlichen Forschung nur die aristotelische Logik, die euklidische Geometrie und die Newtonsche Physik in Frage, sodass die Einsteinsche Relativitätstheorie abzulehnen war.

Sowohl in Europa als auch im angelsächsischen Sprachbereich haben sich in den letzten Jahrzehnten antirealistische Richtungen ausgebreitet, die einer gemeinsamen pragmatisch-hermeneutischen Wende entstammen und in denen der „Mythos des Rahmens" mehr oder weniger stark zum Ausdruck kommt, teilweise mit relativistischen Tendenzen, teilweise auch mit dem Anspruch auf Letztbegründung. Im deutschen Sprachbereich gehören dazu die schon erwähnte universale Hermeneutik Hans-Georg Gadamers und die anderen Versionen der transzendentalen Hermeneutik, die von Karl Otto Apel und Jürgen Habermas im Anschluß an Gadamer, Horkheimer und Scheler entwickelt wurden, und der an Dingler und Heidegger anknüpfende Konstruktivismus der Erlanger Schule Paul Lorenzens, im angelsächsischen Sprachbereich der so genannte „interne Realismus" Hilary Putnams und andere Versionen des Pragmatismus, auf die ich hier nicht näher eingehen kann.[47] Auch die Konsenstheorien der Wahrheit, die damit verbunden sind, erwähne ich an dieser Stelle nur, ohne auf sie näher einzugehen.[48]

Damit komme ich zurück auf das, was ich über die philosophische Situation zu Anfang des vorigen Jahrhunderts gesagt habe. Ich habe auf die beiden Reformbewegungen hingewiesen, nämlich die analytische und die phänomenologische Bewegung, die sich damals im Rahmen eines erkenntnistheoretischen Realismus und Rationalismus entwickelt hatten. Die damals vertretenen Versionen des Kantianismus hatte ich ausgeklammert. Aber auch unter ihnen gab es eine realistische Auffassung, nämlich den transzendentalen Realismus Oswald Külpes, in dem man einen Vorläufer der Popperschen Philosophie sehen kann. Seine kritische Untersuchung der Kantschen Philosophie und sein Vergleich der vorliegenden erkenntnistheoretischen Auffassungen führten Külpe zu der Auffassung, dass ein hypothetischer Realismus allen in Frage kommenden Alternativen vorzuziehen sei. Bei Külpe tritt an die Stelle des Kantschen transzendentalen Idealismus eine Auffassung, die die Frage nach den Bedingungen der Möglichkeit der Erkenntnis im Rahmen eines realistischen Erkenntnisprogramms behandelt. In ihr wird außerdem schon die klassische Begründungsidee aufgegeben und durch die Annahme ersetzt, eine brauchbare Problemlösung sei nur durch die komparative Analyse möglicher Lösungsversuche an Hand bestimmter Kriterien zu erreichen, die eine Entscheidung zwischen ihnen ermöglichen.[49]

---

[47]Zur Kritik vgl. Gadenne (1998).

[48]Vgl. dazu aber Musgrave (1993), pp. 251-279.

[49]Zu diesem Ergebnis ist auch Popper gekommen, vgl. Popper (1973), pp. 54f. und später ebenso Devitt (1991), p. 61.

Im Gegensatz dazu sind die modernen Formen des Antirealismus, die sich vor allem unter dem Einfluss der Ideen Heideggers und Wittgensteins entwickelt haben, nichts anderes als neue Versionen des transzendentalen Idealismus, in denen die Sprache als konstitutiver Faktor an die Stelle des Erkenntnisvermögens tritt. Allerdings unterscheiden sie sich von der Kantschen Auffassung in einem wesentlichen Punkt. Schon bei Kant spielt die Idee eines kategorialen Rahmens, der nicht nur notwendige Bedingung der Erkenntnis ist, sondern darüber hinaus ihre Gegenstände prägt, eine zentrale Rolle. Im modernen Antirealismus verliert aber dieser Rahmen seine Eindeutigkeit. Er wird kulturell und historisch variabel und bleibt dennoch immun gegen jede Kritik. Das heißt aber nichts anderes, als dass dieser Antirealismus einen wesentlichen Bestandteil des klassischen Rationalismus übernimmt, nämlich die Idee der Kritikimmunität so genannter letzter Voraussetzungen, aber diese Idee mit den prinzipiell variablen Resultaten der Erkenntnispraxis verbindet. Dabei wird die Wahrheit auf den jeweils akzeptierten Rahmen relativiert. Dieser Rahmen ist aber nur für eine Gemeinschaft verbindlich, in der ein Konsens über seine Geltung erzielt wurde. Mit dem Idealismus der Kantschen Konstitutionstheorie verbindet sich der Relativismus der modernen Konsenstheorie. Die Idee der objektiven Wahrheit als regulative Idee der Erkenntnispraxis wird mehr oder weniger offen der Konsensidee geopfert. Es geht nicht mehr um die zutreffende Darstellung wirklicher Zusammenhänge, sondern um die Fabrikation von Aussagensystemen, die aus irgendwelchen Gründen auf die Zustimmung einer Gemeinschaft rechnen können. Damit hat der Pragmatismus über den Realismus gesiegt.

Der kritische Rationalismus Popperscher Prägung ist jedenfalls mit allen diesen Auffassungen unvereinbar. Er verbindet, wie schon gesagt, eine realistische Metaphysik und Erkenntnislehre mit einem konsequenten Fallibilismus und einem methodologischen Kritizismus, ist also sowohl mit Letztbegründungen als auch mit einem Wahrheitsrelativismus nicht zu vereinbaren. Er lehnt daher den „Mythos des Rahmens" ab und setzt der Suche nach Gewissheit und nach Konsens um jeden Preis die durch keinen Rahmen eingeschränkte Suche nach Wahrheit entgegen. Er setzt damit unter modernen Bedingungen die Tradition der Aufklärung fort, und zwar sowohl hinsichtlich des Strebens nach Erkenntnis als auch in Bezug auf die moralischen und politischen Konsequenzen, die damit verbunden sind.

Damit komme ich schließlich zu einer Frage, die ich bisher noch nicht behandelt habe, nämlich zu der Frage, inwieweit der Poppersche kritische Rationalismus eine Antwort auf ethische Probleme enthält. Popper selbst hat bekanntlich erklärt, dass die Ethik keine Wissenschaft ist, dass aber die Wissenschaft ethische Grundlagen hat. Das bedeutet natürlich keineswegs, dass man ethische Probleme nicht rational behandeln kann, denn der von ihm vertretene methodologische Kritizismus bezieht sich ja keineswegs nur auf wissenschaftliche Probleme, sondern auf Probleme aller Art. Er hat darauf hingewiesen, dass wir ebenso wie im Bereich der wissenschaftlichen Erkenntnis auch im Bereich der Ethik aus unseren Fehlern lernen und auf diese Weise unsere Maßstäbe verbessern können, ohne dass wir über ein Kriterium für absolute moralische Richtigkeit verfügen.[50] Wir sind zum Beispiel in der Lage, mit Hilfe geeigneter Brückenprinzipien wie „Sollen impliziert Können" wissenschaftliche Erkenntnisse zur Kritik ethischer Auffassungen zu verwenden.[51] Auch in ethischer Hinsicht lässt sich ein Rückfall in den Relativismus vermeiden, wenn man den von Popper vertretenen Kritizismus auch in diesem Bereich praktiziert, der die prinzipielle Revidierbarkeit von Maßstäben einräumt.[52]

Bekanntlich hat sich Popper außerdem explizit für bestimmte Antworten auf ethische Probleme ausgesprochen und ist zum Beispiel für eine Ethik der Toleranz eingetreten, die im Einklang steht mit seiner fallibilistischen Erkenntnislehre. Diese Lehre ist nicht nur einem Pluralismus theoretischer Traditionen, sondern auch mit einem Wertepluralismus vereinbar. Sie steht im Gegensatz zu der Forderung nach einem umfassenden Konsens,[53] wie sie zum Beispiel charakteristisch ist für die Auffassungen von Denkern, die sich an der Idee einer im Glauben einigen Gemeinschaft orientieren. Eine solche Gemeinschaft hat jedenfalls mit dem Popperschen Ideal der offenen Gesellschaft nichts zu tun.[54]

Damit komme ich zurück auf die erwähnten Versuche, den „kritischen Rationalismus" Popperscher Prägung in Einklang zu bringen mit den Versionen eines hermeneutischen Pragmatismus, die heute vor allem im europäischen Denken zu finden sind. Ich glaube, dass wir der von Popper vertretenen Tradition der Aufklärung einen schlechten Dienst erweisen, wenn wir uns bemühen, die Unterschiede zwischen philosophischen Auffassungen zu verwischen, um gewissermaßen eine Versöhnung der streitenden Parteien herbeizuführen. Ein illusionärer Konsens, wie er auf diese Art zu erreichen wäre, ist jedenfalls mit dem Streben nach Wahrheit und Klarheit unvereinbar, das für die Tradition der Aufklärung charakteristisch ist. Eine fruchtbare Diskussion kann, wie Popper mit Recht betont hat, damit enden, das die streitenden Parteien zwar keinen Konsens erreicht haben, aber sich über die zur Diskussion stehenden Alternativen klarer geworden sind.

---

[50] Vgl. dazu Popper (1992), Anhänge zu Bd. II, „Tatsachen, Maßstäbe und Wahrheit: Eine weitere Kritik des Relativismus (1961)", pp. 460-493; Pralong (1999), und Albert (2000), pp. 76-91.

[51] Vergleiche mein Buch (1968), Kap. III, „Erkenntnis und Entscheidung".

[52] Zum Problem der Revidierbarkeit von Maßstäben vgl. Nilsson (2000).

[53] Hier ist vor allem die von Jürgen Habermas vertretene Idee der „unverkürzten Verständigung" zu nennen, die zentrale Idee seiner philosophischen Konzeption, die insofern eine Variante des durch Hans-Georg Gadamer vertretenen hermeneutischen Denkens ist.

[54] Zur Kritik des Konsensideals vgl. zum Beispiel Rescher (1993); Engländer (2000) und (2002); Steinhoff (2001).

Literatur

Adorno, T. W., Albert, H., Dahrendorf, R., Habermas, J. & Popper, K. R. (1969). *Der Positivismusstreit in der deutschen Soziologie.* Neuwied & Berlin: Hermann Luchterhand Verlag GmbH. 2. Auflage 1970.

Albert, H. (1968). *Traktat über kritische Vernunft.* Tübingen: J. C. B. Mohr (Paul Siebeck). 5. Auflage 1994.

——— (1984). „Transcendental Realism and Rational Heuristics. Critical Rationalism and the Problem of Method". In G. Andersson, editor (1984), pp. 29-46. *Rationality in Science and Politics.* Dordrecht: D. Reidel Publishing Company. Wieder abgedruckt als Kapitel II von Albert (1999a).

——— (1987). *Kritik der reinen Erkenntnislehre.* Tübingen: J. C. B. Mohr (Paul Siebeck).

——— (1994). *Kritik der reinen Hermeneutik. Der Antirealismus und das Problem des Verstehens.* Tübingen: J. C. B. Mohr (Paul Siebeck).

——— (1996). „Der Mythos des Rahmens. Zur Kritik des idealistischen Rückfalls im modernen Denken". In Gadenne & Wendel (1996), pp. 9-28.

——— (1999a). *Between Social Science, Religion and Politics. Essays on Critical Rationalism.* Amsterdam & Atlanta: Editions Rodopi B.V.

——— (1999b). „Der Naturalismus und das Problem des Verstehens". In Kanitscheider & Wetz (1999).

——— (2000). *Kritischer Rationalismus. Vier Kapitel zur Kritik illusionären Denkens.* Tübingen: J. C. B. Mohr (Paul Siebeck).

——— (2002). „Critical Realism and Universal Hermeneutics". In J. Malpas, U. Arnswald, & J. Kertscher, Hrsg. (2002), pp. 15-24. *Gadamer's Century. Essays in Honour of Hans-Georg Gadamer.* Cambridge MA: MIT Press.

Albert, M. (2002). „Kritischer Rationalismus und die Verfassung der Wissenschaft". In Böhm, Holweg, & Hoock (2002), pp. 231-241.

Andersson, G. (1988). *Kritik und Wissenschaftsgeschichte. Kuhns, Lakatos' und Feyerabends Kritik des Kritischen Rationalismus.* Tübingen: J. C. B. Mohr (Paul Siebeck).

Bergmann, G. (1954). *The Metaphysics of Logical Positivism.* New York: Longmans, Green.

Böhm, J. M., Holweg, H., & Hoock, C., Hrsg. (2002). *Karl Poppers kritischer Rationalismus heute.* Tübingen: Mohr Siebeck.

Devitt, M. (1991). *Realism and Truth.* 2nd edition. Oxford: Basil Blackwell.

Edmonds, D. & Eidinow, J. (2001). *Wie Ludwig Wittgenstein Karl Popper mit dem Feuerhaken drohte. Eine Ermittlung.* Stuttgart & München: Deutsche Verlagsanstalt.

Engländer, A. (2000). „The Illusions of Discourse Theory". *Associations* 4, pp. 223-251.

——— (2002). *Diskurs als Rechtsquelle? Zur Kritik der Diskurstheorie des Rechts.* Tübingen: Mohr Siebeck.

Gadenne, V. (1996). „Rationale Heuristik und Falsifikation". In Gadenne & Wendel (1996), pp. 57-78.

——, Hrsg. (1998). *Kritischer Rationalismus und Pragmatismus*. Amsterdam & Atlanta: Editions Rodopi B.V.

Gadenne, V. & Wendel, H. J., Hrsg. (1996). *Rationalität und Kritik*. Tübingen: J. C. B. Mohr (Paul Siebeck).

Grayling, A. C. (1999). *Wittgenstein*. Freiburg, Basel, & Wien: Herder.

Grondin, J. (1999a). *Hans Georg Gadamer – eine Biographie*. Tübingen: J. C. B. Mohr (Paul Siebeck).

—— (1999b). „Die Hermeneutik als Konsequenz des kritischen Rationalismus". In Kanitscheider & Wetz (1999), pp. 38-46.

Hacohen, M. H. (2000). *Karl Popper – The Formative Years, 1902-1945. Politics and Philosophy in Interwar Vienna*. New York: Cambridge University Press.

Hall, J. A. (1999). „The Sociological Deficit of *The Open Society*, Analyzed and Remedied". In Jarvie & Pralong (1999b), pp. 83-96.

Heidegger, M. (1927), *Sein und Zeit*. Tübingen. Max Niemeyer Verlag.

Jarvie, I. C. (1999). „Popper's Ideal Types: Open and Closed, Abstract and Concrete Societies". In Jarvie & Pralong (1999b), pp. 71-82.

—— (2001). *The Republic of Science. The Emergence of Popper's Social View of Science 1935-1945*. Amsterdam & Atlanta: Editions Rodopi B.V.

Jarvie, I. C. & Pralong, S. (1999a). „Introduction". In Jarvie & Pralong (1999b), pp. 3-16.

——, Hrsg. (1999b). *Popper's Open Society after Fifty Years. The Continuing Relevance of Karl Popper*. London & New York: Routledge.

Kanitscheider, B. & Wetz, F. J., Hrsg. (1999). *Hermeneutik und Naturalismus*. Tübingen: J. C. B. Mohr (Paul Siebeck).

Kolakowski, L. (1977). *Die Suche nach der verlorenen Gewissheit. Denk-Wege mit Edmund Husserl*. Stuttgart: Kohlhammer.

Kuhn, T. S. (1962). *The Structure of Scientific Revolutions*. Chicago: University of Chicago Press. 2nd edition 1970.

—— (1967). *Die Struktur wissenschaftlicher Revolutionen*. Frankfurt/Main: Suhrkamp. 2. Auflage 1976; deutsche Übersetzung von Kuhn (1962).

Lorenz, K. (1941). „Kants Lehre vom Apriorischen im Lichte gegenwärtiger Biologie". In Lorenz (1978), pp. 82-109.

—— (1973). *Die Rückseite des Spiegels. Versuch einer Naturgeschichte der menschlichen Erkenntnis*. München & Zürich: R. Piper.

—— (1978). *Das Wirkungsgefüge der Natur und das Schicksal der Menschen*. München & Zürich: R. Piper.

Magee, B. (1999). „What Use is Popper to a Practical Politician?" In Jarvie & Pralong (1999b), pp. 146-158.

Meyer, W. (2002). *Grundlagen des ökonomischen Denkens*. Tübingen: Mohr Siebeck.

Miller, D. W. (1994). *Critical Rationalism. A Restatement and Defence*. Chicago & La Salle IL: Open Court Publishing Company.

Molden, O. (1981). *Der andere Zauberberg*. Wien: F. Molden.

Musgrave, A. E. (1993). *Alltagswissen, Wissenschaft und Skeptizismus. Eine historische Einführung in die Erkenntnistheorie.* Tübingen: J. C. B. Mohr (Paul Siebeck).

———— (1999). *Essays in Realism and Rationalism.* Amsterdam & Atlanta: Editions Rodopi B.V.

Nilsson, J. (2000). *Rationality in Inquiry. On the Revisability of Cognitive Standards.* Umeå: Department of Philosophy and Linguistics, Umeå University.

Popper, K. R. (1930-1933). *Die beiden Grundprobleme der Erkenntnistheorie.* 1. Auflage 1979. Tübingen: J. C. B. Mohr (Paul Siebeck). 2. Auflage 1994.

———— (1935). *Logik der Forschung. Zur Erkenntnistheorie der modernen Naturwissenschaft.* Wien: Julius Springer Verlag. 11. durchgesehene und ergänzte Auflage 2005.

———— (1945). *The Open Society and Its Enemies.* London: George Routledge & Sons.

———— (1957-1958). *Die offene Gesellschaft und ihre Feinde.* Bd. I (1957), Bd. II. (1958). Bern: A. Francke AG. Erste Auflage der deutschen Übersetzung von Popper (1945).

———— (1970). „Normal Science and Its Dangers". In I. Lakatos & A. E. Musgrave, Hrsg. (1970), pp. 51-58. *Criticism and the Growth of Knowledge.* Cambridge: Cambridge University Press.

———— (1973). *Objektive Erkenntnis. Ein evolutionärer Entwurf.* Hamburg: Hoffmann & Campe.

———— (1979). *Ausgangspunkte. Meine intellektuelle Entwicklung.* Hamburg: Hoffmann & Campe.

———— (1992). *Die offene Gesellschaft und ihre Feinde.* Bd. I. & II., 7. Auflage mit weitgehenden Verbesserungen und Anhängen der deutschen Übersetzung von Popper (1945). Tübingen: J. C. B. Mohr (Paul Siebeck).

———— (1994). *The Myth of the Framework. In Defence of Science and Rationality.* London: Routledge.

Popper, K. R. & Lorenz, K. (1985). *Die Zukunft ist offen. Das Altenberger Gespräch. Mit den Texten des Wiener Popper-Symposiums.* München & Zürich: R. Piper.

Pralong, S. (1999). „*Minima Moralia*: Is There an Ethics of the Open Society?" In Jarvie & Pralong (1999b), pp. 128-145.

Rescher, N. (1993). *Pluralism. Against the Demand for Consensus.* Oxford: Clarendon Press.

Schantz, R. (1998). „Verifikationismus und Realismus in der Philosophie des Pragmatismus. Eine Studie zu Peirce und James". *Zeitschrift für philosophische Forschung* **52**, pp. 363-382.

Schmid, M. (1994). *Rationalität und Theoriebildung. Studien zu Karl Poppers Methodologie der Sozialwissenschaften.* Amsterdam & Atlanta: Editions Rodopi B.V.

Steinhoff, U. (2001). *Kritik der kommunikativen Rationalität.* Norderstedt: BoD GmbH 2001.

Vanberg, V. (1975). *Die zwei Soziologien. Individualismus und Kollektivismus in der Sozialtheorie*. Tübingen: J. C. B. Mohr (Paul Siebeck).

Watkins, J. W. N. (1958). „Confirmable and Influential Metaphysics". *Mind* **67**, pp. 344-365.

—————— (1999). „The Truth Will Out". *The Philosophers' Magazine*, Spring 1999, p. 11.

Wittgenstein, L. J. J. (1921). „Logisch-philosophische Abhandlung". *Annalen der Naturphilosophie* **44**, pp. 185-262.

PART 1
Popper's Life and Times

1

The Historical Roots of Popper's Theory of the Searchlight
A Tribute to Otto Selz

Michel ter Hark

As a student at the Pedagogic Institute of Vienna between 1925 and 1927, the young Popper took courses from Karl Bühler at the Psychological Institute. By then Bühler was a Viennese guru who attracted a large number of students and followers, among them the sociologist Paul Lazarsfeld and the Gestalt psychologist and philosopher of science Egon Brunswik. Even Konrad Lorenz took courses under Bühler. By his own account, Popper learnt much from Bühler, and he always credits him for his important theory of language. Bühler was a generalist, writing on psycholinguistics, perception, and child development, yet it is his *Habilitation* (Bühler 1907) on the psychology of thinking, supervised by the founder of the so-called Würzburg School of *Denkpsychologie*, Oswald Külpe, for which he is primarily remembered in the history of psychology. This work is also the starting point for Popper's dissertation under Bühler in 1928, *Zur Methodenfrage der Denkpsychologie*. Popper never published his dissertation, and in *Unended Quest* he recalls that it was 'a kind of hasty last minute affair' (Popper 1974/1976, § 15).

Another psychologist Popper mentions in his autobiography, Otto Selz, was closely related to the Würzburg School. Selz's name occurs much less frequently in histories of psychology, but it becomes increasingly clear, mainly owing to A. D. de Groot's (1965) application of his ideas to the study of chess thinking, that he was by far the most original and important pre-computational cognitive psychologist. The young Popper must have learnt from Selz via Bühler. Referring to his own experiments in the psychological laboratory, Popper, in *Unended Quest*, remarks about Selz: 'Finding that some of my results had been anticipated, especially by Otto Selz, was, I suspect, one of the minor motives of my move away from psychology.' (Popper, 1974/1976, § 15) These results are that humans 'do not think in images but in terms of problems and their tentative solutions' (ibidem).

In their pioneering work *Learning from Error* (1984), William Berkson and John Wettersten were the first to argue in detail that Popper's later philosophy of science rests on an equally interesting psychological theory. In their little book, they compare Popper's psychological theory with the theories of

Selz, Gestalt psychology, and Piaget, without however drawing on historical sources such as Popper's unpublished writings on psychology or specific
authors read by him. When I began to study Popper's unpublished dissertation in the early 1990s, I discovered, contrary to Berkson and Wettersten,
that his psychological and epistemological theories were far from original and
enormously indebted to German *Denkpsychologie*, in particular to Otto Selz.
Unfortunately, my article on Popper and Selz (ter Hark 1993) was not much
read. Recently (ter Hark 2002) I studied Popper's psychological work preceding his dissertation, *'Gewohnheit' und 'Gesetzerlebnis' in der Erziehung*.
Popper submitted this work as a protothesis in the summer of 1927 to the
Pedagogic Institute of Vienna. In fact it is not just a protothesis. As the sub-
title, 'A structural-psychological monograph', indicates, his ambition was to
write a full monograph, which, however, remained incomplete. In his *Conjectures and Refutations: The Growth of Scientific Knowledge* (1963, Chapter
1), Popper translates the title of his thesis as *On Habit and Belief in Laws*,
and maintains that it contains his logical criticism of Hume's psychological
theory of the genesis of belief, his bucket theory of mind and knowledge. To
my surprise the thesis turned out to be in no way involved with the psychological problem of induction. Moreover, his reliance on the sensualistic framework provided by Richard Avenarius only further strengthened my idea that
Popper, in 1927, was still far removed from recognizing the defects of a bucket
theory. Indeed, prior to his reading of Selz, Popper simply had no deductivist or quasi-deductivist psychology of problem solving. His reading of the
work of Selz therefore marks the real watershed in his intellectual life, since
it ultimately led him to abandon the inductive (sensualistic) psychology of
knowledge. My aim in this paper is to argue in detail how the young Popper
gradually transformed Selz's theory of problem solving into his well-known
deductivist theory of knowledge, his theory of the searchlight. In particular,
I argue that this transformation spans a period of three years, beginning
with his dissertation in 1928, taking more definite shape in a short article on
mnemonic exercise in 1931, and culminating in *Die beiden Grundprobleme der
Erkenntnistheorie*, written in 1930-1933 (but not published until 1979).

1   Otto Selz and the Würzburg School

The historical background and genesis of Otto Selz's theory of reproductive
and productive thinking still has to be written, but what is clear so far is that
his theory both elaborates upon and criticizes the programme of the Würzburg
School. This programme, headed by Külpe, was already quite revolutionary.
The method of the Würzburg School is called experimental introspection because it combines introspection and a method of testing. Subjects were asked
not only to respond to a question but also to describe their state of mind during the test. For several reasons applying the experimental method to higher
forms of cognition was a daring enterprise in those days. Sensations, emotions,
reflexes, memory, and association were the proper subject of experimentation,

and it seemed far from likely that it could contribute to the study of thought. Moreover, judgement and reasoning were before long considered properly a part of logic and epistemology, normative rather than empirical studies. Perhaps the insurmountable obstacle for a psychology of thinking was the refusal to recognize any other form of experience than sensations, images, and fragments of images common to the sensualism of Berkeley, Hume, Condillac, and Ernst Mach.

The researches of Külpe's graduates were given direction and point precisely by his determination to show that it is impossible to analyse thought into sensory elements, thereby discrediting Mach, and to contribute to the experimental analysis of thought, thereby departing from Wundt. As Külpe summarizes the first achievements of the School, these were largely negative: the traditional contents of consciousness, sensation, feeling, and images — the very substance of Wundtian psychology — proved inadequate to account for the intellectual processes of thoughtful association and judgement. Yet subjects frequently reported that they experienced certain conscious processes which they could describe neither as definite images nor as acts of will. To these impalpable experiences, which could not be classified under any of the standard categories, various names were given, but the name best remembered — imageless thought — came from a critical reviewer of the programme, Edward Titchener (1909). The significance of these Würzburg experiments is not so much the disproof of images, for that was not attempted; images do exist and are part of thinking. Their real significance is that they demonstrated that thought consists not solely of images and, more importantly, that there are (unconscious) regulatory and selective mechanisms in thinking. Thus Heinrich Watt (1905) conducted experiments in which he demonstrated the role of the *Aufgabe*, or task, as a directive influence in the problem he set for naming super-ordinates for sub-ordinates and parts for wholes. At the same time Narziss Ach (1905) dubbed the directive influence of the task on the outcome of thinking 'determining tendencies'. According to Ach, determining tendencies explain the ordered and purposeful character of thought processes; they rule out irrelevances and prevent chance stimuli from distracting the course of thought processes. They accomplish this by favouring those associations that are in line with the purpose of the subject. For instance, if the instruction is given to add two numbers, the subject's representation of this goal (*Zielvorstellung*) will influence the particular stimulus presented. Thus, given 6 ; 2, the answers 8, 4, or 3 will result according to the goal-representations (corresponding to the instructions) of respectively, adding, subtracting, and dividing. But although critical of association psychology, the regulatory systems postulated by Watt and Ach were still associative in nature.

Although his experimental set-up was in the tradition of the School, Selz's theoretical work deviates from the School in two respects. The first difference is that Selz does not adopt even a modified version of associationism but rejects it completely. The second difference is that in Selz's work the explanandum of psychology is shifted from the content of thinking to the process of thinking. While the elder members of the Würzburg School set themselves the phenomenological task of describing and analysing thought experiences as a mental category *sui generis*, Selz, without denying the importance of image-less thought, believed that the essence of thinking is to be found in a series of 'operations'. Selz, de Groot summarizes, '... read protocols in a different way: he searched for the procedures (methods) by which the subject made progress ...' (de Groot 1965, p. 51).

After his PhD, Otto Selz (1881-1943) went to Bonn where he participated in the seminars of Külpe and Karl Bühler. Above all he was engaged in experimental investigations in the laboratory of Külpe. These investigations resulted in his first major work, his *Habilitationsschrift, Über die Gesetze des geordneten Denkverlaufs. Eine experimentelle Untersuchung* (1913). Taking his cue from Bühler's theory of imageless thought, Selz, according to Külpe, made a significant step forward in the psychology of thought.[1] In fact Selz's drift away from the programme of the Würzburg School was more radical than Külpe acknowledged. Already perceptible in 1910, the incipient rift among Selz and the Würzburg School became more obvious in the wake of a devastating review of Ach's book on willing (Selz 1910).

With his second major work in the psychology of thought, *Zur Psychologie des produktiven Denkens und des Irrtums* (1922a), whose publication was postponed owing to the First World War, Selz's intellectual prestige was incontestably on the increase, and in 1923 he was called to the chair of Philosophy, Psychology, and Pedagogy at the *Handelshochschule* in Mannheim (Baden). From this period too stem two of his short philosophical essays, *Oswald Spengler und die intuitive Methode in der Geschichtsforschung* (1922b) and *Kants Stellung in der Geisteswissenschaft* (1924a), in which he attempts to bridge the gap between the natural sciences and the *Geisteswissenschaften* by means of his naturalistic and evolutionary epistemology.

In his scientific work Selz was increasingly marginalized because of his unremitting criticism of colleagues but also because of his formidably complex style of writing. A biologist disguised as a psychologist, Selz came into conflict with proponents of the *Geisteswissenschaften*, who blamed him for endorsing a mechanist view of man. Seeking to reconstruct psychological wholes on the basis of their elements, Gestalt psychologists considered him an atomist, whereas to others he was a one-sided rationalist. Closely allied to the Würzburg School, he did not shrink back from launching frontal attacks on the ideas of some of its members. Aside from two pupils, Jules Bahle and Adriaan de Groot, he never founded a school and after 1933 his name disappears almost completely from the German psychological literature.[2]

---

[1] Quoted in Seebohm (1970), p. 15.

[2] Julius Bahle applied Selz's psychology of productive thinking to the psychology of musical composition (Bahle 1930, 1936). It is noteworthy that Popper's discussions of music in *Unended Quest* (1974/1976, Chapter 11, 12, 13) bear a striking resemblance to Bahle's theory of musical problem solving, yet he eschews any reference to Bahle. As appears from his references in *The Self and Its Brain* (Popper & Eccles 1977, Chapter 4, § 30) Popper was familiar with Bahle's work, including his relation to Selz.

When Hitler was appointed Chancellor of Germany the Ministry of Culture and Education issued an edict in the spring of 1933 demanding that Otto Selz resign his posts, the official reason being the maintenance of security and order in Baden. Selz was no longer allowed to teach and research at the Institute of Psychology and Pedagogy in Mannheim. On October 25 the *Handelshochschule* was finally closed, and the Institute was incorporated into the University of Heidelberg. Since Heidelberg had made no arrangements for Selz, the official reading goes, Selz was unceremoniously stripped of his career and livelihood. The truth of the matter was of course that Selz was a 'non-Aryan'. Most psychologists expelled from the academy left Germany and migrated to the United States. Not so Selz. He led a withdrawn life in Mannheim, where, the opportunities to do experimental work being gravely diminished, he threw himself into purely theoretical work on the *Aufbau* of the phenomenal world. After the *Reichskristallnacht* he was arrested and deported to the concentration camp of Dachau, from which he was released in December 1938. In May 1939 he finally migrated to the Netherlands, first to Bilthoven, then to Amsterdam, where he lived in a small apartment in the Cliostraat. The one fortunate outcome of this shameful episode was that Selz came into contact with the Dutch pedagogue Phillip Kohnstamm and the psychologist A. D. de Groot. Selz taught at the Amsterdam Teachers Seminar (*Nutseminarium*) on psychology and pedagogy, and participated in scientific discussions at the Faculty of Psychology, hugely enriching the field of psychology there. After the German invasion in May 1940 Selz corresponded with Kurt Koffka, who had emigrated to America, but nothing came of Koffka's efforts (Beckmann 2001). He declined the offer of his Dutch friends to find a hiding place for him, replying that the Iron Cross he had won during the First World War would surely protect him. He would not be spared, however. In July 1943 he was again apprehended by the Nazis and deported to the concentration camp at Westerbork. A postcard saying that he wanted to give courses in Westerbork was the last sign of life. On August 24 he was put on train DA 703 for Auschwitz. He either 'died' in transit from suffocation or exhaustion — he was suffering from heart problems — or was murdered in the gas chambers.

2 Otto Selz's revision of psychology

In his first major work Selz (1913) calls his alternative to association psychology a 'theory of whole-completion through schematic anticipations'. In the synopsis of his two books in cognitive psychology, *Die Gesetze der produktiven und reproduktiven Geistestätigkeit. Kurzgefasste Darstellung* (1924b), the two theories are called, respectively, 'system of diffuse reproductions' versus 'theory of specific reactions'. The core of Selz's detailed criticisms of association psychology can be summarized thus: eschewing any reference to cognitive or meaningful relations between associations, such as 'cause of' or 'solution of', and instead admitting only relations of temporal and spatial contiguity or similarity, association psychology, Selz concludes, by definition cannot exclude irrelevant associations from arising. Indeed, there is no more spatial and temporal contiguity between a specific problem and its specific solution than between that problem and countless other problems and solutions. Accordingly, completely pointless errors should occur rather frequently during problem solving. The fact that such errors do not frequently occur is then inexplicable from the point of view of association psychology. Moreover, what is even less explicable from the perspective of association psychology is that errors are not random, but prove to be systematically related to the structure of the problem. Errors, to put it differently, have meaning.

On Selz's theory of whole completion, (reproductive) thinking is not a matter of associatively reproducing one element with another but rather completing a knowledge complex, a memory structure, guided by schematic anticipations. Selz opens his discussion of schemata by noting that in many cases of memory retrieval, subjects already know that the information at hand is a piece of a larger whole. Indeed, they often know even what kind of whole the piece belongs to. Thus a candidate at an oral exam, Selz illustrates, not only knows that the first phoneme of the first word uttered by the examiner is part of a whole, but also that this whole is a word, and that the word begins with this phoneme. This knowledge, Selz emphasizes, does not consist of two separate elements: on the one hand the awareness of a word, and, on the other, the awareness of the uttered phoneme. Rather, the subject knows that the phoneme is part of a word; that is, a relational whole is involved rather than an aggregate of elements. Being aware of this cognitive whole prompts the subject to anticipate schematically the answer to the question. Giving the example of a candidate in an oral examination trying to remember the *Melanchton*, who is assisted by the examiner's giving the first three letters *Mel*, Selz explains: 'The awareness of the word sought is changed from the awareness of an undetermined word to the awareness of a word beginning with *Mel* .... We must think of it as though the empty scheme of a concrete word is partly filled out by the insertion at its beginning of the sounds spoken in anticipation ....' (Selz 1913, p. 114) Diagrams of schematic anticipations, making clearly visible that the awareness of a problem relates to the cognitive whole to be realized as the scheme of a whole relates to the completed whole, appeared in Selz (1922a, 1924b).

Schematic anticipations then establish a system of provisional relations between the new elements and the cognitive whole they fit into, thereby clearly functioning as hypotheses in the process of problem solving. In Figure 1 below, A and B stand for items in memory, for example, the words 'tiger' and 'cow', γ stands for a relation stored in memory, for example 'coordinate with'. The black spot symbolizes a 'gap' in memory that needs to be filled. In his second, massive, book Selz turns from reproductive to productive thinking. The key to his explanation of productive thinking, in science and art, is the concept of a solving method — the term '*Lösungsmethode*' was coined by him — or a heuristic. Confronted with a new problem, Selz argues, utilizing existing

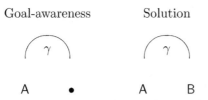

**Fig. 1.1 A schematic anticipation of a cognitive whole
(after Selz 1922a)**

know-how is no longer an option, yet utilizing familiar solving-methods is. Applying familiar solving methods to new problems, changing material, or in different situations, he avers, is the key to understanding creative thinking. In this area, too, earlier problems and schematic anticipations are the tools to explain thinking in a way amenable to the standards of natural science. A philosopher primarily interested in epistemology, Selz sought to use his cognitive psychology as a (naturalistic) foundation for epistemological theories aimed at understanding the nature and growth of scientific knowledge and even of culture. Thus invoking his recent scientific findings in cognitive psychology in explaining creative thinking too, including discoveries in science and art, Selz significantly broadened the objectives of experimental psychology by encompassing an area deemed hitherto the exclusive province of hermeneutic psychology. Indeed the very part of the human mind that is the breeding-ground for products of culture, both Dilthey and Spranger contended, is not subject to the laws of nature. It is this anti-naturalistic stance of hermeneutic psychology that is challenged by Selz's cognitive theory of creativity. Spengler's explicit dismissal of scientific psychology in the study of creative cultural achievements was a special bone of contention for Selz. As Selz sees it, Spengler's concept of the soul belongs to an outdated concept of the mind (1922b, p. 25)

> according to which the mind is merely a formative principle without receiving itself any influences. Contemporary scientific psychology, however, knows that the mind receives again influences from its own products, by means of which it is capable of developing further. Practical and scientific insights form an especially important class of such retro-acting influences that the mind accomplishes, including the discovery of values that can also belong to a past culture.

Rather than being a mysterious *Geist* withdrawn from the laws of nature, the human personality, Selz contends, is functionally interwoven with its biology. As he puts it both in the preface of his work on productive thinking (1922a, p. xii) and in his synopsis of his results in cognitive psychology two years later in a fragment (Selz 1924b, pp. 60f.) quoted approvingly by Popper in his *Zur Methodenfrage* (1928):

The view defended here is diametrically opposed to the teaching of Bergson and of a philosopher who is close to him, Spengler. They conceive of life as a process, as a continuous stream in which nothing occurs twice, but in which continually new forms arise in a mysterious, causally inexplicable way.... By contrast, we have shown here that it is precisely *the constant, systematic linkages of cognitive operations and the recurrence of the same conditions of elicitation that constitute the preconditions for progressive development, for the growth of new operations and the generation of new products of the mind* .... Perhaps our era is witnessing the beginnings of a 'biology of the inner'. Psychology thus enters the ranks of the biological sciences.

In his theory of specific reactions Selz (1924b) applied his theory of whole completion and schematic anticipations to the level of elementary, reflex-like behaviour, to be found among animals and young children, and in human skills, thereby emphasizing the analogy between motor operations and cognitive operations. What Selz sought to achieve with this analogy between motor operations and cognitive operations was nothing less than a biological or evolutionary revision of the then dominant theory of cognitive development that assigns an irreducible place to the intellect. According to this model, espoused above all by Bühler, intelligence gradually arises from the increasing multiplicity of acquired habits or associations. Following this tradition of developmental psychology Selz too distinguished between instinctive learning, automatic learning (habit-formation), and insightful learning, yet he was to argue that even the simplest form of habit cannot be explained in terms of associative learning. On the contrary, he argued, 'acquired reflexes' too are guided by schematic anticipations. Thus conceived the study of the genesis of habits becomes relevant to the study of the development of intelligence for, rather than being a qualitatively different and older stage, cognitive operations are, as he put it, 'a developmental integration of intellectual actions into an existing, more primitive system of specific responses'. (Selz 1927, p. 229) Accordingly, a theory of stages would then be concerned only with 'different developmental stages of a single system of specific responses. In this manner the automatic acquisition of novel modes of behaviour, Bühler's "stage of training", demands no system of diffuse reproduction ...' (Selz ibidem).

It is here that Selz introduces his important notion of trying-out behaviour (*probierenden Verhaltens*). Among the 'trying-out movements', for instance in learning to play tennis, depicted in Figure 1.2 below, a small group will lead to a positive result (R) the others will produce negative results ($N_1, N_2, N_3 \ldots$). In later attempts the subject S cannot anticipate the exact movement that has led to R as a means to achieving his goal, yet, Selz emphasizes, anticipating R prompts only those memory traces of earlier attempts that actually have led to R.

The most important difference between blind trial and error and trying-out behaviour is that in the latter case attempts are based on a partial insight into the situation. Always showing a clear sense of direction the organism tries out within a pre-set, goal-determined and limited domain of solution possibilities;

in Selzian terms, schematic anticipations co-determine the where and what of searching and trying.

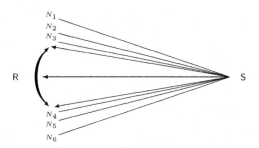

Fig. 1.2 Trying-out behaviour (after Selz 1924b)

3 Popper's *Zur Methodenfrage der Denkpsychologie*

Writing his dissertation in psychology under Bühler, the young Popper was familiar with the most important works in cognitive psychology, including Selz's recent work on creative thinking and evolutionary epistemology. *Zur Methodenfrage der Denkpsychologie* is difficult to read and still far removed from the elegant prose familiar from Popper's later writings. Neither is it a very original piece of writing for rather than elaborating views of his own the author walks dutifully hand in hand with Karl Bühler reproducing blindly the latter's methodological views in his recently published *Die Krise der Psychologie* (1927).

Bühler's main point of criticism is that no school (behaviourism, *Denkpsychologie*, psychoanalysis, hermeneutic psychology) is capable of doing justice to what are the three basic characteristics of human conduct: inner experience (*Erlebnis*), meaningful behaviour (*sinnvolles Benehmen*), and their relation to culture (*Gebilden des objektiven Geistes*). A unitary science of psychology, Bühler maintains, is the science of the triad experience-behaviour-culture. Thereby departing from Selz, Bühler emphatically claims that psychology, although firmly rooted in biology, is also part of the *Geisteswissenschaften*.

Popper's first goal is to defend Bühler's pluralistic methodology against the objections of contemporary physicalism. Demonstrating the indispensability of Bühler's pluralistic methodology for cognitive psychology is his second goal. Yet applying Bühler's methodological insights to cognitive psychology is not Popper's only target; a separate problem that runs through his discussion of cognitive psychology is the biological or evolutionary theory of cognitive development. It is this 'subgoal' that gives the dissertation its unfinished and unbalanced character.[3] For in the course of his discussion of cognitive psychology it becomes clear that Popper is no less interested in the

---

[3]The importance of this subgoal has been overlooked by Hacohen (2000) in his brief discussion of Popper's dissertation. Moreover Hacohen fails to relate both the bucket theory and the searchlight theory to Popper's endorsement of Selz in respectively (1931) and (1928).

evolutionary theory of cognitive development than in the topic, which not
only (formally) deserves, but also receives, the most extensive treatment, to
wit the importance of Bühler's pluralism of aspects for cognitive psychology.

It would be far beyond the scope of this article to deal with Popper's
discussion of Bühler's three aspects here.[4] Under each of these aspects the
name of Selz occurs rather prominently, but especially so when Popper deals
with the aspect of the objective products of the mind, in particular science.
Having earlier dismissed a parallelism of structure between, on the one hand,
subjective experiences and, on the other hand, objective intellectual structures
(his later world 3), Popper now turns to the method of scientific research
(*Forschungsseite*). In this area, he contends, cognitive psychology is on much
firmer ground and can contribute significantly. It is here that the earliest
traces of his later method of trial and error, his theory of the searchlight, are
to be found (Popper 1928, pp. 69f.)

> Perhaps there are important parallels in the methods and operations of scientific
> and 'pre-scientific' induction?
>
> To give just one example: the Selzian concept of trying-out behaviour [*prob-
> ierenden Verhaltens*] seems to me to have important parallels in objective scient-
> ific research. Science tries out its methods, its 'models' (as Bühler puts it), and in
> such a way as to correspond completely with the Selzian scheme [*dem Selzschen
> Schema*]. As is well known the actual ways of scientific research in no way corre-
> spond with the logical principles of the representation; as little as the operations
> [*Operationen*] described by Selz correspond with the objective logical operations.
> Despite this, science is in the end clearly driven by tasks [*aufgabegesteuert*], the
> determining tendencies [*determinierenden Tendenzen*] come clearly to the fore.
>
> Selz himself has several times made use of the example of scientific research;
> although not in the sense in which we here propose. His analysis encompasses
> not the objective intellectual structures, not objective scientific research, but he
> analyses certain scientific discoveries under the aspect of experience.

This passage unmistakably shows that Popper has borrowed his later theory of
trial and error, with its characteristic emphasis on the guiding role of problems
both in individual and in scientific knowledge acquisition, from Selz, yet it also
shows his thoughts to be still rudimentary at this juncture. For one of the most
surprising features of this passage is his speaking of induction as a matter of
course. Embracing induction not only conflicts with his well-known deductivist
methodology and epistemology — as well as with his own portrayal of the
genesis of his philosophy — but also with the epistemological implications of
Selz's psychology. As I have made clear in the preceding section, Selz's detailed
and frontal assault on association psychology, and his defence of a theory of
whole-completion, in fact boiled down to a view of the animal or human
organism as an active cognitive subject constantly putting forward tentative
proposals or hypotheses rather than as a passive recipient, patiently waiting
for the accumulation of information to be inductively safe. Fully embracing

---

[4]See ter Hark (2004).

what he calls the 'Selzian scheme' of problem-solving therefore means that
the material for building a deductivist, and problem-driven, methodology and
epistemology is already available to him in 1928, yet the inductive paradigm
has such a strong hold on Popper that it prevents him from drawing out
the revolutionary implications of Selz's work. In the next section we shall
see how Popper makes a move more in the direction of a deductivist theory
of knowledge and science by first discarding, again within the framework of
Selz's cognitive psychology, the bucket theory of knowledge and science.

4 The bucket theory and mnemonic exercise

The ensuing development of Popper's thoughts on psychology brings us to a
short publication (Popper 1931) in the monthly journal of pedagogical reform,
Die Quelle, edited by Eduard Burger. Scrutiny of this much-neglected article,
entitled 'Die Gedächtnispflege unter dem Gesichtspunkt der Selbsttätigkeit'
('Mnemonic exercise from the perspective of self-activity') shows that the
elaboration of a Selzian evolutionary epistemology takes shape only gradually. After having toyed with the idea of applying Selz's notion of trying-out
behaviour in the philosophy of science we find Popper now appealing to Selz's
theory of whole-completion in a pedagogical debate between, on the one hand,
the *Lernschule*, and, on the other, the *Arbeitsschule* of Eduard Burger concerning the role of memorization in education.[5] The labour schools attempted
to steer education away from a drill school approach, typical of the *Lernschule*,
towards seeking children's active engagement through self-discovery. In fact,
Popper notes, the battle between these two camps has already been decided
in favour of the *Arbeitsschule*, but, he goes on, certain one-sided developments
within the labour school movement have neglected to confront what is in fact
the strong point of the *Lernschule*: the role accorded to memory. He concedes
that the emphasis laid upon the accumulation of dictated knowledge by the
Lernschule has been too strong, yet Popper, following Burger, warns that this
objection can easily invite the *Arbeitsschule* to neglect the role of memory
in favour of the education of the intellect. His goal is not simply to redress
the balance between the intellect and memorization, rather it is to defeat the
Lernschule in its own area and to show that its view of memorization itself is
mistaken.

Having a huge amount of knowledge at one's disposal is the ruling principle
(*Stoffprinzip*) of the *Lernschule*. This principle demands a lot of memorization. Mnemonic exercise is achieved, according to the school, by accumulation of knowledge and frequent repetition of this material. While approving of
the pedagogical importance the *Lernschule* attaches to memorization, Popper
sees the weak point of the school's programme in the way it believes that

---

[5]To the extent that the article is about pedagogy, and especially about certain psychological presuppositions of pedagogy, it is a continuation not of the dissertation on cognitive
psychology but of the thesis on dogmatic thinking of 1927. Indeed, some of the pedagogical
questions left unanswered by Popper in his thesis now receive a clear and definitive answer.
See ter Hark (2002).

mnemonic exercise is achieved. That is, the problem with the *Lernschule* is
not pedagogical but psychological.

The ensuing description of the psychology underlying the pedagogical programme of the *Lernschule* shows Popper using for the first time a metaphor
that will figure prominently in his later writings: 'To the *Lernschule* memory
is nothing but a container of material, a sort of bucket of knowledge.' (Popper
1931, p. 610) The essence of memory, on this view, is to let in and store knowledge. Indeed, the only properties of the bucket are its more or less reliable
storage of knowledge, and its having a certain space. The consequences for
pedagogy are that mnemonic exercise can be achieved only by repeating as
often as possible the process of storing and retrieving information, and by an
accumulation of dictated knowledge, which will enlarge memory space.

Popper's next use of the metaphor of the bucket was to be in 1948, in the
article 'The Bucket and the Searchlight: Two Theories of Knowledge', not
published in English until 1972, in *Objective Knowledge*. One of the striking
differences between these two articles is that while Popper, in 1931, introduces
the bucket theory as a purely psychological theory, the emphasis in 1948 is on
epistemology throughout. Furthermore, there he not only hides the psychological roots of his evolutionary or genetic epistemology from view, but the
pedagogical context in which his criticism of association psychology initially
arose, is totally absent.[6] A third difference is that, in 1931, the bucket theory
is not yet overturned by, or even contrasted with, what Popper regards as
one of his great achievements: the development of a searchlight theory of the
mind.

The theory that does replace the bucket theory in 1931, however, is the
theory of Otto Selz. As Popper goes on (Popper 1931, p. 610):

> This view of the psychology of memory is more or less the same as the outlook of
> association psychology. Unfortunately, association psychology, even though its
> very complete breakdown was the main result of psychological research at the
> turn of the century, is still widespread. This decisive turn in the psychology of
> thought (and of memory) was initiated by Kant and carried through, according
> to strict experimental methods, by the school of Külpe, especially Bühler and
> Selz.

The fundamental mistake of association psychology, Popper argues, is its attempt to derive the whole of human memory, even the whole of intellectual
capacities, from a single and simple form of associative memory (what he
calls the bucket). Popper's alternative account of the genesis of the different
functions of memory follows Selz's cognitive psychology in detail. The role
of associative memory is restricted to the processing of nonsense syllables in
the laboratory, but even in such rather artificial situations, Popper argues,
subjects often establish meaningful connections between stimuli. With this
understanding of meaning, Popper concludes, thinking enters memory: 'The
laws of the mechanisms of association are replaced by the "laws of ordered

---

[6]Popper does not refer to his 1931 article in his later discussions of the bucket theory.

thinking". (Selz)' (ibidem, p. 613) And a few lines further: 'Selz has coined the name "intellectual operations" for the functions of thinking.' That Popper's alternative account of memory and memorization wholly depends for its conception on ideas he takes over from Selz is corroborated by a passage in which the latter's theory of whole-completion is put forward as providing the *Arbeitsschule* with the required notion of psychological activity (ibidem):

> Selz has shown that 'reproductive thinking' is an extremely active process, a production process (*Arbeitsvorgang*). The important method, the important tool of this production process, is the scheme. In this scheme an unoccupied space (*Leerstelle*) takes the place of missing thoughts, thoughts that have to be reproduced. The systematic completion of these unoccupied spaces of the scheme (the 'determinate completion of the complex') leads to reproduction.

Rather than being a passive and mechanical process, Selz has taught, human memory turns out to be a systematic reconstructing of schematic anticipations and their gaps. It is this psychology of memory, Popper believes, that can help steer education away from the *Lernschule*, in which children are treated as empty buckets to be filled by the accumulation of knowledge, towards seeking children's active engagement through thinking, without neglecting the role of memorization in favour of the intellect. Selz's cognitive psychology, as Popper sees it, is a natural psychological foundation for Burger's pedagogical idea that education is the systematic development and perfection of teaching methods ('learning to learn', what is called the *Kraftprinzip* in contrast with the *Stoffprinzip*).

To fight the drill schools, Popper summons pedagogues to abandon not the exercise of memory but the appeal to associative memory. He professes deep scepticism as to the question whether associative memory is capable of developing at all. Perhaps, he says, associative memory is a primitive and rather fixed disposition of the human mind. In any case, the bottom-up attempt of deriving the higher forms of thinking from the mechanisms of association, so characteristic of association psychology and the related constellation theory, Popper recalls, thereby clearly alluding to Selz, has completely failed. Yet abandoning teaching methods based upon associative memory, Popper avers, need not imply a division of labour with, on the one hand, the *Lernschule* inculcating elementary facts of mathematics, language, and history, and, on the other, the *Arbeitsschule* focusing upon the exercise of higher intellectual operations. On the contrary, even getting rows of numbers and words firmly into one's head may profit from the new view of intellectual operations as developed by Selz (Popper, ibidem): 'Inculcating, then, becomes a process of thinking [*Denkarbeit*].' Memorization guided by 'the laws of ordered thinking', Popper is anxious to point out, although equally mechanical, is yet completely different from associative memory; he dubs it 'automatized insightful memory'. The difference turns out to be less an ontological one, as suggested by his categorizing of associative memory and automatized insightful memory in two different layers of the mind, respectively, training and intellect, than a matter of genesis. Indeed, automatized insightful memory is defined by opposition with the (failed) bottom-up approach of association psychology; its genesis proceeds the other way round (ibidem):

> This one consists in a reduction of certain processes, certain chains of ordered thinking, by way of a continual repetition of the course of reactions; indeed, it is even possible that the consciousness of the middle parts of the chain completely fades away, and that finally only the part at the beginning and the one at the end of the chain appear immediately connected with one another.

The key distinction is that in a theory of ordered thinking the process of mechanization sets in later than in an associationist theory. Not until after the pupil has familiarized himself with the relevant piece of memorized knowledge by means of the intellectual operations as described by Selz, mechanization can be initiated. The result in both cases seems to be the same, yet the difference is as big as that between a skilful piano player and a gramophone record (Popper ibidem). As this analogy indicates, insightful memory becoming automatic is a process on a par with the development of skills, of know-how. Although he does not refer to Selz's specific theory of know-how, it is evident that it is this theory to which Popper's theory of mechanization is immensely indebted. Indeed, his specific wording that 'chains of ordered thinking' are reduced by repetition to such an extent that 'only the part at the beginning and the one at the end of the chain appear immediately connected with one another', echoes Selz's (1913) explanation of skills.

Despite the article's mainly practical objectives there are passages in it that point to Popper's later deductivist epistemology. Having repeated that associative memory and automatized insightful memory are fundamentally different processes, he goes on to say that the latter consists merely in an abbreviation of reactions. That is, rather than creating something new (knowledge, belief?), mechanization only makes something disappear. His subsequent remark, 'Where these reactions, these processes of reconstruction, are not shaped yet, there is nothing which can be abbreviated', is, in the context of the article, a pedagogical warning not to let the process of mechanization begin too soon, but at the same time can be seen as conveying the core idea of the later searchlight theory that, since learning (mechanization of skills) can take place only on the basis of already shaped intellectual operations, these intellectual operations have to precede knowledge acquisition (Popper 1931, p. 618) The fully epistemological elaboration of this Selzian view, however, has to wait one or two years. In *Die beiden Grundprobleme der Erkenntnistheorie*, Popper will indeed come to defend the deductivist view that anticipations precede reactions.

5 Popper's deductivist turn

In the section 'The possibility of a deductive psychology of knowledge' of *Die beiden Grundprobleme der Erkenntnistheorie* (1930-1933), Popper undertakes the task of attacking what he calls an inductive prejudice: the idea that only an inductive psychology of knowledge would be feasible.[7] Unlike the philosophical theory of knowledge, which seeks to justify knowledge claims, psychology of knowledge is a theory of the acquisition and genesis of knowledge. These two approaches to knowledge, despite being clearly related, he emphasizes, are yet logically independent, and an inductive stance in epistemology can be associated with a deductivist stance in psychology, and vice versa. Nevertheless, many of those who favour an inductive epistemology, such as Mach and Carnap, subscribe to an inductive psychology of knowledge, which, moreover, is explicitly sensualistic. On this inductive sensualism, humans arrive at knowledge and experience by generalizing from individual experiences, in particular, perceptual experiences. No reference is made in (1931) to what he dubbed the bucket theory, yet this evident connection well explains Popper's eagerly setting himself the problem of providing an alternative to the psychology that he believes underpins the epistemology of many (logical) positivists.

As to the genesis of this alternative theory Popper's account is ambiguous. On the one hand he says that it results from his applying the deductivist theory of knowledge to the area of psychology, his so-called principle of transference, but on the other hand he refers to cognitive psychology. As he begins his sketch (1930-1933, § 4, p. 23): 'In the *psychology of knowledge* properly so called (or '*Denkpsychologie*') deductive lines of thinking are to be found primarily among *biologically* oriented psychologists. While the reader may expect to find here the names of Bühler and Selz, Popper instead mentions Mach, who is clearly not in the tradition of deductivist cognitive psychology but in the opposite camp of 'inductive sensualism'. Quoting Mach's (1896/1900) contention ('What is reacted upon *similarly* falls under *one* concept') Popper now argues that it can be used for the construction of a deductivist psychology of knowledge. Yet the appeal to Mach is scarcely convincing here. For Popper and Mach nurture antithetically different conceptions of the genesis of knowledge, respectively, a deductivist and cognitive theory, and an inductive and sensualistic view. So how can Popper contend that Mach's claim contains the building blocks for a deductivist psychology of knowledge?[8] It is one thing to say that in Mach's explanation a distinction is made between a reactive and a receptive side of the physiological system, but it is another thing to say, as Popper does, that the reactive side is of decisive importance. This latter

---

[7]This prejudice automatically leads to an inductivistic prejudice in the field of the theory of knowledge, according to Popper.

[8]In a footnote added in 1979 (ibidem, p. 24, note *1), Popper correctly observes that Mach's claim is in direct opposition with his sensualistic theory of knowledge as defended in *Analyse der Empfindungen* (1886). Mach's sensualism is not only an inductive theory but also one in which the mind is merely a receptacle and knowledge the passive accumulation of sensory impressions.

claim, crucially important for a deductivist theory, is precisely what is denied by Mach: the new sensations of smell and touch produced by activities
are said to be decisive. It is only in the anti-sensualistic work of Selz that
the idea that our knowledge of the external world is drawn from our mind,
from its anticipatory schemes, and, initially, from behavioural anticipatory
schemes, reaches its clearest expression. Admittedly, Popper does drop the
name of Selz later but in so parenthetical a way as to be out of all proportion
to his real indebtedness to him. Every commentator, however, has to concede
that Popper's sketch shadows Selz's theory of specific responses and anticipations. For the evidence for this is unanswerable. The allusions and parallels
are simply too numerous to be denied.

   To begin with, his conception of cognitive processes exactly parallels Selz,
who, as was recounted by Popper himself in 1931, coined the expression 'intellectual reactions'. As Popper now, but without mentioning Selz, says: 'Our
knowledge and thinking are not to be conceived as a combining or associative
ordering of sensory experiences, of *receptions*, rather our thoughts have to be
characterized as *intellectual reaction*.' (Popper ibidem) That his reliance on
Selz extends itself far beyond the terminological level, and in fact amounts to
a complete assimilation of the 'Selzian scheme', is further testified by Popper's
emphasizing, and elaborating, the analogy between intellectual operations and
motor operations, which was a key element in Selz. Like Selz, Popper contends
that (ibidem): '*Physiological reactions* in general (not only intellectual ones),
although naturally elicited by a stimulus (a reception), are as far as the specific form of the course of their reactions concerned exceedingly dependent upon
the *subjective conditions of the reacting apparatus itself*.' This raises the question of how (intellectual) reactions, drawn from the mind rather than from
the world, nonetheless prove themselves adaptive in objective circumstances.
It is in answering this question that he drops the name of Selz, but only
after first crediting the biologist H. Jennings with the finding of a solution:
'To this question the *theory of trial movements* of Jennings for instance can
provide an answer . . . .' (Popper, ibidem, pp. 24f.) Popper here refers to Jennings's principle of the selection of overproduced movements, which says that
animals learning to deal effectively with some obstacle in their environment
typically try to effect their object in a number of different ways, many of
which are inadequate and hence unsuccessful, but gradually find that certain
efforts are more satisfactory in their results than others; these are repeated,
and thus by successive limitations of the originally numerous and relatively
indefinite trials the exuberant efforts are narrowed down to those that bring
success; these become habitual through repetition. Echoing his earlier pedagogical work and the work of Selz, but now referring to Jennings, Popper
points out that exercise and repetition merely abbreviate the series of trials
and reactions rather than create something new. Yet this reliance on Jennings,
rather than providing further support for a deductivist psychology of knowledge leads only to eroding its basis, for at the bottom of Jennings's theory of

trial movements rules the principle of association.[9] Selz, on the other hand, not only outflanked and discredited association psychology but also provided an alternative theory for both trying-out behaviour and 'associative' memory that shifts the emphasis from the passive reception of sensory impressions to the active restructuring and completing of schematic anticipations. But this seems not to be the reason why Popper finally drops the name of Selz. Rather Selz seems to be named as further supporting the view of Jennings as just outlined by Popper. Subjectively preformed reactions, as the remark in question goes, 'could *adapt* themselves through "trying-out behaviour" [*probierendes Verhalten*)](Selz), through failure and finally fitness, to the objective situation' (Popper 1931, p. 25). It is only in outlining how this adaptation comes about that full justice is done to the deductivist features of this process of knowledge acquisition, but in that phase of the sketch Selz is no longer mentioned, and it is clearly the author of the sketch who wishes to be credited for having elaborated the theory. But here it is also manifest that he is in effect advancing Selz's position. Thus, his remark that the structure of intellectual reactions, like the belief in causality, can be modelled on the structure of physiological reactions echoes Selz's integrative theory of stages (Popper 1930-1933, § 4, p. 25). Finally, his use of the centrally important concept of anticipation exactly parallels Selz's contention that coordinations differ from associations in that the coordination 'is not established by the experienced succession of stimulus and operation, but can precede it' (Selz 1922a, p. 570). Indeed, the following passage (Popper ibidem, § 4, pp. 25f.) contains not a single new idea and is no more than a reworking of Selz:

> If the coordination (*Zuordnung*) between intellectual reactions and objective situations is established via trying-out behaviour, then the coordinations always *precede* their adequacy (*Bewährung*) in time. The coordinations therefore are as regards their adequacy *anticipatory* (as long as the reaction has not proved itself adequate, it can be called an 'unfounded prejudice'). The fulfilment will also often fail to occur: the anticipatory coordination between reaction and stimulus is *tentative*. Therefore I dub the subjectively pre-formed intellectual reactions shortly '*anticipations*'.

This is almost an attempt to freeze Selz's theory of schematic anticipations into oblivion by eschewing all mention of him; indeed Popper even takes credit for having invented the concept of anticipation. Having earlier, in 1931, while explicitly referring to Selz's theory of memorized knowledge, discarded the idea of the mind being nothing but the conduit for sense impressions, he now has come to appropriate Selz's alternative evolutionary theory according to which our knowledge of the external world is drawn from our mind, or, as Popper puts it, 'from trying-out anticipations, which are

---

[9]Indeed the cornerstone element of Jennings's theory is what he calls the law of the resolution of physiological states, saying that the resolution of one physiological state into another becomes easier and more rapid after it has taken place a number of times. This associative law accounts not only for trial-and-error behaviour but even for associative memory. See Jennings (1905).

coordinated tentatively to the "material" of receptions' (Popper ibidem, § 4, p. 26). Rephrasing this theory later, in 1948, as the searchlight theory of mind and knowledge Popper has succeeded in erasing all traces of Selz, yet it can be argued that even this brilliant metaphor is prompted by his reading, and especially his seeing, of Selz's diagrams (see Figure 2). Indeed, this diagram not only looks like a searchlight but, as will be clear by now, also functions as one.

Bibliography

Ach, N. (1905). *Über die Willenstätigkeit und das Denken*. Göttingen: Vandenhoeck & Ruprecht.

Bahle, J. (1930). *Zur Psychologie des musikalischen Gestaltens, eine Untersuchung über das Komponieren auf experimenteller und historischer Grundlage*. Leipzig: Akademische Verlagsgesellschaft.

———— (1936). *Der musikalische Schaffensprozess*. Leipzig: Verlag von Hirzel.

Beckmann, H. (2001). 'Selz in Amsterdam. Der Denkpsychologe Otto Selz (1881-1943) im niederländischen Exil'. *Psychologie und Geschichte* **9**, pp. 3-27.

Berkson, W. & Wettersten, J. (1984). *Learning from Error*. La Salle IL: Open Court Publishing Company.

Bühler, K. (1907). 'Tatsachen und Probleme zu einer Psychologie der Denkvorgänge'. *Archiv für die gesamte Psychologie* **9**, pp. 297-365.

———— (1927). *Die Krise der Psychologie*. Jena: Gustav Fischer.

de Groot, A. (1965). *Thought and Choice in Chess*. The Hague: Mouton.

Hacohen, M. H. (2000). *Karl Popper – The Formative Years, 1902-1945: Politics and Philosophy in Interwar Vienna*. Cambridge & elsewhere: Cambridge University Press.

ter Hark, M. R. M. (1993). 'Problems and Psychologism: Popper as the Heir to Otto Selz'. *Studies in History and Philosophy of Science* **24**, pp. 585-609.

———— (2002). 'Between Autobiography and Reality: Popper's Inductive Years'. *Studies in History and Philosophy of Science* **33**, pp. 79-103.

———— (2004). *Popper, Selz and the Rise of Evolutionary Epistemology*. Cambridge: Cambridge University Press.

Jennings, H. S. (1905). *Behaviour of the Lower Organisms*. New York: Columbia University Press.

Mach, E. (1886). *Beiträge zur Analyse der Empfindungen*. Jena: Gustav Fischer. English translation 1959: *The Analysis of Sensations*: New York: Dover.

———— (1896). *Die Principien der Wärmelehre*. Leipzig: Verlag von Johann Ambrosius Barth. 2nd edition 1900.

Popper, K. R. (1927). *'Gewohnheit' und 'Gesetzerlebnis' in der Erziehung: Eine pädagogisch-strukturpsychologische Monographie*. Hausarbeit, Pädagogisches Institut der Stadt Wien. Hoover Institution Archives, Popper Collection (12, 11).

———— (1928). *Zur Methodenfrage der Denkpsychologie*. PhD dissertation, University of Vienna. Hoover Institution Archives, Popper Collection (17, 1).

———— (1930-1933). *Die beiden Grundprobleme der Erkenntnistheorie*. First published 1979. Tübingen: J. C. B. Mohr (Paul Siebeck). 2nd edition 1994.

—— (1931). 'Die Gedächtnispflege unter dem Gesichtspunkt der Selbsttätigkeit'. *Die Quelle* **81**, pp. 607-619.

—— (1963). *Conjectures and Refutations: The Growth of Scientific Knowledge*. London: Routledge & Kegan Paul. 5th edition 1989. London: Routledge.

—— (1972). *Objective Knowledge*. Oxford: Clarendon Press. 2nd edition 1979.

—— (1974). 'Intellectual Autobiography'. In P. A. Schilpp, editor (1974), pp. 1-181. *The Philosophy of Karl Popper*. La Salle IL: Open Court. Reprinted as *Unended Quest* (1976). London & Glasgow: Fontana/Collins.

Popper, K. R. & Eccles, J. C. (1977). *The Self and Its Brain*. New York: Springer.

Seebohm, H. (1970). *Otto Selz. Ein Beitrag zur Geschichte der Psychologie*. PhD dissertation, University of Heidelberg.

Selz, O. (1910). 'Die experimentelle Untersuchung des Willensaktes'. *Zeitschrift für Psychologie* **57**, pp. 241-270.

—— (1913). *Über die Gesetze des geordneten Denkverlaufs*. Stuttgart: Verlag von W. Spemann.

—— (1922a). *Zur Psychologie des produktiven Denkens und des Irrtums*. Bonn: Verlag von Friedrich Cohen.

—— (1922b). *Oswald Spengler und die intuitive Methode in der Geschichtsforschung*. Bonn: Verlag von Friedrich Cohen.

—— (1924a) *Kants Stellung in der Geisteswissenschaft*. Akademische Rede vom 4. Juli. Mannheim, Berlin, & Leipzig: Bensheim.

—— (1924b). *Die Gesetze der produktiven und reproduktiven Geistestätigkeit. Kurzgefasste Darstellung*. Bonn: Bouvier Verlag.

—— (1927). 'Die Umgestaltung der Grundanschauungen vom intellektuellen Geschehen'. *Kantstudien* **32**, pp. 273-280. English translation: 'The Revision of the Fundamental Conceptions of Intellectual Processes'. In J. M. Mandler & G. Mandler, editors (1964), pp. 225-234. *Thinking: From Association to Gestalt*. New York: Wiley.

Titchener, E. B. (1909). *Lectures on the Experimental Psychology of Thought-Processes*. New York: Macmillan.

Watt, H. J. (1905). 'Experimentelle Beiträge zur einer Theorie des Denkens'. *Archiv für die gesamte Psychologie* **4**, pp. 289-436.

2

Hunting for Roots of Viennese Philosophy

John T. Blackmore

As an increasing number of people are aware, many famous philosophers came
from, studied in, or taught in Vienna during the late 19th and early 20th centuries, including Brentano, Husserl, Meinong, Mach, Boltzmann, Wittgenstein,
Carnap, and the Vienna Circle. They all served to create the intellectual atmosphere in which Sir Karl Popper and his ideas developed. More immediately
he interacted with the Vienna Circle, including Hans Hahn, Philipp Frank,
Otto Neurath, and Victor Kraft. All four of these thinkers and many others
were connected also with an organization that is little-known today, namely,
The University of Vienna Philosophical Society, which existed from 1888 to
1938. I too was ignorant of it until Henk Visser kindly gave me copies of both
a history of the first twenty-five years of the society[1] and a history of the full
fifty years of its existence, which had been published by the Society but only
for its own members.[2]

Indeed, between Boltzmann's death in 1906 and Moritz Schlick's call to
Vienna in 1922 the University of Vienna Philosophical Society was the central
philosophical institution, which helped plant roots for the later developments.[3]
One need mention only that Sir Karl's father, Dr Simon Popper,[4] who would
publish a book on philosophy during this period, was a member of the Society
during part or most of the first two decades of the new century. Indeed, far
from being passive members, all four members of the Vienna Circle mentioned
above had lectured to, led discussion groups at, or even held office in the
University of Vienna Philosophical Society during many of those same years.
Philipp Frank, who later invited Carnap to teach in Prague, was a member
of the 'Ausschuss', or board of directors, in 1911-1912.[5]

Even though it had been very largely students of Franz Brentano who had
originally organized the Society,[6] after he had left Vienna for Italy in 1895,

---

[1] Höfler (?) (1913).

[2] Reininger (with Meister) (1938).

[3] Ibidem. See also Höfler (?) (1913).

[4] Ibidem, p. 45. One of the few yearly 'Berichte' I have seen, which is several years before
the 1913 *Rückblick*, also mentions Simon Popper as a member of the Society.

[5] Ibidem, p. 35.

[6] Ibidem, p. 3. See also Richard Meister in Reininger (with Meister) (1938), p. 4.

the dominant figure, Alois Höfler,[7] shifted his personal and philosophical alle-
giance to Brentano's rival Alexius Meinong in Graz. But as a physicist himself,
Höfler also encouraged other physicists and lovers of science to give lectures
in the Society. Höfler himself lectured on Mach's philosophy. Boltzmann lectured three times, including twice in 1905, Hahn lectured or led discussion
sessions seven times from 1906 to 1927, Frank five times from 1907 to 1915,
Kraft eleven times from 1911 to 1934, and Otto Neurath nineteen times from
1908 to 1924, including two lectures and two discussion sessions on Mach's
views.[8] The last official membership list available to us is for 1913 and all
four were members at that time,[9] but since Frank was then teaching in Prague
and Hahn in Czernowitz, they were only corresponding members. Others in
that category included Husserl in Göttingen, Ehrenfels in Prague, Meinong in
Graz, the economist Schumpeter also in Graz, and the physicists Schweidler
in Innsbruck and Smoluchowski in Cracow.[10]

It may be useful to give an account of the growth in my understanding of the
middle period in the History of the Society, the one between Mach and Boltzmann early in the century and the Vienna Circle in the mid-1920s. Philipp
Frank mentioned the following in his book (1949), p. 1:

> At the time when the first chapter of this book was written (1907) I had just
> graduated from the University of Vienna as a doctor of philosophy in physics.
> But the domain of my most intensive interest was the philosophy of science. I
> used to associate with a group of students who assembled every Thursday night
> in one of the old Vienna coffee houses. We stayed until midnight and even later,
> discussing problems of science and philosophy.

There is no evidence yet that this group was associated with the University
Philosophical Society, but the next quotation from Frank is different and may
well do that, since by that time three of those named by Frank, including
himself, had already given lectures in the Society (1941, pp. 6f.):

> About 1910 there began in Vienna a movement which regarded Mach's posi-
> tivistic philosophy of science as having great importance for general academic life.
> ... To this group belonged the mathematician H. Hahn, the political economist
> Otto Neurath, and the author of this book, at that time an instructor in theor-
> etical physics in Vienna.

My first contact with these two quotations came in the late 1960s. I included
them in my doctoral dissertation of 1970 and on pp. 183f. of *Ernst Mach –
His Life, Work, and Influence* (1972).

---

[7]He was 'Obmann' or head of the Society in 1888-1889, 1898-1903, 1913-1922, assistant
head in 1895-1898, discussion leader in 1906-1912, and in 1903 he was named 'Ehren-
präsident' for life (ibidem). For more details see Blackmore (2001).

[8]Reininger (with Meister) ibidem. See also Blackmore, Itagaki, & Tanaka (2001a), p. 308.

[9]Höfler(?) (1913), pp. 43-47.

[10]Ibidem, pp. 46f.

The next stage came when Henk Visser, a Dutch mathematician and philosopher,[11] discovered, during the 1980s, two key publications by the University of Vienna Philosophical Society.[12] They were discovered in a used bookstore in Vienna, apparently bought from someone who had removed them from the Library of the Philosophy Department at the University of Vienna. They include a full list of lectures given to the Society, a list of members along with the offices held by particular thinkers,[13] and a historical section containing a philosophical discussion and a report on the interaction of some members.[14]

Thomas E. Uebel, in his book *Rediscovering the Forgotten Vienna Circle*[15] rediscovered the old quotations from Philipp Frank (or from later German sources), and it is largely from his book that renewed interest in the period from Boltzmann's death in 1906 to Schlick's arrival in 1922 developed. If information about the University of Vienna Philosophical Society can further clarify Viennese philosophy for this period and especially give insight into Sir Karl Popper's intellectual environment, so much the better.

After Alois Höfler died in 1922, Professor Robert Reininger, the new leader of the University of Vienna Philosophical Society, reduced the number of discussion sessions in the Society down to a mere trickle.[16] They had previously occupied from 30% to 40% of the total sessions given per year by the Society and were clearly more interesting for most members than most of the lectures. They were normally scheduled to take place a few days after any lecture that seemed to be either interesting or controversial. Reininger did not cancel them altogether, but reduced their total number to a small fraction of what they had been. Indeed, from 1923 to 1925 only one discussion session per academic year was scheduled[17] and from 1926 to 1928 none.[18]

It is known that during the middle and late 1920s there were many groups in Vienna that met under the guidance, separately of Moritz Schlick, Victor Kraft, Karl Menger, Edgar Zilsel, Heinrich Gomperz, and even at the home of Reininger himself.[19] Hence it would be natural to suspect that there is a relationship between Reininger's almost complete elimination of discussion sessions in the University Philosophical Society and the creation and flowering of smaller discussion groups outside of the Society two or three years later, when Reininger's new policy had become clear. To be sure, his Kantianism and preference for historical lectures may have played a role, but if the Society had remained the vigorous Debating Society that it had largely been under

---

[11] Henk Visser has a web page and a list of publications on the internet. See http://www.cs.unimaas.nl/h.visser/{vitae.htm, Publications.doc}.

[12] Reininger (with Meister) (1938).

[13] Blackmore (1995), 'Late Appendix', pp. 271-315.

[14] Blackmore, Itagaki, & Tanaka (2001b), pp. 277-314.

[15] Uebel (1991).

[16] Reininger (with Meister) (1938), pp. 37-43.

[17] Ibidem, pp. 37f.

[18] Ibidem, pp. 38f.

[19] Popper (1974/1976), § 16.

Höfler's 'loose' reign, then it seems reasonable to suppose that there would
have been fewer independent discussion groups developing. Even Schlick's Circle, which later became called the 'Vienna Circle', might have been smaller
or might not have even been called into existence.

There is also some misunderstanding about Kant's influence. It is not correct
that his influence in Vienna 'broke through' only after the death of Bolzano
and Zimmermann, the departure of Brentano, and the lingering impact of
Herbart as 'the official' Austrian philosopher. Almost everyone interested in
philosophy in Austria read Kant in the 19th century, including Mach in 1853[20]
and even Boltzmann, though most reluctantly.[21] Nor should we forget that
Höfler had defended Kant against Brentano in the 1880s[22] and that both
he and Jerusalem wrote on Kant, one before and one during the 1904 centenary of Kant's death,[23] which was richly commemorated by the University of Vienna Philosophical Society. It seems probable that Simon Popper
had also read Kant and that his son Karl never fully excised his influence.
Nor should we overlook that Reininger himself, the city's most conspicuous
Kantian or neo-Kantian, became assistant 'Obmann' of the Society as early
as 1906. Our obsession with Mach, Boltzmann, Popper, Wittgenstein, Carnap, Neurath, Feyerabend, and other Viennese methodologists of science or
anti-science should not obscure the fact that Kant and traditional German
philosophy were almost certainly more influential in Vienna during most of
the 19th and 20th centuries than those thinkers we currently honour and treat
as having been the leading philosophers of Vienna and much of the Western
world almost up to the present.

There are probably many reasons why Vienna became so important as a breed-
ing ground for 20th-century methodologists of note. One possibility, however,
is not so pleasant and comes from looking at the situation in retrospect. It
emerges from studying the influence of Kant and Mach in Vienna and their
rather restrictive epistemologies of the physical world. Around the turn of
the century, several scientific discoveries had made the older 'presentist' types
of epistemology difficult to defend, at least for most friends of science. Positions that restricted reference, understanding, reality, or scientific inquiry to
sensory impressions, or to that which could be directly noticed, were incompatible with the reality of atoms and molecules. Overwhelming evidence from
the work of the Curies and the half-lives of radioactive substances pointed out

---

[20] Mach (1886), p. 30.

[21] Boltzmann (1974), p. 155.

[22] Alois Höfler, 'Lebenslauf des Alois Höflers', Schmidt (1921), p. 121.

[23] Höfler (1900) contains a new edition of Kant's *Metaphysische Anfangsgründe der Naturwissenschaft*, and an extended commentary. Wilhelm Jerusalem gave the 'Festrede' to the
Kant Celebration on 12 February 1904. This long speech was given extemporaneously but
was imperfectly preserved on a 'stenogramme'. Using it as a guide, Jerusalem then wrote
out a still longer book version, which was published as his (1904).

that the earth was indeed much older than the animals or any consciousness, as many geologists and biologists had long believed; the work by Külpe, Ach, and others discovered imageless thoughts; and the work of Einstein and Perrin on Brownian motion established that atoms and molecules, even though they were too small for unaided consciousness, were real, and could be largely measured and understood. This seemed incompatible with the basic ideas of both Kant and Mach. Part of what had previously been dismissed as 'metaphysical', as if inconsistent with or inferior to science, had turned out to be true or real, and what was more embarrassing had been proved by science itself to be so.

One solution, perhaps the only fully honest one, was to accept the fact that physical science had determined which epistemology and ontology about the external physical world were most probably true. Arthur Lovejoy in the United States and three Cambridge minds, G. E. Moore, Bertrand Russell, and C. D. Broad all seemed to opt by the 1930s and the 1940s for indirect or representational realism in epistemology, though they did differ in ontology. But this 'surrender' to science may have seemed too tame and unoriginal for most other philosophers. The fourth major philosopher at Cambridge in those days was Ludwig Wittgenstein, and, regardless of how strange or mystical, he soon won a large following.

Some philosophical 'solutions' tried to reduce atoms to 'pictures' (Hertz, Boltzmann), or argued that using the atomic theory was 'the same as believing in the reality of atoms' (Carnap), or made atoms 'theory-dependent' or 'theoretical entities' (many analytic philosophers). The favourite Logical Positivist evasion was to claim that 'everything is either empirical or formal' (which leaves out atoms) and to introduce a linguistic philosophy as if all epistemological differences, including epistemology itself, were 'merely linguistic' or 'outside of science' (Carnap). Indeed, Ludwig Wittgenstein outside, and Rudolf Carnap inside, the Vienna Circle became most famous for these last two 'solutions'. The point is that many Viennese methodologists wanted to be 'pro-science' without believing in the reality of atoms and molecules. Were they successful in squaring this particular circle? In their own opinion, probably yes, but most scientists and historians should perhaps be forgiven for suspecting the incompatibility between most philosophy in Vienna and most real science.

Another suspicious point was their tendency to emphasize the methodology of science as opposed to the concern with the traditional deeper issues of philosophy, such as epistemology, ontology, and value theory. Tell-tale signs of lingering presentism, as sensory or conscious reduction, would become most conspicuous when atoms were called 'theoretical entities' or when à la Carnap *using* 'physical object language' became treated as if it were the same as *believing* in the reality of atoms or even the existence of the atoms themselves.[24]

Sir Karl Popper also tended to focus on methodological questions or rather theories about methodology, even though later in life he would acknowledge

---

[24]Carnap (1947), p. 214.

'three worlds'. [25] This tendency of Viennese theorists to emphasize methodology, language, and, for some members of the Vienna Circle, mathematical
logic, all represented largely unconscious attempts to conceal the major defeat of direct or presentist epistemology, such as had been held by the mature
Kant and Mach, without having to openly recognize the success of indirect
or representationalist epistemology and ontology about the external physical
world as it existed in trans-conscious space and time, which appeared to be
implied by the new scientific discoveries, evidence, and proof.

As a physicist himself, Alois Höfler, head of the Philosophical Society
for most of the period from its founding in 1888 to 1922, played a role in
bringing Mach to Vienna in 1895 and was Boltzmann's friend. Other philosophers resisted the strong influence of these physicists in the Society until
Reininger changed the emphasis to the history of philosophy and recent German thought of a non-scientific kind. Thus Neurath and several other presentist philosophers of science left the Society during the 1920s and joined
Schlick's Circle. But having been influenced by Mach's phenomenalism as
well as by Wittgenstein, most members of the Vienna Circle either took phenomenalism for granted or did their best to ignore epistemology altogether.
Even Schlick himself, who had been a kind of direct realist as Max Planck's
assistant in Berlin, was seduced by Wittgenstein and Carnap and switched to
a position inconsistent with the reality of atoms and molecules.

It is ironic that the Vienna Circle and later the Logical Positivists should
consider their general position '*the* philosophy of science' at a time when
the opinions of most of their members were not even compatible with most
physical science, at least as represented by heliocentrism, atomism, and the
representative theory of perception. One may add that Mach had criticized
all of these positions. Carnap's notion that using a 'physical object language'
proved that they were not presentists or phenomenalists rested on the assumption that epistemology was either merely a language or was 'outside of
science', positions which seem more bizarre than reasonable.

In the real world, most actual physicists, like Einstein and Planck, as
contrasted with the Vienna Circle and later Logical Positivists, had already
attributed a role to physics in determining sound epistemology and ontology.
Let us hope that it will not require another century for most philosophers
to recognize that science has an epistemology and an ontology, which cannot
be reduced to methodology or language. This also applies to other physical
sciences, such as geography, geology, and chemistry, plus an increasing number
of related applied sciences, which along with measurement-based physics are
probably our best guides to reliable epistemology and ontology about the
external physical world.[26]

---

[25] For a most informative biography of Popper see Hacohen (2000).

[26] Alois Höfler like many people in the late 19th century seemed to divide philosophy
into two halves. If one were to make philosophy scientific, then it would become *scientific
psychology* (a notion one can still find in the Dewey Decimal System in libraries where
philosophy and psychology seem to overlap in the numbering system). The second type of
philosophy, following Herbert Spencer, would be 'metaphysics' or 'unscientific philosophy',

But since there is still a huge difference between having or using a sound epistemology and understanding it well, there is still a place for serious philosophers. Current methodologists who call themselves 'philosophers' may not be exactly the right people to trust in attempting to undertake this task. Nevertheless, a new generation reacting against 'anti-foundationalism', against linguistic reduction, against relativism about truth and value, and against originality merely for the sake of originality, could well be in the offing to help improve the situation.[27]

---

whose task would be to relate the different sciences together. But the importance of this odd approach is that for Höfler the *physical* sciences have nothing to do with either type of philosophy, which for him means that each physical science can determine its own epistemological and ontological assumptions, which, as we know, have come to be consciously indirect and to some extent representational. In short, he removes epistemology and ontology from philosophy and gives them to the individual physical disciplines, which in fact is exactly what has happened, even if some theorists of language or methodology still seem to be reluctant to accept or even understand this development.

[27]Much information from the two historical manuscripts put out by the Philosophical Society for its own members can be found in my recent books (1995) and (2001). I should be happy to make copies of the Society's two main publications available to interested readers. My address is: 4932 Sentinel Drive, Apt 201, Bethesda MD 20816, USA. My special thanks again to Henk Visser for help with Alois Höfler and the University of Vienna Philosophical Society during their heyday and to Professor Malachi Hacohen for attempting to waken an old historian from his own rather seedy form of 'dogmatic slumber'.

Bibliography

Blackmore, J. T. (1972). *Ernst Mach – His Life, Work, and Influence*. Berkeley & Los Angeles: University of California Press.

———— (1995). *Ludwig Boltzmann – His Later Life and Philosophy 1900-1906. Book Two: The Philosopher*. Dordrecht: Kluwer Academic Publishers.

———— (2001). 'Alois Höfler – Polymath'. In Blackmore, Itagaki, & Tanaka (2001b), pp. 237-276.

Blackmore, J. T., Itagaki, R., & Tanaka, S., (2001a). 'The University of Vienna Philosophical Society'. In Blackmore, Itagaki, & Tanaka, editors (2001b), pp. 279-314.

Blackmore, J. T., Itagaki, R., & Tanaka, S., editors (2001b). *Ernst Mach's Vienna 1895-1913*. Dordrecht: Kluwer Academic Publishers.

Boltzmann, L. (1974). *Theoretical Physics and Philosophical Problems*. Edited by B. F. McGuinness. Dordrecht: D. Reidel Publishing Company.

Carnap, R. (1947). *Meaning and Necessity*. Chicago: University of Chicago Press.

Frank, P. (1941). *Between Physics and Philosophy*. Cambridge MA: Harvard University Press?

———— (1949). *Modern Science and Its Philosophy*. Cambridge MA: Harvard University Press.

Hacohen, M. H. (2000). *Karl Popper – The Formative Years, 1902-1945: Politics and Philosophy in Interwar Vienna*. Cambridge & elsewhere: Cambridge University Press.

Höfler, A. (1900). *Studien zur gegenwärtigen Philosophie der Mechanik. Als Nachwort zu Kants Metaphysische Anfangsgründe der Naturwissenschaft*. Band IIIA [Kant's book], 108 pages. Band IIIB, 164 pages. Leipzig: Veröffentlichungen der Philosophischen Gesellschaft an der Universität zu Wien.

———— (?) (1913). *Rückblick auf die ersten fünfundzwanzig Vereinsjahre der Philosophischen Gesellschaft an der Universität zu Wien mit dem 26. Bericht für das Jahr 1912/13*. Vienna: Selbstverlag der Philosophischen Gesellschaft. 47 pages.

Jerusalem, W. (1904). *Kants Bedeutung für die Gegenwart [(Kant's Significance for the Present]*. Vienna & Leipzig: Wilhelm Braumüller.

Mach, E. (1886). Beiträge zur Analyse der Empfindungen. Jena: Gustav Fischer. English translation 1959. *The Analysis of Sensations*. New York: Dover.

Popper, K. R. (1974). 'Intellectual Autobiography'. In P. A. Schilpp, editor (1974), pp. 1-181. *The Philosophy of Karl Popper*. La Salle IL: Open Court. Reprinted as *Unended Quest* (1976). London & Glasgow: Fontana/Collins.

Reininger, R. (with Meister, R.) (1938). *50 Jahre Philosophische Gesellschaft an der Universität Wien* 1838-1938. Vienna: Verlag der Philosophischen Gesellschaft an der Universität Wien. 43 pages.

Schmidt, R. (1921). *Die Deutsche Philosophie der Gegenwart in Selbstdarstellungen*, Zweiter Band. Leipzig: Verlag Felix Meiner.

Uebel, T. E., editor (1991). *Rediscovering the Forgotten Vienna Circle*. Dordrecht: Kluwer Academic Publishers.

3

Which Came First,
the Problem of Induction or
the Problem of Demarcation?

Troels Eggers Hansen

A meeting in 1929 or in 1930 was to be of great importance to the young schoolteacher Karl Popper. It was a meeting with Herbert Feigl. The two young philosophers met for the first time and 'spent a whole night in a most exciting discussion'.[1]Feigl found Popper's ideas 'important, almost revolutionary', and he encouraged Popper to publish what he had written. Popper says that this 'meeting ... became decisive for [his] whole life ... [and] without encouragement from Herbert Feigl it is unlikely that [he] should ever have written ... a book'.[2]

So, encouraged by this meeting, Popper undertook to write a book on the fundamental problems of the theory of knowledge.

In the theory of knowledge, there are, according to Popper, *two* fundamental problems: the *problem of induction* and the *problem of demarcation*. These two problems can be described in the following way:[3]

> The *problem of induction* is the question about the *validity* (or about the *justification*) of the universal statements of the empirical sciences. It is the question, whether *empirical statements*, that is, statements about reality, based upon experience, can have *universal* validity.

> The *problem of demarcation* is the question about a criterion demarcating the empirical sciences from non-empirical fields. It is the question, whether there is a criterion that qualifies certain statements or systems of statements as empirical and others as non-empirical.

He called the book *Die beiden Grundprobleme der Erkenntnistheorie*[4] — The Two Fundamental Problems of the Theory of Knowledge.

---

[1]Popper (1966b), p. 343.
[2]Popper (1974a/1976), § 16.
[3]Cp. Popper (1930-1933), Book II, § I, ¶ 3 and ¶ 1.
[4]The title is an allusion to Schopenhauer (1841).

The *first* volume contains a thorough discussion of the *problem of induction*. Popper's conclusion of that discussion is clear and unambiguous:[5]

> ... *there is no induction in an epistemological sense.*

In the first volume, Popper indicates his own criterion of demarcation; but a thorough discussion of the *problem of demarcation* — showing that his criterion is both adequate and very useful — had to be postponed to a *second* volume. Popper completed the first volume; owing to various unfortunate incidents,[6] it is still an open question whether he also completed the second volume.

Popper wrote the first drafts of *Die beiden Grundprobleme* pretty quickly, and as soon as he had a section typed he showed it to Robert Lammer, his

---

[5]Popper (1930-1933), section 48:

... *es gibt keine Induktion im erkenntnistheoretischen Sinn.*

[6]These unfortunate incidents I got to know about while, in 1974-1976, together with Robert Lammer (see text to footnote 7 below), I conducted a search for Popper's early manuscripts.

On Christmas Eve 1936, Popper was appointed to a lectureship at Canterbury University College, Christchurch. In order to arrive at the start of the New Zealand academic year (in March) he and his wife had to leave Vienna within four weeks of the appointment. So, they had to leave a great variety of things behind, unsorted — there simply was no time for anything. (Karl Popper, letter of 20 August 1974, to TEH). Just before leaving Vienna, Popper deposited a wardrobe full of manuscripts in the apartment of his friend Otto Haas (1906-1944) who, in 1942, was arrested by the Nazis and executed for high treason. Otto Haas's apartment was situated in the house where his mother, Frau Philomena Haas (1881-1973), lived, and she took care of her son's belongings after his death.

In 1953, Paul Feyerabend visited London, and before he returned to Vienna, Popper asked him to try to fetch the deposited manuscripts. Back in Vienna, Feyerabend went to Popper's old friend Robert Lammer. Lammer knew Frau Haas very well, and together he and Feyerabend visited her. They were shown into Otto Haas's apartment, and as they pulled out the drawers of his writing table a lot of manuscripts appeared.

While searching the drawers, they found a parcel labeled *Für Robert Lammer!! Dr. Karl Popper*. A little later one more parcel turned up. This parcel was also labelled *Für Robert Lammer!! Dr. Karl Popper*. The two parcels were exactly alike. The first parcel was given to Robert Lammer, the second parcel was not. This was a disaster. Unexamined, the second parcel was put back in one of the drawers and has since disappeared. (Robert Lammer, letter of 30 November 1975, to TEH.)

In the weeks or months following that visit, Feyerabend several times visited Frau Haas; and she gave him many (perhaps all) of the manuscripts deposited early in 1937. Owing to some misunderstandings not all of these manuscripts were sent on to Popper. In 1975, Feyerabend still had some of Popper's early manuscripts, and he kindly sent me all the material to be found in his files. In this material, I found a few minor manuscripts and many important old letters.

Some twenty years after the visit to Frau Haas, Robert Lammer came across the parcel that she did give him. This parcel — which contains a carbon copy of the first volume of *Die beiden Grundprobleme* — was sent on to me. About half a year later, Robert Lammer sent me another carbon copy of the first volume, which he had just received from Feyerabend.

What has happened to the parcel Frau Haas did *not* give to Robert Lammer? Nobody seems to know. The only thing I know is, that, in 1976, Popper was convinced that it contained the manuscript of the second volume of *Die beiden Grundprobleme*.

This account is a short summary of *part* of the story of Popper's early manuscripts; my Postscript to Popper (2006) contains a fuller account. Cp. also Hansen (1998) and Hacohen (2000), pp. 221f. and 238f.

friend and former colleague at the Pedagogic Institute of the City of Vienna. Lammer was a very 'conscientious and critical reader ... he challenged every point which he did not find crystal clear'.[7]

To the best of my knowledge nothing remains of the first drafts of *Die beiden Grundprobleme*; and I do not know more about these drafts than what I have just told you.

That version of the first volume of *Die beiden Grundprobleme* that has been preserved, seems to have been written between February 1931 and the summer of 1932.[8] Of the second volume only a few fragments have been preserved. These fragments — written in 1932 and 1933 — were, in 1979, published together with the completed first volume.[9]

It is a pity, that the publication of the remaining parts of *Die beiden Grundprobleme* took place many years after the abbreviated version, *Logik der Forschung*,[10] had been translated into English and, naturally, had become the standard work on the philosophy of Popper. Of course, *The Logic of Scientific Discovery*[11] is of fundamental importance for an understanding of his philosophy. But, to become acquainted with the background of Popper's philosophy of science, one has to study *Die beiden Grundprobleme*.

In this short presentation, I shall deal with Popper's early work on the two fundamental problems of the theory of knowledge. I shall try to answer a question[12] that seems to be quite simple:

Which came first, the problem of induction or the problem of demarcation?

My discussion of this question is based — not on Popper's later accounts of his intellectual development — but on an early manuscript that will be published soon.[13] Of course, it is based also on *Die beiden Grundprobleme*; from this book, it seems to appear that Popper's *discovery* of the problem

---

[7]Popper (1974a/1976), § 16.

[8]On 13 February 1931, Moritz Schlick's paper (1931) was published in the weekly *Die Naturwissenschaften*. In Popper's discussions of the problem of induction, Schlick's paper plays a *very* important part; and before 13 February 1931, he could not possibly have commenced his work. In the long section 11 on Kant and Fries, a reference (Popper 1930-1933, p. 121, note 53) seems to indicate that the first volume must have been completed between late March 1932 and the summer of 1932 when Popper sent a copy of his manuscript to Egon Friedell (1878-1938) and, in the Tyrolean Alps a few weeks later, showed another copy to Rudolf Carnap and to Herbert Feigl. (Popper 1974a/1976, § 17; 1974b, § 3; 1963, Chapter 11, § 1; see also Hacohen 2000, p. 220, note 27 and text to this note.)
Die beiden Grundprobleme was typed by Popper's wife. In the early 1980s she told me that, when working on the manuscript, they often made excursions to the surroundings of Vienna. Popper carried the typewriter and, in the small restaurant where they used to have their meals, he was for that reason known as 'the man with the gramophone'.

[9]Popper (1930-1933).

[10]Popper (1935/1966a).

[11]Popper (1959).

[12]Malachi Hacohen's pioneer work on Karl Popper prompted this question, on which we seem to disagree. See Hacohen (2000), pp. 198f. and p. 207.

[13]Popper (1927).

of demarcation was the outcome of his work on the problem of induction. Is that true?

As an introduction to my discussion of the question of which fundamental problem came first, I shall give you an outline — a very rough outline — of the contents of *Die beiden Grundprobleme*.

The starting point of Popper's discussion of the *problem of induction* is Hume's argument:[14]

> [Hume] demonstrated that every attempt at *inductive generalization* will be defeated by a *circular inference*.

That is, Hume demonstrated that natural laws cannot be justified by observations. Instead of demonstrating the defeat by a circular inference, Popper demonstrates that every *inductive generalization* will be defeated by an *infinite regress*.[15]

There seems to be no gap in Hume's argument. And one can ask, how are natural laws, that is, universal empirical statements, now to be understood?[16] A discussion of the possible answers to this question is the topic of the *first* volume of *Die beiden Grundprobleme*.

In his discussion of the problem of induction, Popper strives to discuss *all* possible answers to the question raised by Hume's argument; and he proceeds here in a very *systematic* fashion. The various answers or positions are organized according to the following groups:

(1) The standard-statement positions

(2) The probability positions

(3) The pseudo-statement positions.

---

[14]Popper (1930-1933), section 5, text to note 1:

> [Hume] wies nach, daß jeder Versuch einer *induktiven Verallgemeinerung* einem *Zirkelschluß* erliegen muß.

[15]In a new footnote added in 1975, Popper remarks:

> An explicit demonstration of the infinite regress is already to be found in Hume.
> (Der unendliche Regreß findet sich schon ganz explizit bei Hume.)

See Popper ibidem, section 5, note *1.

Popper's demonstration of the *infinite regress* can be summarized as follows:

What we get to know by observation is, that a number — a *finite* number — of singular empirical statements are true. This set of true statements is, however, not sufficient to justify an inductive generalization. In order to justify a set of observations being generalized into a universal law, we need a *principle of induction* that enables us to demonstrate the truth of that universal law — and this need for a principle of induction leads to an *infinite regress*. Whatever such a principle of induction is, it must be a universal empirical statement that says something about the lawlikeness or about the uniformity of nature. Thus, also a principle of induction has to be justified — and, like natural laws, it has to be justified by observations, by singular empirical statements. That is, a *second order* principle of induction has to be introduced and to be justified — and so forth.

[16]Popper ibidem, section 6.

All three groups of positions agree with respect to the type of validity of the *singular* empirical statements; but they disagree as to the type of validity of the *universal* empirical statements.

The *singular* empirical statements — the basic or observational statements — have a *standard* type of validity; they are *'vollentscheidbar'* — they are fully decidable: '...if they are true, their truth is *decidable*, and if they are false, their falsity is *decidable*; that is, decidable by *experience*.'[17]

According to the first group of positions, the *standard-statement positions*, *all* empirical statements have a *standard* type of validity; *all* empirical statements are fully decidable. If there are any *universal* natural laws, that is, if there are any *universal* empirical statements, then these statements — like singular empirical statements — must have a standard type of validity. Whether there are any *universal* empirical statements — this is a question on which the various standard-statement positions disagree.[18]

According to the second group of positions, the *probability positions*, the universal empirical statements do not have a standard type of validity; instead, they have a *probability* value.

According to the third group of positions, the *pseudo-statement positions*, the so-called universal empirical statements are not statements at all; they are *pseudo-statements*. Natural laws are not statements, but they are *'Anweisungen zur Bildung von Aussagen'*,[19] they are 'instructions for the formation of statements', that is, instructions for the formation of *singular* empirical statements.

The first group of positions, the *standard-statement positions*, consists of three positions only: *naive inductivism*, *strict positivism*, and *apriorism*.

According to *naive inductivism*, there is a method — a so-called scientific method — that enables us to establish true universal laws; according to this position, universal natural laws are justifiable, that is, justifiable by experience. *Naive inductivism* has, however, been defeated by Hume's argument, and it must be considered untenable.

Thus, within the *standard-statement positions* we are left with two positions only: *strict positivism* and *apriorism*. There are only two possibilities: either one denies that there are universal empirical statements, or one accepts that there are the existence of *a priori* synthetic statements. According to *strict positivism* (not to be confused with *logical* positivism), there are no universal empirical statements; natural laws are only *summary reports* of our observations.[20] According to *apriorism* — the position of Kant — there are universal empirical statements; there are *a priori* synthetic statements, and these 'most general laws of nature are "just the same" as the most general

---

[17]Popper ibidem, section 7, note *1. See footnote 29 and the text to this note.
[18]Popper ibidem, section 6.
[19]Schlick (1931), p. 151. See also Popper (1930-1933), section 19.
[20]Popper ibidem, section 8.

formal conditions of experience ... '.[21]

The two remaining groups of positions — the *probability positions* and the *pseudo-statement positions* — are more difficult to describe. I refrain from giving you a summary of all the various positions and of the criticisms levelled against them by Popper.[22] I cannot possibly do justice to his very severe criticisms of *logical positivism*; nor can I possibly do justice to his very thorough criticisms of Kant's *transcendental deduction* and *transcendental idealism* or to the subsequent criticisms of Leonard Nelson and of Jacob Friedrich Fries — criticisms that form a whole and lead to Popper's theory of the empirical basis. For my purpose — to give an outline of the book — suffice it to say that *all* positions have to be rejected. Either because they turn out to be logically untenable: like *naive inductivism* they are defeated by an *infinite regress*; or they have to be rejected, because they turn out to be in disagreement with 'the actual procedures of science',[23] or because they turn out to be dependent on a concept of meaning that is not open to discussion[24] that is, because it turns out that these positions are immunized against criticism by a retreat to dogmatism.

Referring to these last positions, Popper concludes his long and very detailed discussions of the *problem of induction* by stating:[25]

> Thus, after a varied wandering between the Scylla of the *infinite regress* and the Charybdis of the *a priori* the rolling ship of inductivism arrives at the safe harbour of dogma.

Thus, all the various positions — all the various answers to the question raised by Hume's argument — have been shown to be defective; and there seems to be no solution to the problem of induction. But there *is* a solution to the problem of induction. There is a solution that is a *downright rejection* of inductivism; this solution is Popper's solution.

Like all positions within the three groups of positions:

---

[21]Kant, *Prolegomena* (1783), § 36, p. 112. See also Popper (1930-1933), section 10, the text to note 9.

[22]One of the many issues discussed by Popper while dealing with the pseudo-statement positions (and also while dealing, in one of the remaining fragments of the second volume, with the problem of methodology) is the thesis that has later become known as the *Duhem–Quine* thesis (Popper ibidem, pp. 259ff. and 390ff.). Dudley Shapere seems to have failed to notice Popper's early discussions of Duhem when he writes (1997, p. 308, my emphasis):

> Even Popper, when he learned of Duhem's objection (*after* having failed to notice it in the original edition of *Logik der Forschung* or in the original English translation), admitted that straightforward logical refutation of a hypothesis is not possible, ...

A failure to notice Popper's rather detailed discussions of Duhem also seems to underlie the criticisms levelled against his 'notion of falsifiability' by Ernan McMullin (1997, p. 607).

[23]Popper ibidem, section 38.

[24]Ibidem, section 45.

[25]Popper (1930-1933), section 45 (concluding remark):

> So landet das schwankende Schiff des Induktivismus nach mancherlei Irrfahrt zwischen der Skylla des unendlichen Regresses und der Charybdis des Apriori im sicheren Hafen des Dogmas.

(1) The standard-statement positions

(2) The probability positions

(3) The pseudo-statement positions

Popper's solution — or his position — is an answer to the question raised by Hume's argument. Considering that every *inductive generalization* will be defeated by an *infinite regress*, one can ask, how are natural laws, that is, universal empirical statements now to be understood? The difference between Popper's position and all other positions can be illustrated by returning to the standard-statement positions.

According to the *standard-statement positions, all* empirical statements must be *fully* decidable. If there are any universal natural laws, that is, if there are any universal empirical statements, then these statements — like singular empirical statements — must have a standard type of validity; these universal empirical statements must be *fully* decidable. Here we get to the root of the matter: it is the idea, that *all genuine* statements must be *fully* decidable,[26] that prevents a solution to the problem of induction. Popper's position is *not* an inductivist position; he does not accept what he calls the *'fundamental thesis of inductivism'*:[27]

All legitimate statements of science must be reducible to basic empirical statements . . . .

Popper's position is a genuine *deductivist* position,[28] that may be characterized as follows:

Natural laws, that is, universal empirical statements, are legitimate statements, but they are not *'vollentscheidbar'*, they are not fully decidable. Natural laws are *'teilentscheidbar'*, they are only *partially decidable*. Natural laws are not verifiable, they are *only falsifiable*; thus, if they are true, their truth *cannot* be decided, but if they are false, their falsity can be decided

---

[26] For the idea, that *all genuine* statements must be *fully* decidable, cp. Schlick (1931), p. 156:

[It is] fundamental to a genuine statement . . . that it can, in principle, once and for all be decided whether it is true or false.

([Es ist] für eine echte Aussage wesentlich . . . , daß sie prinzipiell endgültig verifizierbar oder falsifizierbar ist.)

Cp. also Popper ibidem, section 7, the text to note 1, and section 46; especially note 3 and the text to this note.

[27] Popper ibidem, section 44:

Grundthese des Induktivismus . . . :

Alle legitimen Sätze der Wissenschaft müssen sich auf elementare Erfahrungssätze zurückführen lassen . . . .

[28] By their definition, the pseudo-statement positions seem to be deductivist positions, too. But this is not the case:

. . . the term 'instructions for the formation of statements' does not allow of any conclusion as to how this formation should be performed.

(. . . der Terminus 'Anweisungen zur Bildung von Sätzen' gestattet nicht, Schlüsse daraus zu ziehen, wie diese Bildung vor sich gehen soll.)

(Popper ibidem, section 41.)

by experience, by demonstrating the falsity of some of the prognoses *deduced* from these laws.[29]

Popper's solution of the problem of induction leads to a *criterion* demarcating the empirical sciences from non-empirical fields; that is, his solution of

---

[29] Here, I am varying a much later remark of Popper's (see footnote 17 above and text to this note). Of course, this is somewhat anachronistic. In the early 1930s, Popper did not distinguish clearly between 'to be true' and 'to be shown to be true'; and, in some places, this made him write that natural laws cannot be true — statements to which he later objected. (See, for instance, Popper ibidem, section 34, notes *4 and *5, as well as the text to these notes, and *Einleitung 1978*, pp. XXII ff.)

In the thesis *Axiome, Definitionen und Postulate der Geometrie* (1929), Popper wrote (§ 38, the text to note 2):

... statements of an *a priori* science are pure conceptual constructions and are, therefore, strictly valid, whereas all statements of an *a posteriori* science only after confirmation by observations and experiments, after 'empirical verification', are to be considered *approximately valid*.

(... die Sätze der apriorischen Wissenschaft gelten als rein begriffliche Konstruktionen genau, während alle Sätze einer aposteriorischen Wissenschaft erst auf Grund von Bestätigungen durch Beobachtung und Experiment, auf Grund 'empirischer Verifikation' als *annäherungsweise gültig* betrachtet werden dürfen.)

This view is in agreement with some 'famous words' that, in a footnote (§ 6, note 1) and at the end of the thesis (§ 38, the text to note 6), were attributed to Albert Einstein:

Insofar as statements of geometry are strictly valid, they do not refer to reality; insofar as they refer to reality, they are not strictly valid.

(Sofern die Sätze der Geometrie streng gültig sind, beziehen sie sich nicht auf die Wirklichkeit; sofern sie sich auf die Wirklichkeit beziehen, sind sie nicht streng gültig.)

In fact, Popper did *not* quote Einstein; this 'quotation' as well as the word 'famous' he cribbed from Schlick (1925), p. 326. Unfortunately, Schlick had misquoted Einstein.

In (1921), pp. 3f. — as well as on p. 124 of the first version of this lecture ('Festvortrag', 27 January 1921) — Einstein said:

Insofar as statements of mathematics refer to reality, they are uncertain, and insofar as they are certain, they do not refer to reality.

(Insofern sich die Sätze der Mathematik auf die Wirklichkeit beziehen, sind sie nicht sicher, und insofern sie sicher sind, beziehen sie sich nicht auf die Wirklichkeit.)

What Einstein did say makes *very* good sense; but the 'famous words' that Schlick (and, *in 1929*, also Popper) attributed to Einstein do not make sense.

Insofar as a universal statement referring to reality has not yet been falsified, one cannot exclude the possibility that it is *strictly valid* — or, what is just the same, that it is *true*. However, the essential thing is that such a statement *cannot be shown to be true*; therefore it is *uncertain*. And therefore Einstein said that mathematical statements referring to reality are 'uncertain' and *not* that they are 'not strictly valid'.

In the manuscript of *Die beiden Grundprobleme* (sections 2 and 30), the words attributed to Einstein are the words Einstein did say. By varying and generalizing these words Popper formulated his criterion of demarcation as follows:

Insofar as a scientific statement refers to reality, it must be falsifiable, and insofar as it is not falsifiable, it does not refer to reality.

(Insofern sich die Sätze einer Wissenschaft auf die Wirklichkeit beziehen, müssen sie falsifizierbar sein, und insofern sie nicht falsifizierbar sind, beziehen sie sich nicht auf die Wirklichkeit.)

(See Popper ibidem, section 2, the text to note 1; section 30, the text to note 12; and *Anhang* [Appendix]: *Zusammenfassender Auszug*, V., the text to note 4; 1933, p. 427.)

the problem of induction leads to a solution of the *problem of demarcation* — or rather, it leads to the *first part* of this solution.

Popper's *criterion* of demarcation is as follows:[30]

> Empirical scientific statements or systems of statements are distinguished by the fact that they are empirically falsifiable.
>
> Singular empirical statements, particular statements about reality may also be empirically verifiable; theoretical systems, natural laws, universal statements about reality in principle are only one-sidedly falsifiable.

In the remaining fragments of the *second* volume of *Die beiden Grundprobleme*, Popper emphasizes, that, by itself, a *criterion* is not a solution of the problem of demarcation. By the use of certain stratagems, the risk of falsification can always be avoided. So, a solution to the problem of demarcation has to consist of *two* parts: a criterion of demarcation *and* methodological rules — rules that forbid the use of such stratagems.

Popper rejected inductivist epistemologies and replaced them by a *deductivist* epistemology. In the light of this new epistemology, how is *inductivism* now to be understood?[31]

> Inductivism is nothing but a (primitive) solution of the problem of demarcation. The fear of metaphysics ... leads the (inductively oriented) empiricist to cling as tightly as possible to the immediate data of experience.

Let me present an instance of an *inductivist* criterion of demarcation — a criterion to which I shall return:[32]

> For an empirical science to be taken seriously, it is crucial ... that theories are formed only by induction; that is, that they are abstracted from empirical facts ....

Of course, an *inductivist* criterion of demarcation is not very useful: there is no such thing as induction.

Now, let me turn to the question about the two fundamental problems of the theory of knowledge:

---

[30]Popper (1930-1933), 2nd Book, [V]:

> Empirisch wissenschaftliche Sätze oder Satzsysteme sind dadurch ausgezeichnet, daß sie empirisch falsifizierbar sind.
>
> Singuläre empirische Sätze, besondere Wirklichkeitsaussagen können auch empirisch verifizierbar sein; Theoriensysteme, Naturgesetze, allgemeine Wirklichkeitsaussagen sind grundsätzlich nur einseitig falsifizierbar.

For another version of the criterion of demarcation, see footnote 29 above.

[31]Popper ibidem, section 44:

> Der Induktivismus ist nichts anderes als eine (primitive) Lösung des Abgrenzungsproblems: Aus Angst vor der Metaphysik ... klammert sich der (induktivistisch orientierte) Empirist möglichst fest an die unmittelbaren Daten der Erfahrung.

[32]See footnote 34 below and text to this note.

Which came first, the problem of induction or the problem of demarcation?

From my rough outline of the contents of *Die beiden Grundprobleme*, the problem of demarcation appears to belong to a later stage of the work on the two fundamental problems. At first, Popper seems to have been aware of the problem of induction and to have considered this problem the *only* fundamental problem of the theory of knowledge. While he worked on that problem, he discovered another problem: the problem of demarcation. Moreover, he discovered that inductivism is to be considered an attempt at solving this problem. So, there seemed to be two fundamental problems; but, in fact, there is *only one* fundamental problem: the problem of demarcation.

Presented in this way, Popper's work on induction and demarcation appears to have been very coherent and very systematic. This account agrees with the structure of *Die beiden Grundprobleme* and of *Logik der Forschung*. For this reason, it sounds very convincing; and the question about the two fundamental problems seems to lend itself to a straightforward answer: The problem of *induction* came first.

But the story I have just told you is simply not true; it did not happen that way.

In *Die beiden Grundprobleme*, Popper demonstrated that natural laws are not verifiable, they are only falsifiable. A few years earlier — in 1927 — he held a different opinion:[33]

> As far as ... a psychological theory ... states that some *real experiences* are connected it is just as valuable as the theories (and hypotheses) of the natural sciences, for these connections are verifiable.

That is, he considered natural laws verifiable; in accordance with this view, the Popper of 1927 wrote:[34]

> For an empirical science to be taken seriously, it is crucial ... that theories are formed only by induction; that is, that they are abstracted from empirical facts, and that they are never imposed on empirical facts.

Here, Popper is presenting a criterion of demarcation — a criterion demarcating between scientific theories and non-scientific theories, a criterion demarcating between science and pseudo-science:

---

[33] Popper (1927), § 5, ad 2:

Soweit ... eine psychologische Theorie ... Zusammenhänge *von realen Erlebnissen* behauptet, kann sie an Wert den Theorien (und Hypothesen) der Naturwissenschaften gleichgesetzt werden, denn diese Zusammenhänge sind verifizierbar.

(See also ter Hark 2002. From this paper it appears that, independently of one another, Professor ter Hark and I have both noticed Popper's early inductivism.)

[34] Popper ibidem, § 5, ad 1:

Entscheidend für den Charakter einer ernst zu nehmenden empirischen Wissenschaft ist ..., daß eine Theorie nur induktiv, durch Abstraktion aus empirischen Sachverhalten, gebildet werden darf, niemals aber in die Sachverhalte hineingedeutet sein darf.

For an empirical science to be taken seriously, it is crucial ... that theories are formed only by induction; that is, that they are abstracted from empirical facts ....

To this criterion he added a methodological rule:[35]

... [theories must] never [be] imposed on empirical facts.

Contrary to the criterion presented in *Die beiden Grundprobleme*, the 1927 criterion is an *inductivist* criterion. Nevertheless, this early criterion — like his *deductivist* criterion — is an attempt at solving that problem that, later, Popper called the 'problem of demarcation'; and in general terms, described in the following way:[36]

In case of doubt, how can one decide whether one is dealing with a scientific statement or 'merely' with a metaphysical assertion? (Or, casually speaking, when is a science not a science?)

In 1927, Popper did not talk about a 'criterion of demarcation', nor did he talk about the 'problem of demarcation'. But he certainly had more than 'a vague sense' of this problem.[37] He was aware of the importance of demarcating between scientific and non-scientific theories; and he presented a criterion of demarcation — admittedly, not a very good one.

At this early stage of his intellectual development, Popper was aware also of the importance of methodology: if a theory is imposed on empirical facts, then abstraction from these facts leads to the theory imposed on them; and, for that reason, induction would be defeated by a circular inference.[38] Therefore, to protect his inductivist criterion against circularity, he added a methodological rule that theories must never be imposed on empirical facts. Popper criticized various psychological theories for not adhering to this rule.

Popper's *inductivist* solution of the problem of demarcation was put forward in a thesis — a *'Hausarbeit'* — that, in the early summer of 1927, was submitted to the Pedagogic Institute of the City of Vienna. The title of the thesis is: *'Gewohnheit' und 'Gesetzerlebnis' in der Erziehung*[39] — 'Habit' and 'Experience of Lawfulness' in Education.

Among the various theories criticized by Popper are Alfred Adler's *individual psychology*,[40] Sigmund Freud's *psychoanalysis*,[41] and William James's

---

[35] See also Popper ibidem, § 5, the text to note 3.

[36] Popper (1930-1933), section 1:

Wie kann man im Zweifelsfall entscheiden, ob man einen wissenschaftlichen Satz vor sich hat oder 'nur' eine metaphysische Behauptung? (Oder beiläufig gesprochen: Wann ist eine Wissenschaft keine Wissenschaft?)

[37] Hacohen (2000), p. 198: note 82.

[38] Popper (1927), § 5: the text to note 3. See also note 42.

[39] In Popper (2006).

[40] Popper (1927), § 5: the text to note 3; § 7.1, note 21; § 7.1, *Anhang*, notes 1 and 2 and the text to these notes; and § 7.2: the text to note 10.

[41] Popper ibidem, § 5: the text to notes 3 and 25.

theory of the emotions.[42] Imposing theory on empirical facts, these theories are formed by a *circular* induction; they are not to be taken seriously.

About 1929, the focus of Popper's work no longer was the *psychology* of knowledge, but the *theory* of knowledge.[43] He no longer studied 'Gesetz*erlebnis*' (the '*experience* of lawfulness'), but the *logical status* of natural laws. This change from the *psychology* of knowledge to the *theory* of knowledge was the *first* of three important steps towards a cogent and satisfactory solution of the problem of demarcation.

The *second* step was the introduction of a very important distinction: the distinction between *strictly* universal statements and *numerically* universal statements — or, what is just the same: the distinction between *strictly* universal statements and *singular* statements. Popper demonstrated that this distinction is unequivocal — just as is the distinction between *universal* and *individual* concepts.[44]

---

[42]Popper ibidem, §7.1, the text to notes 30 and 32. William James's idea ('Gedanke')

... is a typical transgression of theory: it is considered a prerequisite of 'empirical' description, and every attempt at explanation must, therefore, be circular ...

(... ist eine typische Grenzüberschreitung der Theorie: da er als Voraussetzung der 'empirischen' Darstellung auftritt, muß er jeden Erklärungsversuch in Zirkelschlüsse stürzen ....)

[43]Cp. Popper (1929). In §§5-8 of this thesis, Popper emphasized the importance of the 'question of validity' (§7) and criticized the confusion of the *theory* of knowledge and the *psychology* of knowledge . See for instance §5:

... instead of asking for the reason for the validity of a statement, it is, in certain philosophical schools, quite common to ask for its origin etc.... thereby seriously confounding *logical*, *historical-genetic*, and *psychological-genetic* issues.

(... in bestimmten philosophischen Richtungen [ist es] ganz allgemein gebräulich, statt nach dem 'Geltungsgrund' eines Satzes, gerne nach seinem 'Ursprung' u.s.w. zu fragen ... [Man] gibt dadurch Anlaß zu schlimmen Verwechslungen von *logischen*, *historisch-genetischen* und *psychologisch-genetischen* Fragen.)

Popper referred (§7) to Heinrich Gomperz in support of this criticism (the text to note 3):

Gomperz shows that many theories of knowledge commit the error of recasting as genetic facts epistemological facts that it is only with difficulty possible — or even impossible — to demonstrate directly. ... With all clarity Gomperz points out that such psychological-genetic assertions have nothing to do with empirical psychology (experimental psychology, genetic psychology of animals and of children etc.), but are pure arbitrary speculations. They are recastings of unprovable epistemological prejudices dressed up as genetic facts.

(Gomperz zeigt, daß viele Erkenntnistheorien in den Fehler verfallen, erkenntnistheoretische Tatbestände, die sich unmittelbar nur schwer oder auch gar nicht nachweisen lassen, genetisch umzudichten ... Gomperz weist mit aller Schärfe daraufhin, daß solche psychologisch-genetische Behauptungen nichts mit empirischer Psychologie (experimenteller Psychologie, genetischer Tier- und Kinderpsychologie u.s.w.) zu tun haben, sondern rein willkürliche Spekulationen sind. Es sind Umdichtungen von unbeweisbaren erkenntnistheoretischen Vorurteilen, die in einem genetischen Gewand auftreten.)

(See Gomperz 1905, pp. 312ff.)

[44]Popper, 1930-1933, section 33:

The *third* and final step towards a solution of the problem of demarcation was his solution of a problem which 'cannot even be formulated' without the distinction between *strictly* universal and *singular* statements.[45] This problem is the problem of induction.

Having got rid of his early inductivism and realizing that natural laws are only *partially* decidable, Popper again faced the problem of demarcation; and, instead of his early *inductivist* solution, he was, at long last, able to present a *deductivist* solution.

So, *which came first, the problem of induction or the problem of demarcation?*

The problem of *demarcation* came first. The *discovery* of the importance of demarcation was *not* the outcome of the work on the problem of induction; but this work proved decisive for a cogent solution of the problem of demarcation.

The analogy between the two distinctions is rather far-reaching. The opposition between universal and singular statements gives rise to the *problem of induction* — the analogous opposition between universal and individual concepts gives rise to the classical *debate about universals.*

(Die Analogie zwischen den beiden Unterscheidungen ist eine sehr weitgehende: Aus dem Gegensatz zwischen allgemeinen und besonderen Sätzen entsteht das *Induktions-problem* — aus dem analogen Gegensatz zwischen Universal- und Individualbegriffen der klassische *Universalienstreit.*)

See sections 32-35, especially section 34, the text to note 1.

[45] Popper, 1930-1933, section 32:

The opposition between 'strictly universal' statements and 'singular' statements is fund-amental for the *problem of induction*. It cannot even be formulated without this distinc-tion ... Almost everything that was stated ... in the presentation of Hume's argument ... and has been said since would fall to pieces if this opposition proved to be untenable.

(Der Gegensatz zwischen den 'streng allgemeinen' und den 'besonderen' Sätzen ist für das *Induktionsproblem* grundlegend: Es läßt sich ohne diese Unterscheidung gar nicht formulieren ... Fast alles, was ... in der Darstellung von Humes Argument ... und seitdem gesagt wurde, würde zusammenbrechen, wenn diese Gegenüberstellung sich als unhaltbar erweisen sollte.)

Bibliography

Duhem, P. M. M. (1996). *Essays in the History and Philosophy of Science.* Translated and edited by R. Ariew and P. Barker. Indianapolis: Hackett Publishing Company.

Einstein, A. (1921). 'Geometrie und Erfahrung'. *Sitzungsberichte der Preußischen Akademie der Wissenschaften*, Erster Halbband, pp. 123-130. Published separately as *Geometrie und Erfahrung*. Berlin: Verlag von Julius Springer.

Gomperz, H. (1905). *Weltanschauungslehre* I: *Methodologie.* Jena & Leipzig: Eugen Diederichs.

Hacohen, M. H. (2000). *Karl Popper – The Formative Years, 1902-1945. Politics and Philosophy in Interwar Vienna.* Cambridge & elsewhere: Cambridge University Press.

ter Hark, M. R. M. (2002). 'Between Autobiography and Reality: Karl Popper's Inductive Years'. *Studies in History and Philosophy of Science* **33**, pp. 79-103.

Hansen, T. E. (1998). 'Popper's Early Work on the Theory of Knowledge'. Lecture given in Vienna on 30 October 1998 in the *Ringvorlesung* organized by the Karl Popper Institute.

Kant, I. (1783). *Prolegomena zu einer jeden künftigen Metaphysik die als Wissenschaft wird auftreten können.* Riga: Johann Friedrich Hartknoch.

McMullin, E. (1997). Review of Duhem (1996). *The British Journal for the Philosophy of Science* **48**, p. 607.

Popper, K. R. (1927). *'Gewohnheit' und 'Gesetzerlebnis' in der Erziehung.* Unpublished. To appear in Popper (2006).

⸻ (1929). *Axiome, Definitionen und Postulate der Geometrie.* Unpublished. To appear in Popper (2006).

⸻ (1930-1933). *Die beiden Grundprobleme der Erkenntnistheorie.* Edited by T. E. Hansen. First published 1979. Tübingen: J. C. B. Mohr (Paul Siebeck). 2nd edition 1994. 3rd edition to appear in *Gesammelte Werke in deutscher Sprache*, Volume 2. Tübingen: Mohr Siebeck.

⸻ (1933). 'Ein Kriterium des empirischen Charakters theoretischer Systeme: Vorläufige Mitteilung'. *Erkenntnis* **3**, 1933, pp. 426f. Reprinted as 'A Criterion of the Empirical Character of Theoretical Systems' in appendix *i of Popper (1959) and in the 2nd edition (1966a) of Popper (1935).

⸻ (1935). *Logik der Forschung.* Vienna: Julius Springer Verlag. 2nd edition, Popper (1966a).

⸻ (1959). *The Logic of Scientific Discovery.* London: Hutchinson. Enlarged English translation of Popper (1935).

⸻ (1963). *Conjectures and Refutations.* London: Routledge & Kegan Paul. 5th edition 1989.

———— (1966a). *Logik der Forschung*. 2nd edition. Tübingen: J. C. B. Mohr (Paul Siebeck). 11th edition 2005. Edited by H. Keuth. *Gesammelte Werke in deutscher Sprache*, Volume 3. Tübingen: Mohr Siebeck.

———— (1966b). 'A Theorem on Truth-Content'. In P. K. Feyerabend & G. Maxwell, editors (1966), pp. 343-353. *Mind, Matter, and Method: Essays in Philosophy and Science in Honor of Herbert Feigl*. Minneapolis: University of Minnesota Press.

———— (1974a). 'Intellectual Autobiography'. In Schilpp (1974), pp. 1-181. Reprinted as *Unended Quest* 1976. London & Glasgow: Fontana/Collins.

———— (1974b). 'Replies to My Critics'. In Schilpp (1974), pp. 959-1197.

———— (2006). *Frühe Schriften*. Edited by T. E. Hansen. *Gesammelte Werke in deutscher Sprache*, Volume 1. Tübingen: Mohr Siebeck.

Schilpp, P. A., editor (1974). *The Philosophy of Karl Popper*. La Salle IL: The Open Court Publishing Company.

Schlick, F. A. M. (1925). *Allgemeine Erkenntnislehre*. 2nd edition. Berlin: Julius Springer Verlag.

———— (1931). 'Die Kausalität in der gegenwärtigen Physik'. *Die Naturwissenschaften* **19**, Heft 7, 13 February, pp. 145-162.

Schopenhauer, A. (1841). *Die beiden Grundprobleme der Ethik, behandelt in zwei akademischen Preisschriften*. Frankfurt/Main: Joh. Chr. Hermannschen Buchhandlung (F. A. Suchsland). 2nd edition 1860. Leipzig: F. A. Brockhaus.

Shapere, D. (1997). 'What Is Truth?' *Annals of Science* **54**, pp. 305-310.

4

Karl Poppers erste Schritte in die Philosophie
Leonard Nelsons Paradoxien der Souveränität und Nelsons sowie Poppers Lösungsversuche

Hans-Joachim Dahms

1 Poppers Weg in die Philosophie

Dass Karl Popper einmal einer der berühmtesten Philosophen des 20. Jahrhunderts werden würde und dass man zu seinem 100. Geburtstag Anlass haben würde, in seiner früheren Heimatstadt Wien eine Tagung zu seinen Ehren abzuhalten, war in seiner Jugendzeit noch absolut nicht abzusehen. Denn zunächst hatte er aus Frustration und Langeweile schon im Alter von 16 Jahren das Gymnasium verlassen, um unter anderem eine Tischlerlehre zu beginnen, sich als Betreuer in einem Kindergarten zu betätigen und sich einer als „Kommunistenbaracke" bekannten Wohngemeinschaft anzuschließen:[1] alles Entscheidungen, die eher auf einen linksalternativen Lebensweg hindeuten als auf eine akademische Philosophenkarriere. Und auch als er sich, nach all diesen Abenteuern, doch entschloss als „Externer" das Abitur nachzumachen, um an dem neu gegründeten Pädagogischen Institut in Wien ein Lehrerstudium aufnehmen zu können, hatte dies mit Philosophie noch wenig zu tun. Zunächst wäre er bei der Externistenprüfung schon fast gescheitert, weil das spätere Wiener-Kreis Mitglied Edgar Zilsel als Prüfer mangelnde Kenntnisse in Logik beanstandete. Und auch als Popper schließlich — übrigens zusammen mit Marie Jahoda, der Autorin der berühmten sozialpsychologischen Studie über die Arbeitslosen von Marienthal — sein Studium aufnahm, war sein Plan keineswegs, ein akademischer Philosoph zu werden. Vielmehr bestand sein Traum darin, sich als Schulreformer um benachteiligte Bevölkerungsschichten verdient zu machen und vielleicht eine experimentelle Versuchsschule zu gründen. Was also hat ihn zur Philosophie gebracht?

---

[1] Diese und die folgenden Informationen über Poppers Leben stammen aus zwei Gesprächen, die ich 1991 mit Popper führen durfte. Teile des zweiten Interviews, an dem auch Friedrich Stadler teilnahm, wurden aufgezeichnet und zum Teil als „Popper und der Wiener Kreis — Aus einem Gespräch mit Sir Karl Popper" in Stadler (1997), pp. 525-545 publiziert. Vergl. dazu die erste, vor allem aus dem Nachlass gearbeitete genaue Biographie Poppers von M. Hacohen (Hacohen 2000).

Das waren, wie seinem autobiographisch gefärbten Aufsatz „Science: Conjectures and Refutations" (Popper 1957b/1963) zu entnehmen ist, zunächst
einmal die Bildungseindrücke der spektakulären Bestätigung der Einstein-
schen Allgemeinen Relativitätstheorie einerseits und die negativen Eindrücke
von Marx' historischem Materialismus, Freuds Psychoanalyse und Adlers Individualpsychologie andererseits. Der Kontrast zwischen diesen beiden Klassen
von Theorien führte zur Entdeckung des Abgrenzungsproblems zwischen Wissenschaft und Pseudowissenschaft und zur Formulierung seines Falsifizier-
barkeitsprinzips als Abgrenzungskriterium. Ob diese Selbstdarstellung zutrifft,
kann ich hier nicht untersuchen.[2]

Wie Poppers 'Intellectual Autobiography' (Popper 1974) zu entnehmen
ist, gehörten zu seinem Weg in die Philosophie aber auch zwei persönliche
Bekanntschaften mit professionellen Philosophen. Sie begannen schon Jahre,
bevor er von der Existenz des Wiener Kreises erfuhr. Ich meine seine Kon-
takte zu dem Wiener Heinrich Gomperz und zu dem gebürtigen Hannoveraner
Julius Kraft (nicht zu verwechseln mit dem Mitglied des Wiener Kreises Victor Kraft). In seiner Autobiographie hat er über Julius Kraft, einen entfernten
Verwandten Poppers und in akademischer Hinsicht ein Schüler des Göttinger
Philosophen Leonard Nelson geschrieben, dass seine Freundschaft mit ihm
bis zu dessen Tod im Jahre 1960 angedauert habe (Popper 1974, § 15). Krafts
persönliche Bedeutung für Popper geht unter anderem auch daraus hervor,
dass er der einzige Mensch gewesen ist, dem er je einen Nachruf gewidmet hat
(Popper 1962). Über die Themen der Diskussionen mit Julius Kraft schreibt
Popper in seiner Autobiographie (ibidem, pp. 58f.):

> Julius Kraft, like Leonard Nelson, was a non-Marxist socialist, and about half
> our discussions, often lasting in the small hours of the mornings were cen-
> tred on my criticism of Marx. The other half were about the theory of know-
> ledge: mainly Kant's so-called „transcendental deduction" (which I regarded as
> question-begging), his solution of the antinomies, and Nelson's „Impossibility of
> the Theory of Knowledge".

----

[2]Ich beschränke mich hier auf ein Beispiel: das Abgrenzungsproblem und die Falsifizierbarkeit als seine Lösung: Unmittelbar nach dem Erscheinen von Oswald Spenglers *Untergang des Abendlandes* (Spengler 1918), jenem spektakulären Erfolg der Popularphiloso-
phie, die die Niederlage der Mittelmächte im Ersten Weltkrieg geradezu im Kontext eines
allgemeinen Weltuntergangszenarios einbettete, hat Leonard Nelson eine lange satirische
Abrechnung mit Spengler verfasst (Nelson 1921). Sie besteht im wesentlichen darin, in
mehreren Anläufen jeweils die *Unwiderlegbarkeit* der Spenglerschen Lehre zu beweisen.
„Umso besser für Spengler", wird der unbeleckte Leser zunächst denken. Aber Nelsons
Pointe verläuft genau umgekehrt: die Unwiderlegbarkeit von Spenglers Theorien wird
nicht als Qualitätsbeweis für seine Lehren hingenommen, sondern als ein Zeichen ihrer
nicht zu reparierenden Schwäche erwiesen. Der Grundsatz des Falsifikationismus musste
Popper also nicht erst „dämmern", wie er in seinem *Personal Report* (Popper 1957b)
schrieb. Vielmehr besteht sein Verdienst allenfalls darin, ihn auf *weitere Beispiele* wie
den Marxschen historischen Materialismus, die Freudsche Psychoanalyse, die Adlersche
Persönlichkeitspsychologie etc. *angewandt zu haben*.

Diese beiden Themen haben in letzter Zeit in der Literatur eine gewisse Aufmerksamkeit erfahren.[3] Zu meiner Überraschung erzählte Popper mir nun von einer sozusagen dritten Hälfte (oder sogar mehr) seiner Diskussionen mit Kraft: „Es hat sich in diesen Diskussionen hauptsächlich um das Führerprinzip gehandelt". Und diese dritte Hälfte werde ich im Folgenden thematisieren. Dass dieses Thema eine solch große Rolle gespielt haben soll, ist aus einer Reihe von Gründen durchaus verständlich, zu deren Erläuterung ich allerdings etwas ausholen muss.

Poppers erster philosophischer Gesprächspartner, Julius Kraft, war nicht nur im akademischen Sinne Schüler von Leonard Nelson,[4] sondern auch dessen politischer Gefolgsmann. Nelson hatte schon in jungen Jahren als Erkenntnistheoretiker, vor allem der Naturwissenschaften und Mathematik, auf sich aufmerksam gemacht und unter anderem das lebenslange Interesse des berühmten Mathematikers David Hilbert auf sich gezogen (Peckhaus 1990). Später wandte sich Nelson mehr und mehr der Ethik und der politischen Philosophie zu. Damit ging eine politische Radikalisierung einher. Nachdem er politisch ursprünglich vor dem ersten Weltkrieg als Linksliberaler begonnen hatte (Dahms 1996, pp. 230f.), war er durch Weltkrieg und Revolution radikalisiert worden und hatte sich immer stärker nach links entwickelt. Er zog als einer der ganz wenigen deutschen Philosophen nach dem Weltkrieg aus seinen sozialphilosophischen Ansichten auch unmittelbar praktische Konsequenzen und gründete unter anderem auch politische Organisationen: zuerst den Internationalen Jugendbund (IJB) und später, 1925, den Internationalen Sozialistischen Kampfbund (ISK). Beide Organisationen folgten programmatisch seinem Konzept eines nichtmarxistischen, auf Gerechtigkeitsprinzipien basierenden Sozialismus. Die Atmosphäre dieser Gruppierungen war weithin durch das Postulat einer weitgehenden Einheit von politischer Haltung und praktischer Lebensführung bestimmt. So hatten die Mitglieder, die einer strikten Schulung unterworfen wurden, auch „Mindestforderungen" (wie Abstinenz von Alkohol, Nikotin, zölibatäre Lebendweise) zu erfüllen. Die beiden Organisationen waren ganz auf die charismatische Führerfigur Nelson ausgerichtet, und in ihnen herrschte eine Art von Führerprinzip. Organisatorisch waren die beiden Bünde als strikte Kaderorganisationen aufgebaut und versuchten als solche jeweils in den größeren Arbeiterparteien beziehungsweise deren Jugendorganisationen Fuß zu fassen. Dank straffer Organisation, exzellenter Präparation der Mitglieder und gezielter Vorbereitung auf wichtige Anlässe hatten sie damit zeitweise auch einen relativen Erfolg.

Seit 1925 machte der ISK enorme Anstrengungen, sich tatsächlich als internationale Partei zu etablieren. In diesem Sinne trat Nelson in Kontakt zu bekannten Figuren der Zeitgeschichte wie etwa zu dem tschechoslowakischen

---

[3]Siehe die ausführliche Darstellung und Diskussion in Hacohen (2000), sowie die Beiträge von pp. 99-110 in diesem Band.

[4]Nach der juristischen Promotion Krafts im Jahre 1922 war Nelson Doktorvater der 1924 anschließenden philosophischen Promotion, die u.a. zu Streitigkeiten einiger Mitglieder der philosophischen Fakultät mit Nelson führte. Die Promotionsakte Krafts befinden sich im Göttinger Universitätsarchiv.

Präsidenten Thomas Masaryk, aber auch zu Leo Trotsky (Franke 1991, p. 210 und pp. 217f.). Als prominenter westlicher Philosoph sollte Bertrand Russell für eine Mitgliedschaft im ISK gewonnen werden. Alle diese Versuche blieben allerdings erfolglos.

Wie Popper mir nun erzählte, sollte auch er — der als 23jähriger noch keine solche Prominenz erreicht hatte — als Mitglied des ISK angeworben werden. Unplausibel erscheint dieser Rekrutierungsversuch nicht, da Popper seit seiner Abkehr vom Kommunismus weiterhin linkem Gedankengut anhing und in diesem Sinne etwa bis zum Verbot der austromarxistischen SDAPÖ deren Mitglied blieb. Kraft habe also Nelson auf ihn (Popper) aufmerksam gemacht und die Folge war: „Er hat mir einen, den Willi Eichler, geschickt; der Nelson hat den Willi Eichler zu mir geschickt". Eichler war im ISK Stellvertreter Nelsons und später sein Nachfolger.[5]   Nach Poppers Erinnerung hat das Gespräch mit Eichler etwa ein Jahr vor Nelsons frühem Tod am 29. Oktober 1927 stattgefunden, also im Jahre 1926.

Popper, der ohnehin schon selbst für sich einen nichtmarxistischen Sozialismus im Auge hatte und für seine Lebensführung schon die meisten „Mindestforderungen" des ISK praktizierte, bevor er sie als solche kennenlernte, wäre auch bereit gewesen, der Organisation beizutreten, wenn nicht ein Punkt ihn daran gehindert hätte: das antidemokratische Führerprinzip und der dahinterstehende politische Platonismus Nelsons.[6] Über diesen Konflikt gibt es nun zwei Darstellungen. Die eine wurde von Maria Hodann, die Eichler nach Wien begleitet hatte, sofort nach dem erfolglosen Anwerbeversuch als offizieller Bericht aufgesetzt und liest sich unter anderem so:[7]

> ... Das, was er an Kritik unserer theoretischen Grundlagen, z.B. Demokratie, vorbrachte, war nicht besonders tief durchdacht... Unser Eindruck also: für praktische IJB Arbeit kommt Popper kaum in Frage — vorläufig wenigstens. Denn wie soll er junge Menschen in unserem Sinne erziehen?

Die andere stammt von Popper und wurde mir von ihm mitgeteilt. Nach seinen Worten hatte ihn noch nie jemand vorher danach gefragt.[8] Sie lautet so: Nachdem er schon mit Kraft viel und ergebnislos über das Wesen und den Wert der Demokratie debattiert hatte, habe die Auseinandersetzung mit Eichler ihn dazu veranlasst, den Dissens über den Wert der Demokratie und das Führerprinzip auch schriftlich zu formulieren. Aus diesen Aufzeichnungen sei dann schließlich fast 20 Jahre später das Kapitel über das Führerprinzip in *Die offene Gesellschaft und ihre Feinde* geworden, in dem unter anderem die Paradoxie der Demokratie diskutiert und eine Lösung angegeben wird.

---

[5] Eichler hat später nach dem zweiten Weltkrieg großen Einfluss auf die programmatische Entwicklung der deutschen Sozialdemokratie, insbesondere auf das Godesberger Programm der SPD und deren Abrücken vom Marxismus als alleiniger weltanschaulicher Grundlage, gehabt.

[6] Über diesen Punkt hat sich Nelson auch mit Masaryk und Russell nicht einigen können.

[7] Zitiert nach Franke (1991), p. 164.

[8] Die erste Erwähnung in der Literatur ist Franke (1991).

Bevor ich zu den mehr systematische orientierten Teilen meiner Bemerkungen übergehe, möchte ich einige Konsequenzen thesenartig zusammenfassen, die sich aus dem Gesagten für das Werk Poppers ergeben:

(1) Das philosophische Nachdenken Poppers hat in der politischen Philosophie einen ersten schriftlichen Niederschlag erfahren, nicht in der Wissenschaftsphilosophie. Insofern sind Darstellungen von Anhängern und Gegnern Poppers zu korrigieren, die davon ausgehen, er habe die Prinzipien seiner Wissenschaftstheorie später auf die Sphäre der Politik übertragen.

(2) Poppers *Die offene Gesellschaft und ihre Feinde* wird meist so verstanden, als sei ihr erster Band mit ihrer Platon-Kritik als Auseinandersetzung mit den geistigen Wurzeln des Nationalsozialismus und ihr zweiter Band mit ihrer Marx-Kritik als Auseinandersetzung mit den geistigen Wurzeln des Kommunismus zu verstehen, so, wie es Popper auch später selbst dargestellt hat.[9] Demgegenüber muss festgehalten werden, dass ein zentraler Teil des ersten Bandes, nämlich die Kritik am Führerprinzip, sich eben nicht der Auseinandersetzung mit rechtem, sondern mit linkem Autoritarismus, nämlich dem Nelsons, verdankt.

2 Die Ausgangslage

Das zentrale Stück der Nelsonschen Demokratiekritik ist die Idee, dass sie mit ihren eigenen Mitteln, nämlich dem Mehrheitsbeschluss, abgeschafft werden kann. Diese Paradoxie der Demokratie wird — wie auch andere Paradoxien der Souveränität — ausführlichst dargestellt und begründet in Nelsons 1924 erschienenem dritten Band seiner *Vorlesungen über die Grundlage der Ethik*, nämlich in seinem *System der philosophischen Rechtslehre und Politik* (Nelson 1924, Bd. 3). Poppers Gesprächspartner Julius Kraft hat Teile dieser Thematik schon in seiner im selben Jahr erschienenen juristischen Dissertation besprochen und zwar im Zusammenhang mit dem staatsrechtlichen Problem des Verfassungswechsels. Auch hat er Nelsons Werk noch im gleichen Jahr in der Kant-Festschrift rezensiert (Kraft 1924). Er war also als Übermittler der entsprechenden Gedankengänge Nelsons bestens geeignet.

Was die beiden nun konkret über Demokratie und das Führerprinzip diskutiert haben und zu welchem Ergebnis sie gekommen sind, ist mir nicht bekannt. Aus dieser frühen Zeit, in der sie beide in Wien wohnten, existiert nur ein einziger Brief, und der beschäftigt sich nicht mit dieser Materie.[10]

Deshalb werde ich mich nun nicht mehr mit historischen Hintergründen befassen, sondern folgende Fragen diskutieren:

---

[9]Er schreibt nämlich im Vorwort zur siebenten deutschen Auflage zu (1992): „So ging ich auf Spurensuche in der Geschichte; von Hitler zurück zu Platon: dem ersten großen politischen Ideologen, der in Klassen und Rassen dachte und Konzentrationslager vorschlug. Und ich ging von Stalin zurück zu Karl Marx. Mit meiner Kritik an Marx wollte ich auch mich selbst kritisieren, da ich in meiner frühen Jugend selbst Marxist gewesen war und für einige Wochen sogar Kommunist" (Popper 1992, Band I, p. IX).

[10]Nach einer Information von Malachi Hacohen.

(1) Worin besteht die von Nelson behauptete Paradoxie der Demokratie?

(2) Worin besteht Nelsons Lösung der Paradoxie? Ist sie ebenfalls von einer Paradoxie betroffen? Ist sie haltbar?

(3) Was ist Poppers Version der Paradoxie?

(4) Kann Poppers Lösung überzeugen?

3 Nelsons „Paradoxie der Demokratie" und seine Lösung

3.1 Nelsons Formulierungen der Paradoxie

Nelson beginnt seine Betrachtungen mit einem Widerspruchsbeweis nicht für den Fall der Demokratie, sondern des *Autoritarismus*. Dieses Argument ist allerdings so formal gehalten, dass es ohne weiteres auf jede andere Regierungsform zu übertragen ist und von ihm in der Tat im Fortgang der Argumentation auch auf die *Demokratie* übertragen wird: „Nehmen wir also an, es sei irgend eine Person durch das Rechtsgesetz als Autorität ausgezeichnet, d.h. als ausschließlich verfügungsberechtigt, so dass ihre Verfügungen verbindlich sind. Wir haben dann den Satz „A: N ist berechtigt, zu verfügen." (Nelson 1924, pp. 227f.)

> Wenn dieser Satz wirklich gelten soll, N also schrankenlos verfügungsberechtigt ist, so führt dies auf einen Widerspruch. Denn dann wäre auch die Geltung dieses Satzes selbst seinem Verfügungsrecht nicht entzogen. Vermöge dieses Verfügungsrechts könnte er die Geltung des Satzes A willkürlich aufheben, d.h. die übrigen Mitglieder der Gesellschaft von der ihnen aufgrund dieses Satzes obliegenden Verpflichtung entbinden und also sein eigenes Verfügungsrecht aufheben. Dieses besteht also nicht unbeschränkt; im Widerspruch zu dem behaupteten Satze.

Die Grundidee dieses Beweises wendet Nelson dann, wie gesagt, auch auf den Fall der Demokratie an. Man braucht im Grund ja auch nur in Satz A die Person N durch „die Mehrheit" (beziehungsweise durch „von der Mehrheit beauftragte Repräsentanten") zu ersetzten. Da beide Beweise auf ein und derselben Grundidee beruhen, gelangt er denn recht schnell zur Verallgemeinerung seiner Resultate.

Nun könnte man natürlich auf die — ganz nahe liegende — Idee kommen, der Paradoxie dadurch zu entkommen, dass man den Satz A von der Verfügungsberechtigung des N ausnimmt. Aber auch für diesen Fall hat Nelson vorgesorgt und sich zu zeigen bemüht, dass sich der Widerspruch dann auf höherer Stufenleiter reproduziert. Nehmen wir seine Kritik des Autoritätsprinzips, also des Grundsatzes „A: N ist berechtigt zu verfügen.", und dessen Einschränkung „B: N ist berechtigt, zu verfügen, ausgenommen über A." Nelson kommentiert die durch die Einführung von B entstandene Lage so (ibidem):

> Ausgenommen über A, das heißt: die Geltung von A ist seiner Willkür entzogen. Dann würde aber gerade gelten, dass, gemäß A, N ausnahmslos verfügungs-

berechtigt ist, somit wir nicht nur auf den ursprünglichen Widerspruch zurück-kommen, sondern auch auf einen Widerspruch mit B. Der Satz B widerspricht sich also ebenso wie der Satz A. In der Tat würde nunmehr das neue Gesetz B dem (nur durch A eingeschränkten) Verfügungsrecht von N verfallen.

Dieser neue (und eine Reihe von weiteren Widersprüchen) entsteht aber nur, weil A nicht in der Formulierung, aber in der Erläuterung, den Anspruch auf schrankenlose Gültigkeit enthält. Mit anderen Worten: *wirkliche Geltung* und *Schrankenlosigkeit des Geltungsbereichs* werden von Nelson miteinander identifiziert. Dies ist aber keineswegs selbstverständlich. Warum sollte eine Regel oder Vorschrift nicht einerseits strikt sein und andererseits Ausnahmen zulassen? Man denke etwa an ein striktes Fahrverbot für Autos mit Ausnahmen, etwa für Krankenwagen und die Feuerwehr. Insofern ist die Gültigkeit von A durchaus mit der „Ausnahme" des Verbots der Selbstanwendung der Regel verträglich. Bei einer Beschränkung von A auf *materiale* Abstimmungen fällt aber die Möglichkeit der Selbstanwendung fort, sodass der Schein einer Paradoxie nicht entstehen kann. Natürlich dürfen solche Ausnahmen (wie im Beispiel des Fahrverbots) nicht willkürlich gesetzt werden. Das ist natürlich besonders von einer Regel zu fordern, die die Substanz der Demokratie auszusprechen beansprucht. Aber das Verbot der Selbstanwendung ist nicht willkürlich, weil es die Möglichkeit aller materialen Abstimmungen unangetastet lässt und nur dafür sorgt, dass die Aufhebung der Regel ausgeschlossen bleibt.

Es gibt von Nelson noch eine zweite Version der Paradoxie der Demokratie. Diese hat er im Sommer 1926 bei Gelegenheit einer Diskussion über ein Referat von Hans Kelsen beim fünften Deutschen Soziologentag in Wien vorgetragen.[11] In ihr wird dargestellt, was der brave Demokrat zu tun gedenkt, wenn er mit ansehen muss, dass die Demokratie, die Herrschaft der Mehrheit, durch Anwendung der Mehrheitsregel selbst abgeschafft wird. Soll er sich dann als Demokrat der neuen nichtdemokratischen Staatsform beugen, oder sich ihr widersetzen, obwohl ihre Einführung Resultat einer Mehrheitsentscheidung war? Diese Formulierung ist als ethische Paradoxie eingekleidet, also als unlösbarer Handlungskonflikt. Es ist nicht unwichtig, sich den Unterschied der beiden Formulierungen klarzumachen. Die erste Formulierung ist eine strikte Antinomie, die der Russellschen Antinomie ähnelt. Bei A handelt es sich nur um die Behauptungen über Tatsächliches, nämlich hier um die Frage: *ist* N im Fall der Selbstanwendung von A nun verfügungberechtigt oder nicht? Bei der zweiten Formulierung dagegen geht es um eine ethische Frage: was soll der von Ns Verfügungen Betroffene *tun*?

Wie wir sehen werden, stand Popper offenbar nur die zweite Formulierung vor Augen. Ich komme in Abschnitt 4.1 darauf zurück.

---

[11]Siehe Näheres zu dieser Diskussion und ihrem Einfluss auf die politische Philosophie Poppers bei Dahms (2001).

3.2 Nelsons „Lösung" der Paradoxien der Souveränität

Als Ausweg zu diesen fundamentalen Kritiken der Souveränitätstheorie, die
sich aus den genannten Paradoxien ergeben, von denen die Demokratie nur
eine ist, verkündet Nelson dann in § 101 (Nelson 1924) als „Positive Lösung des
Problems der Souveränität" „Das Postulat der Herrschaft der Weisen" und formuliert: „Auf die Frage also, wer der Regent im Staate sein soll, ist die einzig
bündige Antwort die alte Platonische: der Weiseste." (Nelson 1924, p. 274).
Was ist von dieser Lösung zu halten? Zunächst einmal: sie ist — anders,
als das Popper angenommen zu haben scheint[12] — selbst paradoxiefrei. Denn
dem Weisesten kann nicht passieren, was dem Demokraten oder auch dem
autoritär Herrschenden sehr wohl passieren kann: nämlich durch negative
Selbstanwendung seiner Legitimationsgrundlage die Regierungsgewalt an jemand anderen übergehen zu lassen. Und zwar kann dies nicht passieren, weil
der Weiseste sonst nicht mehr der Weiseste wäre. Seine Weisheit schließt das
Wissen darum ein, dass es keine bessere Regierung geben kann als die von
ihm selbst angeführte. Insofern „reduziert" sich für Nelson die Problematik
legitimer Herrschaft auf zwei praktische Probleme:

(1) dem Weisesten zur Herrschaft zu verhelfen

(2) seine Sukzession zu sichern.

Die Lösung des ersten Problems stellt sich Nelson so vor, dass der Weiseste
seine Fähigkeiten erkennt und schlichtweg sozusagen „die Macht ergreift". Es
muss ihm zufolge „wohl oder übel dem Weisesten selbst überlassen bleiben,
seinen Beruf zu erkennen und ihn aus eigener Einsicht in seine Berufung zu
ergreifen." (Nelson 1924, p. 274). Dazu bedarf es entsprechender organisato-
rischer Vorkehrungen wie etwa der Gründung einer Partei und einer entsprechenden Aufklärung der Bevölkerungsmassen, sodass der Machtübernahme des
Weisesten der Weg geebnet wird. Das zweite Problem ist ein pädagogisches,
nämlich das der geeigneten Führerauslese zum Zwecke einer rationalen Sukzessionssicherung. Nelson hat versucht, diese beiden Probleme auch durchaus
ganz praktisch anzugehen. Durch die Gründung des „Internationalen Sozialistischen Kampfbundes" das erste, durch die Gründung des Erziehungsheims
„Walkemühle" das andere. Wie diese Projekte verlaufen sind, braucht uns aber
hier nicht weiter zu interessieren.

Denn es scheint klar, dass Nelsons „Alternative" zwar einerseits nicht von
einer Paradoxie betroffen wird, aber andererseits doch nur eine verbale ist.
So hat der berühmte Wiener Staatsrechtler und Rechtsphilosoph Hans Kelsen
den Standpunkt Nelsons auch 1926 beim oben erwähnten 5. Deutschen Soziologentag in Wien kritisiert. Er habe aus Nelsons zahlreichen Schriften (Kelsen
1927b, p. 14 unten).

---

[12]Popper schreibt von „... genau analoge(n) Einwände(n) gegen alle besonderen Formen der *Theorie der Souveränität oder des Führertums* ..." (Popper 1992, Kapitel 7, Anmerkung 4).

nichts anderes ... herauslesen können als die billige Weisheit, daß der Beste herrschen solle. Wenn man nichts anderes als dieses Prinzip der Demokratie entgegenzusetzen weiß, so muß festgestellt werden, dass dies nur eine inhaltslose Tautologie ist, die nichts anderes sagt, als daß geschehen soll, was geschehen soll. Ich weiß wohl, dass Nelson ein bestimmtes Mittel im Auge hat, das seiner Ansicht nach geeignet ist, den Besten zur Herrschaft zur bringen: die Erziehung zum Führer. Aber das heißt in Wirklichkeit nur, das Problem hinausschieben, aber nicht es lösen. ... Dem Streit um die richtige Herrschaft wird der Streit um die richtige Erziehung zur richtigen Herrschaft vorangeschickt und es ist im Grunde genommen derselbe Streit.

Kelsen hat sich mit diesen Bemerkungen nur auf den Aspekt der Sukzessionssicherung des „Weisesten" bezogen. Aber der erste Komplex, nämlich der der Machtübernahme des „Weisesten", stellt natürlich kein geringeres Problem dar. Aus Sicht der Ereignisse nach 1933 in Deutschland muß man wohl sagen, dass Nelson die Möglichkeit zu leicht genommen hat, dass ein *eingebildeter* Weisester „seine Berufung ergreift",[13] und dann vielleicht ein viel größeres Unglück über die von ihm Regierten bringt, als es jede andere Regierung je vermocht hätte, und zwar, ohne dass man ihn ohne Waffengewalt wieder loswerden kann. Es ist kein Wunder, dass die Nelsonianer nicht erst nach 1945 die Führerideologie verworfen und sich dem Gedanken der Demokratie angeschlossen haben.

Als Zwischenergebnis kann damit festgehalten werden, dass Nelson und seine Anhänger die Ausgestaltungsmöglichkeiten der Demokratie (insbesondere die einer Abschwächung der Mehrheitsregel auf nur materiale Abstimmungen) und gleichzeitig die Probleme einer Herrschaft des Weisesten unterschätzt haben. Aber nehmen wir kontrafaktisch einmal an, alle Regierungsformen seien in gleicher Weise von Paradoxien betroffen. Dann böte die Widerspruchsfreiheit jedenfalls kein Entscheidungskriterium zwischen diesen. Und Nelsons eigene „Lösung" scheidet aus, da es sich dabei im Theoretischen um eine verbale Scheinlösung und im Praktischen um eine Gefahr handelt, die der autoritären Regierungsform vergleichbar ist.

4 Poppers Version der Paradoxie und seine Lösung

4.1 Poppers Formulierung der Paradoxie

Poppers Formulierung einer geradezu „logischen" Demokratiekritik, also einer Paradoxie der Demokratie ist im 7. Kapitel von *Die offene Gesellschaft und ihre Feinde* zu finden. Popper schreibt dort, dass es außer empirischen Befunden und persönlichen Meinungen auch ein logisches Argument gegen die Demokratie gebe (Popper 1992, Kapitel 7, Abschnitt I, Text zu Anmerkung 5; meine Hervorhebungen.)

> Eine besondere Form dieses logischen Argumentes richtet sich gegen eine zu naive Fassung des Liberalismus, der Demokratie und des Prinzips der Herrschaft

---

[13]Er diskutiert diese Möglichkeit kurz in Nelson (1924, p. 275).

der Majorität. Und es hat eine gewisse Ähnlichkeit mit dem wohlbekannten
„Paradoxon der Freiheit", das Platon als erster und mit Erfolg verwendet hat.
Anläßlich seiner Kritik der Demokratie und in seiner Darstellung des Aufstiegs
des Tyrannen stellt Platon *implizit* die folgende Frage: Was tun wir, wenn es der
Wille des Volkes ist, nicht selbst zu regieren, sondern statt dessen einen Tyrannen regieren zu lassen? Platon *legt* die Möglichkeit *nahe*, daß der freie Mensch,
seine Freiheit gebrauchend, zuerst den Gesetzen Widerstand leistet, schließlich
die Freiheit selbst missachtet und einen Tyrannen verlangt. Diese Möglichkeit ist
nicht an den Haaren herbeigezogen: Fälle dieser Art sind oft genug eingetreten.
Und immer, wenn sie sich ereigneten, kamen alle jene Demokraten in eine hoff-
nungslose intellektuelle Situation, die das Prinzip der Herrschaft der Mehrheit
oder eine ähnliche Form des Prinzips der Souveränität als die Grundlage ihres
politischen Glaubensbekenntnisses akzeptieren. Einerseits verlangt das von ihnen
akzeptierte Prinzip sich jeder Herrschaft zu widersetzen außer der Herrschaft der
Majorität, also auch der Herrschaft des neuen Tyrannen; andererseits fordert
dasselbe Prinzip von ihnen die Anerkennung jeder Entscheidung der Majorität
und damit auch die Anerkennung der Herrschaft des neuen Tyrannen. Es ist
natürlich, daß der Widerspruch in ihrer Theorie ihre Handlungen lähmen muß.

Beginnen wir mit der Vorfrage, nämlich der nach der historischen Pri-
orität bei der Entdeckung der Paradoxie der Demokratie. Im obigen Zitat
wie im übrigen Text des Kapitels sowie zu Beginn einer langen Anmerkung
wird die Erfindung des „Paradoxons der Demokratie" von Popper auf Platon
zurückgeführt (Popper 1992, Kapitel 7, Abschnitt I). An sämtlichen von
Popper angeführten Platonstellen, die das Paradoxon der Demokratie enthalten sollen, geht es aber jeweils nur um den *kausalen Übergang* von der
Demokratie zur Diktatur. An keiner Stelle ist dort davon die Rede, dass dieser
Übergang durch die Anwendung des Prinzips der Demokratie selbst zustande
kommt, nämlich durch eine Abstimmung der Mehrheit, als deren Resultat
das Mehrheitsprinzip selbst abgeschafft wird. Erst diese Selbstanwendung ver-
leiht dem Paradox der Demokratie aber erst seinen *quasi logischen* Charakter
(bzw., wie ich im Folgenden behaupten möchte: seinen paradoxen Schein).

Etwas verklausuliert und indirekt hat Popper den Einfluss Nelsons auf
seine Formulierung des Paradoxon der Demokratie eingeräumt. Im vorletz-
ten Absatz jener langen Anmerkungen zu seiner Formulierung der Paradoxie
der Demokratie heißt es nämlich hinsichtlich der historischen Vorläuferschaft
(Popper 1992, Kapitel 7, Anmerkung 4):

> Daß sich die Kritik Platons an der Demokratie in der hier gegebenen Weise
> deuten lässt und daß das Prinzip der Herrschaft der Majorität zu einem Selbst-
> widerspruch führen kann, wurde meines Wissens nach zuerst von Leonard Nel-
> son ... bemerkt. Ich glaube jedoch nicht, daß Nelson, der trotz seiner leiden-
> schaftlich humanitären Gesinnung und trotz seines glühenden Kampfes für die
> Freiheit vieles aus den politischen Theorien Platons übernommen hat (vor allem
> übernahm er das platonische Prinzip des Führertums), den Umstand bemerkte,
> daß sich genau analoge Einwände gegen alle besondere Formen der Theorie der
> Souveränität oder Führertums erheben lassen.

Warum es Popper so schwerfiel, den Einfluss zuzugeben, den Nelson auf seine politische Philosophie gehabt hat, kann man nur vermuten. Abgesehen von möglichen persönlichen Eigenheiten Poppers hat es wahrscheinlich mit der Situation zu tun, in die die Veröffentlichung der *Offenen Gesellschaft* fiel. Damals wäre es sicher keine gute Idee gewesen, sich auf einen ausgewiesenen Antidemokraten und Anhänger eines Führerprinzips zu beziehen, wie es Nelson nun einmal gewesen ist. Es überrascht deshalb nicht, dass Julius Kraft in eine amerikanische Ausgabe von Schriften Nelsons keinen einzigen Text aus dessen politischer Philosophie aufgenommen hat (Nelson 1949).

Abgesehen von der historischen Prioritätsfrage fällt an Poppers Präsentation der Paradoxie der Demokratie auf, dass er sich nicht an Nelsons ausführliche Diskussion aus dessen Ethik-Vorlesungen gehalten hat, sondern nur an dessen knappe Diskussionsbemerkungen vom Wiener Soziologentag. Auf meine entsprechende Frage erklärte er mir, dass er an diesem nicht teilgenommen hatte und zwar schon deswegen nicht, weil er die Soziologen immer für Schwindler gehalten habe, „für unbewusste Schwindler natürlich", wie er sich beeilte hinzuzufügen.

Wie steht es nun mit dem Gehalt der Nelson-Popperschen Paradoxie der Demokratie? Ich möchte behaupten, dass die Unmöglichkeit eine nur scheinbare ist. Die Möglichkeit des angegebenen Widerspruchs scheint zunächst — als abstrakte Möglichkeit — wie ein Damoklesschwert über der Demokratie zu hängen. Sobald man sich aber die reale Situation einer Abstimmung über das Mehrheitsprinzip konkret vorstellt, verfliegt dieser Schein. Jene Demokraten nämlich, die durch ihre Stimmabgabe zu einem Mehrheitsbeschluß beitragen, der die Demokratie abschafft, hören damit ipso facto auf, Demokraten zu sein. Nur jene, die dagegen stimmen, bleiben Demokraten. Während die ersteren verpflichtet sind, sich von nun an der Herrschaft des Tyrannen zu beugen, haben die letzteren dazu keinen Anlass. Denn die Anwendung des aus dem Mehrheitsprinzip abgeleiteten Prinzips der Unterordnung der Minderheit unter die Mehrheit erlischt gleichzeitig mit der Abschaffung des Majoritätsprinzips selbst.

Insofern ist der von Popper geschilderte Gewissenskonflikt nicht in ein und derselben Person zu lokalisieren, also kein sozusagen interner, logischer, der dazu angetan wäre, die Handlungen dieser Personen zu lähmen, sondern es handelt sich um einen (externen) Konflikt zwischen verschiedenen Personen, denen nämlich, die von der Demokratie zur Tyrannis übergelaufen sind und jenen, die ihr treu geblieben sind. Und dieser Konflikt muss zwischen diesen politisch ausgetragen werden.

Was also die angebliche „Paradoxie der Demokratie" zeigt, ist kein Widerspruch, sondern nur eine gewisse Anfälligkeit gegen die Gefahr der Selbstaufhebung (die sie, wie wir gesehen haben, mit allen anderen Regierungsformen teilt). Diese Anfälligkeit kann aber rechtlich — soweit man durch gesetzliche Vorkehrungen hier überhaupt etwas verhindern kann — dadurch behoben werden, dass man in einer Verfassung das Prinzip der Demokratie von einer Änderungsmöglichkeit ausnimmt (wie das zum Beispiel im Grundgesetz der Bundesrepublik Deutschland der Fall ist).

4.2 Poppers Lösung für die Paradoxie der Demokratie

Eigentlich erübrigt es sich, Poppers Lösung für die Paradoxie zu betrachten, wenn es sich bei dieser, wie ich meine, nur um einen Scheinwiderspruch handelt. Aber es ist auch instruktiv für Poppers gesamte Philosophie, zu sehen, dass es sich dabei um keine Lösung handelt und warum das so ist.

Poppers Lösung für die Paradoxie der Demokratie muss natürlich eine andere sein als die autoritäre Nelsons. Sie besteht vor allem in einer Mäßigung der Erwartungen, die man der Demokratie entgegenbringen soll. Es soll in Zukunft nicht mehr darum gehen, eine Antwort auf die Frage zu finden, wer legitimerweise herrschen soll. Denn das kann von niemand erwartet werden. Der Weiseste ist ebenso eine Chimäre wie ein aufgeklärter Volkswille. Vielmehr soll man sich nach Popper fragen, ob eine gegebene Herrschaftsform Mechanismen vorsieht, mit denen man einen Wechsel der Herrschaft ohne Gewalt herbeiführen und dauerhaft einen Rückfall in die Tyrannis vermeiden kann. Und *nur in dieser Hinsicht* ist die Demokratie jeder anderen Staatsform vorzuziehen. Das reicht nach Popper aber auch hin. Denn (Popper 1992, Kapitel 7, Abschnitt III).

> So betrachtet, beruht die Theorie der Demokratie nicht auf dem Prinzip der Herrschaft der Majorität; die verschiedenen Methoden einer demokratischen Kontrolle — die allgemeinen Wahlen, die parlamentarische Regierungsform — sind nicht mehr als wohlversuchte und, angesichts eines weitverbreiteten traditionellen Mißtrauens der Diktatur gegenüber, ziemlich wirksame institutionelle Sicherungen gegen die Tyrannei, Sicherungen, die stets der Verbesserung offen stehen und die sogar Methoden für ihre eigene Verbesserung vorsehen.

Reicht nun Poppers — sehr wesentlich von Hans Kelsen geprägte Verteidigung der Demokratie aus?[14] Wenn es nur darum ginge, die möglichst reibungslose Abschaffung bestehender Regierungen zu befördern, so könnte das durch eine radikale Begrenzung der Wahlperioden und zusätzlich vielleicht noch durch ein Verbot der Wiederwahl geschehen. Und das Wahlverfahren könnte, wenn es wirklich nur um Elitenrotation ginge und nicht auch um inhaltliche positive Legitimation für Programme und Personen, durch andere Mechanismen wie etwa eine Verlosung ersetzt werden. Aber bei Wahlen geht es eben nicht nur um die Chance der Ablösung bestehender Regierungen und die möglichst nachhaltige Vermeidung von Tyrannei, sondern auch um die Legitimation des zukünftigen Regierungshandelns für einen übersehbaren Zeitraum.[15]

Poppers Theorie der Demokratie ist seiner (allerdings nur rudimentär entwickelten) Ethik verwandt. In dieser Konzeption gibt es bekanntlich ein Prin-

---

[14]Siehe dazu Kelsen (1920), (1927a) sowie Dahms (2001).
[15]Siehe in diesem Sinne schon Pickel (1991, pp. 217f.).

zip, demzufolge es nicht auf das größte Glück der größten Zahl oder ähnliche utilitaristische Regel ankommt, sondern auf die Vermeidung und Eindämmung von Unglück und Leid, also eine Art von negativen Utilitarismus. Dagegen gibt es bekanntlich den schon fast trivial zu nennenden Einwand, dass die einfachste und nachhaltigste Vermeidung von Unglück darin bestünde, die Menschheit als Ganzes abzuschaffen. Poppers *Ethik* ist insofern zu negativistisch.

Auf Poppers Wissenschaftstheorie trifft Analoges zu. Wenn Bestätigung von wissenschaftlichen Theorien überhaupt keine Rolle spielen würde, sondern nur die möglichst rasche Ablöse einer gegeben Theorie durch eine revolutionäre neue, gäbe es keinen vernünftigen Grund, überhaupt an irgendwelchen Theorien, und sei es auch nur provisorisch, festzuhalten.

In dieser hier nur angedeuteten Perspektive scheint Poppers Begründung der Demokratie durch einen Nachteil charakterisiert, an dem seine Philosophie im Ganzen leidet: eine zu starke Betonung des Negativen. Genauso, wie seine Ethik an der Überbetonung der Vermeidung von Unglück leidet und seine Wissenschaftstheorie an einer Überbetonung der Falsifizierbarkeit, so ist die Achillesferse seiner politischen Philosophie die Verabsolutierung der Frage, wie man eine Regierung wieder loswerden und die Entstehung einer Tyrannis vermeiden kann. Poppers Philosophie, dem einige Kritiker in den 60er Jahren Positivismus vorgeworfen haben,[16] sollte insofern besser mit dem Vorwurf des Negativismus konfrontiert werden.

5 Die Aktualität der Popperschen Verteidigung der Demokratie

Wenn man viele Festreden von Politikern und auch Wissenschaftlern und Philosophen verfolgt, dann scheint es oberflächlich, als sei Poppers Verteidigung der Demokratie besonders zeitgemäß. Immer wieder ist von den Prinzipien einer offenen Gesellschaft die Rede, die gegen ihre Feinde und Verächter zu verteidigen sei. Aber seit Poppers Streitschrift haben sich die Zeiten gründlich geändert. Als er *Die offene Gesellschaft und ihre Feinde* begann, traten die Feinde der Demokratie noch offensiv als solche auf. Sie beteiligten sich allenfalls an den demokratischen Wahlen, weil sie nach einem eventuellen Wahlsieg die Demokratie auf parlamentarischem Wege abschaffen und durch eine Diktatur ersetzen wollten. Heute sind dagegen die *erklärten* Feinde und Verächter der Demokratie keine Bedrohung mehr, jedenfalls nicht von vergleichbarer Größenordnung.

Die Bedrohung der Demokratie geht dagegen von denen aus, die sich als Demokraten ausgeben, aber in Wahrheit — etwa zu Zwecken der inneren Sicherheit oder der Terrorismusabwehr — nach und nach alles aushöhlen und Zug um Zug alles abschaffen, was diese ausmacht: demokratische Grundrechte, den Schutz von Minderheiten, die Gewaltenteilung und besonders die Pressefreiheit. In einigen Ländern des Westens besteht die Gefahr, dass sich die Demokratie in Plutokratie und/oder Telekratie verwandelt. Es ist inter-

---

[16]Das war damals natürlich hauptsächlich im erkenntnistheoretischen Sinne gemeint.

essant zu sehen, dass Karl Popper, aufgeschreckt durch die Beobachtung der telekratischen Tendenzen, wie sie seinerzeit vor allem durch Alexander Schirinowski in Russland und Silvio Berlusconi in Italien gegeben waren, in einem seiner letzten Aufsätze auf die Gefahr der Unterwanderung der Demokratie durch Medienmanipulation mittels der Massenmedien hingewiesen hat. Es wäre interessant zu wissen, wie er gegebenenfalls auf kriegschürende Irreführungen der demokratischen Öffentlichkeit durch einige westliche Regierungen reagiert hätte.

Allerdings sind Übergänge von der Demokratie in autoritäre Strukturen häufig fließend und in ihren Dimensionen, ihrer jeweiligen Dauerhaftigkeit und Tragweite nur schwer zu beurteilen. Dass jedenfalls ein *erklärter* Anhang autoritärer Herrschaft durch die Teilnahme an Wahlen die Demokratie beseitigt und an die Macht kommt, scheint mir im Vergleich zur *schleichenden* Entdemokratisierung mittlerweile die kleinere Gefahr.

Literatur

Dahms, H.-J. (1996). „Über religiösen und politischen Liberalismus". In G. Lüdemann, Hrsg. (1996), pp. 225-242. *Die „religionsgeschichtliche Schule". Facetten eines theologischen Umbruchs.* Frankfurt/Main & Berlin: Peter Lang Verlag.

——— (2001). „Die Philosophen und die Demokratie in den 20er Jahren des 20. Jahrhunderts". In Jabloner & Stadler (2001), pp. 209-230.

Franke, H. (1991). *Leonard Nelson. Ein biographischer Beitrag unter besonderer Berücksichtigung seiner rechts- und staatsphilosophischen Arbeiten.* Ammersbeck bei Hamburg: Verlag an der Lotbek.

Hacohen, M. H. (2000). *Karl Popper – The Formative Years, 1902-1945. Politics and Philosophy in Interwar Vienna.* New York: Cambridge University Press.

Jabloner, C. & Stadler, F., Hrsg. (2001). *Logischer Empirismus und Reine Rechtslehre. Beziehungen zwischen dem Wiener Kreis und der Hans Kelsen-Schule.* Wien & New York: Springer Verlag.

Kelsen, H. (1920). *Vom Wesen und Wert der Demokratie.* Tübingen: J. C. B. Mohr (Paul Siebeck).

——— (1927a). „Demokratie". In Verhandlungen (1927), pp. 37-68.

——— (1927b). „Schlußwort". In Verhandlungen (1927), pp. 113-118.

Kraft, J. (1924). Rezension von Nelson (1924). In F. V. Wieser, Hrsg. (1924), pp. 288-294. *Kant-Festschrift. Zu Kants 200. Geburtstag am 22. April 1924.* Berlin: Rothschild Verlag.

——— (1953). „Leonard Nelson und die Philosophie des XX. Jahrhunderts". In M. Specht, & W. Eichler, Hrsg. (1953), pp. 13-18. *Leonard Nelson zum Gedächtnis.* Frankfurt/Main & Göttingen: Verlag Offentliches Leben.

Link, W. (1964). *Die Geschichte des internationalen Jugendbundes (IJB) und des Internationalen Sozialistischen Kampfbundes (ISK). Ein Beitrag zur Geschichte der Arbeiterbewegung in der Weinmarer Republik und im Dritten Reich.* Meisenheim am Glan: Hain Verlag.

Nelson, L. (1919). *Die Rechtswissenschaft ohne Recht. Kritische Betrachtungen über die Grundlagen des Staats- und Völkerrechts, insbesondere über die Lehre von der Souveränität.* Leipzig: Felix Meiner Verlag.

——— (1921). *Spuk. Einweihung in das Geheimnis der Wahrsagerkunst Oswald Spenglers und sonnenklarer Beweis der Unwiderleglichkeit seiner Weissagungen nebst Beiträgen zur Physiognomik des Zeitgeistes. Eine Pfingstgabe für alle Adepten des metaphysischen Schauens.* Leipzig: Verlag Der Neue Geist.

——— (1924). *Vorlesungen über die Grundlagen der Ethik,* dritter Band: *System der philosophischen Rechtslehre und Politik.* Leipzig: Verlag Der Neue Geist.

────── (1927). „Diskussion über Demokratie". In Verhandlungen (1927), pp. 83-87.

────── (1949). „Socratic Method and Critical Philosophy". In *Selected Essays*. Vorwort von B. Blanshard. Einführung von J. Kraft. New Haven CT & London: Yale University Press.

Peckhaus, V. (1990). *Hilbertprogramm und Kritische Philosophie. Das Göttinger Modell interdisziplinärer Zusammenarbeit zwischen Mathematik und Philosophie*. Göttingen: Vandenhoeck & Ruprecht.

Pickel, A. (1991). „Fallibilismus und die Grundprobleme der politischen Theorie. Zu Poppers Kritik der Souveränitätstheorie und seinem Neuansatz für die politische Theorie". In Salamun (1991), pp. 225-254.

Popper, K. R. (1945). *The Open Society and Its Enemies*. London: George Routledge & Sons. 5. Auflage 1966. London: Routledge & Kegan Paul.

────── (1957a). *Die offene Gesellschaft und ihre Feinde*. 1. Auflage der deutschen Übersetzung von Popper (1945). Bern: Francke.

────── (1957b). „Philosophy of Science: a Personal Report". In C. A. Mace, Hrsg. (1957), pp. 155-191. *British Philosophy in the Mid-Century: A Cambridge Symposium*. London: Allen & Unwin.

────── (1962). „Julius Kraft 1898-1960". *Ratio* 4, pp. 2-15.

────── (1963). *Conjectures and Refutations*. London: Routledge & Kegan Paul. 5th edition 1989.

────── (1974). 'Intellectual Autobiography'. In P. A. Schilpp, Hrsg. (1974), pp. 1-181. *The Philosophy of Karl Popper*. La Salle, IL: Open Court. Wiederabgedruck als *Unended Quest* (1976). London & Glasgow: Fontana/Collins. Deutsche Übersetzung 1979. *Ausgangspunkte. Meine intellektuelle Entwicklung*. Hamburg: Hoffman & Campe.

────── (1992). *Die offene Gesellschaft und ihre Feinde*. 7. erweiterte und verbesserte Auflage von Popper (1957a). Tübingen: J. C. B. Mohr (Paul Siebeck).

Salamun, K., Hrsg. (1991) *Moral und Politik aus der Sicht des Kritischen Rationalismus*. Amsterdam & Atlanta: Editions Rodopi B.V.

Spengler, O. (1918). *Der Untergang des Abendlandes. Umrisse einer Morphologie der Weltgeschichte*. Wien & Leipzig: Braumüller.

Stadler, F. (1997). *Studien zum Wiener Kreis. Ursprung, Entwicklung und Wirkung des Logischen Empirismus im Kontext*. Frankfurt/Main: Suhrkamp.

Verhandlungen (1927). *Verhandlungen des Fünften Deutschen Soziologentages vom 26. bis 29. September 1926 in Wien*. Tübingen: J. C. B. Mohr (Paul Siebeck).

5

The Young Popper as a Scholarly Field
A Comment on Dahms, Hansen, and ter Hark[*]

Malachi Haim Hacohen

Our symposium on the intellectual development of the young Popper signals that Popper has finally, and belatedly, become a subject of historical research. Even prominent philosophers rarely become subjects for historical work during their lifetimes. Scholarly interest usually focuses on their theoretical contributions, not their lives or intellectual development. Historical scholarship on Popper was especially late in coming. His philosophy was formed in the interwar Central European milieu but became popular in the postwar trans-Atlantic world. Few people outside Austria know interwar Vienna well. The major archival sources for his early intellectual development — his manuscripts and correspondence — had remained inaccessible until his archives opened in 1990. His early articles were buried in obscure interwar Viennese journals, and his first book (1930-1933), when finally published in 1979, appeared only in German. Popper always worked alone, leaving a patchy public record. His intellectual autobiography — a rational reconstruction leading from 1919 to *Logik der Forschung* (1935) — obstructed as much as helped the historian. He was a difficult thinker to research.

All the same, pioneers attempted to retrieve Popper's neglected early works and investigate aspects of the interwar Viennese milieu relevant to his work. Popper's student, W. W. Bartley, entrusted with writing his biography, collected rich material on Popper's early life and milieu. In his published work, he pointed to the role Viennese School Reform and psychologist Karl Bühler played in Popper's development.[1] Bartley's untimely death in 1990 put an end to his work, and the material is still inaccessible to researchers. William Berkson and John Wettersten endeavoured to reconstruct, in their *Learning from Error*, the context of cognitive psychology for Popper's early work.[2] Wettersten expanded and deepened the inquiry in his *The Roots of Critical Rationalism* (1992) and offered ingenious conjectures about the formation of *Die*

---

[*]This was the closing comment in a symposium that featured also papers by Dahms, Hansen, and ter Hark, an introductory comment by Blackmore, and a comment by Gattei. Gattei's comment is included in his (2004). The other papers and comments appear in this volume.

[1]Bartley (1974).

[2]Berkson & Wettersten (1984).

beiden Grundprobleme der Erkenntnistheorie, conjectures that the archives later corroborated. Jürgen Alt[3] and others have endeavoured to establish parallels between Popper's early and later works. And, of course, Troels Eggers Hansen's exemplary scientific edition of *Die beiden Grundprobleme* has provided researchers with an invaluable tool for tracing the development of Popper's philosophy in the early 1930s. Still, only the opening of the archives made Popper's 1927 and 1929 theses and his correspondence from 1932-1935 accessible, and thereby ushered in a new period in Popper scholarship. Some of the results we see in the symposium today.

Popper maintained that his philosophy was closer to the Kant–Fries school than to the Vienna Circle, but he could not quite show why and how. The school's foremost contemporary representative was Leonard Nelson (1882-1927). In my book, I tried to show how Nelson's work set the problem situation that made possible Popper's breakthrough in the philosophy of science and emphasized Nelson's formative influence on Popper's cosmopolitanism and on his view of the history of philosophy.[4] Dahms suggests that Nelson also played a crucial role in the formation of Popper's political philosophy, especially his critique of Plato and the paradoxes of sovereignty and democracy. Popper's brief laudatory comments on Nelson in his notes to *The Open Society* make it clear that he had carefully thought through his relationship to Nelson. He comments on Nelson's independent socialist movement, his critique of democracy (especially the paradox of democracy), and his Platonic leader principle, 'the rule of the wise'.[5] Popper admired Nelson and his disciples but rejected their elitism.

Was Nelson Popper's point of departure for the critique of Plato and his theory of democracy? I think he was, although not exclusively. In an exquisite interview with Dahms and Stadler in 1991, only part of it published, Popper said that he declined to join Nelson's movement on account of its anti-democratic ideas.[6] Significantly, his second published essay, the 1927 'On the Philosophy of the Idea of Heimat' which reflects a refined Nelsonian vision of socialist internationalism, contained a critical comment on Platonic education.[7] His 1927 thesis 'On Habit and the Experience of Lawfulness in Education' was likewise suffused with Nelsonian terminology.[8] Dahms enriches our understanding of the early development of Popper's political ideas by reconstructing the context of the political discussions between him and Julius Kraft.[9] He leaves little doubt that Plato, the theory of democracy, and the leadership principle were of major concern to Popper already in the mid-1920s and corroborates Popper's recollection in later years of the early origins of the ideas developed in *The Open Society*.

---

[3]Alt (1982).

[4]See Hacohen (2000). pp. 117-127.

[5]Popper (1945), Chapter 7, notes 4, 25(2).

[6]Popper (with Dahms & Stadler) (1991), § 10.5.

[7]Popper (1927a), p. 907.

[8]Popper (1927b).

[9]Popper (1962), an obituary for Julius Kraft (1898-1960).

As Dahms notes, we have limited evidence of the state of Popper's reflections on Plato and democracy in the 1920s. We know him to be a nonorthodox socialist, internationalist, an avowed democrat, and hostile to Plato's educational theory and leadership ideals, but we know little else. We do not know how much he read of Nelson's political work and certainly not how much he retained and what, if anything, he committed to writing. We know him to be preoccupied, in the same period, with epistemology, and to be writing critiques of Kraft, so science and politics were intertwined in his philosophy from the start. His political concerns seem to have gone through a period of dormancy, when he was preoccupied with the philosophy of science from the late 1920s to the mid-1930s. They resurged in 1937-1938, when he began teaching Greek philosophy in Canterbury College, New Zealand, and became his focal concern in the *Open Society*, written in the early 1940s. Our evidence for Nelson's influence comes mostly from a text fifteen years removed from Popper's first encounter with his ideas.

All the same, there are sufficient traces in *The Open Society* to support Dahms's view of Nelsonian inspiration. Popper's very idea of Socratic dialogue, the bedrock of critical rationalism, seems to rework Nelson's 'Socratic Method'. Both Nelson and Popper identified Socrates with critical dialogue and awareness of the limits of cognition, but Nelson emphasized Socrates' search for the foundations of knowledge, Popper, the Socratic claim for 'not knowing'. Unlike Nelson, Popper dissociated Plato completely from Socrates.[10] Following Dahms, we need to reread Popper's early works from the 1920s and his lecture notes from Canterbury College and ask: Does Popper engage, or rework, Nelson's ideas in places where we did not expect?

At the same time, the context for the reception and working out of Nelson in *The Open Society* changed radically from the 1920s. The critique of fascism and the analysis of the Left's failure to withstand the fascist assault provided a new broader framework for discussing Plato and democracy. Popper's democratic theory now reflected also his philosophy of science: Democracy provides a public sphere that emulates the critical scientific community. No wonder Popper declined to take seriously Nelson's 'resolution' of the paradox of sovereignty: The 'Wise' will neither abuse nor renounce their own rule. Not only was the 'solution', as Dahms correctly observes, a mere verbal quibble with a disastrous political potential, but critical rationalism challenged Nelson's understanding of knowledge and wisdom. To Popper, knowledge could emerge only from critical exchange in a free democratic sphere. Nelson was wrong about first things and toying with ideas Popper considered fascist. All the same, Popper's target was Plato, and not Nelson. He explained away Nelson's elitism as misguided humanitarianism and moved on.

Reformulating old concerns in a new framework, Popper provided an alternative theory of democracy: not majority rule but government that can be

---

[10]Nelson (1949); Popper (1945), Chapter 7; (1974), § 1, pp. 961-963; (1930-1933), Einleitung (1978), § 1, 'Eine kurze historische Bemerkung über das wissenschaftliche Wissen als ein sokratisches Nichtwissen', pp. xv-xxi.

peacefully removed. Dahms emphasizes the theory's limits and its negative
utilitarian character — minimizing evil rather than maximizing good. I have
a more generous view and regard it as quintessentially liberal. Dahms's correc-
tives, such as a *Grundgesetz* (foundational law) à la Federal Republic of Germany that rules out overturning democracy, are problematic from a Popperian
perspective, and can be at most a provisional expedient. Everything, including democracy, is open to debate and change. This is the novelty of the Open
Society.

Dahms focuses on the genesis of Popper's political philosophy, Hansen on
the formation of his philosophy of science. Hansen takes us to the core of
Popper's epistemological revolution — the demarcation problem. He has just
completed a scientific edition of Popper's early writings,[11] a huge accomplish-
ment rivaling his contribution to the study of *Grundprobleme*. His work on
Popper's 1927 thesis produced the bold conjecture offered today. Popper did
not solve either the induction or the demarcation problem before 1929: He accepted induction unproblematically as the scientific method all the way to his
1929 geometry thesis and, in 1927, provided an inductivist demarcation criterion. But, by 1927, Popper had formulated the demarcation problem, prior
to the induction problem. In his autobiographical narratives, Popper may
have read back his solutions by a decade or so but at least he got the order
right: The demarcation problem came first. Contrary to my account, Popper
planned, from the start of his epistemological revolution, to write about both
induction and demarcation. For reasons that still need to be explored, he
chose to write first on induction.[12]

Hansen's reading of Popper's early works and my own are close. We agree
that, reading *Grundprobleme*, it seems that Popper first discovers the demarcation problem in the early 1930s, while working on induction. The evidence
Hansen brings from the 1927 thesis demonstrates that Popper accepted induction unproblematically as a demarcation criterion, but also that demarcation
had not yet become quite a *problem* for him. To be sure, critical of the non-
empirical character of Freud's, Adler's, and James's theories, Popper does
question their scientific character by repeating the conventions as to what
constitutes a scientific theory. But these conventions themselves are unproblematic: Theories must never be imposed on facts. Both Gattei (2004) and ter
Hark (this volume) suggest that his demarcation efforts focus on disciplinary
and sub-disciplinary boundaries, distinguishing between the different types
of psychology, and not on demarcating the boundaries of science as such.
Still, Hansen is prescient in discerning that Popper raised, if only in passing,
concerns that, in a few years, would become central to his philosophy.

---

[11]Popper (2006).

[12]His statement at the end of the volume on induction that demarcation is science's most
basic problem suggests that he would have written on it first, had he recognized the problem
from the start. His focus while writing on induction was on the status of natural laws, and
he sought to demonstrate the impossibility of induction as a scientific procedure, *not* as a
demarcation criterion.

Popper was more aware of the difficulties with induction than of those with demarcation. In Nelson's work, which Popper read as early as 1925, Hume's problem and, to Nelson, the impossibility of an epistemological solution to it, are set out clearly. Other formulations of the induction problem were available elsewhere. But, like everyone else, Popper decided to continue and live with induction. Around 1930, he found a revolutionary solution. Having considered deductivist models in physics in his 1929 geometry thesis, it occurred to him the following year that he could offer an empirico-deductivist model for science that would dispense with induction altogether. If we drop the requirement for the full decidability, or verifiability, of scientific theories, and opt instead for partial decidability, universal statements, or natural laws, can be falsified, although they remain unverified. He, then, pushed the distinction between numerical and universal statements, which Hansen correctly regards as crucial, to make it clear that the inductivist game is over. Philosophers can no longer live with solutions to the induction problem that conflate the two, pretending that science somehow approaches the universal by verifying the numerical.

Popper's solution found its application in a critique of the avant-garde of the philosophy of science — the Vienna Circle. His lengthy engagement of Schlick's 1931 essay on 'Causality in Contemporary Physics' led him to develop a fabulous critique of conventionalism that moved falsifiability from the margins of his revolution — a crucial aspect of decidability — to the centre, the defining moment of his philosophy. Schlick's view that natural laws (or theories) were not genuine statements reflected Wittgenstein's meaning criterion, so Popper next assailed meaning as a dogmatic and metaphysical demarcation criterion. But 'meaning', it turned out, involved verifiability — 'the sense of a proposition is the method of its verification' — hence, induction. The two problems came together: The Circle was desperately holding to induction, despite its problems, because they had no alternative demarcation criterion. He did: falsifiability. The first stage in his epistemological revolution was complete.

Things just did not happen this way, says Michel ter Hark. Hacohen's account of Popper's epistemological revolution diminishes, as previous accounts have diminished, the role of Otto Selz and German psychology. In both his paper and recent book (2004), ter Hark reconstructs in great detail Popper's encounter with German cognitive psychology (*Denkpsychologie*), especially with Otto Selz, Karl Bühler, and the Würzburg School. He enriches our knowledge of interwar discourses providing the context for Popper's early works and traces Popper's intellectual trajectory from his 1927 thesis, discussed by Hansen, to his 1928 dissertation 'On the Methodology of Cognitive Psychology', to the 1931 article 'Memorization from the Perspective of Self-Activity', to the tentative deductivist psychology in *Die beiden Grundprobleme*. ter Hark demonstrates that Popper's concern with biologically oriented evolutionary psychology dated back to 1928 and that, already at the time, he was familiar with Selz's 'trying out behavior', that is, with the theory of a biologically guided mind, advancing from one task to another through trial and error.

By 1931, Popper accepted Selz's psychology of learning, and, in *Die beiden Grundprobleme*, he offered the rudiments of the evolutionary psychology of knowledge he would advance in postwar years. In 1948, in 'The Bucket and the Searchlight', Popper seemed to deploy Selzian psychology to support his epistemology and to explain the growth of knowledge, and in the 1961 Spencer Lecture, 'Evolution and the Tree of Knowledge', he brought together evolutionary biology, psychology, and epistemology in a manner highly evocative of Selz.[13] But Selz has meanwhile disappeared from the stage, and ter Hark wonders where he has gone.

ter Hark's narrative hinges on the interaction of psychology and epistemology in Popper's epistemological revolution of 1931-1932. It deserves a closer look. According to ter Hark, Popper's revolutionary breakthrough first occurred in psychology, then was applied to epistemology. Selz is responsible for Popper's epistemological revolution.[14]

> Popper's theory of knowledge clearly emerges in the process of appropriating and integrating Selz's theory of anticipations into the deductive operations of philosophical reason . . . [, establishing a] linkage . . . between . . . the classical epistemological notions of synthetic a priori knowledge and . . . the (Selzian) notion of anticipation. . . . Precisely this (psychological) notion of a priori knowledge, of anticipations, . . . [enables Popper to break through] the deadlock between classical rationalism and classical empiricism, thereby making room for . . . the hypothetical and fallible nature of all human knowledge.

Popper said that 'what holds in logic must also hold in psychology', invoking a methodological principle that gives a clue to his intellectual progression from the logic of research to evolutionary psychology. On the contrary, says ter Hark, 'the historical facts show an immensely fertile interaction between psychology and epistemology. . . . [T]he encounter with Selz in psychology has been the decisive factor contributing to Popper's deductive epistemology.'[15]

I do not think so. I find ter Hark's narrative sophisticated and suggestive but not altogether persuasive. Popper engaged Selz during the four crucial years, 1928-1932, when his philosophy went through an epistemological revolution, accepting ever growing parts of Selz's psychology, incorporating them into his philosophy. Scholars, who have long noticed the similarities between their views, have been trying to determine Selz's role in Popper's revolution. This is tricky, because he played a different role at each stage, and the temptation to read back Popper's postwar psychology to the interwar years is great.

No doubt Popper was fascinated, in 1928, by Selz's task-oriented mind, the possibilities of evolutionary biological explanation, and the parallels between scientific and psychological problem solving. But he was exploring biological explanations in cognitive psychology *not* because he was concerned

---

[13]Popper (1949); Popper (1972), Chapter 7.
[14]ter Hark (2004), p.143.
[15]Ibidem, p. 22.

with evolutionary epistemology — or, indeed, with epistemology at all — but because he was developing Gomperz's idea of a meta-science that would, at one and the same time, demarcate epistemology, psychology, and biology from each other, translate between them, and guard the integrity of each. He was also eager to defend Bühler's biologically oriented psychology against physiological approaches, especially Schlick's and *Gestalt* physicalism. He seemed willing to accept Selz's idea that the mind reworked knowledge into new schemes to solve problems, but he expressed reservations about his use of psychological experience to explain scientific breakthroughs. There was no transference between epistemology and psychology, science, and thought processes. Selz, he argued, can explain higher thought-processes but Bühler, who made room for instinct and training, did better with primitive ones. Between Selz's active mind and association psychology, Popper took a middle position. Just as ter Hark suggests: 'the material for building a deductivist, and problem-driven, methodology and epistemology is already available to him in 1928' (p. 47) but Popper refused to move in this direction.

The truth is, Popper was in trouble, and, contrary to ter Hark and Hansen, I think his major problem was not induction but transference: He insisted on methodological and disciplinary pluralism. He described 'objective intellectual structures' as logical in character, in a manner not dissimilar to his later views of science and World 3. At the same time, he maintained that the mind, and psychological processes, did not conform to logic. Yet, he wanted psychology to explain the formation of intellectual structures. How could it? He opened a gap between logic and psychology that seemed impossible to bridge. Cognitive psychology could not possibly explain science. Either psychology or epistemology had to give in before a solution emerged. In 1928, it was clear that Popper was not willing to give up on scientific autonomy. The question was how long he would persist in attempting to reach a solution in psychology.

He did not. In his 1929 geometry thesis, his investigation shifted to the logic and method of science, and, then, in *Grundprobleme* he confronted the Vienna Circle with an empirico-deductivist model that emerged as a solution to Nelson's problem of the foundation of knowledge. In my view, the breakthrough occurred in epistemology, not psychology, and Selz was not responsible. Inspired by his deductivist solution to the problem of the growth of knowledge in epistemology, Popper returned momentarily to psychology and had little difficulty adopting Selz's active mind in his 1931 article on memorization. But, as ter Hark points out, true to his anti-psychologism, Popper confined Selz's model to the psychology of learning. In section 4 of *Grundprobleme*, Popper provided a brief and tentative excursus on a deductivist psychology of knowledge, a counterpart to deductivist epistemology, but he argued that it was irrelevant to epistemology and could not explain the growth of knowledge: He could not see how the mind created new material that had not previously been there.[16] About a year later, in section 11 of *Grundprobleme*, rewritten

---

[16]Popper (1930-1933), pp. 26-30.

during the fall of 1932, he accepted Selz's idea of inborn anticipations as the origin for the search for knowledge. His later evolutionary psychology is already there, but he proceeded carefully, all the same: Evolution seemed too erratic for the orderly progress of science, and he dreaded psychologism.

ter Hark is right to emphasize the interaction between psychology and epistemology in Popper's revolution and to point out the potential of an evolutionary epistemology in *Grundprobleme*. Contemporaries, too, were aware of the potential: Herbert Feigl commended the 'pragmatic biological' orientation of Popper's epistemology to Moritz Schlick, after he had met with Popper and Carnap in the summer of 1932.[17] But there is little evidence in Popper's work that Selz's psychology led him to reject induction — Selz himself did not — and much evidence that an epistemological problem, formulated first in 1929 and 1930 as a problem in the logic and method of natural science, led him to do so. ter Hark diminishes the significance of the philosophical problem-situation. He reads Popper's postwar psychology back to 1931-1932 and transfers, or translates, Selz's (and Popper's postwar) psychology — biologically generated anticipations (the genetic a priori) modified through trial and error — into epistemology to create Popper's intellectual breakthrough. It is not difficult: Popper himself translated (transferred) in the other direction in 1948 (and partially already in 1931-1932), and the essential concepts are there. But, in the early 1930s, Popper adamantly refused to explore the epistemological potential of deductivist psychology or an evolutionary epistemology. ter Hark dismisses his refusal as an effort to downplay his psychological past.[18] Popper's view, expressed in *Logik der Forschung* (1935), § 2, that scientific discovery has an irrational element may renounce, as ter Hark suggests, any *Denkpsychologie* or evolutionary epistemology, but radical anti-psychologism was his reasoned position at the time. ter Hark is wrong to override the resistances and diminish the significance of the philosophical problem situation.

All the same, it is not impossible that Selz's vision of inborn anticipations modified by experience provided the insight enabling Popper to see through the epistemological problem of the synthetic a priori (or the validity of scientific hypotheses — universal laws). But the insight was then absorbed into an elaborate ready-made epistemological problem situation. Selz provided no epistemology, and Nelson, Heinrich Gomperz, and the Vienna Circle informed Popper's laborious philosophical work from 1929 to 1932. Popper rejected Selz's view of a genetic a priori until late in 1932, by which time the epistemological revolution was complete, but the vision could have helped him reshape the epistemological field.[19] ter Hark and I reach here the limits of the

---

[17] Herbert Feigl to Moritz Schlick, 14 September 1933, *Schlick Nachlaß, Philosophisches Archiv*, University of Konstanz (original at the *Wiener-Kreis Archiv*, Haarlem, Netherlands).

[18] ter Hark (2004), pp. 22f.

[19] ter Hark's dismissal of Popper's anti-psychologism in 1931-1934 is therefore unnecessary. Notwithstanding Popper's anti-psychologism, Selz could have still informed his philosophy, which is ter Hark's major point.

models intellectual historians use to explain discovery: The logic of the situation can rarely reconstruct all the initial conditions.[20] The evidence requires that we foreground epistemology, but the crucial insight could have still come from psychology.

The advantage of ter Hark's narrative is that it provides a conjecture for the *deus ex-machina* of the epistemological revolution, explaining how Popper saw through the epistemological murk. ter Hark's narrative is more linear and orderly than mine — there is one crucial transference in 1931 from a fully blown psychology to epistemology. I am as much impressed by Popper's refusals, his blind spots, and the obstacles to the interaction of psychology and epistemology, as ter Hark is by 'the fertility of the interaction'. The more ter Hark lets the epistemological and psychological narratives run concurrently, and the more clues he finds in the epistemological formulations that permit his psychological reading — as he found in section 3 of *Grundprobleme*, where Popper dubs conjectures 'anticipations' — the more convincing his narrative will become. At this time, I remain unpersuaded, but I am delighted that he has offered his counter-narrative, and I have learnt a great deal from him. His book is an outstanding contribution to Popper scholarship.

ter Hark's insistence on viewing Popper's epistemological revolution through the lenses of evolutionary psychology accounts for the discordant tone of his paper — his allegation that Popper borrowed heavily from Selz but covered his tracks. In 1931-1932, Popper regarded his project as radical reconstruction of the epistemology of science. He constructed a tentative deductivist psychology, he said, merely to demonstrate that inductive psychology was not the only one possible. In the process, he used his earlier work, on Mach and Jennings among others, occasionally relying, as ter Hark notes in his book, on his 1928 dissertation. His use of Mach and Jennings obfuscated his debt to Selz only if we assume that Selz had replaced previous psychologists in his mind, that he accepted his psychology completely, and that developing evolutionary psychology was his task, in short, if we accept ter Hark's narrative. On the contrary, Popper rejected evolutionary psychology and saw himself as translating from epistemology to psychology, arbitrating epistemological issues raised by psychology. Selz had no epistemology. Popper may not have recognized the extent of Selz's contribution to his work, but it is not unusual for intellectuals more self-aware than Popper to be unclear about the sources and implications of their intellectual moves.

In the 1940s, Popper saw his psychology as an extension of his philosophy. Selz had had only embryonic ideas on the evolutionary growth of scientific ideas, and Popper failed to recognize that the evolutionary epistemology he was developing was Selzian in character. The philosophy was unmistakably his; the psychology he saw as working out his ideas. He did not delve back into interwar psychology. Selz vanished from his 1941 Canterbury lectures, where the searchlight idea appeared for the first time (and the bucket for the

---

[20]This may, indeed, be the 'irrational' element in discovery of which Popper speaks in (1935), § 2, irrational insofar as it escapes the historian's rational reconstruction.

second, as ter Hark has shown), and from the 1948 Alpbach lecture where he brought psychology and epistemology together to explain the growth of knowledge.[21] Popper himself suffered from the convoluted process of the making of his philosophy. When the 'Positivist Legend' emerged, he was not able to mount an effective response, partially because Nelson's and Selz's contributions to his philosophy were not clear to him. Selz suffered immeasurably greater neglect, and it is to ter Hark's credit that he may be gaining now some of the recognition he deserves. But ter Hark need not advance Selz's fortune by discrediting Popper. Blind, self-righteous, self-focused and proprietary about his ideas, even ungenerous about acknowledging his intellectual debts, Popper could surely be, but he would not knowingly cover his tracks so he could claim credit for ideas that were not his. He would have been pleased, I think, to see the Centenary Congress pay a tribute to the memory of Selz. He regarded him as a remarkable and under-appreciated psychologist who tragically perished in Auschwitz. He continues to live through Popper's work.

Our symposium approached the philosophy of the young Popper as historically developing, and modified his autobiography. Dahms, Hansen, and ter Hark, as well as the two commentators, Blackmore and Gattei (2004), traced with great sensitivity Popper's intellectual development. We are all aware of the need to resist the temptation to read Popper's later philosophy into his early works. The problem situation in the early works shifts quickly and is radically different from the later ones. We agree on method, and there is room for competing narratives on the course of Popper's epistemological revolution. I hope the historiographical direction presented here continues and contributes to Popper's scholarship. We all agree also on the need for a close reading of Popper's early works. So, in closing, I would plead for undertaking a scientific edition of the drafts of *Logik der Forschung*. The symposium brought Popper's revolution today up to mid-1932 and the completion of the first volume of *Grundprobleme*. Parts of this volume were radically rewritten during the fall of 1932, ushering in a non-foundationalist philosophy. Popper planned to undertake a second volume. Having received a contract from Springer in June 1933, he launched *Logik der Forschung*, which was radically edited in 1934. Major historiographical questions remain as to what he wrote and to what manuscripts were lost. The remaining fragments of the ur-*Logik* are all we have got, and they deserve a scientific edition. I wish Hansen could undertake the project, but we have no right to impose on him any more. Willing scholars and sponsors must be found. This would be a great tribute in Popper's memory. The appearance of the Collected Works on the shelf marks a philosopher's entry into the Pantheon no less decisively than does the unveiling of a bust in the *Arkadenhof*.

---

[21]WEA syllabus. Hoover Institution, Popper Collection (366, 24), pp. 16, 24, 45.

Bibliography

Alt, J. (1982). *Die Frühschriften Poppers: der Weg Poppers von der Päd-agogik und der Psychologie zur Spätphilosophie*. Frankfurt/Main: Peter Lang.

Bartley, III, W. W. (1974). 'Theory of Language and Philosophy of Science as Instruments of Educational Reform: Wittgenstein and Popper as Austrian School Teachers'. In R. S. Cohen & M. W. Wartofsky, editors (1974). *Meth-odological and Historical Essays in the Natural and Social Sciences*. Boston Studies in the Philosophy of Science, volume 14. Dordrecht & Boston MA: D. Reidel Publishing Company.

Berkson, W. & Wettersten, J. (1984). *Learning from Error: Karl Popper's Psychology of Learning*. La Salle IL: Open Court Publishing Company.

Gattei, S. (2004). 'Karl Popper's Philosophical Breakthrough'. *Philosophy of Science* **71**, pp. 448-466.

Hacohen, M. H. (2000). *Karl Popper – The Formative Years, 1902-1945: Poli-tics and Philosophy in Interwar Vienna*. New York: Cambridge University Press.

ter Hark, M. R. M. (2004). *Popper, Selz and the Rise of Evolutionary Epi-stemology*. Cambridge: Cambridge University Press.

Nelson, L. (1949). 'The Socratic Method'. In T. K. Brown III, translator (1949). *Socratic Method and Critical Philosophy*. New Haven: Yale Uni-versity Press,

Popper, K. R. (1927a). 'Zur Philosophie des Heimatgedankens'. *Die Quelle* **77**, pp. 899-908.

——— (1927b). *'Gewohnheit' und 'Gesetzerlebnis' in der Erziehung: Eine pädagogisch- strukturpsychologische Monographie*. Hausarbeit, Pädagog-isches Institut der Stadt Wien. Hoover Institution Archives, Popper Col-lection (12, 11).

——— (1928). *Zur Methodenfrage der Denkpsychologie*. PhD dissertation, University of Vienna. Hoover Institution Archives, Popper Collection (17, 1).

——— (1930-1933). *Die beiden Grundprobleme der Erkenntnistheorie*. First published, 1979. Edited by T. E. Hansen. Tübingen: J. C. B. Mohr (Paul Siebeck). 2nd edition 1994.

——— (1931). 'Die Gedächtnispflege unter dem Gesichtpunkt der Selbsttätig-keit'. *Die Quelle* **81**, pp. 607-619.

——— (1935). *Logic der Forschung*. Vienna: Julius Springer Verlag.

——— (1945). *The Open Society and Its Enemies*. London: George Rout-ledge & Sons. 5th revised edition 1966. London: Routledge & Kegan Paul.

—— (1949). 'Naturgesetze und theoretische Systeme'. In S. Moser, editor (1949), pp. 43-60. *Gesetz und Wirklichkeit*. Innsbruck: Tyrolia Verlag. Translated into English as 'The Bucket and the Searchlight: Two Theories of Knowledge'. Appendix 1 to Popper (1972).

—— (1962). 'Julius Kraft 1898-1960'. *Ratio* [Oxford] **4**, pp. 2-12.

—— (1972). *Objective Knowledge*. Oxford: Clarendon Press. 2nd edition 1979.

—— (1974). 'Replies to my Critics'. In P. A. Schilpp, editor (1974), pp. 959-1197. *The Philosophy of Karl Popper*. La Salle IL: Open Court Publishing Company.

—— (2006). *Frühe Schriften. Gesammelte Werke*, volume 1. Edited by T. E. Hansen. Tübingen: Mohr Siebeck.

Popper, K. R., with H.-J. Dahms & F. Stadler (1991). 'Popper und der Wiener Kreis – Aus einem Gespräch mit Sir Karl Popper (1991)' ['Popper and the Vienna Circle. Excerpt from an Interview with Sir Karl Popper (1991)']. In Stadler (1997/2001), § 10.5.

Stadler, F. (1997). *Studien zum Wiener-Kreis. Ursprung, Entwicklung, und Wirkung des Logischen Empirismus im Kontext*. Frankfurt/Main: Suhrkamp. English translation (2001). *The Vienna Circle. Studies in the Origins, Development, and Influence of Logical Empiricism*. Vienna & New York: Springer.

Wettersten, J. (1992). *The Roots of Critical Rationalism*. Amsterdam: Editions Rodopi B.V.

6

Popper and Hayek
Who Influenced Whom? *

Bruce Caldwell

This paper attempts to address the question of who had the greater influence on the other, the polymath philosopher of science Karl Popper, or the polymath social theorist Friedrich A. Hayek.

It is evident that the two are suitable candidates for such an investigation. Both of the protagonists were giants in their respective fields, and both of them to varying degrees claimed that the other was an important figure in his own intellectual development. Thus Popper stated in a much-quoted letter to Hayek that 'I think I have learnt more from you than from any other living thinker, except perhaps Alfred Tarski' (Popper to Hayek, 15 March 1944, quoted in Hacohen 2000, p. 486). This is really quite a remarkable statement given the circles that Popper ran in and the people whom he encountered. Popper also dedicated his most famous collection of papers, *Conjectures and Refutations* (Popper 1963), to Hayek. For his part, Hayek first cited Popper in a paper published in the 1930s, then began citing him repeatedly in the 1950s and 1960s, referring to one of his own papers as 'little more than an elaboration of some of Popper's ideas' (Hayek 1955/1967, p. 4). Hayek dedicated his own 1967 collection, *Studies in Philosophy, Politics and Economics* to Popper, mentioning him explicitly in the Preface. And in a 1982 retrospective, Hayek said of Popper's thought, '...ever since his *Logik der Forschung* first came out in 1934, I have been a complete adherent to his general theory of methodology' (Hayek 1982, p. 323).

A further reason for beginning such an investigation is the availability of new source materials. The archives of both men are now open, and through the work of scholars such as Jeremy Shearmur and Malachi Hacohen we have begun to have a better appreciation of the relationship between them. So the time seems right to try to figure out which one had the greater influence on the other.

*I thank Jeremy Shearmur, who chaired my session at KARL POPPER 2002, as well as other session participants for many useful comments. I subsequently received additional helpful comments from seminar participants at George Mason University, the Université du Québec à Montréal, and at the University of Toronto – York University Joint Seminar on the History of Economic Thought.

Were it only all so simple. It turns out that even raising the question of 'who influenced whom' raises all sorts of questions itself. There is first of all the general problem surrounding any investigation of 'influence'. Though the question of influence is always a popular one, some believe that it is also probably one that responsible scholars should make a point to resist trying to answer. In some cases, of course, the whole notion of 'influence' is wrong-headed because it gets the concept of agency reversed. This can be the case if one is referring to the influence of earlier writers on later ones — for example, what kind of sense does it make to say that Menger set out to influence Hayek? More generally, when one thinks not just of all the earlier writers, but also of all the contemporary people who could have had an impact on a person's thought, and also of the influence of the milieu in which the person worked, it does not take long before the mind boggles. There are good general reasons, then, to be very cautious when speaking in terms of 'influence'.[1]

But there are specific reasons, too, why unraveling the question of influence is particularly difficult when it comes to Popper and Hayek. In order to make credible claims about influence, one must have a reasonably clear picture of both the content of each person's thought and of its development through time. There are problems here for both of our protagonists. In the case of Popper, the convoluted publishing history surrounding his works, in which various pieces when published in book form (or, in the case of *The Logic of Scientific Discovery*, 1959, when translated) contain additions, or the fact that the last published of his major works, though circulating in galley proofs, remained unpublished for decades, makes it hard to know exactly what Popper thought when. The problem is compounded if Malachi Hacohen is right that Popper, in crafting his autobiography as a series of problems and solutions, may have forgotten or neglected certain important episodes that did not fit neatly into his framework (Hacohen 2000, pp. 18-21). (I hasten to add that Hacohen's biography does an extraordinary, if sometimes controversial, job, at straightening many of these matters out.)   As for Hayek, I will simply mention Ludwig Lachmann's storied response to the question of 'What did Hayek think about subject x?' Lachmann's wonderful riposte was, 'Which Hayek?' — which was meant to indicate that one might get different answers to the question depending on which part of Hayek's *oeuvre* one consulted.

A further layer of complications is added when one recognizes that though each man was fulsome in his praise of the other, each would also typically add qualifiers when it came to specific points, qualifiers that make attribution of influence extremely difficult. Thus Hayek in the sentence immediately preceding his acknowledgement that he had since 1934 been a complete adherent of Popper's methodology said that this was because Popper's formulation was 'a statement of what I was feeling', implying that he had already had similar

---

[1] I thank Mary Morgan for pointing out to me the general problems that surround the question of 'influence'. Her commonsense solution is to avoid the word altogether, and to speak instead of earlier writers as *resources* upon which the person in question *might* have drawn.

ideas, even if he had never articulated them (Hayek 1982, p. 323). And Popper more than once made a point of emphasizing that he had had certain insights before he had read similar sounding ideas in Hayek (Shearmur 1996, p. 27; cf. also Popper 1957, § 29). So it turns out that, despite their many statements of their debt to one another, in the specific case of Popper and Hayek the question of influence is as tricky as it can be more generally.

It is thus with considerable trepidation that I nonetheless forge ahead. I shall state my conclusions in advance. My own reading of the evidence is that neither Popper nor Hayek had much of an influence on the other, at least if we restrict ourselves to speaking in terms of their ideas about how to do social science. To the extent that any influence exists, it is mostly in terms of the *language* in which each came to express his ideas, the way they came to put things.

I shall support this thesis by examining four episodes drawn from their long relationship. The first is their initial encounter in the 1930s, one that led to Hayek's first citation of Popper's work. Next, I shall look at the extent to which Hayek's writings influenced Popper's final draft of 'The Poverty of Historicism' during the war years. Third, I shall examine certain of Hayek's methodological writings from the 1950s and 1960s in which Popper is prominently cited. Finally, I shall look at the interpretative puzzles surrounding Hayek's last book, *The Fatal Conceit*, which again contains certain new and apparently very Popperian themes.

In what follows I shall concentrate on the influence that each man might have had on the others' writings about *the methods of the social sciences*. I shall not deal with questions of influence on political outlook, and neither shall I address Malachi Hacohen's fascinating counterfactual that, had Popper not met Hayek, he might have gone on to contribute more in the area of political philosophy (Hacohen 2000, p. 450). However, at the end of the paper I shall speculate on why two such apparently different thinkers should be so taken with each other.

The first episode has to do with Hayek's first citation of Popper, which occurred in a paper entitled 'Economics and Knowledge' published in 1937. Though both were born in Vienna, Hayek being three years the elder, they never met there. It seems that their paths did cross, however. Both of them apparently witnessed the shootout in April 1919 between a communist-inspired crowd of workers and the police force, an incident that, according to Hacohen, helped begin to wean Popper from his youthful commitment to communism (Hacohen 2000, pp. 80-83). Hayek was a student returning home from university and got caught in the crossfire, though obviously he escaped unharmed (Bartley 1989, p. 44). Anyway, Hayek spent the 1920s mostly in Vienna and then, in a story that itself is not without interest, managed in the early 1930s to get appointed to the Economics faculty of the LSE as holder of the Tooke Chair. Hayek heard about Popper's work when, soon after its publication,

Gottfried Haberler put a copy of Popper's *Logik* into his hands. This ultimately led to an invitation by Hayek for Popper to present a paper in Hayek's
seminar in June 1936.[2]

With that background, we can now turn to Hayek's paper, 'Economics
and Knowledge', which was apparently written in the late summer or early
fall of 1936, that is, soon after Hayek had met Popper. Hayek stated in his
paper that the 'empirical element in economic theory' is that part that leads
to conclusions that are capable, at least in principle, of verification — at
which point he added a footnote, 'Or rather falsification' and cited Popper's
Logik (Hayek 1937/1948, p. 33). This, then, is Hayek's first citation of Popper
in print. The same paper also contained a criticism, though an extremely
diffident one, of Ludwig von Mises's apriorism. (Mises believed that what
he called 'the axioms of the science of human action' were a priori true yet
capable, via a 'verbal chain of logic', of yielding apodictical claims about the
world.) The combination led one observer, Terence Hutchison, to propose that
'Economics and Knowledge' represented Hayek's turning away from Misesian
apriorism and towards Popperian thought (Hutchison 1981, Chapter 7). If one
takes into account certain of Hayek's later remarks (for example, he once called
the paper a turning point, after which he began to ask 'all kinds of questions
usually regarded as philosophical' (Hayek 1964a/1967, pp. 91f.); also recall his
comment that he immediately accepted Popper's methodology after reading
the *Logik*), one can see how Hutchison might reach such a conclusion.

It is a conclusion, though, with which I disagree. Though Hutchison is
right that Hayek is critical of Mises's apriorism in the article, I disagree that
he was ever an apriorist, and certainly never one of the type that Mises was.
Furthermore, it was not until much later that Popper's ideas seem to play an
important role in Hayek's written work. I argued these points in an earlier
sequence of papers (Caldwell 1988, 1992a, 1992b; cf. Hutchison's reply in his
1992), and shall just summarize the main points here.

Concerning Hayek's commitment to apriorism: When Mises claimed that
the fundamental postulates or axioms of the science of human action were a
priori true, he was discussing what might be called today the assumptions of
microeconomic theory. Hayek's early work in economics principally focused on
monetary theory and the theory of the trade cycle, fields quite different from
microeconomics, so the question of the a priori basis of microeconomic theory
never came up. Furthermore, in those few places that Hayek used the terms
'a priori' or 'a priorism' in writings in the 1930s and 1940s, his use appears to
be quite different from that of Mises. Finally, in a letter in which he offered a
retrospective reflection on the question, Hayek flatly stated that he had never
been an apriorist (Hayek to Hutchison, 26 November 1981, Hayek Collection,
Box 26, folder 8, Hoover Institution Archives).

---

[2]I originally stated that Popper presented his paper in the joint seminar run by Lion-
el Robbins and Hayek. Her examination of archival material at the LSE, enabled Susan
Howson to correct my mistake. I offer her my thanks.

As for traces of Popper's ideas on Hayek's subsequent writings, there is little to be found in either of Hayek's next two major projects, the first being on the Abuse of Reason, one that ultimately would include both his essay on 'Scientism and the Study of Society' (1942-1944) and *The Road to Serfdom* (1944), and the second being his book on psychology, *The Sensory Order* (1952). Had Hayek begun becoming a Popperian in 1937 the philosopher's ideas would presumably have been discernible somewhere in these works. They are not, and indeed, Popper had reservations about at least parts of each project. I can finally add that in a letter to the author Hayek noted that his reference to falsification in 'Economics and Knowledge' was added in the galley proofs, mostly in recognition of the fact that the term 'verification' was, given recent developments in philosophy, 'no longer adequate' (Hayek to Caldwell, 29 September 1984, Hayek Collection, Box 13, folder 30, Hoover Institution Archives).

Let us move next, then, to the 1940s, and Hayek's impact on Popper's thought during the period that the latter was working on 'The Poverty of Historicism'. In his autobiography Popper called the essay one of his 'stodgiest pieces of writing' (Popper 1974, § 24). A better description might be that it is 'brilliant but disorganized'. The book starts out very systematically. In the first two Parts the anti-naturalistic and the pro-naturalistic doctrines of historicism are described. The only complaint that one might have about these sections is that it is not always clear exactly which particular writers Popper had in mind when he wrote about each doctrine. On the other hand, he addresses this problem in the book's introduction by noting that he was trying to present historicism as a well-considered and complete doctrine, so that in some instances he was *constructing* arguments for the historicists rather than *describing* the ideas of concrete individuals (Popper 1957, Introduction).

In the third Part, though, things begin to go awry. Though his table of contents promised that the third and fourth Parts would contain Popper's critique of the anti-naturalist and pro-naturalist doctrines of historicism, this is not what he provides. A good part of the third Part has nothing to do with the anti-naturalist doctrines, but instead is a defence of what Popper called piecemeal social engineering, something he contrasts with utopian social engineering. In addition, rather than criticize anti-naturalist doctrines as a whole, Popper's chief target seems to be Karl Mannheim and his *Man and Society in an Age of Reconstruction* (1940). (Mannheim is lacerated in no fewer than fourteen different footnotes.) Things get better for a while in Part four, the first section of which is devoted to a discussion of the difference between laws and trends, which fits as a part of the critique of the pronaturalist doctrines. But when Popper gets to his defence of the unity of scientific method in § 29, he switches from criticisms of the pro-naturalist doctrines to criticisms of certain anti-naturalist ones. In short, the structure of the essay breaks down in Parts three and four. The first two very orderly and systematic Parts seem to have little relationship to the last two.

Now that the archives have been opened, various scholars have been able to document just what was going on. It turns out that Popper worked on the 'Poverty' during three different periods. He first conceived of the project in 1936 or so, then worked on it again between 1938 and 1940. He then set it aside to work on *The Open Society*. The first two parts were published with minor changes in *Economica* in 1944, but then Popper extensively revised the last two parts before sending them in for publication. And it is here that Hayek comes unmistakably into the picture (Hacohen 2000, p. 354).

Popper had by this time read Hayek's 1935 edited collection, *Collectivist Economic Planning*, as well as a number of his articles. The most important of the latter was Hayek's long piece, published in parts in *Economica* in 1942-44, 'Scientism and the Study of Society'. In the article Hayek criticized both historicism and the engineering mentality. In a series of letters in late 1943 and early 1944 Popper repeatedly responded to ideas that Hayek had expressed in his writings, and this is what caused Popper to revise his essay. So, what do these letters tell us about Hayek's influence?

The answer is — it depends on how you read them. Though it is clear that Popper is responding to Hayek, it is less clear just what his response *is*. His responses seem to fall into three general categories. One is praise for Hayek's erudition, usually coupled with the remark that he, Popper, is learning a lot from him. Secondly, Popper marvels at the similarity of their positions on various issues. Finally, Popper points out areas where they differ. It is not atypical to find all three sorts of statements in a single letter. Depending on which part of a letter one chooses to emphasize, one can come away with very different answers to the question of the extent of Hayek's influence.

And indeed, different scholars have given different answers. My own view comes closest to that of Jeremy Shearmur, who tends to minimize the effect of Hayek's influence. Shearmur points out that Popper had every reason to be grateful to Hayek personally, because he was helping him get a publisher for *The Open Society* and, as editor of *Economica*, was also responsible for the 'Poverty' being published. As such, he may have added citations to Hayek's work more out of gratitude than anything else. This is reason enough, says Shearmur, for one to 'be careful of reading too much into Popper's discussion of Hayek' in the 'Poverty' (Shearmur 1996, p. 29).

The actual content of the 'Poverty' provides further support for Shearmur's thesis. Though there are sixteen references to Hayek listed in the index, if one separates out the passing *references* from the more substantive *discussions*, arguably there are only two of the latter. One of these comes in § 21 in the third Part of the 'Poverty', where Popper appears to be trying to convince Hayek that piecemeal social engineering (which Popper endorses) is different from the 'engineering mentality' that Hayek had criticized in 'Scientism'. For Popper, piecemeal social engineering is simply the application of the scientific method, conceived by Popper as a non-dogmatic method of trial and error, to the realm of social policy. The method is non-dogmatic in that it does not rule out a priori any sort of social arrangement, but also in that it requires decision makers always to be ready to learn from experience and to be prepared to adapt their reforms in the face of contrary evidence.

The second major reference comes in § 29 in the fourth Part of the 'Poverty', where Popper states that the 'Scientism' essay could be used to defend the thesis of the unity of the methods of science that Popper endorsed. This was much more of a stretch, because for Hayek 'scientism' meant the application of the methods of the natural sciences in areas where they did not belong. Popper's argument is that the methods Hayek criticized were not the real methods of the natural sciences, but the illegitimate fabrications of natural scientists that social theorists in their efforts to be 'scientific' mistakenly accepted.

Whatever we think of these arguments, it is pretty clear that Popper's main point in both of his extended citations of Hayek is to argue that, *appearances notwithstanding*, their views are very similar. He nowhere suggests that Hayek caused him to change his mind. What shines through is not any particular thesis of *Hayek's*, but Popper's own original thesis, that the method of trial and error is applicable to the social sciences. Hayek did not so much cause Popper to change his mind as to change his *manner of presentation* so as to show that their apparent differences were in fact not so great. Because he ended up spending so much time responding to Hayek, my conclusion is that Hayek's major impact on the 'Poverty' was to cause Popper in rewriting them to destroy the orderliness of his last two Parts!

Let us now move to the next period, the 1950s and 1960s. If one were going to make a case for Popper's influence on Hayek, it is in two papers that Hayek reprinted in his 1967 collection that one should look. These are 'Degrees of Explanation', first published in 1955, and 'The Theory of Complex Phenomena', first published in 1964 as Hayek's contribution to *The Critical Approach to Science and Philosophy: Essays in Honor of K. R. Popper*. It was in the former that Hayek stated that 'In many respects what follows is little more than an elaboration of some of Popper's ideas' (Hayek 1955/1967, p. 4). In the paper Hayek accepts Popper's dictum that to be scientific a theory must be falsifiable, meaning that it must forbid certain outcomes so that, if they occur, the theory stands as falsified (Hayek 1955/1967, p. 4; 1964b/1967, p. 29). He cites Popper again in claiming that 'prediction and explanation are merely two aspects of the same process' (Hayek 1955/1967, p. 9). Another key Popperian idea is that science follows the hypothetico-deductive model, not induction; a related one is that science does not start with pure observation but with a problem that shapes our interests in data of a certain kind (ibid., p. 4; 1964b/1967, p. 23). Finally, in the preface (Hayek 1967, p. viii) Hayek notes yet another place where Popper helped him:

> Readers of some of my earlier writings may notice a slight change in the tone of my discussion of the attitude which I then called 'scientism'. The reason for this is that Sir Karl Popper has taught me that natural scientists did not really do what most of them not only told us that they did but also urged the representatives of other disciplines to imitate.

Given all of this, it will be doubtless be surprising that even here I do not see that much influence. More precisely, I will argue rather that Popper was only one of many influences on Hayek at this time. (For a fuller version of my alternative story, see Caldwell 2004, Chapter 13.)

We must first go back to the 'Scientism' essay, an essay that Hayek had written without any discernible influence from Popper. In that essay, Hayek criticized the collectivism, objectivism, and historicism of the scientistic approach. He also presented a positive account of what he called, after Menger, the compositive method, something that he thought was appropriate in the social sciences. That approach implied strict limits on prediction: when dealing with the subject matter studied by the social sciences, often pattern prediction is the best one can do, or an explanation of the principle by which complex social structures form. Finally, throughout the essay Hayek always distinguished the sciences according to the natural science – social science dichotomy. It was a crucial distinction for him because, recall, Hayek defined 'scientism' as the illegitimate attempt to apply the putative methods of the natural sciences in areas they did not belong.

After the war Hayek began working on a book on theoretical psychology, *The Sensory Order* (1952). Initially his major goal in the book was to provide a scientific critique of behaviorism. But in the course of his investigations he began to see the mind as another example of a spontaneously forming order, analogous to the social orders that formed as the result of the unintended consequences of human action.

In 1950 Hayek moved to the Committee on Social Thought at the University of Chicago. Beginning in the fall of 1952 he ran a seminar there in which *The Sensory Order* and the 'Scientism' essay were the major readings. Hayek later called the seminar 'one of the greatest experiences of my life' (Hayek 1983, p. 134), and he seemed particularly pleased that it attracted natural scientists from around the University. A handout from the seminar indicates that he was beginning to pay more careful attention to evolutionary theory. This is significant because in 'Degrees of Explanation' evolutionary theory is identified as yet another example of a science in which only pattern predictions are possible. During this period Hayek also began exploring other fields, among them cybernetics, made popular by Norbert Wiener; the systems theory of Ludwig von Bertalanffy (Bertalanffy had offered Hayek comments on *The Sensory Order* when it was still in manuscript form); communication theory; and John von Neumann's theory of automata. Finally, he read Warren Weaver, whose distinction between sciences that study simple versus complex phenomena he ultimately adopted. This distinction would replace the natural science – social science dichotomy that he had used in the 'Scientism' essay.

In short, Hayek drew on many different resources in the 1950s. To be sure, Popper was one of them. But it was Hayek's own research, in the first instance — and in particular, his effort to provide a framework for the idea that in economics only 'explanations of the principle' and 'pattern prediction' are possible — that was the driving force behind any changes he underwent. The twin notions of pattern prediction and explanations of the principle were his core ideas, ones that predated his change from the natural science – social science distinction to the simple phenomena – complex phenomena one, and remained after the switch. With the new terminology, a terminology that derives most directly from Warren Weaver, Hayek could present his original ideas in a way that was more consistent with the most up-to-date philosophy of the time, including not just Popper's, but also that of Ernest Nagel, whom he also cites (1964b/1967, pp. 25, 28, 36). He could argue that economics was one of *many sciences* that study complex phenomena. Both the 'many' and the 'sciences' are important; economics was fully scientific, but that did not imply that it should follow the methods of physics and other 'simple' sciences, as his positivist foes had for so long insisted. Economics was a science, but it was one among the sciences that studied complex phenomena. That is why we can do no better than to make pattern predictions. And *that* implies limits on what social planners and other constructivist rationalists could accomplish.

Note finally that though Hayek clearly accepted Popper's key idea that a theory must be falsifiable to be scientific, he also always emphasized that theories that deal with complex phenomena are necessarily less falsifiable. He put it this way (1964b/1967, p. 29):

> The advance of science will thus have to proceed in two different directions: while it is certainly desirable to make our theories as falsifiable as possible, we must also push forward into fields where, as we advance, the degree of falsifiability necessarily decreases. This is the price we have to pay for an advance into the field of complex phenomena.

So Hayek supported the notion of falsifiability, but at the same time he claimed that in sciences that study complex phenomena, progress is linked to a decrease in falsifiability. I suspect that the two different emphases account for the different readings that Professor Hutchison and I have offered of these papers.

There is a final episode that deserves at least a brief mention. In his last book, *The Fatal Conceit* (1988), Hayek occasionally sounds Popperian themes. He describes the book in the introduction as 'an evolutionary account of moral traditions', one meant to complement Popper's evolutionary epistemology (Hayek 1988, p. 10). Another prominent bow to Popper comes in his section on morals in Chapter 5, where he argues that morals are not justifiable (ibid., pp. 67-69). To my knowledge, this is the first time that either of these ideas appears in Hayek's work. Did he, late in life, come to accept evolutionary epistemology and the notion that neither knowledge nor our moral code is justifiable?

Once again, it is hard to say. Hayek began work on what would become *The Fatal Conceit* in the late 1970s, and by the early 1980s envisioned a book of 21 chapters, the first four of which were written. Some of the remaining chapters were also in various stages of completion. Work stopped in 1985, when Hayek's health deteriorated significantly. The book probably would not have been finished had the philosopher William Bartley, who was by then both the general editor of *The Collected Works of F. A. Hayek* and Hayek's officially designated biographer, not stepped in to assist Hayek in putting together the final manuscript.

Bartley's considerable efforts on Hayek's behalf raise the question, though, of how much of *The Fatal Conceit* should be attributed to Bartley and how much to Hayek. Neither of the themes just identified appeared in the early drafts of *The Fatal Conceit*. Indeed, most of the planned sections that had to do with economics, even those that Hayek had already written up, did not make it into the final edition. Both the addition of new material and the cutting out of material already written suggest that Bartley's role as editor was not a passive one.

Other bits of evidence should make one leery of putting too much emphasis on Hayek's apparent new enthusiasm for Popperian themes in *The Fatal Conceit*. One is struck, for example, by Hayek's use of italics in the book. Though he occasionally used them for emphasis, in previous writings Hayek typically only used italics when he was introducing a new term. Anyone who has read Bartley, on the other hand, knows that he was far more promiscuous in his use of italics. This certainly points towards a conclusion that the book was a product more of his pen than of Hayek's.

This intuition was supported by Sudha Shenoy, who in an e-mail reported to me that a colleague of hers, John Burrows, had undertaken a preliminary computer textual analysis of the book, comparing selected chapters with bits of the book that Hayek had written before *The Fatal Conceit*, namely *Law, Legislation and Liberty* (1973-1979). Shenoy told me, 'The results showed a definite divergence — i.e., some other hand definitely played a clear part in the published text of FC. Specifically, on early 'crude' tests, the text of FC clearly separated itself from the texts of LLL' (e-mail, Shenoy to Caldwell, 6 September 1999).[3]

Of course, the fact that Bartley may have written the book does not rule out the possibility that Hayek signed off on all the new materials in it. But again, he would have been in ill health when he made those decisions, and also very much in Bartley's debt for having carried out what all admit was a huge editorial task. It certainly is not inconceivable that *acquiescence* rather than *endorsement* might best describe Hayek's attitude towards the new additions to his original manuscript.

To sum up: I have argued that, statements made by each man notwithstanding, a plausible case can be made that neither Popper nor Hayek had a real influence on the other's writings. I have offered arguments for my interpretation, though it is also clear that the evidence at hand is capable of supporting alternative interpretations. If my interpretation is to be at all

---

[3]Jeremy Shearmur has told me, however, that Hayek frequently asked others to check his writings over before publication and to make suggestions for grammatical or stylistic changes. If this was indeed his standard practice, it would undermine any attempts to do computer analyses of his texts.

convincing, I must also address the question of why each man was apparently so taken with the other. What explains their mutual attraction? If I can explain this, it may help to explain why each was so eager to praise the other in ways that could lead outside observers to assume that one or the other of them was an influence.

I think that in the first instance each was fascinated by the fact that someone else, someone coming from a very different disciplinary background, had come up with an argument that complemented his own. Imagine Hayek's reaction, for example, when he first read the opening chapters of *Logik der Forschung* in 1935 or so. Hayek would have immediately been taken with those chapters. He was, after all, part of the Austrian tradition in economics, a tradition that had fought in the *Methodenstreit* against the German historical school economists at least some of whom had argued that the careful collection of facts would someday, by means of induction, lead to the creation of a theory. Hayek had just published his inaugural lecture, 'The Trend of Economic Thinking', and in it he had argued that many of the bad ideas about economics then current in British society found their origins in the writings of the German historical school (Hayek 1933/1991). Those first few chapters would resonate with Hayek because he would read them as a modern scientific philosopher's rebuttal to views that the Austrian economists had so long been opposed. It is in this respect that Hayek is exactly right to say that when he first read Popper he immediately accepted his views, but that also what Popper had put into words was something that Hayek had long felt. For his part, Popper had developed a critique of historicism before he had studied the social science literature, so he too must have been amazed to find that another scholar in a very different field should come up with arguments so similar to his. Both of them were impressed with each other because both of them saw in the other's work further support for his own arguments. Hayek gave Popper access to the past, to a set of methodological debates within the history of social science, knowledge of which could buttress his case. And Popper gave Hayek access to arguments from within contemporary philosophy of science to buttress his claim that economics was fully a science, but because it studies complex phenomena, one that could not follow the supposed methods of physics.

There was perhaps another dimension to their mutual attraction. As many writers have shown, for most of their lives Popper and Hayek were pretty far apart as far as politics is concerned. But they also had some things in common. One was a classical liberal in a world in which few existed, the other, if we accept Hacohen's characterization, was an outsider in both the Jewish and the German-speaking communities and a socialist, but a disgruntled socialist. Both were secular, and both were cosmopolitan in outlook, at times idealistically so, particularly given the times in which they lived. Their views made them outsiders in Vienna, and then they became outsiders of a different sort again when they lived in English-speaking countries that were at war with the country of their birth. And though each held to certain bedrock views tenaciously, both were committed to the ideal of the importance of rational discussion and debate. All of this, I submit, helps to explain their mutual attraction. I conclude that though each found the other impressive, their ideas were *sui generis*. On the question of who influenced whom, we must answer: no one.

Bibliography

Bartley, III, W. W. (1989). 'Music and Politics: Karl Popper Meets Arnold Schönberg and the Eislers and Gives Up Communism'. Unpublished manuscript.

Caldwell, B. J. (1988). 'Hayek's Transformation'. *History of Political Economy* **20**, pp. 513-41.

―――― (1992a). 'Hayek the Falsificationist? A Refutation'. *Research in the History of Economic Thought and Methodology* **10**, pp. 1-15.

―――― (1992b). 'Reply to Hutchison', *Research in the History of Economic Thought and Methodology* **10**, pp. 33-42.

―――― (2004). *Hayek's Challenge*. Chicago: University of Chicago Press.

Hacohen, M. H. (2000). *Karl Popper: The Formative Years, 1902-1945*. Cambridge: Cambridge University Press.

Hayek, F. A. (1933). 'The Trend of Economic Thinking'. In *The Collected Works of F. A. Hayek*, Volume 3, *The Trend of Economic Thinking: Essays on Political Economists and Economic History*, pp. 17-34. Edited by W. W. Bartley, III and Stephen Kresge. London: Routledge, 1991.

―――― (1937). 'Economics and Knowledge'. In *Individualism and Economic Order*, pp. 33-56. Chicago: University of Chicago Press, 1948.

―――― (1942-1944). 'Scientism and the Study of Society'. In *The Counter-Revolution of Science: Studies in the Abuse of Reason*, pp. 17-182. Glencoe IL: The Free Press, 1952.

―――― (1944). *The Road to Serfdom*. Chicago: University of Chicago Press, 1976.

―――― (1952). *The Sensory Order: An Inquiry into the Foundations of Theoretical Psychology*. Midway Reprint. Chicago: University of Chicago Press, 1967.

―――― (1955). 'Degrees of Explanation'. In Hayek (1967), pp. 3-21.

―――― (1964a). 'Kinds of Rationalism'. In Hayek (1967), pp. 82-95.

―――― (1964b). 'The Theory of Complex Phenomena'. In Hayek (1967), pp. 22-42.

―――― (1967). *Studies in Philosophy, Politics and Economics*. Chicago: University of Chicago Press.

―――― (1973-1979). *Law, Legislation and Liberty*. Three volumes. Chicago: University of Chicago Press.

―――― (1982). '*The Sensory Order* after 25 Years' and 'Discussion'. In *Cognition and the Symbolic Processes*, Volume 2, edited by Walter Weimer and David Palermo, pp. 287-93, 321-39. Hillsdale NJ: Lawrence Erlbaum Associates.

——— (1983). *Nobel Prize Winning Economist*. Transcript of an interview conducted in 1978 under the auspices of the Oral History Program, University Library, UCLA. Edited by Armen Alchian. Copyright © Regents of the University of California.

——— (1988). *The Fatal Conceit: The Errors of Socialism*. Edited by W. W. Bartley, III. Chicago: University of Chicago Press.

———, editor (1935). *Collectivist Economic Planning: Critical Studies on the Possibility of Socialism*. London: Routledge and Kegan Paul. Reprint 1975. Clifton NJ: Kelley.

Hutchison, T. W. (1981). *The Politics and Philosophy of Economics: Marxians, Keynesians and Austrians*. Oxford: Blackwell.

——— (1992). 'Hayek and "Modern Austrian" Methodology: Comment on a Non-Refuting Refutation'. *Research in the History of Economic Thought and Methodology* **10**, pp. 17-32.

Mannheim, K. (1940). *Man and Society in an Age of Reconstruction: Studies in Modern Social Structure*. London: Kegan Paul.

Popper, K. R. (1935). *Logik der Forschung*. Vienna: Julius Springer Verlag.

——— (1945). *The Open Society and Its Enemies*. London: George Routledge & Sons. 5th edition 1966. London: Routledge & Kegan Paul.

——— (1957). *The Poverty of Historicism*. London: Routledge & Kegan Paul.

——— (1959). *The Logic of Scientific Discovery*. New York: Basic Books.

——— (1963). *Conjectures and Refutations*. London: Routledge & Kegan Paul. 5th edition 1989.

——— (1974). 'Intellectual Autobiography'. In P. A. Schilpp, editor (1974), pp. 1-181. *The Philosophy of Karl Popper*. La Salle IL: Open Court. Reprinted as *Unended Quest* (1976). London & Glasgow: Fontana/Collins.

Shearmur, J. F. G. (1996). *The Political Thought of Karl Popper*. London: Routledge.

7

A Tour of Popper's Vienna[*]

Heidi König

This guide identifies a number of places in Vienna that are, in one way or another, associated with Karl Popper's life. Some, such as the barracks at Grinzing where he lived after the First World War, and the cemetery in Hietzing where his ashes are laid, are too far from the city centre to be reached on foot, but they are here identified, and brief instructions are given on how to get to them (and all the other places mentioned) by public transport.

Synagogue Stadttempel
1010, Seitenstettengasse 2-4
Built 1824-1826 by Josef Kornhäusel
U1 SCHWEDENPLATZ

The building escaped destruction, though on 10 November 1938, the inner room of the synagogue was devastated by the National Socialists. Karl Popper's parents, Dr Simon Siegmund Carl Popper and Jenny Popper (née Schiff), married here on 3 April 1892.

His parents were Jewish, but had converted to the Protestant faith. His mother, who was born in Vienna in 1864, came from a richly musical family; her parents were founder-members of the *Gesellschaft der Musikfreunde*, and she and her two sisters were talented pianists. Popper's father, whose family came from Kolin, was born in Roudnice nad Labem (Raudnitz) in what is now the Czech Republic. ... He was a cultivated man, historian, poet, social theorist, 'really more a scholar than a lawyer' according to his son.
(Miller 1997, p. 370; 2006, pp. 2f.)

Bauernmarkt 1
1010, Freisingergasse 4
U1 STEPHANSPLATZ

The Popper family lived in the centre of Vienna in the handsome 18th-century house at the corner of Freisingergasse and Bauernmarkt where Popper's father maintained his successful law practice.
(Miller 1997, p. 370; 2006, p. 3)

[*]For providing valuable information on Karl Popper's life in Vienna between 1902 and 1937, I am greatly indebted to Malachi Hacohen, Christian Mertens, Karl Milford, David Miller, Alfred Klahr-Gesellschaft, Institut Wiener Kreis, Wiener Kinderfreunde, Wiener Stadt- & Landesarchiv.

The house has been declared a historical monument. The front has not been changed since the time when Popper's family — Simon and Jenny Popper, and their children Dora, Annie, and Karl — lived there on the top floor, in apartment 22. After her husband's death in 1932, the apartment remained Jenny Popper's residence until 1938. Popper reports that she lost it shortly after the Anschluss in March 1938. She died after a long illness in the Herzklinik (hospital) in the 9th district in May 1938.

Großloge Wien
Großloge von Wien der alten freien und angenommenen Maurer
1010, Dorotheergasse 12
U1 STEPHANSPLATZ

Sometime after 1904, Simon Popper apparently became Master (*Meister vom Stuhl*) of the Masonic lodge *Humanitas*. Established in 1871, Humanitas was the oldest and largest lodge, and had a few hundred members. ... In Vienna, the Freemasons organized as charitable and educational societies, promoting social welfare and secular popular education. They were especially proud of the orphanage (*Kinderasyl Humanitas*) they opened in 1875 in Kahlenbergerdorf near Vienna for about sixty children. Simon Popper ran the association's affairs from his office, as he did with other non-Masonic, charitable organizations.
(Hacohen 2000, pp. 41f.)

A colour painting of Simon Popper was hanging in the Großloge in Vienna (Hoover Archives).

Freie Schule
1080, Albertgasse 23
TRAM LINE 5, 33; BUS 13A

The Verein Freie Schule *had been established by a coalition of Freemasons, progressives and socialists in 1905 as a reaction to Christian Socialist inspired school laws. In 1906, a school was opened in Vienna. In interwar years the* Freie Schule *and the socialist movement* Kinderfreunde *('Childrens' Friends' — dedicated to welfare and pedagogical work among working class youth) became one organization. The office of the* Wiener Kinderfreunde *is still in Albertgasse 23.*

Popper went to the *Freie Schule* for five years, from 1908 to 1913. It was a private elementary school providing an alternative educational environment, free from clerical influence. ... Popper, who hated discipline but loved learning, recalled fondly his teacher Emma Goldberger, who first taught him reading and writing. ... the *Freie Schule* was the only teaching environment in which he ever felt comfortable as a student. In interwar years, he would join the socialist

school-reform effort, designed to extend the *Freie Schule*'s educational methods throughout Viennese schools.
(Hacohen 2000, pp. 65f.)

Franz Josef Gymnasium
(today: Bundesgymnasium Stubenbastei)
1010, Stubenbastei 6
U1 STEPHANSPLATZ

Popper attended this school in about 1914-1915. Other famous students at this school were Karl Kraus, Paul Wittgenstein, and Edgar Zilsel, who would some years later examine Popper on logic when he tried to pass his entrance examination for the University (Matura).

Bundesrealgymnasium
1030, Radetzkystraße 2A
TRAM LINES N, O

Until 1918, and probably also 1913-1914. At one time Popper represented the school in the socialist student organization.

[Popper] attended the Franz Josef Gymnasium. But he reports that, desperately bored in most of his lessons, he effectively left school at the age of 16. His first attempt at the *Matura* ... was unsuccessful, as he failed in two subjects: logic and Latin. In logic he was examined by Edgar Zilsel, later a member of the Vienna Circle, with whom he had a disagreement about Aristotelian logic. ... The Latin examination required the oral translation of an unseen Horace ode. In 1922, the second attempt at the *Matura* was successful.
(Miller ibidem)

Parliament Building
1017, Dr Karl Renner Ring 3
Built by Theophil von Hansen 1873-1883
U1, U2 VOLKSTHEATER; TRAM LINES 1, 2, D PARLAMENT

The proclamation of the First Austrian Republic took place here on 12 November 1918. It was accompanied by riots, which claimed two dead and numerous injured.

It was a time of upheavals, though not only political ones. I was close enough to hear the bullets whistle when, on the occasion of the Declaration of the Austrian Republic, soldiers started shooting at the members of the Provisional Government assembled at the top of the steps leading to the Parliament building. (This experience led me to write a paper on freedom.)
(Popper 1974/1976, § 8)

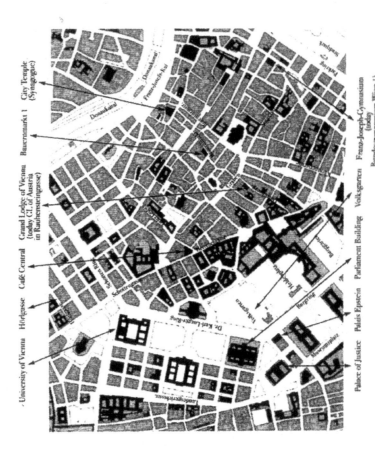

Fig 7.1 Map of central Vienna

University of Vienna · Hörlgasse · Café Central · Grand Lodge of Vienna (today Gl. of Austria in Rauhensteingasse) · Bauernmarkt 1 · City Temple (Synagogue)

Palace of Justice · Palais Epstein · Parliament Building · Volksgarten · Franz-Joseph-Gymnasium (today Bundesgymnasium Wien 1)

Donaukanal · Franz-Josefs-Kai · Graben · Schwarzspa... · Schottengasse · Dr. Karl-Lueger-Ring · Volksgarten · Heldenplatz · Burgring · Ring · Burgtheater · Maximilianplatz · Landesgerichtsstr.

Hörlgasse
1090 Wien
U2 Schottentor-Universität

From about 1917 [Popper] had been actively concerned in progressive politics, even for a short time thinking of himself as a communist. But after the callous shooting of unarmed demonstrators by the police in Hörlgasse in 1919, he turned against the cynical readiness of Marxists to sacrifice others' lives for indeterminate ideals.

(Miller 1997, pp. 370f.; 2006, p. 3)

Headquarters of the Communist Party
in 1919
1010, Stubenring 4
U3 Stubentor

Shortly after the peace, in 1919, I went to the Communist Party office and offered them my services as an errand boy. Among the leaders there were three children of an Austrian philosopher Rudolf Eisler: Gerhardt, Hans and Fritti (short for Elfriwade) Eisler, whose married name was Friedlander, although she may already have been divorced by then. Gerhardt later became the main leader of the American Communists and was expelled from the United States after the Second World War. His younger brother, Hans, became one of the most important musicians in East Germany. And Fritti Friedlander, under the name of Ruth Fischer, became one of the leaders of German Communism. ... It was an interesting meeting I had with them. They were very nice to me, spoilt me a little, and at first I trusted them. But very soon I found that a telegram from Moscow was enough for them to turn 180 degrees and say the opposite of what they had been saying the day before. ... So when I found that out, my attitude to Communism was thrown into cris[i]s.

(Popper 1997, Chapter 1)

Café Akazienhof
1090, Thurngasse 2
Restaurant 'Intermezzo'
Tram lines 37, 38, 40, 41, 42

In 1901, the educational reformer and pioneer in the fight for women's education, Eugenie Schwarzwald, opened the first Lyzeum for girls to prepare them for university. Several other 'Schwarzwaldsche Schulanstalten', including a co-educational school and a 'Realgymnasium' for girls, were to follow. Arnold Schönberg, Oskar Kokoschka, Adolf Loos, and Hans Kelsen, among others, supported the project and taught and lectured at her schools. Schwarzwald's social projects included also the organization of summer vacation colonies for children (Popper visited one of them in 1919) and of not-for-profit eateries during and after the Great War: 'Akazienhof' was the first one to be opened, in 1917.

> For a few months Popper saw [Otto Neurath] at Akazienhof, a pleasant
> not-for-profit eatery (*Gemeinschaftsküche*) that Schwarzwald opened near the
> university for students and professors, a meeting place for the radical
> intelligentsia, including Hungarian émigrés. The two met again eight years
> later, during Neurath's lecture to the *Verein Ernst Mach*, and, apparently, once
> or twice when Popper had his class visit ... Neurath's Economic Museum.
> (Hacohen 2000, p. 89)

Grinzing Barracks
1190, Grinzinger Allee 7
TRAM LINE 38

In the interwar period, the Grinzing barracks became residences for impov-
erished intellectuals, socialist youth, students, exiles. The Kinderfreunde *ran*
an orphanage and primary school for neglected children in one of the barracks
(directed by Alois Jalkotzy); communist refugees lived in another, students in a
third. Popper lived in Barrack 29 . Among others, Popper met here his lifelong
friend Paul Ostersetzer, who was working as a carpenter at that time, making
toys for a Montessori orphanage; — Popper was soon to follow his example
and become a cabinetmaker. Popper participated in the educational reforms
initiated by the Social Democratic movement, worked in Alfred Adler's child
guidance clinic, and did social work with neglected children.

> During the winter of 1919-20 I left home to live in a disused part of a
> former military hospital converted by students into an extremely primitive
> students' home. I wanted to be independent, and I tried not to be a burden to
> my father, who was well over sixty and had lost all his savings in the runaway
> inflation after the war. My parents would have preferred me to stay at home.
> (Popper 1974/1976, § 9)

Arnold Schönberg Center
Palais Fanto
1030, Schwarzenbergplatz 6
U1, U2, U4 KARLSPLATZ, TRAM LINE D

The Arnold Schönberg Center, founded in 1997, houses the Schönberg
Archives and is situated in the Palais Fanto, built by Ernst von Gotthilf-
Miskolczy and Alexander Neumann in 1917-1918.
At the age of 17, Popper joined Schönberg's Society for Private Musical
Perfomances; Hans Eisler, his friend from the Communist Party, was one of
Schönberg's students. Popper attended a series of rehearsals and performances,
many of which took place in the Schwarzwald-Lyzeum, where Schönberg was
teaching. Popper got to know closely the first Chamber Symphony and Pier-
rot Lunaire, and (in a letter to Kurt Blaukopf in 1992) he remembers having
even sung in the choir at a perfomance of Gurrelieder in the Vienna Opera. In
the end, however, he disagreed with Schönberg's concept of performing music

privately, in order to protect musicians from both the public and from criticism. In Popper's view, this ...

> ... promoted infallibility and self-aggrandizement. Popper's experience with Schoenberg recapitulated the one with the Marxists. He distrusted artists' claims to superior talent, just as he doubted revolutionaries' claim for special knowledge. ... To [him], both the political and cultural avant-garde became forever suspect. Popper left the Schoenberg circle late in 1921, but he still contemplated a career in music. For about a year, he became a student of church music in the Vienna *Konservatorium* (Academy of Music).
> (Hacohen 2000, pp. 102f.)

For admission to the Academy of Music, Popper submitted an organ fugue in F sharp minor, written in 1922 or 1923 and considered by him as an attempt to honour Bach. On 5 July 2002, during the congress to celebrate the centenary of his birth, Popper's fugue was performed by Wolfgang Fritzsche in the church of St Michael in Heiligenstadt.

University of Vienna
Main Building
1010, Dr Karl Lueger Ring 1
Built by Heinrich von Ferstel in 1873-1884
U2 SCHOTTENTOR-UNIVERSITÄT

Karl Popper started attending lectures at the age of 16 and remained at the University until 1928. He studied mathematics with Hahn, Helly, Furtwängler and Menger, among others, physics with Thirring and Arthur Haas, psychology with Bühler, and philosophy with Gomperz and Moritz Schlick, who was shot by a former student on the stairs of the main building on 22 June 1936.

To mark Popper's centenary, a bust by Christine Pillhofer was unveiled in the Arkadenhof *of the University main building on Sunday, 7 July 2002.*

> At the University I sampled lecture courses in various subjects: history, literature, psychology, philosophy, and even some lectures at the medical school. But I soon gave up going to lectures, with the exception of those in mathematics and theoretical physics. The University had, at that time, most eminent teachers, but reading their books was an incomparably greater experience than listening to their lectures.
> (Popper 1974/1976, § 9)

> [Instead he] began studying with a group of socialist friends he had known since the revolution. They composed their own reading list, discussed books, debated politics, climbed the Alps, and went to concerts. Circles of young intellectuals who found the university stifling were common in Vienna both before and after the war, but socialist students moved the center of activities from the coffeehouse to the scoutlike group. (Popper, especially, despised the coffeehouse milieu....)
> (Hacohen 2000, p. 104)

Palais Epstein
1010, Dr Karl Renner Ring 1
Built by Theophil von Hansen in 1868-1872
U2, U3 VOLKSTHEATER

The Pedagogic Institute, which Popper attended between 1925 and 1927,
the Wiener Stadtschulrat *controlled by Otto Glöckel, the pedagogical library*
Popper visited, and Karl Bühler's psychological laboratory were in the Palais
Epstein from 1922-1934. Here Popper first met Josefine Henninger ('Hen-
nie'), who had been in the first class of women training at the Pedagogic
Institute.

> At the institute, Popper expanded his social and intellectual circle. His
> class included Robert Lammer, who would help him to write his first book;
> Otto Haas, to whom he would entrust his papers, upon leaving Vienna; Ludwig
> Krenek; and Fritz Kolb. He established long-term friendships with all. Most
> significantly, he met his future wife, Josefine Anna Henninger (1906-1985)
> there. She and Karl were members of a student group that studied, hiked, and
> mountaineered together. Karl became their intellectual leader. ... Popper gave
> the group informal seminars, reviewing class material and helping them
> prepare for exams. He did well. ... [Bühler] related to Popper, in their first
> personal conversation, that these were the best-prepared students he had ever
> encountered.
> (Hacohen 2000, p. 135)

Karl and Charlotte Bühler
(residence)
1190, Weimarerstraße 100
TRAM LINE 38 PETER-JORDAN-STRASSE

> Karl Bühler was the first professor Popper managed to engage. Their styles
> of thinking differed from the start, but Bühler's spontaneous generosity drew
> Popper. He felt that he could learn much from the erudite and cultivated
> master. ... He sat in on all his lectures in psychology and logic and managed to
> find his way to his colloquium as early as in the first semester. (He also took
> Charlotte Bühler's courses in youth and social psychology.)
> (Hacohen 2000, p. 140)

Palace of Justice / Justizpalast
1010, Schmerlingplatz 10-11
U2, U3 VOLKSTHEATER

On Friday 15 July 1927 the morning papers in Austria gave the news of
the recently pronounced sentence in the case of 'the Schattendorf killers'. This
report gave rise to a mass demonstration of workers who left their work places
and marched to the centre. The police failed to block their way and opened fire.
The crowd reacted violently, and the Palace of Justice was seized and set on

fire. At noon the police intensified the shooting: As a result, 85 of the workers gathered on the square in front of the Palace of Justice were killed, and several hundred wounded. Popper and Hennie were amongst the crowd, caught between the demonstrators and the police.

They watched incredulously as the police opened fire on 'peaceful and un-armed social democratic workers and bystanders. We were lucky to escape.' [Popper] thought the police's attack was unprovoked, but, all the same, blamed the socialist leaders for the 'massacre'. Their 'suicidal' policies gave the government opportunity to use violence. He understood well the event's historical significance. From then on, he was sure of the demise of Austrian democracy.

(Hacohen 2000, p. 300)

Heinrich Gomperz
(residence)
1120, Grünberggasse 25
U4 SCHÖNBRUNN

Gomperz was a professor of philosophy at the university. He had an enormous breadth of interests and published extensively on epistemology and classical philosophy. ... A circle of intellectuals met on Saturdays at his Viennese villa, but Popper did not participate in these meetings. Rather, for the next two years, he met Gomperz privately to discuss psychology. ... Gomperz was never scathing and ironical with him, Popper said, as he had been with other students. All in all, they may have met only eight to ten times. But Popper also took Gomperz's course on Plato in the spring of 1926 and read all his works. They provided Popper with an incomparable guide to epistemology, psychology, and the methodology of science.

(Hacohen 2000, p. 149)

Popper visited Gomperz several times in the late 1920s and early 1930s.

Mathematisches Institut der Universität Wien (Department of Mathematics)
1090, Boltzmanngasse 9
TRAM LINES 37, 38, 40, 41, 42

Only the department of mathematics offered really fascinating lectures. The professors at the time were Wirtinger, Furtwängler, and Hans Hahn. All three were creative mathematicians of world reputation.... But I learned most from Hans Hahn. His lectures attained a degree of perfection which I have never encountered again. Each lecture was a work of art: dramatic in logical structure; not a word too much; of perfect clarity; and delivered in beautiful and civilized language.

(Popper 1974/1976, § 9)

From 1924 on, Moritz Schlick held here the Thursday evening seminars that constituted the Vienna Circle.

... the group met weekly for a Thursday evening seminar .... As the holder of Mach's chair in philosophy, Schlick presided as *primus inter pares*. Regular participants included Carnap, Feigl, Hahn, Olga Hahn-Neurath, Kraft, Menger, Neurath, and Waismann; social theorist Felix Kaufmann; young mathematicians Gustav Bergmann and Kurt Gödel; Schlick's students Béla Juhos, Marcel Natkin, Heinrich Neider, Rose Rand, and Josef Schächter. Zilsel maintained a critical distance, but kept current. Gomperz made an occasional appearance. Frank came frequently from Prague, von Mises and Reichenbach from Berlin. Visitors from abroad abounded with the years: philosopher A. J. Ayer and mathematician Frank Ramsey from England, philosophers Ernest Nagel and W. V. O. Quine from the United States, Kurt Grelling and Carl Hempel from Berlin, Polish logician Alfred Tarski, Danish philosopher Jørgen Jørgensen, and Norwegian philosopher Arne Naess. A number of epicycles formed around Schlick's seminar, most notably Karl Menger's Mathematical Colloquium. The core group, however, remained quite exclusive. A personal invitation by Schlick was required to attend. Popper never received one.

(Hacohen 2000, pp. 187f.; dates omitted)

Sir Karl Popper Schule, Hauptschule Schweglerstraße
1150, Schweglerstraße 2-4
U3 SCHWEGLERSTRASSE

In 1930 Popper finally obtained a teaching position at the Schwegler Hauptschule in the fifteenth district. A generation earlier, few intellectuals had opted for school teaching as a career, but economic circumstances, and enthusiasm for school reform, made teaching a popular career among Popper's cohort.

(Hacohen 2000, p. 178)

Café Central
1010, Herrengasse 14
U3 HERRENGASSE

Meeting place of the Viennese intelligentsia, of artists and writers such as Karl Kraus, Peter Altenberg, Adolf Loos, Egon Friedell, Franz Werfel, Alfred Polgar, Leon Trotsky. In 1934, Popper met Richard von Mises in Café Central.

I didn't like going to coffee-houses, but two people got me to the coffee-house. One was [Philipp] Frank, the other one (Richard von) Mises.
(Popper (with Dahms & Stadler) 1991, § 10.5, italics omitted)

Karl and Hennie Popper
(residence)
1130, Anton Langer Gasse 46
Tram lines 60, 62 Speising

After his marriage with Josefine Henninger (Hennie) on 11 April 1930,

> Karl moved into the small house where Hennie and her mother lived, in
> Hietzing, a single-family residence area — distinctly non-Jewish — in the
> westernmost part of Vienna. ... After a turbulent decade, he seemed to be
> settling down.
> (Hacohen 2000, p. 178)

*The original house was replaced in the 1970s. On the initiative of Dipl.
Ing. Wilfried Tepser and Dr Heinz Schuster, who live in the present house on
the site, a plaque bearing the words:*

> *Der große österreichische Philosoph*
> *Sir Karl Popper*
> *(28.7.1902 Hietzing – 17.9.1994 London)*
> *wohnte hier mit seiner Frau Josefine*
> *von 1930 bis 1935*
> *Sein Grab befindet sich am Lainzer Friedhof*

*was unveiled on 24 September 2004, in the presence of the District Mayor,
Dipl. Ing. Heinz Gerstbach. A short talk was given by Professor Karl Milford.*

Walter Schiff
(residence)
1090, Kolingasse 9
U2 Schottentor, bus 40A

*Walter Schiff, a statistician and economist, and Jenny Schiff's brother,
helped Popper to edit* Logik der Forschung *in 1934. Several years earlier, he
had introduced him to Herbert Feigl, contact with whom was to become crucial
for Popper's career as a philosopher:*

> Popper's uncle, Walter Schiff, arranged the first Feigl-Popper meeting by
> inviting Feigl and his fiancée, Maria Kaspar. ... The two set out for a nightlong
> walk around Vienna, ending in Feigl's apartment. Other all-night sessions
> followed. Popper drove home every intellectual victory. Feigl was impressed,
> but exasperated. He suggested that Popper publish his ideas in a book. Popper
> had previously ruled out a career as a professional philosopher. Gomperz had
> discouraged him from trying to publish .... His father and wife, too, dissuaded
> him from undertaking a book. ... Hennie was happy with their new life as
> teachers. She wished to continue their skiing and mountain climbing. But
> Popper was possessed. ... Sometime in 1930, he began writing.
> (Hacohen 2000, p. 185)

An active social democrat since 1928, Schiff became a member of the Austrian Communist Party in 1934. During the Ständestaat *his apartment became a meeting place for the Communist underground. The Gestapo searched it shortly after the* Anschluß. *Schiff escaped to Britain on 12 March 1938.*

Volksgarten
1010, Dr Karl Renner Ring
U2, U3 VOLKSTHEATER

About 1929, Karl Popper and Victor Kraft met in Volksgarten several times. But the most decisive meeting Popper had there was with Alfred Tarski.

As mentioned before, I first met Tarski in July 1934 in Prague. It was early in 1935 that I met him again in Vienna, in Karl Menger's Colloquium, of which Tarski and Gödel were members, and in which I also met such great men as Skolem and Abraham Wald. It was in those days that I asked Tarski to explain to me his theory of truth, and he did so in a lecture of perhaps twenty minutes on a bench (an unforgotten bench) in the *Volksgarten* in Vienna. ... No words can describe how much I learned from all this, and no words can express my gratitude for it. Although Tarski was only a little older than I, and although we were, in those days, on terms of considerable intimacy, I looked upon him as the one man whom I could truly regard as my teacher in philosophy. I have never learned so much from anybody else.

(Popper 1972, Chapter 9, § 1)

Lainzer Friedhof
1130, Küniglberg (Hietzing)
U4 KENNEDYBRÜCKE, BUSES 58B, 8A

Karl and Hennie Popper's grave is situated near the entrance, on the right hand side.

[Popper] died early in the morning of 17 September. His body was cremated, and some weeks later his ashes were laid, as he had requested, in his wife's grave in the Lainzer Friedhof, a small cemetery in Vienna. In 1992 Karl Popper had been made an honorary citizen of the City of Vienna, and the grave is to be maintained in perpetuity by this city of innumerable illustrious names.

(Miller 1997, p. 402; 2006, p. 43)

Bibliography

Hacohen, M. H. (2000). *Karl Popper – The Formative Years, 1902-1945. Politics and Philosophy in Interwar Vienna*. Cambridge & elsewhere: Cambridge University Press.

Miller, D. W. (1997). 'Sir Karl Raimund Popper C.H. F.B.A., 28 July 1902 – 17 September 1994'. *Biographical Memoirs of Fellows of the Royal Society of London* **43**, pp. 367-409. Reprinted as Chapter 1 of D. W. Miller (2006). *Out of Error*. Aldershot: Ashgate.

Popper, K. R. (1972). *Objective Knowledge*. Oxford: Clarendon Press. 2nd edition 1979.

———— (1974). 'Intellectual Autobiography'. In P. A. Schilpp, editor (1974), pp. 1-181. *The Philosophy of Karl Popper*. La Salle IL: Open Court. Reprinted as *Unended Quest* (1976). London & Glasgow: Fontana/Collins.

———— (1997). *The Lesson of This Century*. London: Routledge.

Popper, K. R., with H.-J. Dahms & F. Stadler (1991). 'Popper und der Wiener Kreis – Aus einem Gespräch mit Sir Karl Popper (1991)' ['Popper and the Vienna Circle. Excerpt from an Interview with Sir Karl Popper (1991)']. In Stadler (1997/2001), § 10.5.

Stadler, F. (1997). *Studien zum Wiener-Kreis. Ursprung, Entwicklung, und Wirkung des Logischen Empirismus im Kontext*. Frankfurt/Main: Suhrkamp. English translation (2001). *The Vienna Circle. Studies in the Origins, Development, and Influence of Logical Empiricism*. Vienna & New York: Springer.

8

Sir Karl Popper School
More than just a Name?

Renate Wustinger

> Those who have an excessive faith in their ideas are not well fitted to make
> discoveries.
> Claude Bernard *An Introduction to the Study of Experimental Medicine*,
> 1865/1927, Part One, Chapter II, §III

1 The framework of the School

The Sir Karl Popper School is not actually a school in itself but a department
of the upper division of a general high school. The pupils who are taught
in the classes of this department (school years 9–12) are between 13 and 18
years old, and have achieved above-average results in various intelligence tests.
The department is run as a school experiment, meaning that there is more
freedom for innovation. The 'experiment' aims to develop methods of learning
that promote the gifted. The school is a state school and there are no school
fees. It has been in existence for six years.

2 The School's relationship to Sir Karl Popper

'Why did you choose this name?' ask many visitors to the Sir Karl Popper
School. On the one hand this can be quickly answered — *we* (the Principal
and the Management Team of the school) did not choose it. It was chosen
by the initiators of the school with Popper's explicit consent. On the other
hand, there is an interesting question here that is asked less frequently: what
does this name mean for this school? What does Karl Popper's thought
mean for those who shape this school, that is, the pupils, the teachers and
the management team?[1] Do they feel committed to his theories? A quick
answer at the outset from the point of view of the management team: we feel
committed to examination of his theories, and indeed with his own approach
of making 'critical attempts at falsification'.

---

[1]Three Assistant Directors support the Director as a team — one Assistant Director for
administration, one for financial matters and myself as Assistant Director for pedagogical
matters. Other high schools in Austria do not have this structure.

The question, 'What does this or that answer of Popper's to particular problems mean for a school, for our school?' can be one of the ways in which we constantly re-evaluate our own model ourselves. It is one of the most attractive ways.... An example:

3 The conjectural character of human knowledge

In a lecture on 'The Rationality of Scientific Revolutions' Popper compared the three levels of adaptation — genetic adaptation, adaptive learning behaviour and scientific discovery (as a special case of adaptive learning behaviour). The main point is in the assertion that on all three levels every proposed 'solution' to a problem (instruction) comes from the *inside of the structure* and that conjectures on the third level (scientific 'tentative solutions') can be handed down in language. However, since these are always only 'conjectures', we should immediately attempt to falsify them if we want to approach the 'truth', because they are to be all the more favoured the longer they stand up to these attempts at falsification. The more creatively we can depict these various tentative solutions (conjectures about reality), the more important testing will naturally be.[2]

> The growth of imagination enhances of course the need for some control, such as, in science, interpersonal criticism — the friendly-hostile co-operation of scientists which is partly based on competition and partly on the common aim to get nearer to the truth. This, and the role played by instruction and tradition, seem to me to exhaust the main sociological elements inherently involved in the progress of science.

What does this mean for a school, for a school experiment? — We want to live out this attitude and pass it on. On the one hand in learning, in our basic didactic attitude, we want to give mistakes, criticism and the elimination of errors the same status as they have with Popper. The pupils should be able to rely upon this attitude: problems require solutions and only if we continually search out whether there are not better, more adequate, more sustainable solutions, only then is there an approach to the 'truth'. Whoever tries not to make a mistake does not become free and does not come up with creative answers and then go on with curiosity to subject them to severe tests. Whoever is afraid of falsification will become apprehensive and stubbornly hold to his theories or only hesitantly tread new and bolder paths. — However this also applies to ourselves outside the classroom, to all those involved in the continual development of this school experiment. We have conjectures about how learning supporting the gifted 'works' best. We are 'experimenting' in fact, and therefore we must ourselves observe the realization of our principles with the same alert eye the scientist uses to falsify his theories. The most searching question is: what could make us realize that our approach is not

---

[2]Popper (1975). The lecture is reprinted in part in selection 5 of Popper (1985). See § III.

correct? — And since it is still more difficult for us INSIDE the system, because perception is influenced by attitudes, we must see all criticism as valuable support. Somebody helps us in an attempt at falsification? Thank you, we take every train of thought into consideration, and if we have to reject it, then our approach has proved itself a little further. When we can also understand something of this criticism ourselves, then it was a valuable tip and we can introduce a small correction.

4 Piecemeal social engineering

'Small correction' because if we follow another of Karl Popper's thoughts:[3]

> The characteristic approach of the piecemeal engineer is this. Even though he may perhaps cherish some ideals which concern society 'as a whole' ... he does not believe in the method of redesigning it as a whole. ... The piecemeal engineer knows, like Socrates, how little he knows. ... Accordingly, he will make his way, step by step ... always on the look-out for the unavoidable unwanted consequences of any reform; and he will avoid undertaking reforms of a complexity and scope which make it impossible for him to disentangle causes and effects ....

School is an important and particularly sensitive part of our social world, and especially here the policy of small steps is the more cautious way. We are dealing with children and young people who could also feel like 'guinea pigs' in experiments of our size. It appears all the more important to initiate the changes on a scale that means that in the case of a possible 'falsification' of the theses no real damage is done to the young people. If we were to realize after four years that a particular way was not the right one after all, we could not simply say to these pupils, 'Back to the beginning. Now we know how it goes.' We have the responsibility to ensure that in the years in which they work with us they receive the best of school that we are able to give.

Isn't such an education experiment fainthearted? — Yes, if it lacks vision. However, one does not exclude the other. 'Piecemeal social engineering' and vision must work in partnership. The vision sets the course, piecemeal engineering determines the tempo and the size of the steps we take as we move towards this aim. Without vision, piecemeal engineering would merely become tinkering around. For our school this means: the vision is there — as described in the mission statement of the Sir Karl Popper School — we see a school in which young and older people together try, in the sense of Popper's theory of knowledge, to get a little bit closer to the 'truth' (whereby in various fields one can know more than the others), in which these people work together, in the sense of piecemeal social engineering, on the social world in which they live and in which the older people also pass on responsibility for this world piece by piece to the younger people. Existing structures partly

---

[3]See Popper (1944/1957), § 21, 'Piecemeal Social Engineering'. Reprinted in Popper (1985), selection 24, § II.

stand in the way of this vision, as to some extent do existing procedures and attitudes. It is a question of changing these — but in small steps that also allow for small corrections. Cautiously in fact. This does not necessarily mean that the aim is approached more slowly — it takes more time to return long distances if one has taken the wrong path. The demands should be 'high'. It is also the more responsible way, for the aims that school as an institution can set for itself and the ideals that it perhaps follows are not set up for it alone. They are linked to other developments in institutions of the social world, and whoever rebuilds in small steps can keep a regular check on whether the aims are still compatible with each other.

5   What do we need as a school in order to be able to live this out?

It is difficult for the individual to expose himself immediately to the attempt at falsification and the criticism connected with it. Popper, the scientist, knows that we never stand on solid ground, that everything is uncertain and shaky — but this should not be misconstrued as an attitude to life. It is especially young people who need exactly the opposite, they must be able to have confidence in reliable constants, in 'something that will always be there'. Here too it is not about 'one or the other' but the question, 'When the one, when the other and when a third thing?' If we bring together Popper's concept of shaky ground with the image of a ship that has sailed out to chart new territory and also learn something about the sea that makes this ground so shaky, then from time to time this ship also needs an anchor to stabilize it, and at certain intervals also a port. Solid ground would be an illusion where learning is about content and young people can be expected to be aware of this fact (and especially the teachers). The anchor must be reliably to hand where, in this learning together, it is about the contact, about the relationships and the values that regulate and steer this cooperation, and it must be possible to set course for port at any time. As Popper always emphasized, it is the scientist's theory, separated from him as a person, that is subjected to the 'error elimination process' and the possible falsification says nothing about the scientist but only about the usefulness of his tentative solution. Likewise, we hope that our pupils always feel that their learning and their courage to make mistakes (precisely in learning, and that should be clearly separated from assessment) is a third thing between them and their teachers and their fellow learners, which does not affect their relationship but only connects people for a time. However, it must not be the only connection.

6   Where do the young people get support in this?

The subject 'personal competence' (communication and social competence, personality building and project management, coaching) is an attempt to make a contribution in this direction. In these lessons it is not a question of 'compensation [for what?] through social action' and also not of training 'social engineers' in a negative sense.[4] It is much more about gaining insight into how conjectures about reality come about, insight into the processes resulting from it in communication about these conjectures, about reflection on one's own attitude to those making mistakes and those who think differently.... Here we confront the question, 'How much uncertainty may there be, must there be, if I really want to get a bit closer to the truth, and where do I find the certainty that I need in order to be able to expose myself to this uncertainty?' Karl Popper gives the answer so simply, but we know how difficult it is to live it out in everyday life, and we are working on it:[5]

> Scientific method in politics means that the great art of convincing ourselves that we have not made any mistakes, of ignoring them, of hiding them, and of blaming others for them, is replaced by the greater art of accepting the responsibility for them, of trying to learn from them, and of applying this knowledge so that we may avoid them in future.

7 How does it work?

Of course, the pupils have to get used to this unusual freedom. When they start their learning at this school, they feel a little bit lost by having the choice of what they would like to learn, and very often they misjudge their capabilities. Therefore we think that the coaching system — during the first two years, five pupils and one coach have one coaching lesson per week, planning their work — is not only very helpful, but very necessary to accompany this kind of education. In this context they can also think about what it means to make a 'mistake'. They have 8 years of experience of traditional thinking in traditional schools; in many of them, mistakes are still the thing to avoid because of the consequences. It takes time to rediscover the courage of a very young child who was learning naturally by trial and error. But it's worth persisting, and they learn to take decisions and to set priorities, plan their work and 'go through till the end'. Some of them (very few) do not get along with this freedom, they continue to ask for the traditional guidelines they are familiar with. Only one or two of them (out of more than 40 pupils) find out that this is not the right school for them.

Two classes graduated in 2002 and 2003. As our school is a public (or state) school, the graduation procedure is identical with that of other Austrian schools. Of course, there are some excellent examination results *at every* school — it is just that, at our school, *more* students achieve such outstanding results and win prizes and awards. The main source of frustration for the examinees is that they sometimes have to realize that they cannot show the wide range of their knowledge and, even more importantly, their abilities in

---

[4]If it is a question of processes of social change, the social engineer is in demand. If it is about communication and contact between individual people, the technological aspect would be doubtful and fortunately also ineffective.

[5]Popper (1944/1957), § 24, 'The Holistic Theory of Social Experiments'. Reprinted in Popper (1985), selection 24, § III.

the given examination time and structures. We are working on creative ways of modifying the situation. Nevertheless, both our team and the examination inspectors have been able to see that we are on the right track. Our basic principles are sound, there are many possibilities of improving our ways of implementing them — which means we should focus even more on independent and open learning — more searchlight and less '*Kübeltheorie*' [bucket theory].

8   Feedback and discussion

The discussions following the presentation at KARL POPPER 2002 showed a high level of agreement about the didactic methods of the Sir Karl Popper School. The pupils themselves influence the planning of the curriculum, they participate in the decision making about *what* and *how* learning will be done. One question was, 'And why do you give the children a suggestion at all, to which they can respond? Why don't you start with the children and first ask them what they want to learn? Then you can react to their suggestions.' We immediately took up this idea and put it into practice — it has proved very successful. The highly individual character of the teaching — by no means need everybody be learning the same thing at the same time — also met with great approval. In my opinion the most important objections related to the question 'segregational versus integrational promotion of gifted pupils'. Do the highly gifted need their own classes? And — how does this fit in with Popper's oft-stated aversion to everything elitist?

In our opinion the highly gifted do not need their own classes when schools are more prepared to give time and attention to the individual learning personalities, irrespective of their IQ. In a kind of laboratory situation the Sir Karl Popper School can try out such didactic methods and make its observations and findings available to other schools. (The Vienna Education Authority has a special programme for this purpose.) Of course, such observations about the development of learning capabilities — how does a child get from A to B in realizing his possibilities, wherever A is — may be made just as well or perhaps even better in heterogeneous classes. However, public interest and therefore also the financial means for such an experiment are currently easier to attract under the appealing label of the highly gifted. One can use this interest and at the same time play one's own game.

Bibliography

Bernard, C. (1865). *An Introduction to the Study of Experimental Medicine*. English translation 1927. New York: Henry Schuman, Inc.

Popper, K. R. (1944). 'The Poverty of Historicism, Part II. A Criticism of Historicist Methods.' *Economica* NS **XI**, pp. 119-137. Reprinted as Part III of Popper (1957). *The Poverty of Historicism*. London: Routledge & Kegan Paul.

———— (1975). 'The Rationality of Scientific Revolutions'. In R. Harré, editor (1975), pp. 72-101. *Problems of Scientific Revolution. Progress and Obstacles to Progress in the Sciences*. Clarendon Press, Oxford.

———— (1985). *Popper Selections*. Princeton: Princeton University Press. Originally published 1983. *A Pocket Popper*. London & Glasgow: Collins/ Fontana.

9

Popper in Iran

Ali Paya

Popper is a well-known figure in post-revolutionary Iran. Many of his books and short articles have been translated into Persian in the past two and half decades. Moreover, hot debates concerning his views have been going on in Iranian society since the victory of the Islamic revolution in 1978/1979.

In comparison, only a handful of Popper's works have been translated into the languages current in other Islamic countries, for example, Arabic and Turkish, and Popper's fame and influence in these countries are nowhere near the status he is enjoying in Iran.

Since I have discussed the political, cultural, and historical background to Popper's rise to fame in Iran elsewhere (Paya 2003, Paya & Ghaneirad 2006), in this paper I shall concentrate on a more critical assessment of Popper's impact. I shall do so by briefly discussing the quality of some of the Persian translations of Popper's works and the works produced by the Iranian writers on Popper. I shall also briefly evaluate the intellectual level of the debates concerning Popper's views. However, the material produced here should be regarded only as a supplement to the above papers.

Prior to the Islamic revolution in Iran only one of Popper's books, *The Poverty of Historicism* was translated into Persian.[1] Due to the unsatisfactory quality of the translation, the book was not received well by either the general public or the intellectuals. No review of the book appeared in the scholarly magazines and no discussion on its content ensued among the book-reading class (mostly students and academics). After the revolution, the same translator, Ahmad Ārām, who was a well-established translator with many translations from either English or French to his credit, translated five of Popper's other books.[2] According to many observers, the poor quality of these translations in which, apart from many unintelligible phrases, occasionally some paragraphs were missing, played some role in hampering the smooth reception of Popper's ideas among the educated public.

Other circumstantial evidence show that before the revolution, Popper was unknown to the majority of the educated public in Iran and to those who had a rudimentary familiarity with his name, he was an obscure pro-capitalist reactionary writer whose views were not worth pursuing.

---

[1] Popper (1944/1945). Details of the Persian translations of Popper's works can be found in the Bibliography.

[2] Popper (1959), (1963), (1972), 1982), (1983). See the Bibliography.

The following two examples are good cases in point. In 1974, Dr Houshang Nahavandi, the then chancellor of the University of Tehran and an ex-Marxist who had become a staunch supporter of the Royal regime, in pursuing a policy authorized by the shah, whose objective was to combat the influence of the Soviet-inspired left-wing propaganda on Iranian students, launched a project of translating a number of books by well-known European writers critical of Marxism. However, the translation of one of these books, namely, Popper's *Open Society and Its Enemies* was aborted through the influence exerted by the head of the Department of Political Sciences of the University, Dr Hamid Enayat, who was a first-rank political scientist with left-wing religious tendencies.[3] Similarly, when in 1976 Marcuse's & Popper's *Revolution or Reform?* was translated by a well-known Marxist translator, the impression it produced of Popper, in the heavily charged anti-Imperialism atmosphere of the day, was that Popper is a right-wing reactionary writer.

However, this situation was completely reversed during the first few years after mid-1978. A talented pharmacologist turned philosopher of science, Abdolkarim Soroush, published a series of short books that were based on Popper's views or the views of some his successors or peers. These books, *Dar Āmadi Enteghadi bar Tazad-e Dialectiki [A Critical Introduction to Dialectical Logic]* (1978a), inspired and informed by Popper's paper 'What is Dialectic?'; *Ideology-ye Sheitani (Dogmatism-e Neghabdar) [Satanic Ideology (Masked Dogmatism)]* (1978b), modelled on Heinz Post's 'Against Ideologies'; and *Falsafe Tarikh [Philosophy of History]* (1979), based on Popper's 'Prediction and Prophecy in the Social Sciences' and 'Utopia and Violence' (both in his 1963) and on Hempel's 'The Function of General Laws in History' (1942), which provided the young Muslim revolutionaries with a much needed theoretical tool in their ideological battle against various Marxist groups who were vying with the Islamic groups, drew the attention of the educated class, especially Muslim intellectuals with left-wing tendencies to the importance of themes in the Philosophy of Science in general and Popper's views in particular.

However, while various Marxist groups found it difficult to fight back against the ideas of the Viennese philosopher, another group of intellectuals, who came to be called 'the Heideggerians' and who were courting the more conservative clergy in the power hierarchy, launched a direct attack on Popper. The Heideggerians, were then and still are now, the most vociferous opponents of Popper's ideas in Iran.

The father figure of the group, an emeritus university Professor with a colourful background, Ahmad Fardid, in series of lectures at the University of Tehran that started barely three months after the victory of the revolution, expounded a theory that he claimed to be the true theoretical foundation of the Islamic revolution. In the course of these lectures, which made a considerable impact on some powerful sections of the conservative clergy, their

---

[3] This incident was related to me by Dr Ali Mortazaviyan, a sociologist and the elder brother of the would be translator of the book.

hard-line followers, and also some other intellectual groups with strong senti-ments for the 'Irano-Islamic tradition', Fardid criticized Popper for 'being one of those right-wingers who defends the *status quo* and is against all types of revolutions' (2003).

Fardid's theory, which was a mixture of themes from Hegel, Heidegger, and some Muslim mystics, couched in a pseudo-etymological wrapping, in a nutshell was that the history of mankind goes through distinct periods or eras, each being governed by one dominant 'name', which manifests the main features of that era. Each older era is replaced by a newer one whose time has come. The replacement takes place by means of a 'revolution' in the Aristotelian sense, namely through a change of essence. The names of the superseded eras would become the 'matter' for the new era whose 'form' is the new name. The latest era, which started in the Renaissance, is under the rule of the name of *Taghout* (devil) some of whose attributes are democracy, liberalism, human rights, and pluralism. With the appearance of this name history has come to an end. The history of tomorrow, which is akin to the history of the first era, belongs to the Imam Mahdi (the occult Imam who would reappear at the end of the Time). The Islamic revolution is not a 'revolution' in the proper sense of the word. It is a revolt that heralds and paves the way for the emergence of the rule of the occult Imam.

Fardid maintained that the liberals, both Iranian and foreign, are against Islam and the Islamic 'revolution', and he took it upon himself to expose those, in his view, who were representatives of such corrupting ideology. In this endeavour, Fardid had no qualms about resorting to ad hominem attacks and verbal abuse while talking about those personalities he regarded as being under the influence of the corrupt and corrupting Western ideologies.

For him Popper was a neo-positivist who was against holistic approaches to politics, history, art, and philosophy. In Fardid's view Popper's philosophy was the ideological weapon of the Western oppressors who intended to dominate the world through corrupting the minds of the people. 'The End of the Time is the time of *Dajjal* (the impostor, the deceiving leader). A time in which creatures like Popper defend Imperialism, the bourgeoisie, and the policy of "piecemeal reform" ' (Fardid 2003, p. 257). 'Open society is a society devoid of all the holy books and in which everything is expressed in the language of logic. The present era, in which false ideas and material desires rule, is such an open society. Closed society, is a society which contemplates the Absolute, the Whole and the Truth.'

Though a controversial, and certainly (in some quarters) an influential figure, Fardid rarely published his views and little has been written in critically assessing his ideas.[4]

---

[4]For a partial list for some such critical appraisals see my (2003) and Paya & Ghaneirad (2006). Recently, one of Fardid's ex-followers, Darius Ashouri, has produced a scathing attack (2004) on his mentor's ideas.

A young researcher, Mohammad Mansur Hashemi, who has obtained his PhD from the University of Tehran and has attended both my lectures and Davari's at the Department of Philosophy in that university, has published a book on Fardid and some of his most

Other Heideggerians, however, have not shied away from putting pen to paper. One of the most influential followers of Fardid, Dr Reza Davari, a Professor of Philosophy at the University of Tehran, Head of the Iranian Academy of Science, and a leading member of a number of other important bodies including the powerful 'Council for the Cultural Revolution', which oversees the activities of the universities, research centres, and other higher education institutes, has written extensively about Popper accusing him of being a propagandist for the hegemony of the West and a writer whose ideas are against religious beliefs and Islamic sentiments.

In a review of two partial translations of Popper's *Open Society and Its Enemies*[5] Davari claimed that Popper 'is a sophist who belongs to the Enlightenment movement of the Eighteenth century' (Davari 1985). '*Open Society* is a book in defence of the capitalist faction of the West and political liberalism and the enemies of this book are, in the first place, the thinkers and philosophers and in the second instance, Marxists and Fascists' (ibidem). 'Popper's school is critical rationalism (that is, idle inquisition).... Such reason is not compatible with any religious belief.... This reason is alien towards religion and is in line with the technological science that has replaced philosophy. However, this reason cannot render a noticeable service for Western civilization. Defence of the West in a world in which revolution has arrived is a difficult task, which cannot be done by an abject reason borrowed from the Eighteenth century' (ibidem).

In a reply to Davari, I pointed out that he has not only misrepresented many of Popper's key ideas by means of his misquotations, but also that he himself has failed to appreciate Popper's political views as well as his views concerning the methodologies of physical as well as social sciences. I tried to explain why, contrary to Davari, Popper is not a positivist, and why critical rationalism is not a reactionary school of thought in the service of Imperialism (Paya 1985).

Some other writers also responded to Davari's criticisms. Soroush criticized the views of those who ascribe essences to socially constructed entities such as Imperialism or Capitalism (Soroush 1984), and Akbar Ganji, an investigative journalist argued that the views of the Heideggerians, far from being a theoretical support for the revolutionaries, pave the way for Fascism (Ganji 1986).

In subsequent years Davari has consistently continued his attacks on Popper. In a recent book,[6] Davari, while trying to justify his own much criti-

---

prominent followers, including Davari. Hashemi's own position vis-à-vis these writers is critical. He has tried however to give equal space in his chapter on Fardid to the views of Fardid's opponents and sympathizers while expanding his own criticisms in a separate section (Hashemi 2004).

[5] At present three different Persian translations of *Open Society* are available. Only one, by Ezzatollah Fouladvand, is complete and definitive.

[6] *On a Critical Excursion into Carl Popper Philosophy* (Davari 2000). This English title appears on the cover of the book itself, but the correct translation of the Persian title seems to be: *A Critical Examination of Karl Popper's Philosophy*.

cized position vis-à-vis Popper's views and to repudiate some of his own earlier rather flimsy objections to Popper, has claimed that Popper is not a great philosopher and his views will not have any lasting effect on the future of philosophical thinking.

His fame in Iran after the revolution should be compared with that of Gustav le Bon (a second-rate French philosopher) popular in Iran in the 1930s and 1940s.

In Davari's view the reason for Popper's reputation in Iran is manyfold. He writes in a way that is easily comprehensible; does not tackle profound issues; never discusses the nature of things and regards the question of meaning as irrelevant; his philosophy is based on uncomplicated views; he is a critic of Marxism, which in the context of Iran gives him a favoured position; and he writes in the style of the writers of scientific books and therefore his books are appealing to those with a scientific background.

According to Davari, Popper, though against ideology in theory, has, in practice, the temperament and attitude of the ideologists. His fame in Iran is mainly due to the distinctions he makes between people's 'motives/intentions' and their 'asserted views' [that is, the distinction between the context of discovery and the context of justification] and between 'is' and 'ought'; his support of piecemeal engineering against revolution; the possibility of dialogue among various groups regardless of their differing fundamental principles; his criticism of induction, his principle of falsifiability and his theory of the three worlds. However, in Davari's views none of these issues can be regarded as significant philosophical themes.

Davari concluded that while some of Popper's works may have shed some light on methodological problems of modern science, this is not enough to make him a great philosopher. Whereas Heidegger *is* a truly great philosopher to the extent that any attempt to make a comparison between him and Popper should be regarded as a result of either ignorance or misunderstanding.

Davari maintains that while Heidegger has tackled profound philosophical issues, for example, the identification of modern science as one of the attributes of modernity and has discussed this issue at length and in depth, Popper has done nothing comparable. Popper, as Habermas has correctly observed, is a positivist.

While Davari's book is long on its list of superficial criticisms it is woefully short on proper argumentation. There are many occasions in which the author, rather innocently, betrays his complete lack of understanding of the issues at hand. Thus for instance, in criticizing the distinction that Popper adopts between the contexts of discovery and justification, Davari after a confused discussion states that one of the flaws of this theory is that 'it gives an opportunity to the wrong-doers to justify their wrong actions and claim that they had good intentions' (p. 47). Davari even approvingly quotes Fardid's claim that 'Popper is an existentialist [in the Sartrean tradition]' (ibidem, pp. 61f.). Fardid maintained that Sartre's philosophy, contrary to that of Heidegger, was devoid of deep understanding. While the goal of the Heideggerian philosophy was to go beyond the debates about objectivity and subjectivity, Sartre has remained in the realm of subjectivity. In this sense his philosophy is 'one-eyed' (2003, p. 256).

> Popper is just like this. This man has not even read the basics of philosophy. However, he shares a similar position with Sartre in being 'one-eyed'. The task of all these *philosophers* is to shepherd the people into the deceit of the End of the Time. ... *Dajjal* is a dodderer who has an ass. ... Now Jean-Paul Sartre and these philosophers are the asses on which Dajjal is mounted. These are the asses of the End of the Time whose dung they have fed into the mouths of the people.

In 1997 a younger member of the Heideggerian group, Bijan Abdolkarimi, who had studied philosophy in India, published a book entitled *Thought and Politics*, in which he tried to develop a political philosophy based on the ideas of Plato re-interpreted in the light of Heidegger's views. The second appendix of this book was devoted to a critical assessment of Popper's portrayal of Plato. Abdolkarimi's main objections, reminiscent of some of Davari's criticisms, are that Popper's criticisms of Plato are mostly ideological and political without proper attention to the philosophical basis of Plato's views; Popper has not considered the relation between Plato's objectives and his philosophical principles and therefore has produced a caricature of Plato's philosophy, for example, without paying attention to the Platonic theory of 'the Good' Popper has accused Plato of being racist and elitist; Popper, despite his own criticism of sociologism, falls into the trap of this type of explanation in his discussions of Plato, Marx, and Hegel; Popper accuses Plato of historicism, whereas Plato acknowledges the role which can be played by chance or unknown forces; Popper, in his assessment of Plato's views does not apply his own criterion of fasifiability in a consistent way (*sic*) in that he disregards the refuting evidence and only concentrates on cases that could 'prove his own ideological understanding' of Plato; and finally, Popper accuses Plato of being utopianist while he himself is one of the greatest utopianists of our age.

While Popper himself has acknowledged that his treatment of Plato's philosophy in his *Open Society* was not meant to cover all aspects of Plato's thought, it seems that his most outspoken Iranian critics have found no better argument than to hold the philosophical high moral ground of assuming the mantle of Plato's defenders without in any substantial way engaging with Popper's complex views.

In today's Iran, Popper's views are, by and large, and to varying degrees, known to a large portion of the educated public. His views have inspired a good number of the decision-makers since 1978. However, the ultra-conservative religious establishment and their hard-line followers, as well as some groups of intellectuals, still regard his views as dangerous and troublesome. It remains to be seen whether in the wake of the recent victory of the hard-liners in the Presidential election the theories of the Viennese thinker will still be tolerated and regarded as sources of inspiration or will be considered as an unwelcome intellectual heritage.

Bibliography

Abdolkarimi, B. (1997). *Tafakkor va Siyasat* [*Thought and Politics*]. Tehran: Entesharat-e Elmi va Farhangi.

Ashouri, D. (2004). 'Ustore-ye Falsafeh Fardid dar Miyan-e Ma' ['The Myth of Fardid's Philosophy Amongst Us']. http://www.Nilgoon.org/cgibin/ashouri_on_Fardid.pl/.

Davari, R. (1985). 'Molahezati dar bareh *Jameh Baz va Doshmanan-e An*' ['Observations Concerning *The Open Society and Its Enemies*']. *Kayhān-e Farhangi* **2**, 8, pp. 23-26.

———— (2000). *Seyri Enteghadi dar Fasefeh Carl Popper* [*A Critical Examination of Karl Popper's Philosophy*]. Tehran: Cultural Institute for Contemporary Knowledge and Thought

Fardid, S. A. (2003). *Didar-e Farrahi va Futuhat-e Akher al-Zaman* [*The Idea of Charisma and the Openings of the End of Time*]. Edited by M. Madadpur. Tehran: Nazar Publications.

Ganji, A. (1986). 'Gharb Setizi, Dindari, va . . .' ['Challenging the West, Keeping Faith, and . . .']. *Kayhān-e Farhangi* **3**, 5, pp. 11-16.

Hashemi, M. M. (2004). *Hoviyat Andishän va Miras-e Fekri-ye Ahmad Fardid* [*The Essentialists and the Intellectual Legacy of Ahmad Fardid*]. Tehran: Enteshart-e Kavir.

Hempel. C. G. (1942). 'The Functions of General Laws in History'. *The Journal of Philosophy* **39**, pp. 35-48. Reprinted as Chapter 9 of C. G. Hempel (1965). *Aspects of Explanation*. New York: Free Press.

Marcuse, H. & Popper, K. R. (1971). *Revolution oder Reform?: eine Konfrontation*. Munich: Kösel-Verlag. English edition, 1976. *Revolution or Reform: A Confrontation*. Chicago: New University Press. Persian translation by H. Vaziri (1976). *Enghelab Ya Eslah?* Tehran: Khawrazmi Publications.

Paya, A. (1985). 'Jāmeh-e Bāz va Jāmeh-e Basteh' ['The Open Society and the Closed Society']. *Kayhān-e Farhangi* **2**, 12, pp. 18-22.

———— (2003). 'Karl Popper and the Iranian Intellectuals'. *American Journal of Islamic Social Sciences* **20**, pp. 50-79.

Paya, A. & Ghaneirad, M. A. (2006). 'The Philosopher and the Revolutionary State: How Karl Popper's Ideas Shaped the Views of Iranian Intellectuals'. *International Studies in the Philosophy of Science* **20**, pp. 185-213.

Popper, K. R. (1944-1945). 'The Poverty of Historicism'. *Economica* NS **XI**, 1944, pp. 86-103, 119-137; NS **XII**, 1945, pp. 69-89. Reprinted as K. R. Popper (1957). *The Poverty of Historicism*. London: Routledge & Kegan Paul. Persian translation by A. Ārām (1971). *Faghr-e Tarikhigari*. Tehran: Khawrazmi Publications.

———— (1959). *The Logic of Scientific Discovery*. London: Hutchinson. Persian translation by A. Ārām (1985). *Manteqh-e Ekteshāf-e Elmi*. Tehran: Soroush Publications.

———— (1963). *Conjectures and Refutations*. London: Routledge & Kegan Paul. Persian translation by A. Ārām (1986). *Hads-hā va Ebtalhā: Roshd-e Shenakht-e Elmi*. Tehran: Soroush Publications.

———— (1972). *Objective Knowledge*. Oxford: Clarendon Press. Persian translation by A. Ārām (1996). *Ma'refat-e E'ini*. Tehran: Soroush Publications.

———— (1982). *The Open Universe*. London: Hutchinson. Persian translation by A. Ārām (1996). *Jahan-e Bāz*. Tehran: Soroush Publications.

———— (1983). *Realism and the Aim of Science*. London: Hutchinson. Persian translation by A. Ārām (1996). *Vāgh' Grāee va Hadaf-e E'lm*. Tehran: Soroush Publications.

———— (1994). *The Myth of the Framework*. London: Routledge. Persian translation by A. Paya (2000). *Ostoreh-e Charcoob*. Tehran: Tarh-e Nou Publications.

Post, H. R. (1976). 'Against Ideologies'. *Inaugural Lecture*, Chelsea College London.

Soroush, A. (1978a). *Dar Amadi Enteghadi bar Tazad-e Dialectiki* [*A Critical Introduction to Dialectical Logic*]. Tehran: Yärän Publications. 2nd edition 1981.

———— (1978b). *Ideology-ye Sheitani (Dogmatism-e Neghabdar)*[*Satanic Ideology (Masked Dogmatism)*]. Tehran: Yärän Publications.

———— (1979). *Falsafe Tarikh* [*Philosophy of History*]. Tehran: Yärän Publications.

———— (1984). 'Voojud va Mahiyat-e Gharb' ('The "Existence" and the "Essence" of the West']. *Kayhān-e Farhangi* **1**, 5, pp. 19-22.

PART 2
Values in a World of Facts

10

Popper and Nationalism

Andrew Vincent

In one of his last public lectures, in Prague in 1994, Popper remarked in glowing terms upon the figure of Tomáš Masaryk, seeing him as 'the great founder of the Republic of Czechoslovakia, and its Liberator President'. Popper continued, 'I deeply admire Masaryk. He was one of the most important pioneers of what I have called, . . . the open society. He was a pioneer of an open society, both in theory and in practice — indeed, the greatest of its pioneers between Abraham Lincoln and Winston Churchill.' However, the glowing tribute had a sting in the tail. He noted that[1]

> there was from the beginning an unnecessary weakness built into the structure of the Czechoslovakian open society. I am alluding to the so-called 'principle of national self-determination', a principle that had acquired an almost absolute moral authority in the West . . . . And Masaryk's open society was unable to give these claims a deeply considered moral and political response.

Popper continues: 'I think that all lovers of peace and a civilized life should work to enlighten the world about the impracticability and inhumanity of that famous — or shall I say it notorious? — "principle of national self-determination", which has now degenerated into the ultimate horror of ethnic terrorism'.[2] From the 1950s Popper articulated a deeply influential perspective on nationalism, which was uniformly negative, and, fortuitously, encapsulated a cold war mentality. Nationalism was considered a characteristically 'closed ideology' — akin to totalitarianism — and the precise opposite of liberalism. In 2002, Popper's views are doubly interesting, since the last decade has not only seen a practical renaissance of nationalism in the politics of Europe and elsewhere, but also growing, and, at times, immensely enthusiastic

---

[1] See Popper (1999), Chapter 14. The lecture may be read also on line at the website www.lf3.cuni.cz/aff/p2_e.html/.

[2] Ibidem. The grounding of this idea in 1994 can be found clearly stated in the much earlier *Open Society*. Popper asks in this book, 'how anybody . . . could ever have put forward such an inapplicable principle, is hard to understand'. His answer is that Wilson (and Masaryk) 'fell a victim to a movement that sprang from the most reactionary and servile political philosophy that had ever been imposed upon meek and long-suffering mankind. He fell a victim to his upbringing in the metaphysical political theories of Plato and of Hegel, and to the nationalist movement based upon them' (1945, Chapter 12, § III).

academic literature, trying to provide a distinctively benign benediction to nationalism.[3]

This paper focuses, first, on Popper's critical views of nationalism and examines his reasons as to why it should be seen as a suspect mode of thought and practice. The second section of the paper analyses Popper's political solutions to the nationalist mentality. The third section offers some critical evaluations.

1 Popper and nationalism

Popper's indictment of nationalism is wholesale. There are no distinctions in his work between acceptable and unacceptable nationalisms.[4] All nationalist beliefs are considered absurd. He comments, for example, that, in speaking of national self-determination, he is not just alluding to 'Hitler's racial myth', or the like. He continues, 'What I have in mind is, rather, an alleged natural right of man — *the alleged right of a nation to self-determination*. That even a great humanitarian and liberal like Masaryk could uphold this absurdity as one of the natural rights of man is a sobering thought'.[5] However, it would be true that he never formally structured his ideas on this issue, except via certain critiques, such as that of Hegel in *The Open Society*. However, Popper's objections to nationalism can be broken down into four sets of claims: philosophical, sociological, moral, and historico-practical.

1.1 Philosophical

First, much of what Popper has to say on nationalism is underpinned by his conception of *philosophy* (and the role of the human mind in knowledge

---

[3]Contemporary liberal interest in nationalism is premised upon a twofold classification — which Popper does not appear to acknowledge. John Plamenatz, and the slightly earlier work of Hans Kohn, typify this classification. Kohn, for example, divided nationalism into two opposed types: Western and Eastern. His distinction keeps reappearing — in slightly different dress — in debate through the 1990s. The former, premised on Enlightenment values of reason and universalist humanism, was aimed at a more open, plural, outward-looking society. It tended towards democracy, liberalism, and constitutional rule. The latter was more overtly authoritarian, closed, inward-looking, bellicose, and xenophobic. Plamenatz echoed this distinction directly. He distinguished, like Kohn, between an acceptable 'moderate' Western liberal nationalism and a more bellicose East European cultural nationalism. For Plamenatz, many critics (Popper may well have been in his mind) saw the whole of nationalism as tainted with illiberalism. See Kohn (1945) and Plamenatz (1976), pp. 23ff. It is usually the liberal variant that has been enthusiastically picked up by academic political theorists during the 1990s. There appear to be three major elements to the liberal nationalist case. First, there is the communitarian-like argument that we are socially contextual or embedded beings. We are constituted through the community and its values. Second, nations make up a part of our identity. Identity is deserving of respect. The principle of respect obliges us to respect that 'which in others constitutes any part of their sense of their own identity'. The third component of liberal nationalist argument, which follows closely upon the previous points, entails specific recommendations for political arrangements. Nationalism can underpin liberal individuality and democracy, although some add that nations are not necessarily coincidental with states (Vincent 2002, Chapter 4).

[4]See Vincent (2002), pp. 87f.; Spencer & Wollman 2002, Chapter 4.

[5]Popper (1963), Chapter 19, p. 367.

construction). For Popper,[6]

> the rise of philosophy itself can be interpreted,... as a response to the breakdown of the closed society and its magical beliefs. It is an attempt to replace the lost magical faith by a rational faith; it modifies the tradition of passing on a theory or a myth by founding a new tradition — a tradition of challenging theories and myths.

Philosophy, quite bluntly, arises from the questioning of and progress away from doctrines such as nationalism. Philosophy, as a discipline, may well be embedded in a tradition, but it is, unlike any nationalist understanding, a 'critical rationalist tradition'. It is thus a concept of tradition that is intrinsically antagonistic to the conception of a closed society. Thus, to practise genuine philosophy is, by definition, to move outside nationalism. One cannot therefore be a nationalist and a genuine philosopher. Popper suggests that the singular importance of tribe or nation inevitably becomes suspect as soon as more sophisticated rational intelligence develops. At the most simple level, careful observation of the differing taboos of other tribes or nations is enough to alert us to their ontological and epistemological constraints.[7]

Further, for Popper, the development of philosophy should be regarded as an individual and not a collective enterprise. This implies that philosophy, as a practice, ought to work against the grain of the collective sentiment. It is not surprising, in this context, that Socrates symbolized for Popper the philosophical enterprise — an enterprise betrayed of course by Plato. Consequently, as philosophy replaces magic and irrationalism, so it must also replace nationalism.[8] Tangentially, it is not surprising, in the context of nationalism's link with the irrational, that Popper (with his early Viennese interests in psychology) should also suggest a connection between nationalism and neurosis and collective hysteria.[9] Nationalism, in his sense, might best be considered a pathology, rather than a legitimate theory of politics. In this sense, the best way to understand nationalism (and the nationalist) might be through some form of psychoanalytic study.

If one extrapolates here, there is also a theory of mind that underpins Popper's conception of the nation. Popper calls this the 'bucket theory'. It envisages the mind as 'a container — a kind of bucket — in which perceptions and knowledge accumulate'; essentially the mind is seen as a passive recipient.[10] It is not too much of a leap to seeing this as a theory of mind more compatible with the closed society, namely, where the mind is simply filled up, uncritically, with, for example, national norms, traditions, and prejudices. Popper favours, conversely, what he calls the 'searchlight view of mind',

---

[6](1945), Chapter 10, § IV.

[7]Ibidem, Chapter 5, § II.

[8]For Popper, the nationalist lives in a 'charmed circle' embodying 'unchanging taboos, ... laws and customs which are felt to be as inevitable as the rising of the sun'. See (1945), Chapter 5, ¶ 2.

[9]Ibidem, Chapter 12, note 19.

[10]Popper (1949a/1972), p. 341.

namely, where the mind is considered an active constructive participant in knowledge of the world, both reacting to sense perceptions and organizing experience in certain ways. As Popper notes, this latter theory implies that 'we must most actively engage ourselves in searching, comparing, unifying, generalizing, if we wish to attain knowledge'.[11] The searchlight theory also has direct connections to Popper's conjecture and falsification thesis. Consequently it implies genuine science and philosophical rationalism. The searchlight theory is therefore incompatible with the 'closed mentality' of nationalism.

Popper also sees an indirect connection between the passive theory of mind, nationalism, and the sociology of knowledge. He focuses, for example, on one facet of Hegel's thinking here — which also underpins the historicism thesis — namely the idea that human reason 'must coincide with the historical development of his society, i.e. of the nation to which he belongs'.[12] In other words, reason is not an independent faculty, it rather mutates historically. Knowledge and reason therefore become historically relativized. The mind of the individual is consequently seen as passively 'filled up' by the norms of the historical moment. If one shifts this argument to Marx, then the individual's mind is occupied by the norms of their social class. For Popper, the upshot of this whole position is the Mannheimian sociology of knowledge thesis, namely, that all knowledge claims become sociologically conditioned. For Popper this thesis is fundamentally flawed. Reason is not something dependent on class or historical circumstance, it is rather an ahistorical and asocial 'attitude of readiness to listen to critical arguments and learn from experience'. We should not therefore be misled by the idea of learning about rationality *within* a society. As Popper comments: 'if I say, for example, that we owe our reason to "society", then I always mean that we owe it to certain concrete individuals'.[13] In other words, reason is always concerned with mature individuals, within a society, coming to decisions through a rigorous process of self-criticism and communicating that method to others.

For Popper there is one marked difference between Marx and Hegel. For Popper, Marx, unlike Hegel, was a committed 'rationalist'. Popper notes: 'With Socrates, and with Kant, he [Marx] believed in human reason as the basis of the unity of mankind.'[14] Marx had the great virtue of being contemptuous of nationalism. For this view Popper was prepared to forgive a great deal. However Marx's fundamental mistake was to suggest that our reason was 'determined by class interest'; this, in turn, hastened the decline of reason into the sociology of knowledge. As Popper notes, 'Like Hegel's doctrine that our ideas are determined by national interests and traditions, Marx's doctrine tended to undermine the rationalist belief in reason'.[15] This argument effectively destroyed the possibility of intellectual discussion.[16] As Popper observes,

[11] (1945), Chapter 23.
[12] Ibidem.
[13] Ibidem, Chapter 24, § I.
[14] Ibidem, Chapter 24, proem.
[15] Ibidem.
[16] Ibidem, Chapter 23.

discussion in this 'sociology of knowledge' always rapidly moves away from rational criticism towards a form of 'socio-therapy', which becomes obsessed with unveiling the repressed motives of the thinkers — an idea not unfamiliar to postmodern deconstruction and genealogy.[17]

1.2 Sociological

One central dimension of nationalist thinking is the now familiar idea (specifically from recent communitarian thought) that human beings are embedded within their communities, that is, human identity is constituted through and by membership.[18] This constitutive process is achieved through different media, although language and culture are most commonly cited by nationalists. Admittedly, this contention is not particularly clear; however, Popper has a number of general objections to this whole sociologically-inspired way of thinking. The most obvious objection is that the idea of collective moral identity is just false. Identity can never be collective. It is always individual. Even if nations collapse or disappear, one can and should still defend individual human identity. He thus notes that 'human individuals and not states or nations must be the ultimate concern even of international organizations'.[19] For Popper, nothing of significance attaches to national identity. Those who try to attach identity claims to nations are peddling falsehoods.

The most common adjective that Popper attaches to nationalism is the term 'tribal' — to which he also often appends the word 'instinct'. He suggests that 'tribal instinct' is the most primitive form of human drive. In a similar vein to writers such as Spencer, Maine, Tönnies or Hayek, Popper suggests that this instinctive drive is something that we need to *evolve* away from. Parallel to the manner in which philosophy develops, Popper equates the movement away from the closed society as a form of social evolution. In fact, he characterizes this movement as one of the most significant processes through 'which mankind has passed'.[20] Mature, evolved, and rational societies no longer manifest this tribal instinct. The 'tribal urge' remains though as a threatening subtext — a regressive possibility within the human species. There is, therefore, what Popper calls, a 'perennial fight against it' and a need for continuous philosophical vigilance.[21] In this context, phenomena such as nationalism and totalitarianism are both grouped under the 'tribal instinct' category. In *The Open Society* Popper also saw ancient Greek theories (Plato) manifesting this 'tribal' character. The tribalist baton is then seen picked up by eighteenth- and early nineteenth-century German thinkers — Hegel and

---

[17]Popper comments that the sociology of knowledge 'can be considered as a Hegelian version of Kant's theory knowledge' (ibidem, text to note 2).

[18]For an analysis of the relation between nationalism and contemporary communitarianism, see Vincent 2002, Chapter 6.

[19]Popper (1945), Chapter 9, § VII.

[20]Ibidem, Chapter 10, § 1.

[21]Ibidem, Introduction, p. 1. Popper comments: 'the magical or tribal or collectivist society will also be called the *closed society*, and the society in which individuals are confronted with personal decisions, the *open society*'. Ibidem, Chapter 10, § I.

Fichte being singled out. The important point to note here is that Popper saw *all* assertions of nationalism as evolutionary regression.

The other worrying aspect of the 'national' mentality for Popper was its link with the concept of race. Racial identification often had a direct conceptual and practical connection to nationalism (and thus European anti-Semitism in Popper's mind) during the later nineteenth and twentieth centuries. Racialism and nationalism were thus frequent bedfellows, rather as Isaiah Berlin noted, 'racial hatreds seem to be at the core of the most hideous expressions of violent collective emotion'.[22] It is worth reminding ourselves here that for Popper, unlike Berlin, Zionism was the worst example of nationalism. In fact, Zionism was also a form of racism. In an interview Popper remarked, for example, that 'Of all the countries benefiting from European civilizations, only South Africa and Israel have racial laws that distinguish between rights of different groups of citizens. The Jews were against Hitler's racism, but theirs goes one step further. They determine Jewishness by mother alone. I opposed Zionism initially because I was against any form of nationalism, but I never expected the Zionists to become racists. It makes me feel ashamed in my origin'.[23] Thus, not all nationalists are overtly racist; nonetheless, the nationalist perspective opens the door to the racial idea.[24]

For Popper, nationalism — as a clear example of a closed tribal mentality — contradicts a basic fact about modern societies, namely, that individuals are primary, both morally and methodologically. True individualism is therefore incompatible with nationalism. In this context, it is important to emphasize that Popper would have regarded the more recent claim that nationalism can underpin individualism and liberal democracy as simply laughable.[25] Popper, of course, would not deny the widespread instinctive appeal of the 'nation', however it 'owes its popularity solely to the fact that ... it is the cheapest and surest method by which a politician who has nothing better to offer can make his way'.[26] Thus, it is crude *Realpolitik* and political vacuity that ensures the continual reappearance of nationalist sentiment.

1.3 Moral

Another substantive nationalist claim focuses on the purported moral significance of nations. The basic argument is that if nations make up a part of our identity and identity is deserving of respect, then the principle of respect obliges us to respect what in others constitutes any part of their sense of their own identity. Thus, if the nation constitutes a significant part of human identity, this implies the necessity of a basic respect for nations. However, Popper contends that the principle of collective identity is spurious. Identity is *always* an individual matter. Further, for Popper, morality can be only a

---

[22]Berlin (1990), p. 252.

[23]Interview with Popper quoted in Hacohen (2000), p. 305, note 49.

[24]The concept race though remains slightly vague.

[25]For a critical discussion of recent liberal nationalism, see Vincent (2002), Chapter.4, and also Vincent (1997).

[26]Popper (1945), Chapter 9, note 7.

matter of individual, not collective, responsibility. Thus it is false to locate any moral considerations within nations. To place morality into a national setting is a duplicitous way of relieving 'men of the strain of their responsibilities'.[27] Nationalist argument about morality shuffles off moral responsibility to collective entities.

Popper can see why this kind of nationalist argument appears. He notes, for example, that in more primitive societies the 'tribal community (and later the "city") is the place of security for the member of the tribe'.[28] To appeal to the nation takes the moral weight off the shoulders of the individual. However, as societies mature, rationality should grow and individuals are asked increasingly to take moral responsibility upon themselves. Therefore genuine civilization creates, as Popper notes, a 'straining away from the social', by the demand for individuals rationally to control their own lives. This, he says, is the price of growing knowledge. The reality is that 'the future depends on ourselves', it does not depend upon any historical or national necessity.[29] Popper is adamant on this issue of individual moral responsibility and condemns all suggestions either that nations are the source of morality, or that they are morally significant in themselves. He remarks that '[m]any are ready to die for [the nationalist religion], fervently believing that it is morally good, and factually true. But they are mistaken; just as mistaken as their communist bedfellows. Few creeds have created more hatred, cruelty, and senseless suffering than the belief in the righteousness of the nationality principle'.[30] Nationalism basically indicates a lack of moral sense and civilization.

1.4 Historico-practical

A fourth line of substantive criticism focuses on the purported *historical* and *practical* reality of nations. For Popper, no one seems to be able to explain precisely what a nation is empirically or historically. Furthermore, there is no adequate account of how nations actually relate to politics. He comments that 'none of the theories which maintain that a nation is united by a common origin, or a common language, or a common history, is acceptable, or applicable in practice'. On the practical side, Popper continues that the 'principle of the national state is not only inapplicable but it has never been clearly conceived. It is a myth. It is an irrational, a romantic and Utopian dream, a dream of naturalism and of tribal collectivism'.[31] His case is that if one observes empirically (via presumably a falsification method) the majority of societies in the world, the fact is that they virtually all contain multiple subgroups. He continues, 'no doubt, a homogeneous population that speaks one language has a tremendous advantage for the purpose of industrial collaboration; but where do you find this in Europe? Europe just is not like this, except in very

---

[27] Ibidem, Introduction.
[28] Ibidem, Chapter 10, § II.
[29] Ibidem, Introduction.
[30] Popper (1963), Chapter 19, pp. 368f.
[31] Popper (1945), Chapter 12, § III.

few countries where it has been brought about, by political and educational means, to suppress minorities or dialects.' The only exceptions are Iceland and Malta. In consequence, Popper expresses stark amazement that the idea of national self-determination should still be spoken of so readily in politics. He continues that, 'just a little thought should have told us all that this "principle" is totally inapplicable in Europe, where even islands like Great Britain, Ireland, or Cyprus are populated by several so-called nationalities ... '.[32]

In terms of certain Austrian and German sensibilities in the 1920s and 1930s, Popper adds an idiosyncratic historical rider to the above point, namely, that the Versailles Treaty (1919) was not actually mistaken or wrongheaded at all, except insofar as it promulgated, with President Wilson's absurd blessing, the idea of nationalism and self-determination. He continues 'the terrible effect of Wilson's attempt to apply this romantic principle to European politics should be clear by now to everybody. That the Versailles settlement was harsh, is a myth. ... Versailles failed mainly because of the attempt to apply Wilson's inapplicable principles'.[33] The concept of national self-determination, which in his estimation, caused major problems wherever it occurred, is something that should be unceremoniously dumped from international relations. As Popper opined, 'I refuse to abandon the hope that the absurdity and cruelty of this alleged moral principle will one day be recognized by all thinking men'.[34]

These historical and practical points are reinforced by Popper's insistence on what he frequently refers to as the conceptual nonsense of 'nation state' compound.[35] For Popper, 'nation-states', at an empirical level, 'do not exist'.[36] States remain but they do not coincide with nations. There are no empirically identifiable unified homogenous ethnic groups coinciding with states. The overt empirical evidence supporting this point is that ethnic groups, dialects, and different linguistic assemblages mingle everywhere. Popper raises a further point here, namely, that given that most human beings encounter multiple forms of group life on an everyday basis, then it is not at all clear why nationalism is more important than other loyalties.[37] What, in other

---

[32] See Popper (1999), Chapter 14; and also http://www.lf3.cuni.cz/aff/p2_e.html/.

[33] Popper (1945), Chapter 13, note 2.

[34] Popper (1963), Chapter 19, p. 369.

[35] He remarked that 'the utter absurdity of the principle of self-determination must be plain to anybody who devotes a moment's effort to criticizing it' (ibidem, p. 368).

[36] For Popper, states unlike individuals can never be 'natural' (1945, Chapter 9, note 7): *'there are no natural boundaries to a state'* and

> the attempt to find some 'natural' boundaries for states, and accordingly, to look upon the state as a 'natural' unit, leads to the *principle of the national state* and to the romantic fictions of nationalism, racialism, and tribalism. But this principle is not 'natural', and the idea that there exist natural units like nations, or linguistic or racial groups, is entirely fictitious. Here, if anywhere, we should learn from history; for since the dawn of history, men have been continually mixed, unified, broken up, and mixed again.

[37] This point has (I believe) wider ramifications vis à vis his views on the Habsburgs. See Popper, ibidem, Chapter 12, § III.

words, are the grounds for allotting nationalism some kind of priority? For Popper no adequate answers exist to any of these questions.

2 Popper's alternatives

Popper's alternatives to nationalism are contained in three basic overlapping themes, all rooted in early twentieth-century Viennese politics. The three themes are, again, never really systematized by Popper and become obscured in the cold-war era. The three themes are Kantian socialism, cosmopolitanism, and a deep-rooted admiration for the political and juristic idea of multicultural federation. The underpinning for the latter theme is embedded in his peculiar esteem for the Habsburg Empire.

2.1 Kantian socialism

The first point to note about Popper, which is one often remarked upon by commentators, is that in *The Open Society*, Marx comes off far better than Hegel. This was not just because Marx was a rationalist and anti-nationalist who went 'socially' wrong; rather that, at a certain stage, Popper was both politically and morally very sympathetic to Marx. However, this should not be misinterpreted. For Popper, crudely, there were two Marxes. The first was a dogmatic heavily positivist Marx, caught in a crude materialist teleology, a debilitating historicist legacy (culminating in the sociology of knowledge), a class-based determinism (collapsing into a form of relativism equally as damaging as nationalism), a form of pseudo-science embodying false prophetic utterances (historicism) and containing deeply ambiguous and confused views concerning important values such as individualism, democracy, and freedom. This Marx was rejected by Popper. The other Marx — who was not the 'young Marx', since this perspective was not available to Popper — was a fellow rationalist and progressive. This second Marx was appealing to Popper for certain very basic reasons. This was the Marx who was motivated by issues of social adversity and poverty and advocated forms of social engineering to deal with them. As one recent scholar remarks, the Popper (of *The Open Society*) was genuinely distressed by 'the poverty that he had witnessed in his youth and during the depression' (that is, in Vienna); consequently, '[e]liminating poverty would be the major goal of his future proposed reforms, and he would see the disappearance of poverty from much of the Western Hemisphere as one of humanity's greatest achievements'. Thus, '[r]ather than condemning Marxism as secular religion and pseudoscience, Popper maintained that Marxism's failure was the result of an improper synthesis of faith and reason, prophecy and science.'[38]

Another reason why this second version of Marx comes to the fore, for Popper, was connected to a significant change within European Marxism in the late nineteenth and the early part of the twentieth century. This was the philosophical rapprochement between Marxism and Kantian philosophy,

---

[38]Hacohen (2000), pp. 46, 64, and 447.

which was an aspect of a much larger revival of Kantianism. The initial leaders in Germany were Friedrich Albert Lange and Otto Liebermann, although a number of distinct schools of Kantianism in fact developed. Kantianism was, amongst other things, an attempt to rehabilitate philosophy against the claims of positivism, as well as standing firm against philosophical idealism. Kantians also saw philosophy as an indispensable, if constrained activity, focusing on the critique of knowledge. However, in defending philosophy, Kantianism also offered a profound response to critics of the natural sciences. All these tendencies were deeply attractive for Popper, who resolutely refused to take either the linguistic turn or the move to logical positivism. The other important dimension of Kantianism was its rational validation of a universal ethics. This latter tendency is well known. However, what is of greater interest, in terms of Popper's own sentiments in the 1920s and 1930s, is another adjunct to Kantian ethics, namely, the development a philosophical rapprochement between Kantian ethics and Marxian socialism.

There were two dimensions to this latter rapprochement. The initial ideas developed in the Marburg Kantian school, that is, in the writings of Hermann Cohen and Paul Natorp. Cohen particularly held that Kant's ethics provided a quite definite foundation for socialism. Kantian ethics argued that all humans should be treated as ends and never as means, which, for Cohen, translated into the principle that no worker should be treated as a commodity. Kantian ethics also implied that socialism and equality were something that rationally *ought to be*. The second dimension of the socialism/Kantianism rapprochement came from within Marxism itself, that is Marxists who found within Kantianism a serviceable epistemology and moral philosophy. In Germany, Eduard Bernstein was probably one of the higher profile converts to Kantian Marxism, although in terms of more systematic writing on this issue, Carl Vörlander was the more sophisticated theoretician in writings such as *Marx und Kant* (1911). In addition, Kant's ideas were associated with radical notions of social democracy and moral and social progress to greater social and economic equality. They were also seen as compatible with many of the themes scientific socialism. These general themes on a Kantian-based socialism were influential in the school of Austro-Marxists in the early 1900s, for example, Max Adler. The same radical Kantian movement can be seen in Britain in terms of new or social liberal theorizing — although that is tangential to the present discussion.

It is in the above context that we should view Popper's socialist interests. Popper clearly viewed his own perspective (in epistemology and politics) as radically neo-Kantian. Thus, Hacohen is correct, I believe, to remark that Popper's *The Open Society* and *The Poverty of Historicism* make 'no sense when read in the cold war context'. Popper's political perspective was rooted in a German and Austrian neo-Kantianism, a detail that Popper later omitted to say much about. Popper also admired Eduard Bernstein — the arch-Kantian revisionist. Like Bernstein, Popper believed that Kant showed the way forward for socialism.[39] Hacohen observes here that Popper's philosophical roots were clearly in neo-Kantian writers such as Leonard Nelson and Julius Kraft. He thus remarks that in terms of Kraft's *Von Husserl zu Heidegger* (1932) and *Die Unmöglichkeit der Geisteswissenschaft* (1934) '[t]oday, these books read almost as sequels to *The Open Society*'. Thus, he continues, Popper's central ideas during this early period 'belonged to Kant'.[40]

In this context, Popper's *Open Society* can be viewed as 'the work of an unorthodox socialist coming to terms with his ambivalence about socialism'.[41] Although some of these themes had become submerged by the 1940s and *The Open Society* took on a different hue, certainly for his American audience, nonetheless, the themes of Kantian ethical socialism still underpin Popper's political sensibilities. They certainly informed his post-1945 — what I would call — 'social liberalism'. In essence — as in British social liberal debates in the early part of the twentieth century — Popper was concerned to eliminate poverty, constrain free markets, protect individual liberty, and uphold public order and the rule of law. *The Open Society* was therefore part of a social democratic (or social liberal) structure of ideas, which provided a social-reform platform for the welfare state. Popper's first alternative to nationalism is therefore a workable social liberal welfare state.[42] Such a state had no need of nationalism — a nationalism that thrived on poverty and social dislocation. It is worth noting here, in passing, that although Popper's anti-nationalism and stress on the open society endeared him to Friedrich Hayek, nonetheless,

---

[39] See Hacohen (2000), pp. 12ff. Popper's 'Kantian socialism was less anomalous, but it had unique features. Austro-Marxists, notably Max Adler, assimilated Kant to socialism' (ibidem, p. 129). For Popper's admiration for Bernstein see ibidem, pp. 299f.

[40] Namely that 'the state as a legal and political entity (not a cultural-historical one); the parallel between civil, national and cosmopolitan rights; the universality of the moral imperative and its expression in law ...'. Hacohen (2000), pp. 124 and 130.

[41] 'Once completed, Popper separated himself from the Austrian socialist past, and embarked on a new political course in the West. The nexus of progressivism and socialism was unique to Vienna' (Hacohen 2000, p. 334).

[42] Popper's own views here on freedom and markets are fairly balanced and correspond loosely with the views that one finds in many twentieth-century 'social liberals'. Thus in commenting on the role of the market Popper notes (1945, Chapter 20, note 26):

> The problem of the *free market* ... is paradoxical. If the state does not interfere, then other semi-political organizations such as monopolies, trusts, unions, etc., may interfere, reducing the freedom of the market to a fiction. On the other hand, it is most important to realize that without a carefully protected free market, the whole economic system must cease to serve its only rational purpose, that is, *to satisfy the demands of the consumer*. If the consumer cannot choose; if he must take what the producer offers; if the producer, whether a private producer or the state or a marketing department, is master of the market, instead of the consumer; then the situation must arise that the consumer serves, ultimately, as a kind of money-supply and rubbish-remover for the producer, instead of the producer serving the needs and desires of the consumer.

He continues (ibid):

> Here we are clearly faced with an important problem of social engineering: the market must be controlled, but in such a way that the control does not impede the free choice of the consumer and that it does not remove the need for the producers to compete for the favour of the consumer.

his submerged social liberalism seemed to have remained an enigmatic barrier that both thinkers continually tiptoed around.[43]

2.2 Cosmopolitanism

The consideration of Kant's ethics leads to a second alternative to the nationalist perspective, namely, cosmopolitanism. Democratic Kantian socialism or social liberalism were viewed by Popper as essentially adjuncts to cosmopolitanism. Like-minded social liberal states were the most appropriate vessels for facilitating a cosmopolitan moral or legal structure. Outside of these Kantian philosophical roots, there were also strong biographical grounds, in Popper's Viennese social milieu, which account for his interests in cosmopolitanism. The idea of cosmopolitanism itself originated as one solution to the dilemmas of ethnic identity faced by the assimilated Jewish-Viennese intelligentsia. Popper's *Open Society* expressed in many ways 'their hopes of integration into a community that discounted religion, ethnicity, and nationality'. Thus, '[c]osmopolitanism tended to be the ideology of those who lived in between cultures and saw no ethnic future for themselves'.[44]

---

[43]There is a very strange longish mutating footnote (Chapter 9, note 4) in the later edition of *The Open Society*, which meanders, in a slightly bizarre manner, around Hayek's sentiments. Popper notes:

> What I call 'Utopian engineering' corresponds largely, I believe, to what Hayek would call 'centralized' or 'collectivized' planning. Hayek himself recommends what he calls 'planning for freedom'. I suppose he would agree that this would take the character of 'piecemeal engineering'. One could, I believe, formulate Hayek's objections to collectivist planning somewhat like this. If we try to construct society according to a blueprint, then we may find that we cannot incorporate individual freedom in our blueprint; or if we do, that we cannot realize it. The reason is that centralized economic planning eliminates from economic life one of the most important functions of the individual, namely his function as a chooser of the product, as a free consumer. In other words, Hayek's criticism belongs to the realm of social technology.

Popper then adds to this commentary, in a later edition, the following:

> ... readers of Hayek's *Road to Serfdom* (1944) may feel puzzled by this note; for Hayek's attitude in this book is so explicit that no room is left for the somewhat vague comments of my note. But my note was printed before Hayek's book was published; and although many of his leading ideas were foreshadowed in his earlier writings, they were not yet quite as explicit as in *The Road to Serfdom*. ... In the light of what I know now about Hayek's position, my summary of it does not appear to me to be mistaken, although it is, no doubt, an understatement of his position.

Popper thus modifies slightly, remarking that

> Hayek would not himself use the word 'social engineering' for any political activity which he would be prepared to advocate. He objects to this term because it is associated with a general tendency which he has called 'scientism' — the naïve belief that the methods of the natural sciences ... must produce similarly impressive results in the social field.

He continues, 'Terminology apart, I still think that Hayek's views can be interpreted as favourable to what I call "piecemeal engineering".

[44]Hacohen continues 'Neither the majority of German-Austrians nor the Czechs nor the Zionists went for it. ... Emerging from a life-and-death struggle against ethnonationalism, Popper's cosmopolitanism ignored the legitimate claims of community' (2000, p. 5 and pp. 20f.).

However, what did cosmopolitanism imply? I would contend that Popper, again, did not really work this idea out in any detail. It had a number of connotations and it is not always clear exactly what Popper had in mind. Certainly, he thought that liberal-minded states could be vessels for some form of more acceptable international legal and political order, as developed after 1945 with institutions such as the United Nations. He suggested that with the decline of nationalism there was no overriding reason not to find some common ground amongst liberal states. Cosmopolitanism also implied a world brought together (somewhat loosely) by a concern for rationalism and science. For Popper, there could be no barriers between genuine scientists — other than ignorance.

Cosmopolitanism was still open to the charge of lacking any sense of realism about the actual character of international relations. Yet Popper did obviously believe that it was a viable option, on a legal and institutional scale. This was not only foreshadowed in his neo-Kantianism, but also in his overall contempt for nationalism. The idea that an international or cosmopolitan *legal order* was possible, was in fact mooted by Popper. He remarked, for example,[45]

> I believe that the parallelism between the institutional problems of civil and of international peace is most important. Any international organization which has legislative, administrative and judicial institutions *as well as an armed executive which is prepared to act* should be as successful in upholding international peace as are the analogous institutions within the state.

In other words, legal and political authority could be transposed on to an international stage. For Popper, there is nothing insuperable in such an enterprise. Those who contend that a cosmopolitan legal order could *not* deal with the actions of 'rogue' states, and the like, are only speaking of contingent issues concerning will and capabilities. He notes that in the same way that crime can be reduced within all states, but it can never be eliminated, analogously, we should not expect anything more from a cosmopolitan legal order. Thus, although a cosmopolitan order could not end wars or conflicts, it could limit 'international anarchy', and, furthermore, it should be 'ready to go to war against any international crime'.[46] The difference between domestic states and the cosmopolitan order is simply the nature of the agent who performs the criminal act. In the domestic order it is the individual citizen; in the cosmopolitan order it is the state. In summary, the cosmopolitan order negates any need for nationalism.

2.3 Popper's Habsburgs

Popper's third alternative to nationalism is slightly stranger and, in someway a little unexpected, although there are conceptual connections with the cosmopolitan theme. This is the model provided by the Habsburg Empire,

---

[45] Popper (1945), Chapter 9, note 7.
[46] Ibidem.

namely the idea of a multinational federation. Popper looked back with nostalgic admiration to this solution on a number of occasions throughout his life. The model propounds a particular institutional theory of how 'national subcultures' can be tolerated and incorporated within a broad, moderately open, political federation.[47] The Habsburg structure of political organization, in his experience, actually made a positive, and for a time, quite successful attempt at dealing with nationalities. Further, there was no reason why such a multinational federation could not be a subject of legitimacy and loyalty. Popper frequently asked the question here — why should nationalism be considered more important than religion, birth, or loyalty to a dynasty.[48] The Habsburg solution was one which was, in Popper's view, opposed to nationalism. Popper regarded 'the dissolution of the Habsburg Empire as an unmitigated disaster and held nationalism, especially German nationalism, responsible'.[49]

This point connects up with Hacohen's more general thesis, namely, that Popper's admiration was part of a nostalgia that many assimilated central European Jews felt for the Habsburg Empire under Franz Joseph. Although suffering a long history of persecution in Austria, by the 1880s Jews were widely accepted and prospering in the various professions under the Empire, and it should not be forgotten that Popper came from this assimilated Jewish background. Thus, for Popper, the Habsburg empire represented an 'idyllic multiculturalism'. Whereas 'nationalities were false, reactionary, and utopian. Individuals, empires, and cosmopolitan federations were true, progressive, and possible'.[50] In many ways, the more positive vision underpinning *The Open Society*, and other essays during the 1950s, reflected a cosmopolitanism (in science and political practice) that, at the same time, also reflected the Viennese Jewish progressives' lost hopes for Habsburg monarchy.[51] Thus, in terms of his reading historical events in Europe, during the early decades of the twentieth century, Popper believed that 'An inter-national federation in the Danube basin might have prevented much'.[52] Thus, for Popper multinational federations, premised on something like the Habsburg model, obviated the demands of nationalities. It accommodated them and nullified their enthusiasm.

---

[47]For Popper, 'The oppression of national groups is a great evil; but national self-determination is not a feasible remedy' (1963, Chapter 19, p. 368; italics suppressed).

[48](1945), Chapter 12, § III.

[49]See Hacohen (2000), p. 53. Popper remarked that its 'dissolution ... proved a disaster for Europe and the world' (1994, Chapter 9, § I; quoted by Hacohen 2000, p. 75). In effect, the empire was lost between January and October 1918, when the various nationalities moved to independence from Vienna encouraged by President Wilson's Fourteen Points.

[50]Ibidem, pp. 26, 75, 437f.

[51]Ibidem, p. 6. Hacohen (pp. 34f.) comments that Popper watched in the 1920s and 1930s the collapse of the liberal politics of his father's generation. German-Austrian-Jewish identity reached a crisis, and German, Czech, and Hungarian nationalisms were undermining the multinational empire. Popper devoted his political philosophy to reconstructing liberalism, and provided a radical cosmopolitan solution to the predicament of his youth: the Open Society.

[52]Popper (1945), Chapter 1, note 53.

In being criticized in later years by, for example, Israelis, for his myopic nostalgia for the Habsburgs, Popper's response was blunt and to the point: 'Those Jews who criticize me for my tolerance of remaining inequalities under the Habsburgs should show me how many Arab university professors, army officers, and cabinet ministers the Jewish state has today.'[53]

3 Evaluation

There is much that could be said about Popper's arguments on nationalism and his alternatives. However, I wish to concentrate on one specific issue, namely, his views on the Habsburgs and multinational federation as kind of 'idyllic multiculturalism'.

The first point to note is that his views, referred to earlier, on Kantian socialism and cosmopolitanism — particularly the idea of a cosmopolitanism of rational science or international juristic development — do not correspond with his views on the Habsburg federation or multiculturalism. This may be obvious, but it is worth reminding ourselves. It would true to say — as Popper reminded his Israeli critics — that the professoriate, bureaucracy, and officer core of the army of the Habsburgs were multinational and indeed, for a time, were tolerant towards all groups within the empire, including Jews. However, a pragmatic political tolerance has no link with moral, scientific or legal cosmopolitanism, let alone extensions in social democracy or egalitarianism. The Habsburgs were simply a more benevolent, but nonetheless autocratic, imperial, and dynastic regime, who had found a workable pragmatic *modus vivendi* for dealing with the diversity of subnationalities.

In one sense, Popper's view of the Habsburgs, as well as his rather unexpected view of classical Athenian society (which had odd parallels in Popper's mind with the Habsburgs), was a fastidious and selective vision.[54] Presumably, Popper was not implying that a cosmopolitan equivalent to the Habsburgs was a prerequisite for the achievement of the open society. In addition, his views on the Habsburgs have no links with his views on science, democracy or cosmopolitanism. It is difficult to know exactly what Popper was suggesting here, unless it was just an observation on the contingent or momentary effectiveness of the Habsburgs, in comparison to other solutions. However, I strongly suspect that Popper did see something normatively attractive and rational in the Habsburg federal multicultural model. Part of his critique of the nation state idea (as already noted) was that all states contain multiple subnationalities, thus, something like the Habsburg model is of much wider relevance.

The Habsburg idea was therefore attractive on a number of levels to Popper. Firstly, it was premised on the actual reality of most polities in the world. It did not dream of spurious unified state-based national groups and it did not ignore the actual empirical existence of sub-nationalities. Thus, the

---

[53]Hacohen (2000), p. 305, note 49.
[54]Hacohen (2000), p. 426.

diversity of cultures was the background assumption. Second, a diversity of cultural perspectives, regularly subject to rational challenge within a rule of law framework, corresponded very *loosely* to his conception of what rational social (or scientific) existence should actually be about. Popper thus often inveighed against, what he called, the myth of the 'univocal voice'.[55] He argued that we should always distrust any overarching sense of intellectual, social or moral unanimity. The Habsburg idea was thus almost an instantiation of political possibility of rational dialogue. As Hacohen comments, Popper thus often spoke 'nostalgically of Habsburg (and classical Athenian) multiculturalism, praising culture clash as productive of great intellectual advances. Culture clash was conducive to critical dialogue that transformed identities, transgressed boundaries, and changed communities' (2000, p. 541). Popper clearly accepted the idea that pluralism and internal difference, as facts of political life, generated intellectual benefits. Thus, Hacohen comments, 'Popper acknowledged "diversity" and ... assailed any effort to suppress difference' (ibidem, p. 426).

However, it is important to note that Popper clearly did not celebrate difference or pluralism for its own sake. It was a more of an empirical fact than a value. I suspect that Popper would not have been sympathetic to the more recent 'group or cultural rights' arguments that have appeared in the last decade.[56] In this sense, the rights of cultural minorities could not be special or differentiated rights. His strong individualism and suspicion of collective identity were enough to make him deeply suspicious of all such claims. Openness and tolerance were however to be afforded to cultural difference, but the actual differences were not celebrated. They were also open to continuous rational contestation within a legal framework. Again, this would appear to be the general implication of Popper's arguments on social and scientific life, although it is worth noting that it is doubtful that this practice could or would have existed in the Habsburg framework.[57]

There appears to me to be two significant weaknesses in Popper's position here. The first is that nationalism, although considered febrile, tribal, and hysterical is clearly accepted by Popper, on another level, as an inevitable detail of the political life of most states, even if it is far more internally fragmented than most of its proponents would acknowledge. Therefore Popper accepted that nationalisms (ethnic and cultural) did constitute the multi-national federation of the Habsburgs. In fact they constitute most societies in the world. Yet, at the same time, he did not consider such attachments as intrinsically valuable or authoritative. Thus, cultural attachment was not accorded any special status — if anything, it was frowned upon by Popper. However, at the same time, Popper would be one of the first to admit that it was nationalism that actually challenged and undermined the Habsburgs and eventually

---

[55]Popper 1963, Chapter 17, § 1.

[56]For a critical discussion of this literature, see Vincent (2002), Chapters 6f.

[57]Hacohen (2000), pp. 541 and pp. 246f.

'turned multiculturalism on its head by reifying national identity as race'.[58]
This presents a very peculiar scenario, namely, where nationalism is seen, on
the one hand, as an unnecessary, tribal, and primitive form of association that
is of no value. It is something that Popper gives every impression of wishing
to do away with as an exemplification of the 'closed society'. However, on the
other hand, nationalism(s) is an ever-present reality within every state in the
world, in fact, it is given virtual international status in terminology such as
'self-determination', as Popper was painfully aware. If one views this state of
affairs through the lens of the 'open society' theory, then every society for
Popper is, by definition, a unusual mix of the open and closed, in fact probably more closed than open. Given that Popper gives a very strong impression
that this blending cannot and ought not to happen, something seems to be
wrong here. Nationalism is a primitive, irresponsible, irrational, and neurotic
mentality that we should be progressing away from, yet it swamps virtually
every known state, by Popper's own blatant admission.

A second weakness concerns Popper's implied distinction between nationalism and multiculturalism. One way for Popper to meet the first criticism
is to suggest that multicultural federations are distinct from nationalisms.
Nationalism implies a claustrophobic unity. What presumably characterizes
multiculturalism, for Popper, is that it implies the possibility of rational dialogue between internally diverse cultures. This critical dialogue will facilitate,
in its wake, not only a more comprehensive or cosmopolitan understanding
in the participants (which could almost be read as a form of 'intellectual assimilation'), but also greater equality of opportunity for all groups. In the
Habsburg situation, it allowed German-acculturated Jews to proceed through
the various professional sectors of society and the same would presumably
apply ideally to all minority groups. Thus, in Popper's mind, with some social democratic tweaking, and the development of a welfare state (which was
not a hopeful prospect under the Habsburgs), inequalities of power would be
addressed and this, in turn, would enable such a multicultural dialogue to
work more effectively.[59] However, all of Popper's ideas here sound uncharac-
teristically speculative and idealistic.

The problem is: can one make a clear distinction between nationalism
and multiculturalism? Multiculturalism is, in effect, internally diverse micro-
nationalisms. If one culture dominates, it becomes a macro-nationalism or
univocal voice. As Popper acknowledged, it was the warring and restive nationalisms of the 1920s that actually allowed the German ethno-nationalist
to come to power as the dominant form in Austria. Thus, multiculturalism
is not an avoidance of nationalism, just an acknowledgement of its pervasive-
ness and fragmentariness. Multiculturalism is also the seedbed of nationalist

---

[58]Thus, '[d]iversity existed [for Popper] but unlike universal humanity, it was no cause
for celebration. His refusal to celebrate diversity reflected determination not to eliminate
difference but to ensure it does not infringe on universal humanity'. Both quotations are
from Hacohen (2000); see p. 53 and pp. 426f.

[59]Some of these ideas have some passing resonance with very recent debates about difference theory and deliberative democracy.

aspiration. In addition it may well undermine rather than enable basic justice
and equal treatment of minorities. It is in this kind of context that a number
of recent social democratic and liberal writers such as Brian Barry, Stephen
Macedo, Susan Okin, and Amy Gutman, amongst others, have expressed deep
reservations about the whole multicultural enterprise.[60]

Given what Popper has to say about the nationalist mentality — that is, it
is primitive, insular, irrational and neurotic — it is difficult to see how cultural
clash (read as sub-national clash) could solve any problems. It could be seen
as just an empirical realistic acknowledgement of diversity, but one suspects
that Popper hoped for more from this scenario. If one considers that many of
the cultural minorities might well have singularly odd or restricted views on
what is reasonable, valuable, or acceptable, it is difficult to see how they could
participate in rational dialogue, certainly in the form that Popper portends.
Given that many cultural groups often have idiosyncratic perspectives on what
they would consider fundamental truths, it is also difficult to see how they
would participate in any open rational rigorous dialogue about comparative
truth. They certainly would not all acknowledge Popper's strong sense of the
importance of the natural sciences. For Popper, clearly the search for truth
requires imagination, trial and error, and gradual discovery of our prejudices
through critical discussion. Thus, the critical rational method is not about
final truth or complete proof. Rather, for Popper, the 'value lies, rather, in
the fact that participants in a discussion will, to some extent, change their
minds'. In this sense, Popper's focus on rational method, and his interests in
a form of multiculturalism, have links with his later conception of liberalism:
namely, as he put it '[t]he liberal does not dream of a perfect consensus of
opinion; he only hopes for the mutual fertilization of opinions'.[61]

In sum, the crucial weakness here is that nationalism *cannot* be easily
drawn distinct from multiculturalism. Both come from the same 'identity-
based stable'. Further, Popper's more idyllic sense of multiculturalism, as a
form of critical open dialogue, does not really square with the multicultural
reality of any societies. It also does not, for example, cohere with what he
has to say about the mentality of cultural nationalist groups — namely they
are often narrow-minded, febrile, and immature. Multiculturalism itself might
be deeply disruptive and socially illiberal. There is little indication therefore
that Popper thought through the social, moral, and ontological character and
conditions for such a critical polylogue. The idea presumably is that 'reasonableness' indicates an 'attitude of readiness to listen to critical arguments and

---

[60]Barry (2001), Gutman (1993), Macedo (1993), and Okin (1998).

[61]Popper (1963), Chapter 17 ('Public Opinion and Liberal Principles'), §4. Popper's
commitment to rationalism is though vulnerable in terms of the challenge of nationalists.
He notes (1949b/1963, p. 357) that 'I choose rationalism because I hate violence, and I do
not deceive myself into believing that this hatred has any rational grounds. Or to put it
another way, my rationalism is not self-contained, but rests on an irrational faith in the
attitude of reasonableness. I do not see that we can go beyond this. One could say, perhaps,
that my irrational faith in equal and reciprocal rights to convince others and be convinced
by them is a faith in human reason; or simply, that I believe in man.'

learn from experience'.[62] Popper assumes this reasonableness in participants, as a necessary condition for multiculturalism. But, at other points, he pours scorn on the mentality of such cultural groups.

4 Conclusion

In summary, Popper obviously wanted to make a case against nationalism. Despite the fact that it was not systematically developed, it remained very influential for a long period. Nationalists, of all stripes, were seen as narrow and primitive exemplars of closed minds and closed societies. In fact, nationalism was considered more of a social pathology than a political theory.[63] Since the 1990s nationalism has bounced back into political theory. However, Popper remained adamant, into the 1990s, in his condemnation. Popper's alternatives to nationalism are, in some cases, predictable. Most relate to the intellectual milieu of early twentieth century Vienna. In this context, I have interpreted Popper as a Kantian-inspired socialists or social liberal — certainly in *The Open Society* — committed to a vision of a liberal welfare state. This also has link with his vision of cosmopolitanism. The most unexpected alternative is Popper's admiration for the Habsburgs and his vision of some form of idyllic multicultural federation. This, at one eccentric extreme, appears to exemplify a form of open critical dialogue between cultures. One might even suggest here that this vision sounds distinctly utopian. However, Popper basically neither resolved the relation of nationalism to contemporary politics, nor its relation with multiculturalism. He assumes some form of distinction between nationalism and multiculturalism, which is never adequately explained. In his somewhat dreamy association of multiculturalism with critical cultural dialogue, he never faced the question as to whether multiculturalism itself could be socially disruptive, illiberal, and antagonistic to the very values he cherished.

---

[62] (1945), Chapter 24, § I.

[63] Oddly Popper attacks the sociology of knowledge proponents for engaging in this type of reductionist social therapy.

Bibliography

Barry, B. (2001). *Culture and Equality*. Cambridge MA: Harvard University Press.

Berlin, I. (1990). *The Crooked Timber of Humanity*. London: John Murray.

Gutman, A. (1993). 'The Challenge of Multiculturalism in Political Ethics'. *Philosophy and Public Affairs* **22**, pp. 171-206.

Hacohen, M. H. (2000). *Karl Popper – The Formative Years, 1902-1945. Politics and Philosophy in Pre-war Vienna*. Cambridge & elsewhere: Cambridge University Press.

Kohn, H. (1945). *The Idea of Nationalism: A Study in its Origins and Background*. New York: Macmillan.

Macedo, S. (1993). 'Transformative Constitutionalism and the Case of Religion: Defending the Moderate Hegemony of Liberalism'. *Political Theory* **26**, pp. 56-80.

Okin, S. (1998). 'Feminism and Multiculturalism: Some Tensions'. *Ethics* **108**, pp. 661-684.

Plamenatz, J. P. (1976). 'Two Types of Nationalism'. In E. Kamenka, editor (1976). *Nationalism: The Evolution and Nature of an Idea*. London: Edward Arnold.

Popper, K. R. (1945). *The Open Society and Its Enemies*. London: George Routledge & Sons. 5th revised edition 1966. London: Routledge & Kegan Paul.

——— (1949a). 'Naturgesetze und theoretische Systeme'. In S. Moser, editor (1949), pp. 43-60. *Gesetz und Wirklichkeit*. Innsbruck: Tyrolia Verlag. Reprinted as Appendix 1 ('The Bucket and the Searchlight: Two Theories of Knowledge') in K. R. Popper (1972). *Objective Knowledge*. Oxford: Clarendon Press. 2nd edition 1979.

——— (1949b). 'Utopia and Violence'. *The Hibbert Journal*, **46**, pp. 109-116. Reprinted as Chapter 18 of Popper (1963).

——— (1957). *The Poverty of Historicism*. London: Routledge & Kegan Paul.

——— (1963). *Conjectures and Refutations: The Growth of Scientific Knowledge*. London: Routledge & Kegan Paul. 5th edition 1989.

——— (1999). *All Life Is Problem Solving*. London: Routledge.

Spencer, P. & Wollman, H. (1997). *Nationalism: A Critical Introduction*. London: Sage Publications.

Vincent, A. (1997). 'Liberal Nationalism: An Irresponsible Compound?'y *Political Studies* **45**, pp. 275-295.

——— (2002). *Nationalism and Particularity*. Cambridge: Cambridge University Press, 2002.

Vörlander, C. (1911). *Marx und Kant: Ein Beitrag zur Philosophie des Sozialismus*. Tübingen: J. C. B. Mohr (Paul Siebeck).

11

The Enlightenment Programme and Karl Popper

Nicholas Maxwell

1 Popper's contributions to the Enlightenment programme

By the Enlightenment Programme I mean the eighteenth century French Enlightenment idea of learning from scientific progress how to go about making social progress towards world enlightenment.

Three steps need to be got right to put the basic Enlightenment idea into practice correctly:

(i)   The progress-achieving methods of science need to be correctly identified.

(ii)   These methods need to be correctly generalized so that they become fruitfully applicable to any worthwhile, problematic human endeavour, whatever the aims may be, and not just applicable to the endeavour of improving knowledge.

(iii) The correctly generalized progress-achieving methods then need to be exploited correctly by the great human endeavour of trying to make social progress towards an enlightened, civilized world.

Unfortunately, the *philosophes* of the Enlightenment got all three points disastrously wrong. They failed to capture correctly the progress-achieving methods of natural science (in that they defended inductivist, or at least verificationist, conceptions of science); they failed to generalize these methods properly; and, most disastrously of all, they failed to apply them properly so that humanity might learn how to become more civilized or enlightened by rational means. Instead of applying the generalized progress-achieving methods of science to *social life itself*, so that social progress might be achieved, the *philosophes* sought to apply scientific method merely to *social science*. Reason (as construed by the *philosophes*) got applied, not to the task of making social progress towards an enlightened world, but to the task of making intellectual progress towards greater knowledge about the social world. Social inquiry was developed, not as social methodology or social philosophy, but as social science.

This traditional but botched version of the Enlightenment Programme was immensely influential. It was developed throughout the nineteenth century by

Comte, Marx, Mill and many others, and was built into the institutional structure of academic inquiry in the twentieth century with the creation of departments of social science: anthropology, economics, psychology, sociology, linguistics, political science. Academic inquiry as it exists today, devoted primarily to the pursuit of knowledge, is the outcome.

Much of the importance of Karl Popper's work, especially of his first four books, stems from the fact that it does much to correct defects of the traditional, bungled Enlightenment Programme that we have inherited from the eighteenth century — although Popper does not himself formulate his contribution in these terms. In *The Logic of Scientific Discovery* (1959), Popper goes some way towards correcting step (i) above. Science does not, and cannot, verify its theories. Science makes progress by proposing bold conjectures in response to problems, which are then subjected to sustained attempted empirical refutation. This falsificationist conception of scientific method is then generalized, in accordance with step (ii) above, to form Popper's conception of (critical) rationality, a general methodology for solving problems or making progress. As Popper puts it, 'inter-subjective *testing* is merely a very important aspect of the more general idea of inter-subjective *criticism*, or in other words, of the idea of mutual rational control by critical discussion' (1959, § 8, note *1: see also Popper 1963, Chapter 8, § 2; 1972, Chapter 3, § 3, and Chapter 6, § XVIII).

In *The Open Society and Its Enemies* (1945) and *The Poverty of Historicism* (1957) Popper applies critical rationalism to problems of civilization, in accordance with step (iii) above. From all the riches of these two books, I pick just two points, two corrections Popper makes to ideas inherited from the Enlightenment.

First, there is Popper's devastating criticism of historicism. Pro-naturalistic historicism is the outcome of an especially defective attempt to put step (iii) of the Enlightenment Programme into practice. If one seeks to develop social science alongside natural science, and if one takes the capacity of Newtonian science to predict states of the solar system far into the future as a paradigmatic achievement of natural science, one may be misled into holding that the proper task of social science is to discover laws governing social evolution. Historicism is the doctrine that such laws exist. Popper decisively demolishes historicism, and demolishes the above rationale for adopting historicism. In doing so, he demolishes one influential and especially defective version of the traditional Enlightenment Programme.

Second, Popper's revolutionary contributions to steps (i) and (ii) of the Enlightenment Programme lead to a new idea as to what a 'rational society' might be, one that is fully in accordance with liberal traditions, rather than entirely at odds with such traditions. A major objection to the Enlightenment programme is overcome. If one upholds pre-Popperian conceptions of science and reason, and construes reason, in particular, as a set of rules that determine what one must accept or do, the very idea of 'the rational society' is abhorrent. It can amount to little more than a tyranny of reason, a society in which spontaneity and freedom are crushed by the requirement that the rules of reason be obeyed. When viewed from the perspective of Popper's falsificationism and critical rationalism, however, all this changes dramatically.

Popper's falsificationist conception of science requires that theories are *severely* tested empirically. But, in order to make sense of this idea of *severe* testing, we need to see the experimentalist as having at least the germ of an idea for a rival theory up his sleeve (otherwise testing might degenerate into performing essentially the same experiment again and again). This means experiments are always *crucial experiments*, attempts at trying to decide between two competing theories. Theoretical pluralism is necessary for science to be genuinely empirical. And, more generally (implementing step (ii)), in order to *criticize* an idea, one needs to have a rival idea in mind. Rationality, as construed by Popper, requires plurality of ideas, values, ways of life. Thus, for Popper, the rational society *is* the open society, the society in which diverse ways of life can flourish. In short, given pre-Popperian conceptions of science and reason, the Enlightenment idea of creating a rational society guides one towards a kind of tyranny of reason, the very opposite of a free or open society. Adopt improved Popperian conceptions of science and reason, and the Enlightenment ideal of the rational society is one and the same as the ideal of the free, open society. At a stroke, a major objection to the Enlightenment Programme is overcome.

Despite the enormous improvements that Popper has made to the traditional Enlightenment Programme, his version of the Programme is still defective. I now discuss two ways in which Popper's version of the Programme needs to be improved. Both involve changing dramatically Popper's conception of social science. It is important to note that Popper defends a highly traditional conception of social science. According to him, the methods of social science are broadly the same as those of natural science (Popper 1957, § 29). But it is this key element of the eighteenth-century Enlightenment, so profoundly influential over subsequent developments, that constitutes the traditional Enlightenment's greatest blunder. Popper endorses, and fails to correct, this blunder.

2 The New Enlightenment, first version

Let us, then, consider again the basic Enlightenment idea of learning from scientific progress how to go about making social progress towards an enlightened world. And let us consider what form academic inquiry ought to take granted that it has, as a basic aim, to help promote human welfare, help humanity learn how to become more enlightened or civilized, and granted, too, that it seeks to implement the three steps of the Enlightenment Programme, (i)-(iii), with which we began.

As a minor improvement to Popper's critical rationalism, I suggest we take the following as basic 'rules of reason', arrived at by generalizing the methods of science (in accordance with step (ii)):

(1) Articulate, and try to improve the articulation of, the problem to be solved.

(2) Propose and critically assess possible solutions.

(3) When necessary, break up the basic problem to be solved into a number of preliminary simpler, analogous, subordinate, or specialized problems (to be tackled in accordance with rules (1) and (2)), in an attempt to work gradually towards a solution to the basic problem to be solved.

(4) Interconnect attempts to solve basic and specialized problems, so that basic problem-solving may guide, and be guided by, specialized problem-solving (see Maxwell 1980, pp. 20f.; 1984, pp. 67-75).

Popper's critical rationalism consists of rules (1) and (2); problem-solving rationality (as (1) to (4) may be called) improves on this by adding on rules (3) and (4), which become relevant when we are confronted by some especially recalcitrant problem — such as the problem of understanding the nature of the universe, or the problem of creating a civilized world — that can be solved only gradually and progressively, bit by bit, and not all at once. Popper was too hostile to specialization to emphasize the need for rule (3); he did not appreciate that the evils of specialization can be counteracted by implementing rule (4).

Two preliminary points now need to be made.

First, in order to create a more civilized, enlightened world, the problems that we need to solve are, fundamentally, problems of *living* rather than problems of *knowledge*. It is what we *do* (or refrain from doing) that matters, and not just what we *know*. Even where new knowledge or technology is needed, in connection with agriculture or medicine for example, it is always what this enables us to *do* that solves the problem of living.

Second, in order to make progress towards a sustainable, civilized world we need to learn how to resolve our conflicts in more cooperative ways than at present. A group acts cooperatively in so far as all members of the group share responsibility for what is done, and for deciding what is done, proposals for action, for resolution of problems and conflicts, being judged on their merits from the standpoint of the interests of the members of the group (or the group as a whole), there being no permanent leadership or delegation of power. Competition is not opposed to cooperation if it proceeds within a framework of cooperation, as it does ideally within science. There are of course degrees of cooperativeness, from its absence, all out violence, at one extreme, to settling of conflicts by means of threat, to agreed procedures such as voting, to bargaining, to all out cooperativeness at the other extreme. If we are to develop a sustainable, civilized world we need to move progressively away from the violent end of this spectrum towards the cooperative end.

Granted, then, that the task of academic inquiry is to put the four rules of problem-solving rationality into practice in such a way as to help humanity learn how to make progress towards a civilized, enlightened world, the primary intellectual tasks must be:

(1) To articulate, and try to improve the articulation of, those social problems of living we need to solve in order to make progress towards a better world.

(2) To propose and assess critically possible, and actual, increasingly cooperative social actions — these actions to be assessed for their capacity to resolve human problems and conflicts, thus enhancing the quality of human life.

These intellectually fundamental tasks are undertaken by social inquiry, at the heart of the academic enterprise. Social inquiry also has the task of promoting the increase of cooperatively rational tackling of problems of living in the social world — in such contexts as politics, commerce, international affairs, industry, agriculture, the media, the law, education.

Academic inquiry also needs, of course, to implement the third rule of rational problem solving; that is, it needs:

(3) To break up the basic problems of living into preliminary, simpler, analogous, subordinate, specialized problems of knowledge and technology, in an attempt to work gradually towards solutions to the basic problems of living.

But, in order to ensure that specialized and basic problem solving keep in contact with one another, the fourth rule of rational problem solving also needs to be implemented; that is, academic inquiry needs:

(4) To interconnect attempts to solve basic and specialized problems, so that basic problem solving may guide, and be guided by, specialized problem solving.

There are a number of points to note about this 'rational problem solving' conception of academic inquiry. Social inquiry is not, primarily, social science; it has, rather, the intellectually basic task of engaging in, and promoting in the social world, the increase of cooperatively rational tackling of conflicts and problems of living (see Maxwell 1984, pp. 162-166, for further details). Social inquiry, so conceived, is actually intellectually more fundamental than natural science (which seeks to solve subordinate problems of knowledge and understanding). Academic inquiry, in seeking to promote cooperatively rational problem solving in the social world, must engage in a two-way exchange of ideas, arguments, experiences, and information with the social world. The thinking, the problem solving, that really matters, that is really fundamental, is the thinking that we engage in, individually, socially and institutionally, as we live; the whole of academic inquiry is, in a sense, a specialized part of this, created in accordance with rule (3), but also being required to implement rule (4) (so that social and academic problem solving may influence each other). Academic inquiry, on this model, is a kind of people's civil service, doing openly for the public what actual civil services are supposed to do, in secret, for governments. Academic inquiry needs just sufficient power to retain its independence, to resist pressures from government, industry, the media, religious authorities, and public opinion, but no more. Academia proposes to, argues with, learns from, attempts to teach, and criticizes all sectors of the social world, but does not instruct or dictate. It is an intellectual resource for the public, not an intellectual bully.

The basic intellectual aim of inquiry may be said to be not knowledge, but wisdom — wisdom being understood to be the desire, the active endeavour and the capacity to realize what is desirable and of value in life, for oneself and others ('realize' meaning both 'to apprehend' and 'to make real'). Wisdom includes knowledge, know-how, and understanding but goes beyond them in also including the desire and active striving for what is of value, the ability to experience value, actually and potentially, in the circumstances of life, the capacity to help realize what is of value for oneself and others, the capacity to help solve those problems of living that need to be solved if what is of value is to be realized, the capacity to use and develop knowledge, technology, and understanding as needed for the realization of value. Wisdom, like knowledge, can be conceived of not only in personal terms but also in institutional or social terms. Thus, the basic aim of academic inquiry, according to the view being indicated here, is to help us develop wiser ways of living, wiser institutions, customs and social relations, a wiser world.

It is important to appreciate that the conception of academic inquiry that we are considering is designed to help us to see, to know, and to understand, for their own sake, just as much as it is designed to help us solve practical problems of living. It might seem that social inquiry, in articulating problems of living and proposing possible solutions, has only a severely practical purpose. But engaging in this intellectual activity of articulating personal and social problems of living is just what we need to do if we are to develop a good empathic or 'personalistic' understanding of our fellow human beings (and of ourselves) — a kind of understanding that can do justice to our humanity, to what is of value, potentially and actually, in our lives. In order to understand another person *as a person* (as opposed to a biological or physical system) I need to be able, in imagination, to see, desire, fear, believe, experience and suffer what the other person sees, desires, and so on. I need to be able, in imagination, to enter into the other person's world; that is, I need to be able to understand his problems of living as he understands them, and I need also, perhaps, to understand a more objective version of these problems. In giving intellectual priority to the tasks of articulating problems of living and exploring possible solutions, social inquiry thereby gives intellectual priority to the development of a kind of understanding that people can acquire of one another that is of great intrinsic value. In my view, indeed, personalistic understanding of this kind is essential to the development of our humanity, even to the development of consciousness. Our being able to understand each other in this way is also essential for cooperatively rational action.

And it is essential for science. It is only because scientists can enter imaginatively into one another's problems and research projects that objective scientific knowledge can develop. At least two rather different motives exist for trying to see the world as another sees it: one may seek to improve one's knowledge of the other person; or one may seek to improve one's knowledge of the world, it being possible that the other person has something to contribute to one's own knowledge. Scientific knowledge arises as a result of the latter use of personalistic understanding — scientific knowledge being, in part, the product of endless acts of personalistic understanding between scientists (with the personalistic element largely suppressed so that it becomes invisible). It is hardly too much to say that almost all that is of value in human life is based on personalistic understanding. (For further details see Maxwell 1984, pp. 172-189 and pp. 264-275; 2001, Chapters 5-7.)

The basic intellectual aim of the kind of inquiry we are considering is to devote reason to the discovery of what is of value in life. This immediately carries with it the consequence that the arts have a vital *rational* contribution to make to inquiry, as revelations of value, as imaginative explorations of possibilities, desirable or disastrous, or as vehicles for the criticism of fraudulent values through comedy, satire, or tragedy. Literature and drama also have a rational role to play in enhancing our ability to understand others personalistically, as a result of identifying imaginatively with fictional characters — literature in this respect merging into biography, documentary, and history. Literary criticism bridges the gap between literature and social inquiry, and is more concerned with the content of literature than the means by which it achieves its effects.

Another important consequence flows from the point that the basic aim of inquiry is to help us discover what is of value, namely that our feelings and desires have a vital rational role to play within the intellectual domain of inquiry. If we are to discover for ourselves what is of value, then we must attend to our feelings and desires. But not everything that feels good is good, and not everything that we desire is desirable. Rationality requires that feelings and desires take fact, knowledge, and logic into account, just as it requires that priorities for scientific research take feelings and desires into account. In insisting on this kind of interplay between feelings and desires on the one hand, knowledge and understanding on the other, the conception of inquiry that we are considering resolves the conflict between rationalism and romanticism, and helps us to acquire what we need if we are to contribute to building civilization: mindful hearts and heartfelt minds.

All this differs dramatically from academic inquiry as it mostly exists at present, devoted primarily to the pursuit of knowledge. And it differs from Popper's conceptions of social inquiry, and academic inquiry more generally. It deserves to be noted that, when judged from the standpoint of promoting human welfare, a kind of inquiry that gives priority to the pursuit of knowledge violates *three* of the above four rules of reason. Rules (1) and (2) are violated because the intellectual activities of articulating problems of living, proposing and criticizing possible solutions, cannot proceed within the context of the pursuit of knowledge. And once rules (1) and (2) are not implemented, rule (4) cannot be either.

3 The New Enlightenment, second version

I come now to a rather more radical revision of Popper's version of the En-lightenment Programme. This begins with a revision of step (i) of the Pro-gramme. Popper's falsificationism is untenable, and needs to be replaced by a conception of scientific method that I have called *aim-oriented empiricism* (AOE). The reason for this revision can be summarized as follows. Physics only considers (and only accepts) theories that are sufficiently simple, unified or explanatory, and this means that the methods of physics make a persistent metaphysical assumption about the universe, to the effect that it has a simple, unified, explanatory dynamic structure. That such a persistent metaphysical assumption is made by physics, as a part of (conjectural) scientific knowledge, contradicts, and refutes, falsificationism. An improved conception of scientific method is required.

In *The Logic of Scientific Discovery*, Popper claims that the more falsi-fiable a theory is, so the greater its degree of simplicity. (There is a second method for assessing degrees of simplicity, in terms of number of observation statements required to falsify the theories in question, but Popper stresses that if the two methods clash, it is the first that takes precedence.) It is easy to see that Popper's proposal fails. Given a reasonably simple scientific theory, T, one can readily increase the falsifiability of T by adding on an inde-pendently testable hypotheses, h_1, to form the new theory, $T + h_1$. This new theory will be more falsifiable than T but, in general, will be drastically less simple. And one can make the situation even worse, by adding on as many independently testable hypotheses as one pleases, h_2, h_3 and so on, to form new theories $T + h_1 + h_2 + h_3 + \ldots$, as highly empirically falsifiable and as drastically lacking in simplicity, as one pleases. Thus simplicity cannot be equated with falsifiability.

And there is a further, even more devastating point. Popper's methodo-logical rules favour $T + h_1 + h_2 + h_3 + \ldots$ over T, especially if h_1, h_2, and h_3 have been severely tested, and corroborated. But in scientific practice, $T + h_1 + h_2 + h_3$ would never even be considered, however highly corroborated it might be if considered, because of its extreme lack of simplicity or unity, its grossly ad hoc character. There is here a fundamental flaw in the central doctrine of *The Logic of Scientific Discovery*.

Later, in *Conjectures and Refutations* (1963), Popper put forward a new methodological principle that, when added to those of the earlier book, suc-ceeds in excluding theories such as $T + h_1 + h_2 + h_3$ from scientific consid-eration. This principle states that a new theory, in order to be acceptable, 'should proceed from some *simple, new, and powerful, unifying idea* about some connection or relation (such as gravitational attraction) between hith-erto unconnected things (such as planets and apples) or facts (such as inertial and gravitational mass) or new "theoretical entities" (such as field and parti-cles)' (Popper 1963, Chapter 10, § XVIII). $T + h_1 + h_2 + h_3$ does not 'proceed from some *simple, new, and powerful, unifying idea*' and is to be rejected on that account, even if more highly corroborated than T.

But the adoption of this 'requirement of simplicity' (as Popper calls it) as a basic methodological principle of science has the effect of permanently excluding from science all ad hoc theories (such as $T + h_1 + h_2 + h_3$) that fail to satisfy the principle, however empirically successful such theories might be if considered. This amounts to assuming permanently that the universe is such that no ad hoc theory, that fails to satisfy Popper's principle of simplicity, is true. It amounts to accepting, as a permanent item of scientific knowledge, the substantial metaphysical thesis that the universe is non-ad hoc, in the sense that no theory that fails to satisfy Popper's principle of simplicity is true. But this clashes with Popper's criterion of demarcation: that no unfalsifiable, metaphysical thesis is to be accepted as a part of scientific knowledge.

It is, in fact, important that Popper's criterion of demarcation is rejected, and the metaphysical thesis of non-*ad hocness* is explicitly acknowledged to be a part of scientific knowledge. The thesis, in the form in which it is implicitly adopted at any given stage in the development of science, may well be false. Scientific progress may require that it be modified. The thesis needs to be made explicit, in other words, for good Popperian reasons, namely, so that it can be critically assessed, and perhaps improved. As long as Popper's demarcation criterion is upheld, the metaphysical thesis must remain implicit within science, and hence immune to criticism.

As I have argued at length elsewhere (Maxwell 1998; see also Maxwell 1974; 1984, Chapter 9; 1993, 1999; 2001; 2002b; 2004, 2005), in order to facilitate criticism and improvement of metaphysical theses implicit in persistent scientific rejection of ad hoc, disunified physical theories, we need to reject Popper's falsificationism and adopt AOE instead, a view that construes science as accepting, as a part of (conjectural) scientific knowledge, a hierarchy of metaphysical theses concerning the comprehensibility and knowability of the universe, these theses becoming increasingly insubstantial as one goes up the hierarchy, and thus becoming increasingly likely to be true. At any level in this hierarchy of theses, that thesis is accepted that *either* (a) is such that its truth is a necessary condition for the acquisition of knowledge to be possible at all, *or* is such that (b) it is more nearly compatible with the best available thesis immediately above in the hierarchy and (c) it appears to be more fruitful from the standpoint of promoting the growth of empirical knowledge than any rival. Those physical theories are accepted that (a) meet with sufficient empirical success, and (b) are sufficiently in accord with the best available metaphysical thesis at the bottom of the hierarchy of theses. Associated with each metaphysical thesis, M, there is a methodological principle that asserts: accept that thesis or theory lower down in the hierarchy which best accords with M.

If there is a clash between a physical theory and an experimental result, and the result has survived severe, sustained, critical, experimental scrutiny, then the theory is, in general, held to be false. But there is always the possibility that the fault lies, not with the theory, but with the experimental result, and it is the latter that needs to be rejected. Likewise, given a dramatic clash between theory and the best available metaphysical thesis at the bottom of the hierarchy of theses then, in general, the theory will be rejected (whatever its empirical success might be) on the grounds that it is too ad hoc and disunified to be accepted. It is always possible, however, that the fault may lie with the metaphysical thesis rather than the physical theory; the theory may be accepted, and the metaphysical thesis may be revised. This is likely to happen if the theory (a) has met with great empirical success and (b) accords with that metaphysical thesis one up in the hierarchy of theses. In this way, according to AOE, as physics proceeds, clashes between a physical theory and the metaphysical thesis at the bottom of the hierarchy of theses in general result in the theory being rejected, but will, on occasions, result in the metaphysical thesis being revised and the theory being accepted. Examples of such revisions taken from the history of physics are: rejection of the corpuscular hypothesis (which clashes with Newtonian theory); rejection of the view that nature consists of point-atoms interacting by means of rigid, spherically-symmetrical forces (which clashes with Maxwellian electrodynamics given its field interpretation, and special relativity); rejection of the view that nature consists of a self-interacting classical field (which clashes with quantum theory). Metaphysical theses higher up in the hierarchy survive such revisions of theses at the bottom of the hierarchy. The basic idea of this hierarchical view is to concentrate criticism and revision where it seems most likely to be needed, namely low down in the hierarchy of theses. In this way, a relatively permanent, unproblematic framework of assumptions and associated methods is created within which much more specific, substantial, and problematic assumptions and methods can be revised in the light of the empirical success and failure of associated research programmes. As theoretical knowledge improves, assumptions and associated methods improve as well: knowledge-about-how-to-improve-knowledge is improved. There is something like positive feedback between improving knowledge, and improving assumptions and methods, or aims and methods, the methodological key, according to this view, to the immense success of modern science. (For further details see Maxwell 1998; see also the other works cited on p. 185 above.)

This hierarchical, aim-oriented empiricist conception of scientific method can be generalized, in accordance with step (ii) of the Enlightenment Programme, to form a new conception of rationality fruitfully applicable to any worthwhile human endeavour with problematic aims. As we have in effect just seen, a basic and highly problematic aim of science is to discover in what way (and to what extent) the universe is comprehensible, it being presupposed that it is comprehensible in some way or another, to some extent. Precisely because of the highly problematic character of this aim, we need to represent it as a hierarchy of aims, increasingly unspecific and unproblematic as we go up the hierarchy, thus creating a relatively permanent framework of unproblematic aims and associated methods within which more specific and problematic aims and associated methods can be revised and, we may hope, improved, as we proceed, in the light of empirical success and failure.

But it is not just in science that aims are problematic; this is the case in life too, either because different aims conflict, or because what we believe to be desirable and realizable lacks one or other of these features, or both. Above all, the aim of creating global civilization is inherently and profoundly problematic. Quite generally, then, and not just in science, whenever we pursue a problematic aim we need first, to acknowledge the aim; then we need to represent it as a hierarchy of aims, from the specific and problematic at the bottom of the hierarchy, to the general and unproblematic at the top. In this way we provide ourselves with a framework within which we may improve more or less specific and problematic aims and methods as we proceed, learning from success and failure in practice what it is that is both of most value and realizable. Such an 'aim-oriented' conception of rationality is the proper generalization of the aim-oriented, progress-achieving methods of science (see Maxwell, 1976; 1984, Chapter 5; 2001, Chapter 9; 2004, Chapter 3).

Any conception of rationality that systematically leads us astray must be defective. But any conception of rationality, such as Popper's critical rationalism, that does not include explicit means for the *improvement* of aims, must systematically lead us astray. It will do so whenever we fail to choose that aim that is in our best interests or, more seriously, whenever we misrepresent our aim — as we are likely to do whenever aims are problematic. In these circumstances, the more 'rationally' we pursue the aim we acknowledge, the worse off we will be. Systematically, such conceptions of rationality, which do not include provisions for improving problematic aims, are a hindrance rather than a help; they are, in short, defective. (Science specifically, and academia more generally, at present misrepresent basic aims: see Maxwell 1976; 1984; 2002a, 2004.)

AOE and its generalization, aim-oriented rationality (AOR), incorporate all the good points of Popper's falsificationist conception of science and its generalization, critical rationalism, indicated above, but also improve on Popper's notions, in being designed to help science and other worthwhile endeavours progressively improve problematic aims and methods.

We come now to step (iii) of the new Enlightenment Programme. The task, here, is to help humanity gradually get more AOR into diverse aspects of social and institutional life — personal, political, economic, educational, international — so that humanity may gradually learn how to make progress towards an enlightened world. Social inquiry, in taking up this task, needs to be pursued as social *methodology* or social *philosophy*. What the philosophy of science is to science, as conceived by AOE, so sociology is to the social world: it has the task of helping diverse valuable human endeavours and institutions gradually improve aims and methods so that the world may make social progress towards global enlightenment. (The sociology of science, as a special case, is one and the same thing as the philosophy of science.) And a basic task of academic inquiry, more generally, becomes to help humanity solve its problems of living in increasingly rational, cooperative, enlightened ways, thus helping humanity become more civilized. The basic aim of academic inquiry becomes, as I have already said, to promote the growth of *wisdom*. Those parts of academic inquiry devoted to improving knowledge, understanding, and technological know-how contribute to the growth of wisdom. The New Enlightenment Programme thus has dramatic and far reaching implications for academic inquiry, for almost every branch and aspect of science and the humanities, for its overall character and structure, its overall aims and methods, and its relationship to the rest of the social world. (For further details see Maxwell 1976, 1977, 1980, 1987, 1991, 1992a, 1992b, 1997, 1998, 2000a, 2000b, 2001, 2002a, 2002b, 2002c, and especially 1984 and 2004.)

As I have already remarked, the aim of achieving global civilization is inherently problematic. This means, according to AOR, that we need to represent the aim at a number of levels, from the specific and highly problematic to the unspecific and unproblematic. Thus, at a fairly specific level, we might, for example, specify civilization to be a state of affairs in which there is an end to war, dictatorships, population growth, extreme inequalities of wealth, and where democratic, liberal world government and a sustainable world industry and agriculture are established. At a rather more general level we might specify civilization to be a state of affairs in which everyone shares equally in enjoying, sustaining, and creating what is of value in life *in so far as this is possible*. And at a more general level still, we might specify civilization to be that ideal, realizable state of affairs we ought to try to achieve in the long term.

As a result of building into our institutions and social life such a hierarchical structure of aims and associated methods, we create a framework within which it becomes possible for us progressively to improve our real-life aims and methods in increasingly cooperative ways as we live. Diverse philosophies of life — diverse religious, political, economic, and moral views — may be cooperatively developed, assessed and tested against the experience of personal and social life. It becomes possible progressively to improve diverse *philosophies of life* (diverse views about what is of value in life and how it is to be realized) much as *theories* are progressively and cooperatively improved in science.

AOR is especially relevant when it comes to resolving conflicts cooperatively. If two groups have partly conflicting aims but wish to discover the best resolution of the conflict, AOR helps in requiring of those involved that they represent aims at a level of sufficient imprecision for agreement to be possible, thus creating an agreed framework within which disagreements may be explored and resolved. AOR cannot, of itself, combat non-cooperativeness, or induce a desire for cooperativeness; it can however facilitate the cooperative resolution of conflicts if the desire for this exists. In facilitating the cooperative resolution of conflicts in this way, AOR can, in the long term, encourage the desire for cooperation to grow (if only because it encourages belief in the possibility of cooperation).

Bibliography

Maxwell, N. (1974). 'The Rationality of Scientific Discovery'. *Philosophy of Science* **41**, pp. 123-53, 247-95.

——— (1976). *What's Wrong With Science?* Frome: Bran's Head Books.

——— (1977). 'Articulating the Aims of Science'. *Nature* **265**, 6.i.1977, p. 2.

——— (1980). 'Science, Reason, Knowledge and Wisdom: A Critique of Specialism'. *Inquiry* **23**, pp. 19-81.

——— (1984). *From Knowledge to Wisdom.* Oxford: Blackwell.

——— (1987). 'Wanted: A New Way of Thinking'. *New Scientist*, 14.v.1987, p. 63.

——— (1991). 'How Can We Build a Better World?' In J. Mittelstrass, editor (1991), pp. 388-427. *Einheit der Wissenschaften: Internationales Kolloquium der Akademie der Wissenschaften zu Berlin.* Berlin: Walter de Gruyter.

——— (1992a). 'What Kind of Inquiry Can Best Help Us Create a Good World?' *Science, Technology and Human Values* **17**, pp. 205-227.

——— (1992b). 'What the Task of Creating Civilization Has to Learn from the Success of Modern Science: Towards a New Enlightenment'. *Reflections on Higher Education* **4**, pp. 47-69.

——— (1993). 'Induction and Scientific Realism: Einstein versus van Fraassen, Parts I-III'. *The British Journal for the Philosophy of Science*, **44**, pp. 61-79, 81-101, 275-305.

——— (1997). 'Science and the Environment: A New Enlightenment'. *Science and Public Affairs*, Spring 1997, pp. 50-56.

——— (1998). *The Comprehensibility of the Universe.* Oxford: Oxford University Press, 1998.

——— (1999). 'Has Science Established that the Universe is Comprehensible?' *Cogito* **13**, pp. 139-145.

——— (2000a). 'Can Humanity Learn to Become Civilized? The Crisis of Science without Civilization'. *Journal of Applied Philosophy* **17**, pp. 29-44.

——— (2000b). 'A New Conception of Science'. *Physics World* **13**, pp. 17f.

——— (2001). *The Human World in the Physical Universe.* Lanham MD: Rowman & Littlefield.

——— (2002a). 'Is Science Neurotic?', *Metaphilosophy* **33**, pp. 259-299.

——— (2002b). 'The Need for a Revolution in the Philosophy of Science'. *Journal for General Philosophy of Science* **33**, pp. 1-28.

——— (2002c). 'Karl Raimund Popper'. In P. Dematteis & others, editors (2002), pp. 176-194. *British Philosophers, 1800-2000.* Detroit: Gale Group.

——— (2004). *Is Science Neurotic?* London, Imperial College Press.

———— (2005). 'Popper, Kuhn, Lakatos and Aim-oriented Empiricism'. *Philosophia* **32**, pp. 181-239.

Popper, K. R. (1945). *The Open Society and Its Enemies*. London: George Routledge & Sons. 5th edition 1966. London: Routledge & Kegan Paul.

———— (1957). *The Poverty of Historicism*. London: Routledge & Kegan Paul.

———— (1959). *The Logic of Scientific Discovery*. London: Hutchinson.

———— (1963). *Conjectures and Refutations*. London: Routledge & Kegan Paul. 5th edition 1989. London: Routledge.

———— (1972). *Objective Knowledge*. Oxford: Clarendon Press, 1972. 2nd edition 1979.

12

Popper in the Poison Cupboards
The Resonance of his Political Works in the Former GDR

Rachael Knight

In the public libraries of former East Germany, *Giftschrank*, or 'poison cupboard', was the common name for a stockroom of classified literature. In 1961, the government tried to euphemize such terms. *Sperrbibliothek*, or 'locked library', disappeared from official documents and the state secretary ordered that *Giftschrank* be replaced by a term meaning 'section for special research literature' (Ferret 1997, p. 403). Such a phrase was to attract less interest than a book kept in a 'poison cupboard'. Unofficially, however, the word *Giftschrank* stuck.

This paper has three main 'blocks' of interest. The first identifies the official East German response to Popper and so makes clear why his political works were segregated into the so-called poison cupboards. The second discusses in brief the use of Popper's works in East German theology schools — the small bastions of critical discussion. The final section then comments on the significance of Popper's political theory to the 1989 *Wende*.

1 The official response

Philosophy as a whole was given an immense status in the German Democratic Republic (GDR). The centralization of the economy and social structure compelled a parallel centralization of truth. Marxism was hallowed as a singular science and individual cornerstone of the system. It was given a philosophical monopoly and one that the government promulgated in all social areas. In Poland, Hungary, and Czechoslovakia, for example, communism did not so totally confront the individual state traditions. In East Germany, Walter Ulbricht, the leader of the GDR from its formation in 1949, had to convince the people that the very disfavoured occupation army had in fact freed them. This compelled a rigid suppression (at least until the 1980s) of such national traditions as the Reformation, humanist education, and the role of Bismarck. Theories from the West critiquing Marxism were thus all the more denounced as imperialist and/or bourgeois. The official academic perspective warned against Popper as an anti-Marxist whose teaching could threaten the global socialist victory. Thus the regime tried to protect its own ideology and success by barring access to Popper's ideas.

As a rule, visitors to public libraries could not read Popper's political works without a permission slip that verified their purpose as scientific. Consequently, the readership was practically limited to the students and faculty of philosophy departments and a few academics whose studies closely related to Popper's work. Otherwise, Popper's books could occasionally be obtained through underground contacts.

Most published East German material on Popper is from those who remained unequivocal in their rebuke that his political work was a strategic, yet erroneous anti-Marxism. A number of writers, for example, asserted that Popper's theory against historical necessity is based on long since defeated arguments. Others presented Popper's philosophy as promoting unhinged morality and 'moral opportunism'. Critical rationalism and Popper's 'open' theory of knowledge were ridiculed as the basis for an arbitrary and irresponsible moral concept. East German academics within the official realm of academia, asserted that only the developmental laws of society, as discovered by Marx, give an unerring basis for morals and action, whereas Popper's theories preclude principled morals. Evidently, this is a biased misrepresentation, particularly of Chapter 22 of *The Open Society*. As other authors such as Eidlin (1999) and Pralong (1999) affirm, a distinct moral code does underpin Popper's concept of an open society, his choice of critical rationalism — indeed his entire political writings. (I shall return to this point in section 2.)

Much of the official critique against Popper might be regarded as a predictable response from any of the Eastern bloc socialist states. Yet the official GDR criticism also includes points of particular interest: Academics such as Harald Wessel denounced critical rationalism for what was seen as its tangible social influence (Wessel 1971a, p. 6). Wessel made the portentous claim that Popper's ideas effected the key turning point in the West German student protests of 1968. As the *Positivismusstreit*[1] took its course through the 1960s, it became evident that the support for the Frankfurt School's doctrine of critical theory was waning and giving way to Popper's theory of critical rationalism. Bryan Magee, recalls how '[i]nsofar as this would-be revolution had an ideology it was unquestionably Marx-inspired, even if the Marxism was not always orthodox' (Magee 1999, p. 146). The Neomarxism of the Frankfurt School was seen to have sparked the wave of upheaval through its comprehensive criticism of the late bourgeois society. East German academics, such as Joachim Pröhl and Klaus Kneist,[2] argued that it was the growing recognition of Popper's theory that defused the 1968-1969 turmoil; and that the advocates of critical rationalism eliminated the school's influence on the left student movements (Kneist 1981, p. 12). The protests were even depicted as

---

[1] For further background on the *Positivismusstreit* see Adorno et al. (1969).

[2] Klaus Kneist. Lecturer of philosophy at the Academy of Social Sciences at the Central Committee of the East German Communist Party (SED) – Institute for Marxist-Leninist Philosophy, Berlin, East Germany.

an opportunity for a socialist revolt of a far broader impact, yet one effectively foiled by Popper's ideas.

What is certain is that Popper's social theory made a considerable impact in West German politics throughout the 1970s and at least until the end of Helmut Schmidt's term as Chancellor in 1982. Schmidt named Popper alongside Aurel, Kant, and Weber, as one of his four 'in-house medicines' — an evidently unintended, yet neat antithesis to the poison image — and admitted that he consciously referred to thinkers such as Popper in the midst of political decision-making (Rupps 1997, p. 138).

Schmidt wrote with explicit support for piecemeal social engineering as well as the concept of an open society (Schmidt 1996, p. 150). He also highlighted Popper's theory that such a society is incompatible with a Utopian approach and that to protect West Germany from totalitarian tendencies, politicians would have to rely on variations of piecemeal reform. Indeed in an article from 1987 Schmidt suggests that Popper's political philosophy met a characteristic need in the case of Germany, considering a recurring tendency towards a Utopian model (Schmidt 1987, p. 31).

East German writers exaggerated Popper's influence and hailed him as West Germany's state philosopher. Academics loyal to the regime argued that Schmidt favoured Popper's political theory to legitimate fickle politics and evade commitment to social change. A main bone of contention was the endorsement of Popper's argument for reform rather than revolution. Kneist claimed that under Schmidt, the West German Social Democrats (SPD) had so influenced the theory of the working-class movements that they no longer regarded socialism as their end-goal, rather, they had turned to an anti-communist position that openly endorsed bourgeois society.

Even so, some East German authors dismissed the reach of Popper's influence. Wessel scoffed at piecemeal social engineering for lacking efficacy. He compared this theory with the Marxist metaphor of revolutions as the locomotives of history (1971b, p. 67):

> 'left reformism' would like to replace the locomotives of history with small toy trains. The mini-dynamics of 'small steps' which are 'more peaceful' and are 'more according to law', are supposed to replace the mass power of the revolution. But they always go around obediently in a small circle, and such child's play does not at all disturb the real rulers.

Certainly, some of the East German doctoral dissertations and articles written on Popper have a more scholarly register and offer careful analyses of his theories. However, the predominant tone of the official criticism was one of rigid ideological self-defence. As indicated, this included an acute awareness of Popper's influence in West Germany. Popper was branded from the start as a bourgeois philosopher and this precluded a fair consideration of his ideas. Moreover, as the preface to a book against piecemeal engineering reminded its readers, the victory of the working class 'demands not only the political and economic, but *just as much the strict ideological and theoretical dis-empowerment* of the bourgeoisie' (Wessel 1971a, p. 5; italics added).

2 Popper in the theology schools

The East German theological or seminary schools, however, housed a sub-group of academics who typically did not submit to such strict ideological prejudice. These thinkers taught Popper with genuine scientific interest and encouraged students to consider his reasoning against Marxism. The government did not officially recognize these institutes and they often relied on smuggled literature, but they were not illegal. In the philosophy departments of the state universities and academies, the theories of thinkers such as Heidegger, Sartre, and Popper were presented, but students were forbidden to read their works. By contrast, in the theology schools students could freely study the books of these authors.

Richard Schröder lectured at theology schools in both Naumburg and East Berlin. Rather than having any strong empathy for a religious career, Schröder had chosen to study theology as it was one of the few university courses that did not require membership in the state communist party. As in the cases of a number of theologians in East Germany, Schröder's work as a theology professor advanced his dissident tendency and it gave him the freedom to study and teach the works of Popper (Schröder 1999, p. 1):

> I dealt myself with Popper in my lectures ... — above all *Logik der Forschung* and *The Poverty of Historicism*. The latter book was also important for my own examination of Marxist-Leninism. This also left an impression on my students.

This gives evidence of the place of Popper's work within the curricula at such academies and how it was used to develop a critical perspective on Marxism. By 1989, Schröder had become co-founder of an opposition party (the East German Social Democrats[3]) and a key figure striving for political change. As Schröder also highlights, a high proportion of theology students took activist roles in the *Wende* process.

While Schröder points out that he first came to know Popper's philosophy in the early 1980s, Joachim Goetz, a former student at the Naumburg school, affirms that in the late 1970s he and his fellow students were required to make an intensive study of *The Open Society*. While the book did not become a central pillar in his political argument, it did contribute to his political persuasion and Goetz likewise took a leading activist role in the events leading to November 9, 1989.[4]

---

[3]The SDP (founded in September 1989) was the *Sozialdemokratische Partei* (Social Democratic Party). Soon after November 1989 the SDP amalgamated with the West German SPD.

[4]Interview with Goetz, 19 October 1999. (Joachim Goetz, a student of theology at the Advanced Catechist College, Naumburg, was Priest at Bartholomäus Kirche, East Berlin. In the mid-1980s, he was co-founder of the *Arbeitskreis Solidarische Kirche*, an activist group that campaigned for increased democracy.)

Not all lecturers, however, at the theology academies encouraged students to agree with Popper's teaching. Wolfgang Ullmann, for instance, took a decidedly critical position against certain points in *The Open Society* and taught this perspective to his students in East Berlin. This is significant considering that Ullmann was also a key opposition figure throughout the initial and latter stages of the *Wende* and became a minister in Hans Modrow's cabinet,[5] as well as a leading participant of the Berlin Round Table and a Member of Parliament for the Green Party Alliance in the reunified Bundestag (Maleck 1991, p. 143). Ullmann sees Popper as having perpetrated a number of significant misunderstandings of Marx, whom he perceives as a true scientist. He also criticizes, for example, Popper's theory of knowledge by arguing that the ever recurring test of falsification would compel an ever-shifting code of ethics (Ullmann 1995, p. 61).

> The ever new test of falsification is an ever new suspension of verification, exactly what the old sceptics called the postponement of judgement. The critical aspect of this position is its relation to ethics. What should a code of ethics look like in relation to falsifying hypotheses? Obviously, it can also only be in such a way that all behaviour is with the reservation that a better teaching will turn up.

Consequently, we see how despite Ullmann's criticism of the GDR government and his subsequent activism, he shared similar doubts about Popper's moral code as other East German academics who defended the official ideology. This is despite Popper's reproach in *The Poverty of Historicism*, §§ 18, 22, that the belief in historical laws permits compromised morals. As touched on above, Popper evidently favoured a form of moral code that demands far more personal accountability — one that is not determined by social trends or historical circumstances. Pralong argues that Popper's *Open Society* implicitly outlines his political moral standard — an ethical methodology —, which also corresponds to Popper's theory of knowledge (Pralong 1999, pp. 128-135). Certainly we can see that Popper did not intend his falsification method to allow moral standards to give way. Ullmann, however, taught his (mis)understanding to his students. Therefore, although Popper's ideas were read and discussed in the seminary schools, it was not always in a way that would encourage dissident thinking. Indeed, although there was a strong demand for Popper's work immediately after the revolution in 1989, apart from his influence at some of the theological seminaries, there is little evidence that Popper's ideas directly fueled the impetus for change.

It is yet useful here to examine in more detail the question of Popper's moral standpoint. East Germany's *Wende* process from a 'closed society' to a radically more liberal one, can be viewed as an ethical insurrection. East German citizens called for a renewal of ethical standards within the political structure as one of the pivotal requirements for expediting change. By further sketching Popper's ethical expectations here, we have a broader basis both

---

[5]This was the last East German cabinet to be led by a communist.

from which to defend Popper's theory from points of East German academic criticism, and from which to trace the parallels between Popper's political ethics and some of those crucial to the *Wende*.

Popper's critique of Marx helps to reveal his own viewpoint. Popper saw the Marxist political theory as a secondary step from Marx's morality, and reasoned that Marx's ethical standpoint imaged Popper's own (1945, Chapter 22):

> He [Marx] attacked the moralists because he saw them as the sycophantic apologists of a social order which he felt to be immoral . . . . Thus, by implication, he admitted his love for freedom; and in spite of his bias, as a philosopher, for holism, he was certainly not a collectivist, for he hoped that the state would 'wither away'. Marx's faith, I believe, was fundamentally a faith in the open society.

Here Popper links Marx's high moral position with a belief in the open society, implying a parallel with Popper's ethical values. He then attacks Marx for 'betraying' this social conscience with a faulty political theory. Despite the strength of praise for Marx's morals, Popper more distinctly berates what he terms the 'historicist moral theory'. As outlined in *The Poverty of Historicism*, Popper holds Marx's socialist prophecy as culpable for declining moral standards and promoting, for example, the suppression of critical thought, as well as personal social responsibility.

3   Popper and the *Wende*

So what is the significance of Popper's Marxist critique to what took place in East Germany and the Socialist bloc at the end of the 1980s? This final section sketches the argument that much of Popper's political reasoning coincides with the characteristics of the GDR government and its demise; that as the tribal socialism of the Eastern bloc was deconstructed, this unhinged the established political mechanisms, such as those used to prohibit freedom of movement, manipulate information, and repress critical thought.

On 1 May each year, East Germany had its largest national holiday. Children from every school and people from every workplace were expected to attend official rallies together in groups. The largest assembly was the state parade along Karl-Marx-Allee, in Berlin. Here people marched past Erich Honecker,[6] who stood waving from a tiered stage. Over the years, however, support for these official events diminished considerably. People preferred to use the day as they chose — to picnic for instance. In response to the depleted numbers, the Stasi (the secret state police) organized groups of those who did parade to repeat their walk. The Stasi directed these people to go on to the next *U-Bahn* station (Weberwiese), travel back to the station closest to where Honecker stood (Strausberger Platz) and so to parade past him a second time.

---

[6] Erich Honecker succeeded Walter Ulbricht in 1971.

Thus, the national leader was led to believe that a greater number of citizens than was really the case had thronged to greet him and celebrate the state.

This story underscores the network of lies that pervaded East Germany and the socialist bloc. It was a chronic self-infliction of falsehood and one that corresponds directly with key points in Popper's reasoning. The anecdote just mentioned fits, for example, with Popper's binary opposites of the open and closed societies: 'the magical or tribal or collectivist society will also be called the closed society, and the society in which individuals are confronted with personal decisions, the open society' (Popper 1945, Chapter 10, § 1; italics suppressed). The objective of the Stasi was to construct an appearance of healthy collectivism — of mass crowds honouring the state and its ideology. Honecker was not to know what was really going on and thus not to be confronted with genuine political responsibility. There were even particular streets in East Berlin where a few select houses were painted so that Honecker could be chauffeured on a set route where cosmetics disguised the economic predicament.

Popper argued that within a system that subscribes to Utopian engineering 'there is every likelihood' that the government will have to repress objections to the regime and to control information. He also reasoned that holistic planners would need to 'control and stereotype interests and beliefs by education and propaganda' (Popper 1957, § 24). There are numerous examples of all these symptoms in the former GDR. Unfortunately, this paper does not have the scope to treat these in depth, but I will mention a couple to highlight the extent of the deceit. The first coincides with Popper's expectation that it would be very likely for such regimes to pose as protectors of their country and so perpetuate the belief in a national enemy.

Jens Reich points out that the enemy propaganda by the East German government was taken so far that it overtly lacked credibility and even encouraged the reverse of its intended effect. Reich refers in particular to the Berlin Wall and its so-called justification as an 'anti-fascist protection wall'. He writes (1999, p. 12):

> Whatever position you took on the reason for the establishment and continued existence of this fiction, the description was so obviously untrue that it even discredited anti-fascism. Thus, the appeal to anti-fascism provoked either total rejection or even a fascinated turning to radical right-wing ideologies.

The history of prominent figures was also silenced. Quite soon after Ulbricht ceded his position to Honecker in 1971, his existence and relevance to East Germany were largely hushed. A state textbook from 1970 (*Politisches Grundwissen*) mentions Ulbricht approximately one hundred times, yet in its second edition two years later, Ulbricht is not referred to once (Hütter 1998, p. 92). Apparently the government was attempting quickly to distance the nation's attention from Ulbricht's conspicuous endorsement of Stalinism, his political *faux pas*, and his depleted competence after more than twenty years to represent progressive socialism.

When Mikhail Gorbachev came to power in the Soviet Union in 1985, his politics gradually underscored a contrast both with the methods used by previous Soviet leaders, and with the cover-up tactics used in the satellite socialist states. Like his predecessors, Gorbachev would give notice that he intended to visit a particular Moscow hospital. However, he would then deliberately call on a hospital that had not been forewarned. Just as on factory visits, he sought to speak with those people who would candidly complain, rather than with the traditional group of KGB selected workers who would unduly compliment conditions. These tactics were part of Gorbachev's new policy of *glasnost* — openness. It was a policy that at least in spirit coincided both with the characteristics of an *open* society and with critical rationalism. It was also what Gorbachev saw as a prerequisite for his second famous policy of this period — namely *perestroika* (restructuring).[7]

Gorbachev saw the need to end the practice of constructed or falsified statistics, so that he could accurately assess the economic circumstances of the Soviet Union. As with Honecker, such information was even withheld from the highest levels of the Politburo. The new transparency in the Soviet Union ended up running its own course and opened a can of economic and social worms far greater than anticipated. Yet Gorbachev continued this new confrontation with the actual conditions and then permitted the same confrontation and personal responsibility to the other socialist states. Ralf Dahrendorf (1990, pp. 6f.) relates how Gorbachev's Foreign Ministry spokesman, Gerasimov, announced this new Soviet approach on 25 October 1989. Gerasimov was asked

> whether the Soviet Union still adhered to the Brezhnev Doctrine, which threatened recalcitrant allies with military intervention. He replied by introducing the Sinatra Doctrine: 'Sinatra', he said, had a song, "I did it my way ...." So every country decides in its own way which road to take.'

Dahrendorf's examination of the *Wende* uses Popper's 'open society' as an analytical *leitmotif*. He sees Gorbachev as having unlocked political doors for socialist central Europe to an 'open future by abdicating from its hegemonic control'.

In 1992 Popper gave his own analysis of the fall of socialism in Eastern Europe. He asserted that socialist states endeavoured to hide their erroneous theoretical basis under a panoply of lies — one that was sustained by dictatorial power and violence, but which ultimately procured its own end (Popper 1999, Chapter 12, p. 129). Popper's theoretical analysis of Marxism had long agreed with Bertrand Russell's empirically based conclusion that the communist attitude precludes a 'scientific temper' or 'fruitful scepticism' which constitutes the scientific outlook (Russell 1920, p. 8). Thus Popper emphasizes that the socialist regimes not only purveyed deceit, but their Marxist foundation was itself a pseudo-science blind to its own falsehood. Popper argued

---

[7]*Perestroika* can likewise be seen to have parallels with Popper's theory of piecemeal social engineering.

that it was the Soviet Union's internal weakness that impelled Gorbachev's program of reform and prevented any 'disciplinary' intervention against the Hungarian regime when it permitted East Germans to use their land as a passage to freedom.

In another interview, however, Popper saw this Soviet Union – Hungary link as having had a critical *reflex* effect on the USSR, and so speaks of the Hungarian government as having made the key move in the *Wende*. When asked what he would identify as the principal factor causing the collapse of the Soviet regime, Popper answered in 1991 as follows (1997, Chapter 3):

> What brought on the breakdown was the flight of East Germans through Hungary to West Germany. Although the Soviet Union had been reduced to a kind of empty room intellectually, it could have gone on for ever, or at least for a long time. But the decision of the Hungarians ... led to the fall of the East German regime, with everything that has followed from it.

It must be seen, however, that the Hungarians were able to make this choice only because of Gorbachev's new Sinatra Doctrine with its release from Soviet hegemony or tribal socialism. Consequently, the steps leading to the *Wende* in 1989 can also be viewed as the culmination of an increased development of political responsibility — the type of responsibility that is in accord with what Popper saw as requisite for the 'open future' of an open society. Indeed, Popper confirms that the Utopian, Marxist approach 'was a mistake from the very start', describing it as 'hatred instead of responsibility' (1997, Chapter 5). Many East German citizens finally demanded freedom from this ideological oppression and its correlative intellectual repression, from the ubiquitous secret police and a tightly coddled, failing economy. Just as Popper had done through analysis over forty years earlier, great numbers of East Germans demonstrated their rejection of the authoritarianism of a Marxist regime, and so defied its notion of inexorable historical laws and the prophecy of a global socialist future.

Bibliography

Adorno, T. W., Albert, H., Dahrendorf, R., Habermas, J. & Popper, K. R. (1969). *Der Positivismusstreit in der deutschen Soziologie*. Neuwied & Berlin: Hermann Luchterhand Verlag GmbH. 2. Auflage 1970. English translation 1976. *The Positivist Dispute in German Sociology*. London: Heinemann.

Dahrendorf, R. G. (1990). *Reflections on the Revolution in Europe. In a Letter Intended to have been sent to a Gentleman in Warsaw*. New York: Random House.

Eidlin, F. (1999). 'Matching Popperian Theory to Practice'. In Jarvie & Pralong (1999), pp. 203-207.

Ferret, C. (1997). 'Die Zensur in den Bibliotheken der DDR'. *Zeitschrift für Bibliothekswesen und Bibliographie* **44**, p. 403.

Hütter, H. W. (1998). *Bilder die Lügen*. Bonn: Stiftung Haus der Geschichte der Bundesrepublik Deutschland.

Jarvie, I. C. & Pralong, S., editors (1999). *Popper's Open Society after Fifty Years. The Continuing Relevance of Karl Popper*. London: Routledge.

Kneist, Klaus. (1981). *Dialektisch-materialistische oder kritisch-rationalistische Methode der Gesellschaftserkenntnis? (Eine Auseinandersetzung mit dem kritischen Rationalismus)*. Berlin: Akademie für Gesellschaftswissenschaften beim ZK der SED – Institut für Marxistisch-Leninistische Philosophie.

Magee, B. (1999). 'What Use is Popper to a Practical Politician?' In Jarvie & Pralong (1999), pp. 146-158.

Maleck, B. (1991). *Wolfgang Ullmann: 'Ich werde nicht schweigen': Gespräche mit Wolfgang Ullmann/Bernhard Maleck*. Berlin: Dietz Verlag GmbH.

Popper, K. R. (1945). *The Open Society and Its Enemies*. London: George Routledge & Sons. 5th edition 1966. London: Routledge & Kegan Paul.

——— (1957). *The Poverty of Historicism*. London: Routledge & Kegan Paul.

——— (1997). *The Lesson of This Century: with two Talks on Freedom and the Democratic State. Karl Popper interviewed by Giancarlo Bosetti*. London: Routledge.

——— (1999). *All Life Is Problem Solving*. London: Routledge.

Pralong, S. (1999). '*Minima Moralia*: Is There an Ethics of the Open Society?' In Jarvie & Pralong (1999), pp. 128-145.

Reich, J. (1999). 'Die Organisierte Langeweile. 40 Jahre DDR – ein Rückblick aus der Distanz von zehn Jahren'. *Die Zeit*, 41, 17.x.1999, p. 12.

Rupps, M. (1997). *Helmut Schmidt: Politikverständnis und geistige Grundlagen*. Bonn: Bouvier.

Russell, B. A. W. (1920). *The Practice and Theory of Bolshevism*. London: George Allen & Unwin Ltd.

Schmidt, H. (1987). 'Der Mann mit dem Goldhelm'. *Die Zeit*, 31, 24.vii.1987, p. 31.

―――― (1996). *Weggefährten: Erinnerungen und Reflexionen*. Berlin: Siedler.

Schröder, R. (1999). Letter to the author, 3.viii.1999.

Ullmann, W. (1995). *Zukunft Aufklärung. Eine Bestandsaufnahme nach dem Ende der Utopien*. Berlin: Kontext Verlag.

Wessel, H. (1971a). *Für die siebziger Jahre eine Philosophie des Stückwerks? Kritische Anmerkungen zu einem Aufsatz des Mannheimer Neopositivisten Hans Albert*. Cologne: Facit Verlag.

―――― (1971b). *Philosophie des Stückwerks. Eine Auseinandersetzung mit dem neupositivistischen 'kritischen Rationalismus'*. Frankfurt/Main: Verlag Marxistische Blätter GmbH.

13

Can the Japanese Learn to Welcome Criticism Openly?[*]

Kiichi Tachibana

1 Surreptitious changes[1]

Joseph Agassi has emphasized the importance of Popper's critique of surreptitious changes.[2] If we fail to confront the mistakes pointed out by critics, but instead change the original assertions surreptitiously, we cannot learn from our mistakes. Furthermore, the idea of surreptitious changes is closely connected with a closed society.[3] This suggested to me that it would be worthwhile to write a book on surreptitious changes in Japan as an aid to making Japanese society more open, more democratic, more liberal, and more egalitarian. In Popper's view of the open society, freedom, equality, and mutual help are mutually compatible.[4]

As far as I know Popper uses the expressions, 'surreptitious alterations' or 'surreptitious changes' only in two places in his books, one in *The Logic of Scientific Discovery* (1959) and the other in *Conjectures and Refutations* (1963). Popper's argument in his *Logic*, § 20, against surreptitious alterations is too technical to be explained here. I shall therefore restrict myself in this paper to explaining the objections to surreptitious changes presented in *Conjectures and Refutations*.

Popper says almost all schools, except the Ionian School of Thales, Anaximander, and Anaximenes, are founded on the same task, that is, the task of imparting a definite doctrine, and preserving it, pure and unchanged. It is

---

[*]I am grateful to William Berkson and the anonymous referees for many helpful suggestions. Sheldon Richmond and Ivor Ludlam helped to correct my English. In places the content of this paper overlaps with my paper 'Criticism and Surreptitious Changes', *Learning for Democracy* **2**, 2006, pp. 49-58.

[1]In Japan there still exists a fear of change, which may impede surreptitious changes as well as explicit changes. See Koestler's (1961) analysis and my remark on it below.

[2]In October 2000, Agassi gave a lecture in Keio University, Tokyo, on 'Popper's Political Philosophy in the Perspective of Global Politics'. In this lecture he emphasized the importance of avoiding surreptitious changes.

[3]Agassi (1988), p. 331.

[4]Popper, mentioning Rousseau and Kant, says (1945, Chapter 12, § II): '[T]he freedom of each man should be restricted, but not beyond what is necessary to safeguard an equal degree of freedom for all.' See also ibidem, Chapter 6, note 20. Neither freedom nor equality is unlimited, but we can reduce unreasonable unfreedom and inequality as far as possible.

the task of a school to hand on the tradition, the doctrine of its founder, its master, to the next generation, and to this end the most important thing is to keep the doctrine intact. Then he writes:[5]

> In this way all changes of doctrine — if any — cannot but be *surreptitious changes*. They are all presented as re-statements of the true sayings of the master, of his own words, his own meaning, his own intentions.

Let us call such a tradition an 'authoritarian tradition'. By contrast, the Ionian school founded a tradition that allows or encourages critical discussions between various schools and, even within one and the same school. We may call this a 'critical tradition'. This spirit of respecting criticism was clearly expressed in Plato's *Gorgias*.[6]

> Socrates: Of what sort am I? One of those who would be glad to be refuted if I say anything untrue, and glad to refute anyone else who might speak untruly; but just as glad, mind you, to be refuted as to refute, since I regard the former as the greater benefit.

According to Popper, we are all fallible, but we can learn from our mistakes. His respect for criticism or mutual criticism is based on fallibilism. Now, in order to find mistakes we need criticism and refutations. In order to learn from our mistakes, we accept refutations as *refutations*, and try to correct our former views, and try to approach the truth as a regulative idea gradually, by correcting previous mistakes.

Surreptitious changes weaken the power of criticism since they obscure which part of an idea has been successfully criticized, and which part is right and which part is wrong. To learn from our mistakes we must first recognize that mistakes have been made, and this is what surreptitious changes allow us to avoid doing. One who changes his ideas surreptitiously can also give the impression that his ideas have not been refuted, and he can thereby dodge refutations. He learns nothing from his mistakes. Surreptitious change happens, for example, when criticism or refutations of a view are explained away as based on misunderstandings of that view, and the meaning and intentions of that view are reinterpreted to deflect the criticisms or refutations. Such surreptitious changes allow the view to appear to remain unchallenged, unrefuted, and intact. No mistakes appear to have been made by the defender of the view, and there is consequently no possibility of learning from the mistakes actually made. Opposition to surreptitious changes is therefore vitally important to criticism and refutation.

Popper's opposition to surreptitious changes is very important both in the philosophy of science and in social philosophy. I apply this idea to illuminate various political matters in Japan. The following is one of many examples.

---

[5]Popper (1963), Chapter 5, § XI. The italics are mine.
[6]Plato, *Gorgias* 458A.

2 From militarists to democrats: an example of surreptitious changes in Japan

There were many surreptitious changes in Japan after the Second World War. I have in mind such changes as: from militarists to democrats; from militarists to Marxists; war criminals returned to the political world; the process of rearmament; the red purge; from Marxists to militarists; surreptitious changes among some critics of politics and economics, and so on.

Here I shall take up only one example, the surreptitious change from militarists to democrats. Japan's postwar period began as the result of a so-called unconditional surrender.[7] Just before the unconditional surrender most Japanese militarists were forced to be militarists by order of the Japanese powers that be. This fact is exemplified by a well-known government official policy in the time of war, *Ichioku-So-Gyokusai*, which means that all one hundred million Japanese are ready to accept death but never surrender. Even after the Potsdam Declaration of 26 July 1945, this slogan continued to be advocated by the Japanese Army. They tried to continue the war under the illusion that a final battle on the main island of Japan would lead to victory. This idea is fanatical and required literally suicidal acts. It was a sign neither of nationalism, nor of patriotism, though appearing to be so. It was simply nihilism. They chose the way of complete annihilation, the utter destruction of the Japanese nation and way of life. In war, the motto of death and no surrender may regrettably have a point — but in a limited way, and not with regard to the Japanese people as a whole. The USA and its allies feared that this nihilism would be implemented.

The end of war was miserable and painful but nevertheless prevented complete annihilation. Japan surrendered on 15 August 1945. Just after the war Shigeru Yoshida, who later became Foreign Minister and then Prime Minister, frankly admitted that defeat was not necessarily bad.[8] Many Japanese may have felt the same. Such a common sentiment seems to have enabled the swift and peaceful reconstruction of Japan after the war.

After the surrender the slogan of death and no surrender was changed to *Ichioku-So-Zange*, which means that all one hundred million Japanese apologized. In the Diet on 5 September 1945, Prime Minister Naruhiko Higashikuni officially expressed this idea in a speech on his administrative policies.

The Japanese people immediately accepted democracy and welcomed MacArthur's occupation policies. They went to bed, as it were, as militarists and awoke next morning as democrats. In his book, *The Lotus and the Robot*, Arthur Koestler depicts this drastic change with wonder, though he does not use the term democracy:[9]

---

[7] Popper mentions 'unconditional surrender' as a case which should be worthy of careful analysis (1963, Chapter 17, § 7) I hope to find an opportunity to analyse this case.

[8] In his letter to Saburo Kurusu, dated 27 August 1945.

[9] Koestler (1961), p. 178.

The undefeated armies overseas, whose standing orders had been death before surrender, peacefully yielded up their arms at the Emperor's radioed order; there was no fighting on the beaches and no fighting in the streets, and no attempt to 'repel the Barbarian invader with bamboo spears'. The most ferociously warlike foe turned overnight into the most peaceful and affable population which an occupation army ever had to deal with.

Koestler tries to understand this by appealing to the Japanese traditional values of '*chu*', which means 'unconditional loyalty to the head of the social hierarchy' and '*ko*', which means 'the loyalty due to parents and ancestors'. He points out that *chu* was the First Commandment of Japanese ethics and *ko* was the Second and all other rules of conduct came lower in the list. Then he claims as follows:[10]

> The dramatic change which, on 14 August 1945, transformed the nation overnight from a tiger into a lamb was thus, paradoxically, a proof of its basically unchanged character; it showed that, in spite of revolutions and reforms, the traditional code of feudal ethics had never lost its hold; that the ancient pattern had survived underneath the imported, prefabricated superstructure.

Koestler's analysis is very interesting and may be true as an analysis of the situation at that time, especially in regard to the immediate steps taken by the Japanese when they heard Hirohito's order on the radio. If we accept his analysis, however, we have to conclude that the Japanese did not change at all, and that there were not even any surreptitious changes in Japan. In my opinion, once a new policy or a new institution is introduced, people who are subject to such a policy or institution will change their ideas and conduct if only a little and the Japanese are no exception. I hope that since the Second World War the Japanese have changed or are changing, or will change their ideas and conduct. Apparently they accepted democracy as an institution, which did not exist at all in prewar Japan, even though there was a democratic tendency for a short period. At least nowadays quite a few Japanese do not obey the rules of conduct, *chu* and *ko*, and there are some who do not even know what *chu* and *ko* are.[11] Accordingly I shall assume that the Japanese did in fact change their ideas and conduct, even though they might have changed them surreptitiously.

Did the Japanese, then, know what democracy was at that time? I am referring to the Japanese born before the Second World War. Did they regard democracy as important? Did they reflect and apologize? A former militarist who confesses that he was wrong and is now a democrat has changed, but not surreptitiously. Most of them, however, do not seem to me to have reflected and apologized. Or rather, I am afraid they may say they were formerly democrats and were *victims* of militarism, for the excuse was often made that they had been deceived by the military authorities.

---

[10]Ibidem, p. 178.

[11]Moral education is taught in Japanese public elementary schools, but *chu* and *ko* are no longer taught nowadays.

On the other hand, some may argue that all the Japanese apologized, since the saying, *Ichioku-So-Zange*, 'all one hundred million Japanese apologize', shows this fact. If so, my assertion that they did not apologize would be decisively refuted. I do not think my assertion has been refuted. My position is more nuanced. I could of course avoid the refutation by surreptitiously changing my view, or I could admit to making a mistake. I shall do neither.

2.1 Two senses of apology

Let me explain my position. I think there are at least two senses to the word 'apology'. In one of these senses, the Japanese apologized, but in the other sense, they did not apologize. In ordinary life a Japanese person often says 'I am sorry. I made a mistake' when he is *scolded* by another. This may appear to be Popperian,[12] but it is not. You will understand that this is not so from a simple question. 'Where do you think you made a mistake?' The scolded Japanese will not answer. He apologizes, but thinks that it is not he himself but the person who scolded him who should indicate where the mistake lies. He himself does not reflect and does not look for the cause of his mistake. I think the reason the Japanese apologize is that they want to be forgiven, and to say sorry means to beg for pardon. Once they are forgiven, they forget everything they did. The very expression of apology causes the faults of their past deeds to be washed away. There is a Japanese saying, *Misogi wo shite subete wo mizu ni nagasu*. '*Misogi*' means Japanese ablutions, and the saying means to wash and let bygones be bygones, or to be forgiven and forget, not forgive and forget. Apology is only a means to be forgiven by, to win pardon, and to return to the original state. They lost the war and surrendered, and apologized because they were defeated and lost. The reason for their apology was to return to the original state as before. If they had not lost the war, they would not have reflected, though they had made a lot of mistakes.

Now for the second sense of 'apology'. There are at least five conditions for a statement such as 'I am sorry. I made a mistake', to be an apology in the second sense. First, apology must be based on a sincere reflection, not pretence. Second, you have to say concretely where you made a mistake. Third, you must not forget the mistake. Fourth, you learn from the mistake and try to correct it. Fifth, you take responsibility for your mistakes and your attempted solutions.

The apology of *Ichioku-So-Zange* lacks all of the above-mentioned conditions. For this reason I say the Japanese did not apologize. They appear to have apologized and this might seem to refute my assertion, but they apologized in the first and not the second sense. I have not changed the sense of apology from the first sense to the second sense surreptitiously in order to evade refutation. I clearly show the two senses of apology and do not change from the first to the second surreptitiously, so I hope I am true to the spirit

---

[12]In a private conversation, dated 4 July 2002, Sheldon Richmond told me: 'Concerning intellectual mistakes a true Popperian may rather say "Thank you for pointing out my mistakes." '

of Popper. For a Popperian apology is a means not of obtaining forgiveness, but of learning from mistakes and their correction, and of revising one's ideas, deeds, or the society in which one lives. To change society for the better is an important aim, and apology in the second sense is its means. Therefore, the aims are utterly different between apologizing in the first sense and apologizing in the second sense.

Higashikuni, who confessed *Ichioku-So-Zange*, spoke further, 'Now we do not have to blame or condemn anybody or anything, *looking back into the past*.'[13] Therefore, he himself did not reflect, nor apologize; he just pretended to do so. And literally, all the Japanese were made to apologize under the disguise of apology by *him* in his speech. Of course, Higashikuni's idea of *Ichioku-So-Zange* was not accepted by all Japanese. For example, there were some who had been in jail because of their opposition to the war.

Besides, in his radio speech, that is, his Rescript on the End of War, Hirohito did not offer a word of reflection for the victims of Japanese aggression in the countries invaded. For him the reason for stopping the war was 'to avoid the extinction of his race and protect Japanese national polity'. He said that his intention had not been the invasion but rather the emancipation of Asia, and he did not apologize for the invasion as a consequence of this. Not only did he not answer for the invasion, but he apologized to his allies (the Axis), who, he said, had cooperated with Japan towards the emancipation of East Asia. He kept insisting that the war was not one of aggression but of emancipation! Again my assertion has not been refuted. Therefore, the change of most of the Japanese from militarism to democracy was merely surreptitious.

Or rather, it would be more accurate to say as follows. My earlier assertion was refuted. I learnt the errors and corrected them, proposing now that they did not apologize in the second sense. I tried to clarify the differences. I hope this procedure is not a surreptitious change. Further, I should like to propose that we Japanese should change the idea of apology from the first sense to the second sense. This change of attitude, I hope, will be *a first step against surreptitious changes*.

The process of change from militarism to democracy, particularly the process of change from *Ichioku-So-Gyokusai* to *Ichioku-So-Zange* may be compared to a Kuhnian paradigm change, that is, a gestalt switch. However, in the case of the apology in the Popperian sense, it is not a paradigm change but moral progress based on learning from mistakes. It depends on us whether our change is a Kuhnian paradigm change, which is irrational,[14] or a Popperian example of progress.

---

[13] The italics are mine.

[14] Clear evidence of Kuhn's irrationalism is the following: 'If I am right, then "truth" may, like "proof", be a term with only intra-theoretic applications. ... [C]onfusion will only be perpetuated by those who points out ... that the term is regularly used as though the transfer from intra- to inter-theoretic contexts made no difference.' (Kuhn 1970, p. 266).

Feyerabend said that the church was replaced by science and priests were replaced by scientists, but the authoritarian structure was the same.[15] His observation is not true for science, in which Popper sees critical traditions, which are utterly different from authoritarian ones, even though science *de facto* has some authority. However, in the case of Japan it seems right to say that militarism was replaced by democracy, but the authoritarian structure remained the same. Koestler also emphasized this point, as I mentioned above.

3 Militarism and the open society

Just as the open society is able to rid itself of militarism, the closed society is closely connected with militarism. Let me explain this connection with an example.

According to Popper, a tribal society is a closed society. In tribal society there exist fixed laws or customs that are sacred and fundamental to the cohesion and identity of the tribe. That is, they are the absolute criterion of right or wrong for the members of the tribe. They cannot be broken or even criticized, that is, to break or criticize them is taboo, and breaking the taboo is punishable, in the last resort, by death. The most rigid social control is capital punishment. It completely deprives man of his freedom. The function of taboo in tribal society is to regulate and dominate the members and stop them from doing anything on their own initiative. Only the ruler may be beyond restraint. Suppose you were a ruler. If you wanted to force the members to obey your laws rigidly, then you would have to close the society in order to have them believe that your laws are the best. Yet you cannot close your society completely. There will still be some new ideas that are born within the society or introduced from outside. Even having closed the door to new ideas from outside, you must get rid of those members inside who, for reasons of their own, will not obey your orders. You must expel or even kill such free thinkers, and this requires the use of military forces. The result is internal militarism, a terrible case of which existed in Japan before the Second World War.

There is another type of militarism. A country that invades another country is called a militarist country, and a man who supports this policy is also called a militarist. This type of militarism may better be called imperialism. Before the Second World War, Japan was founded on both internal militarism and imperialism. Many other countries were also imperialist countries. There are some Japanese who insist that Japan imitated what other countries did. This insistence is beside the point. If you commit a crime, you are wrong. Even if others commit the same crime, you are still wrong.

---

[15]Feyerabend said (1975, p. 157): 'In society at large the judgement of the scientist is received with the same reverence, as the judgement of bishops and cardinals was accepted not too long ago. ... [Y]ou will see that science has now become as oppressive as the ideologies it had once to fight.'

Now in Japan it became common sense that *invasion in general* is wrong. There have been some Japanese historians who therefore try to prove that Japan did not pursue a war of aggression. Several years ago in some high-school textbooks of Japanese history the authors changed the term 'invasion' to 'advance'. Whether right or not in their rewriting, they did, in fact, recognize that a war of aggression is wrong. Why, however, did they want to claim that Japan was not an invader? One of the reasons appears to be that if they admitted that Japan was an invader, Japanese soldiers and civilians who died in the war would have died in vain, their deaths being meaningless and absurd. In order to make their deaths meaningful, they could not publicly admit that Japan had been an invader, even though they knew this fact privately.

On the other hand, those who admitted that Japan had been an invader also admitted that those deaths had consequently been meaningless. The parties shared a common presupposition that, in my opinion, is mistaken. I think the death of Japanese soldiers and civilians in the war has meaning, because, despite the sorrow and pain, their death and Japanese defeat allow us to learn that Japan really did evil things, that Japan made mistakes. In fact, there was a special attack corps, a kamikaze party, comprising members who were willing to die in order to tell the Japanese people that this war was mistaken and meaningless. Let me mention an example.[16] A second sub-lieutenant in the first reserve who died with his manned torpedo *Kaiten* had left his last message, 'Japan will not win or rather Japan should be defeated. I am not going to die for the sake of the Emperor. I am going to be a foundation stone for the newly born Japan. Once I hit upon this idea, I could resolve my anguish.' I am sure that by being determined never to commit such mistakes, such evil things, we shall be able to mourn for our dead as well as for the victims of the invaded countries.

Recently more than half of ordinary Japanese people have accepted the fact that Japan invaded Korea and China, and so on and were wrong to do so.[17] Did they then reflect on their deeds deeply and apologize[18] to the Koreans and the Chinese in Popper's sense? The answer is no. Let me give you an example. Let us ask a person who says Japan invaded and it was wrong, a simple question, 'Do you think Hideyoshi Toyotomi is a great figure?' He replies yes. Then let us ask him, 'why is he a great man, though he invaded Korea?' He will not understand this question. He does not reflect on the past and just says parrot-fashion that invasion was wrong. Ideas have to be at least internally consistent, or else we can not criticize them, let alone refute them. Or rather, contradictory ideas are in themselves false. Even now quite a lot of

---

[16]This message is quoted in Iwai & Iwai (2002), pp. 193f. A question remains. Why did he attack?

[17]According to the public opinion poll dated 13 November 1993.

[18]A Japanese individual under the age of about 80 has no responsibility for the war and consequently has no need to apologize for it; yet, in my opinion, each individual should take responsibility for the history of the war, and should ensure that it is not falsified.

Japanese refer to Hideyoshi Toyotomi as one of the greatest politicians, as the Asahi Newspaper's periodic public opinion poll shows. And now I am surprised to find that there are some Japanese historians, albeit only a handful, who try to justify Hideyoshi's invasion.[19] If you really think invasion is wrong, you would have to say that Hideyoshi was wrong in his invasion, even though, perhaps, he carried out other good policies for us.

How about Japanese political leaders? Did the Japanese governments, our representatives, reflect on their deeds and apologize to the Asian nations? This is a typical example of surreptitious change.

After Hirohito died in 1989, the Japanese government's policy on war responsibility seemed to change drastically. On 10 August 1993, in a press conference Prime Minister Morihiro Hosokawa all of a sudden frankly referred to 'the war of aggression' and clearly expressed his apology to the Asian nations for the first time in Japanese modern history. Then in a speech on his administrative policies in the Diet two weeks later, on 23 August, he said almost the same thing concerning war responsibility. However, he did not use the expression, 'the war of aggression' but 'aggressive acts', without explaining the difference. This is nothing but a surreptitious change. Since then, succeeding Prime Ministers seem to have followed Hosokawa's view but never used the expression, 'the war of aggression'. Even now one cannot tell whether the Japanese government officially admits the war to have been a 'war of aggression' or not.[20]

Let us go back to the problem of the open society and militarism. What is militarism exactly? The late Masao Maruyama[21] (1914-1996), who was a leading political scientist and a champion of democracy against militarism in Japan, defines militarism as follows:[22]

> In a country or in a society a mode of thought or behaviour that places considerations and institutions for wars and preparations of wars the highest place semi-permanently, and subordinates all the other realms of national life such as politics, economics, education, culture to the militarist values.

I agree with his definition of militarism but I do not agree with his following remark, that is, that militarism is a tendency and that any society is more or less militaristic.[23] I think one should make a difference between militarism

---

[19] Nishio (1999), pp. 369-383.

[20] Suppose, for the sake of argument, that the meaning of 'aggressive acts' is the same as 'war of aggression'. One may then ask which wars are included in the war of aggression. The Asian-Pacific War (1941-1945), the Japan–China War (1937-1941), or the Manchurian Incident and the following wars (1931-1937)? We cannot judge from the speeches of our politicians. This tells us that here the problem is not of surreptitious changes, but worse. One cannot identify clearly what is the official government view!

[21] Herbert Norman (1909-1957), historian and diplomat in Canada, recommended Maruyama to read and review Popper's *The Open Society* in his letter to Maruyama in 1951. Maruyama read Popper's book but did not write the review. If he had written it the Japanese would have been interested in Popper's ideas in the 1950s.

[22] Maruyama (1954), p. 285.

[23] Ibidem, p.,286.

and militaristic tendencies, as well as democracy and democratic tendencies, which are utterly different from each other. Further, as I said earlier, I regard militarism as a characteristic of the closed society. Of course, there is no completely open society, so there are more or less militaristic tendencies in a more or less open society. However, in a more or less open society, there are elements that can suppress and control militarism or militaristic tendencies. Critically important are the thoughts, attitudes, and behaviour, of the members of a society or a country.

In any society there are some who are militarists, others who are anti-militarists, and the remainder who are neither. A society whose members are more or less different in their thoughts, feelings, or behaviour cannot be completely closed. Militarism cannot be imposed on such a society without using military force to oppress the people. If a militarist seizes power, he may successfully force people to be militarists, as happened in Japan.

In Japan most political leaders from the Meiji period onwards were influenced by the two ideas of reverence for the Emperor and the expelling of the barbarians. There was besides a long history in Japan of the rule of the generals and their warriors. The ruled were accustomed to such rule and yielded to the powerful. It was comparatively easy for the political leaders to govern such a people and integrate them into a military organization. This was the seed of the development of militarism.

Opening the country in the Meiji period was not the aim but the means by which the leader could expel the barbarians. The leaders required their country to be rich enough to support a strong national army in order to succeed. It is important to see that militarists are a minority while the majority is anti-militarist. If you ask each person individually, most of them would say it could not have been helped. Before the Second World War there was no choice for Japanese subjects, except revolution, in order to overthrow militarism. The few who countenanced revolution favoured social revolution, not political revolution in Popper's sense.[24] Most did not think of revolution at all.

Concerning individuals, a militarist is one who has absolute loyalty or obedience to the military authority or identifies absolutely with it. For life and death are absolutes. Someone coerced into obedience to the military authority may be called a militarist if there is room for choice (accepting Kant's idea of autonomy), even though it is very difficult to choose. As the case of Adolf Eichmann shows, such a person should be called a militarist, even though he never admits his responsibility on the grounds that he had just obeyed orders from above. The point is that the choice was open to him. At any time, one can try to get rid of militarism by rejecting absolute loyalty.

However, in the wide sense of militarism, the object of the absolute loyalty, obedience, or identity is not necessarily the military authority. It is possible

---

[24]Popper says (1945, Chapter 7, § III): 'In a non-democratic state, the only way to achieve reasonable reforms is by the violent overthrow of the government, and the introduction of a democratic framework.'

to have economic militarism, industrial militarism, and so on.

Military militarism seems to have disappeared in Japan but the problem is that the Japanese have not noticed that they are still militarists of another sort. There are, for example, economic militarists. Some economic leaders support militarist economic activities. In February 1964, Hajime Maeda, a managing director of the Japan Federation of Employers' Associations, frankly said that in Japan from ancient times, the spirit of self-sacrifice and the spirit of loyalty have been fostered, with the Emperor as a focal point, and if Japanese companies are run on these lines, then the Japanese economy will prosper. The recent catch phrase in a TV commercial, 'warriors in the company' is not empty rhetoric. Regrettably, almost every year some Japanese persons in a company or organization commit suicide. This is evidence of militarism. The collapse of the object of one's absolute loyalty or identity leaves a vacuum, the response to which is all too often suicide.

Democracy is the only antidote to militarism in all its guises, since in democracy one can relativize one's subjective absolutism. Democracy is also the only means of getting rid of force, violence, oppression, and discrimination as far as possible. The choice of democracy or militarism depends on us, either the open society or the closed society. Once we choose the former *consciously*, not based on the reasons that democracy is popular or we learnt in school that democracy is of the highest value, we will be democrats and not forced-democrats any longer[25] Our choice will not be a surreptitious change at all.

Popper and Maruyama have some values in common. Democracy is one of the most important things. Democracy is placed at the centre of their social and political philosophy. They tried to defend and develop democracy and make society more open. Maruyama clearly declared in 1947:[26]

> Once again it becomes our task to accomplish the democratic revolution, which the Meiji restoration was unable to carry out.

Maruyama rightly pointed out that democracy was born in order to control power, but he did not say that socialist democracy or people's democracy was not democracy at all. His attitude towards people's democracy in the Soviet Union at that time or in China was ambiguous.[27] It is a pity that Maruyama did not notice the importance of Popper's criterion of democracy, and he did not notice that Popper drastically changed the problem of the forms of government from the problem of 'Who should rule?' to the problem of the elimination of the evil ruler. So I am afraid Maruyama did not understand democracy *in Popper's sense*.[28]

---

[25] Once we choose democracy, precisely by being democrats we will not know automatically what to do, nobody will tell us what to do. It is up to us to choose our values. This is also a function of democracy.

[26] Maruyama (1947a), p. 161.

[27] Maruyama (1959b), pp. 187-195.

[28] In his explanation of democracy, Maruyama does not use Popper but Zevedei Barbu's *Democracy and Dictatorship* and claims that their ideas are almost the same (Maruyama 1959a, p. 47).

Another problem with Maruyama is that he was regrettably an elitist. As he was not a Marxist, he did not divide people into two classes: bourgeois and proletarian, but he had a tendency to see people according to social strata. Here is a typical example of his classification, the division into intellectuals and pseudo-intellectuals. He says:[29]

> We have all met men in barbers' shops, bathhouses, and railway carriages who treat those around them to their lofty opinions on inflation or the American-Soviet question. These men are what I call the pseudo-intellectuals, and on asking them their occupation, we find that they mostly belong to ... the middle stratum.

Then Maruyama hints that supporters of fascism in Japan are not from the group of intellectuals but from the group of pseudo-intellectuals.[30] Historically, this is not necessarily true. How about Hajime Tanabe, a leading philosopher of the Kyoto School? Before the Second World War his philosophy affirmed the war. Herein, I see Maruyama's arrogance, his scorn of the masses. And I find this is the cause of his pessimism. I am afraid that he did not trust ordinary people. He also despised the so-called intellectuals for living in an octopus trap.[31] I am afraid that he and his followers have lived in the same octopus trap as such intellectuals.

On the other hand, from a Popperian point of view, people are more or less knowledgeable or ignorant, so one should not draw a line, for example, between the elite and the masses, and, of course, there is no distinction between the intellectuals and the pseudo-intellectuals.

Maruyama intensively analysed the situation before and after the Second World War, but did not explicitly analyse it from the viewpoint of the closed society and the open society, as he did in his paper, 'The Opening of the Country' (1959a), which treated the periods from the Edo to the Meiji. Nor did he say that after the Second World War, for the first time, Japan had a chance of getting rid of militarism when she attained democracy *in Popper's sense*.

There are many social problems in Japan, for example, homelessness, discrimination between the sexes, the human rights of Korean residents, discrimination against foreigners, minorities, the weak, the old, the handicapped, and so on. Popper's social philosophy can provide various policies to address such urgent problems. In order to do so, however, there must be much discussion among various people with various opinions, without discrimination. In this sense, too, the idea of the open society is very important in Japan. I hope now that there will be a third attempt at reform of Japan towards a more open society and that it will be successful.[32]

---

[29]Maruyama (1947b), p. 68.

[30]Ibidem, pp. 69f.

[31]Maruyama (1961), p. 137.

[32]The first chance was in the Meiji Restoration and the second one was just after the Second World War.

Bibliography

Agassi, J. (1988). *The Gentle Art of Philosophical Polemics*. La Salle IL: Open Court Publishing Company.

Feyerabend, P. K. (1975). 'How to Defend Society against Science'. *Radical Philosophy* **2**, pp. 4-8. Reprinted in I. MacD Hacking editor (1981), pp. 156-167. *Scientific Revolutions*. Oxford: Oxford University Press.

Iwai, Tadamasa & Iwai, Tadakuma. (2002). *Tokko* [*The Special Attack Corps*]. Tokyo: Shin-Nihon Shuppan-sha.

Koestler, A. (1961). *The Lotus and the Robot*. New York: Macmillan.

Kuhn, T. S. (1970). 'Reflection on My Critics'. In I. Lakatos & A. E. Musgrave, editors (1970), pp. 231-278. *Criticism and the Growth of Knowledge*. London & New York: Cambridge University Press.

Maruyama, M. (1947a). 'Nihon niokeru Jiyuishiki no Keisei to Tokushitsu' ['Formation and Characteristics of the Consciousness of Freedom in Japan']. In Matsuzawa & Uete (1995), pp. 153-161.

—————— (1947b). 'Nihonfashizumu no Shiso to Undo' ['Thought and Movement of Japanese Fascism']. In Maruyama (1964), pp. 29-87.

—————— (1954). 'Nashonarizumu, Gunkokushugi, Fashizumu' ['Nationalism, Militarism, Fascism']. In Maruyama (1964), pp. 270-304.

—————— (1959a). 'Kaikoku' ['The Opening of the Country']. In Matsuzawa & Uete (1996), pp. 45-86.

—————— (1959b). 'Minshushugi no Rekishitekihaikei' ['The Historical Background of Democracy']. In Matsuzawa & Uete (1996), pp. 87-95.

—————— (1961). *Nihon no Shiso* [*Thought in Japan*], Tokyo: Iwanami-shoten.

—————— (1964). *Gendai Seiji no Shiso to Kodo* [*Thought and Behaviour in Modern Japanese Politics*]. Tokyo: Mirai-sha.

Matsuzawa, K. & Uete, M. editors (1995). *Maruyama Masao Shu*, Volume 3. Tokyo: Iwanami-shoten.

Matsuzawa, K. & Uete, M. editors (1996). *Maruyama Masao Shu*, Volume 8. Tokyo: Iwanami-shoten.

Nishio, K. (1999). *Kokumin no Rekishi* [*The History of the Japanese Nation*]. Tokyo: Sankei-shinbun-sha.

Plato. *Gorgias*. Quoted from G. P. Goold, editor (1932). *Lysis; Symposium; Gorgias*. The Loeb Classical Library. Cambridge MA: Harvard University Press.

Popper, K. R. (1945). *The Open Society and Its Enemies*. London: George Routledge & Sons. 5th edition 1966. London; Routledge & Kegan Paul.

—————— (1959). *The Logic of Scientific Discovery*. London: Hutchinson.

—————— (1963). *Conjectures and Refutations*. London: Routledge & Kegan Paul. 5th edition 1989. London: Routledge.

14

Karl Popper's Revisionist/Realist Theory of Democracy[*]

Geoffrey Stokes

In its critique of 'classical' democratic theory and its stress on proceduralism, Karl Popper's theory of democracy shares a great deal with that of Max Weber (1864-1920) and Joseph Schumpeter (1883-1950). They were all opposed to utopian political ideas, especially communist and radical socialist ideologies. Within their writings the strong liberal tendencies that valued freedom, individualism, and progress were tempered by conservative fears of social and political disorder. Their revisionist theories of democracy have maintained a certain appeal and provide some of the justification for the currently dominant practices of minimalist forms of liberal democracy. For two writers (Norman 1993, p. 268, and Przeworski 1999, p. 50) at least, there is little more than proceduralism in Popper's democratic theory. Nonetheless, Popper departs from liberal minimalism in a number of crucial ways. First, he provides a more substantive account of the institutional requirements for the effective working of democracy. Second, he accepts that replacing and controlling government is not all there is to maintaining a democratic state. Accordingly, he seeks to establish certain principles for state intervention in society and economy. This paper begins by outlining the main tenets of democratic revisionism. It then reviews the main elements of Popper's theory of democracy and points out his divergence from Weber and Schumpeter. Along the way, the paper deals with a few of the criticisms of Popper's democratic theory. Finally, the paper indicates what can be usefully retained from Popper's writings on the topic of democracy.

1 Theoretical background

The democratic revisionists get their name from their project to revise the theory of democracy away from the idealistic, participatory aspirations evident in the 'classical' heritage, and towards a liberal, representative, procedural model. In most respects, the revisionists are critical of an older republican version of democracy that values the direct rule of the people and seeks to

---

[*]I should like to thank Julie Connolly and Hans Löfgren for providing me with information about Joseph Schumpeter. I am grateful also for the comments of two anonymous referees.

ascertain the common good through rational debate and deliberation (for example, Rousseau 1762, pp. 72f.[1]). Both Weber (1919, p. 152) and Schumpeter (1943, p. 251) recognized that politics involved competing values and that, because these could not be decided rationally, there could be no possibility of rationally determining the common good or means to it. For Schumpeter (ibidem, pp. 250-268), notions such as the 'general will' are meaningless. Furthermore, the revisionists often claim that most citizens are unable to meet the requirements for informed participation and deliberation. That is, the capacities of modern citizens living within complex societies and economies are insufficient for the role laid out for them by classical republican theorists such as Rousseau. Thus democracy theory must adapt to this more 'realistic' assessment of the limits to political participation.

For these reasons, the revisionists articulate what may be called a liberal minimalist theory of democracy and citizenship.[2] Here the main function of democracy is to protect individual rights, while offering a fairly reliable means for changing governments.[3] Such functions require only the participation of citizens in voting at regular elections. More active forms of citizenship participation are generally considered dangerous because the mass of people is too prone to be swayed by emotion and demagogy (Weber 1917, p. 230). Such predispositions are a regular source of social disorder and political instability. The main burden of participation therefore falls upon political leaders and party elites who compete with each for the people's vote. For Weber (ibidem, p. 339), elections become primarily plebiscites upon the performance of leaders, their policies and political records. As Schumpeter (1943, p. 269) famously expressed it:

> the democratic method is that institutional arrangement for arriving at political decisions in which individuals acquire power to decide by means of a competitive struggle for the people's vote.

On this view, democracy ought not to be an end in itself; it is simply a means to other ends.[4] Popper shares most of these views, but puts them into a slightly different and wider problem context that stresses the importance of non-violence and intellectual progress.

2 Popper's problem context

Karl Popper's theory of democracy seeks to offer answers to a number of political *and* epistemological problems. He writes (1945, Introduction) for example: 'only democracy provides an institutional framework that permits reform without violence, and so the use of reason in political matters'. Furthermore,

---

[1] Rousseau, however, favoured the people as legislators rather than as 'rulers'.

[2] See Stokes (2002) pp. 27-31.

[3] See the discussion of Weber, Schumpeter, and competitive elitism by Held (1996, pp. 157-198).

[4] O'Donnell (2001) suggests that Schumpeter is not quite as minimalist as he appears, and Meadaris (1997) points out that he saw democracy as a transformative agent in history.

democracies not only allow political and social changes by means of a particular methodology, but they also provide the necessary foundation for scientific
and intellectual progress (Popper 1944-1945, § 32). That is, democracy performs a vital function for both politics and epistemology. It provides a peaceful
means for reform and change of government (1945, Introduction; Chapter 7,
§ III; Popper 1963, Chapter 17, § 3), while ensuring the freedom of thought and
speech necessary for intellectual progress. This process encourages a pluralism
of ideas and groups (Popper 1972a, Chapter 6, § II):

> For I take it to be one of the characteristics of an open society that it cherishes,
> apart from a democratic form of government, the freedom of association, and
> that it protects and even encourages the formation of free sub-societies, each
> holding different opinions and beliefs.

In this statement we may discern the essential characteristics of what we
now call 'civil society', which provides some of the pre-conditions for liberal
democracy.

Just as such pluralism and toleration of differences are the necessary
pre-conditions for the 'working out of political meanings and aims' (Popper
1968, p. 294), so also it is vital for the processes of critical thought and the
goal of emancipation through knowledge. 'This self-criticism and this self-
emancipation', Popper affirms, 'are possible in a pluralist society, that is, in
an open society which tolerates our errors as well as the errors of others' (ibidem, p. 295). Adherence to the principle of non-violence in both political and
epistemological matters ensures that within a democracy and open society
'ideas have a chance to prevail' (1972b, p. 16).

Popper's theory of democracy typically grows out of his criticism of other
approaches to government, initially that of Plato and later of Marx. This is
not the place to review whether Popper accurately interprets these writers
and I shall simply attempt to lay out his positive programme. Popper (1945,
Chapter 7; 1988, p. 24) denies that the guiding principles of politics should be
determined by answers given to the question 'Who should rule?'. We should
instead take account of the possibility of bad or unwise rulers. This would
result, according to Popper (1945, Chapter 7, § I) in asking the new question:
'*How can we so organize political institutions that bad or incompetent rulers
can be prevented from doing too much damage?*' By contrast to the old question, Popper (1988, p. 24) regards his approach as 'a thoroughly practical,
almost technical problem'.

Popper (1945, Chapter 7, § I) considers that the former question makes the
unwarranted assumption that political sovereignty is unchecked. He also raises
another difficulty in that such an approach leads to the unresolvable paradox
of sovereignty recognized by Plato. On such a theory it is possible that the
democratic will of the people may decide that it wants to be ruled by a tyrant
(Popper ibidem). The opposite possibility also exists that the wisest or best
rulers may decide that the majority should rule (ibidem). In both cases the
result contradicts the original intention.

3 Popper's proceduralism

Instead of being based upon what he sees as a self-contradictory theory of
sovereignty, democracy should be founded upon a *'theory of checks and balances'* (Popper 1945, Chapter 7, § i). Assuming that even the best rulers have
failings, this theory devises institutional means for curbing their power. The
major check is provided by periodic election of governments. This points up
the difference between democracy and its opposite, tyranny (ibidem). Thus
his procedural definition, that people live in a democracy if institutions exist
which enable them 'to oust their government without using violent means'
(Popper 1972b, p. 16).

Although he offers this as a brief guide to democracy Popper denies that
there is any true meaning or essence of democracy. He is adamant, however,
that it does not mean 'the rule of the people' or even that the majority should
rule, if only because this is impossible in any concrete or practical way (Popper
1945, Chapter 7, § ii). He also does not assume that 'we can ever develop
institutions ... which are faultless or foolproof' (ibidem). In Popper's view
acceptance of a bad policy in a democracy is 'preferable to the submission to
a tyranny, however wise or benevolent' (ibidem). Popper (1988, p. 25) argues
that 'we do not base our choice on the goodness of democracy, which may be
doubtful, but solely on the evilness of a dictatorship, which is certain.'

In terms of political method, democracy relies upon general elections and
representative government. Nonetheless, Popper (1945, Chapter 7, § ii) considers these to be no more than 'reasonably effective institutional safeguards
against tyranny', which are always open to improvement. Although democracies may be based upon majority vote this does not affirm that the majority
is right. Accordingly, democracy must also allow individuals both to criticize
these decisions and, within the law, to attempt to revise them (ibidem).

Popper's theory requires that: 'free debate and especially debate about
the wisdom or otherwise of governmental decisions, should be possible ... and
should exert an influence on politics' (1972b, p. 14). This criterion acknowledges the possibility of 'free rational discussion' influencing government,
which Popper (ibidem, p. 15) regards as 'the greatest virtue of democracy'.
Accordingly, within a democracy opportunities ought to be available for ideas
to replace force and violence as the determinants of political decision. There is
also an additional stimulus of organized public opinion (Popper 1963, Chapter
16, § xi).

4 Problems with Popper's proceduralism

The preceding characterization of democracy is, with few exceptions, a
relatively conventional elaboration of liberal democratic principles. Despite
Popper's admirable quest for intellectual and political simplicity, it remains
arguable that, on their own, such principles may not guarantee the maintenance of democracy, even as Popper conceives it. Institutional issues, such as
the method of representation, the size and nature of electorates, and so on,

all have a bearing upon whether citizens would consider themselves to be part of a legitimate democracy.

Popper's approach also avoids important issues in democratic theory that are signalled in the original meaning of the word democracy as 'rule of the people'. Understanding democracy in this way presses one to ask: 'what do we mean by rule?' and 'who are the people?'. Clearly, Popper is most interested in the institutional issues implied in the first question, which leads him to ignore questions about citizens and citizenship. Nonetheless, many of the key political struggles throughout the history of democracy have been over who is to be included as a citizen or not, and over what their rights and responsibilities ought to be. Even Popper's minimalist proposals require some understanding of who ought to be allowed to vote.

Furthermore, in practice, a pluralist system of checks and balances may be so restrictive as to prevent a duly elected government from carrying out its policies. As for the influence of public opinion, the undoubted power of government and business to manipulate public opinion may mean that there is little pressure at all upon those in office to change their policies. The exclusion of large segments of the population from citizenship will exacerbate such tendencies. Open criticism by those without the franchise will surely count for less than that coming from those with the vote.

Perhaps more important, within Popper's theory of democracy two incompatible elements may also may be discerned. Although Popper stresses the importance of free debate, argument, and criticism on public affairs, there are limits to citizens' participation, except perhaps in civil society. Because it is assumed that the mass of people cannot govern, Popperian democracy is reduced to a theory of competing elites. The only means by which critical debate and governing are linked is through periodic elections. Although his theory of scientific change stresses deliberation, his theory of democracy, in typical revisionist fashion, emphasizes the aggregation of votes. Eventually, the force of argument must give way to the force of elections and majorities.

Except on the issue of proportional representation, Popper provides little detail on practical matters, such as methods of representation, size and nature of electorates, and length of terms of office. He rejects strongly the electoral method of proportional representation because of its origins in what he sees as dubious theories of sovereignty, and also because of its alleged propensity to produce unstable coalition governments. In Popper's view, two-party government is preferable if only because it allows for more serious internal self-criticism after election defeats (1988, p. 26).

Nevertheless, what distinguished Popper from the other revisionists, such as Weber and Schumpeter, is his recognition that control over government is not all there is to securing a democratic polity. Unlike the social liberals, his solution is not to encourage more widespread political participation, but to require democratic states to engage in social and economic reforms. That is, Popper gives attention to the social and economic conditions under which democracy must operate.

5   Democracy, social reform, and the state

Popper goes beyond straightforward proceduralism to endorse state intervention in society and economy and indicates principles by which it can be
defended. First, Popper requires the state to protect the institution of democracy. For example, Popper stresses that this principle 'must not be lightly
invoked to defend measures which may endanger the most precious of all
forms of freedom, namely intellectual freedom' (1945, Chapter 7, § IV). Similarly, since democracies must always be open to ideas, this in turn requires
that protection be given to minorities. This condition can be waived, however,
in the case of those 'who violate law and especially . . . those who incite others
to the violent overthrow of the democracy' (Popper 1945, Chapter 19, § V).
Nevertheless, the danger remains that the majority might seek peacefully to
overturn democratic institutions. Popper's firm response is to require that a
'consistent democratic constitution should exclude only one type of change
in the legal system, namely a change which would endanger its democratic
character' (ibidem).

One of the strongest and recurring criticisms of liberal democracy is that
the establishment of formal democratic procedures is futile if the citizens lack
the means or motivation to use them, or if elected governments are unable to
implement the policies they want. In such cases democracy is merely 'formal'
since it does not allow for any substantial social reform leading to improvement
in people's lives that would allow them to make best use of democratic institutions. According to the vulgar Marxist critique, politics in liberal democracies
is largely impotent. The state apparatus including representative government
is simply the managing committee of the ruling class, the dictatorship of the
bourgeoisie. That is, democratic government is an element of the ruling su-
perstructure that is fundamentally determined by the underlying capitalist
economic base. Popper (1945, Chapter 17) attributes such views to Marx and
is concerned to refute them.

Popper's awareness of such criticism presses him to elaborate a more positive doctrine of politics. He needs to show not only the advantages of democratic institutions but also that political change and social reform are possible. This in turn requires him to propose guidelines for the use of state power.
Popper's first step is to recognize the problem of economic power (ibidem,
§ III):

> Even if the state protects its citizens from being bullied by physical violence (as
> it does in principle, under the system of unrestrained capitalism), it may defeat
> our ends by its failure to protect them from the misuse of economic power.

The remedy for this is seen as a political one in which institutions must
be constructed to protect the economically weak against the economically
strong (ibidem). To safeguard freedom, Popper demands 'that unrestrained
capitalism give way to *economic interventionism*' (ibidem). In Popper's view,
'political power is the key to economic protection' (ibidem, § IV). He argues

that unless this political power is exercised in a democratic fashion then one runs the risk of losing both political and economic freedom.

Popper (ibidem, § VII) proposes further that there are two main methods by which state economic intervention may proceed:

> The first is that of designing a 'legal framework' of protective institutions (laws restricting the powers of the owner of an animal, or of a landowner, are an example). The second is that of empowering organs of the state to act — within certain limits — as they consider necessary for achieving the ends laid down by the rulers for the time being.

The first method of 'institutional' or ' indirect' intervention is preferable to the second 'personal' or 'direct' form, which should be used only where the first is inadequate. A Government's financial Budget is a defensible example of direct state intervention. For Popper (ibidem), the advantage of the indirect method is that it introduces certainty and security into individuals' lives and even with substantial changes of policy, allowances can be made for particular individuals during the transition. On the other hand, the direct method of allowing discretionary powers introduces unpredictability into social life and brings less democratic control.

Popper is convinced that economic and social reforms not only are possible, but are necessary ingredients of a democratic order. He (1945, Chapter 18, § III) cites the achievement of Marx's economic programme in the twentieth century as an example of the potency of democratic politics. With a few notable exceptions, such as the abolition of landed property and the '[c]onfiscation of the property of all emigrants and rebels', most of the measures Marx and Engels (1848, pp. 104f.) advocated in *The Communist Manifesto* have been put into practice (Popper ibidem). Popper (ibidem, Chapter 20, § IV) also considers that systematic interference with the trade cycle is possible and defensible. At one stage, he even advocated a guaranteed income for everyone (Shearmur 1996, p. 32). Although there is much wrong with modern societies, Popper believes that there is room for improvement. In moving beyond the narrow boundaries of liberal minimalism he argues 'that institutions should exist for the protection of freedom and the protection of the poor and the weak' (Popper 1972b, p. 14). With this step in his argument, Popper is not just seeking to protect political rights, but recognizing and looking to defend social and economic rights.

Indeed, he goes further to suggest that democratic planning is essential for the protection of freedom. 'Only by planning, step by step', writes Popper (1945, Chapter 18, § IV), 'for institutions to safeguard freedom, especially freedom from exploitation, can we hope to achieve a better world.' This raises problems of increased state power and bureaucracy but these may be tempered by strengthening democratic institutions and by following the principles of piecemeal social engineering (Popper ibidem, Chapter 21). The latter policy is not as restrictive as it is commonly thought to be. It allows for experiments in socialization, especially in the case of monopolies (Shearmur 1996, p. 32), but it does specifically rule out the nationalization and socialization of the *entire* private industry of a country.

A point in favour of piecemeal social engineering is thought to be its scientific character. Popper considers it methodologically superior to holistic and revolutionary programmes, in part because piecemeal social engineers accept the limitations of their knowledge. He (1944-1945, § 24) regards piecemeal social experiments as the basis of all social knowledge, both prescientific and scientific. Such knowledge is being developed all the time for practical rather than scientific purposes. For example, the grocer who opens a new shop or a person who joins a theatre queue is each gaining experimental knowledge that may be useful in the future (ibidem; Popper 1945, Chapter 9). The mistakes made in such endeavours are the essential means whereby progress occurs (1944-1945, § 24). Popper generalizes from this insight to suggest that there is no reason why we should not be more systematic and critical in our social experiments. This is the means whereby the scientific method of trial and error is brought into the study of society and politics (ibidem).[5] In line with his political minimalism, Popper supplies a minimalist value framework for making practical policy decisions. By advocating 'negative utilitarianism' (1945, Chapter 5, note 6, Chapter 9, note 2; Popper 1948, § XI), he proposes that the highest priority ought to be that of choosing the most urgent social evils (Popper 1945, Chapter 9), rather than the greatest good. It is proposed that unavoidable suffering such as that of hunger in times of food shortage, should be distributed as equally as possible (ibidem, note 2). Governments therefore need to conduct a fight against 'avoidable misery' and leave the increase of happiness to private initiatives (1948, § XI). Popper thinks that such a policy would have greater support of the majority of people and that the existence of such evils 'can be comparatively well established' (1945, Chapter 9).

Two common criticisms directed against these minimalist policies are that they may have unanticipated outcomes or be inapplicable in certain contexts. In this vein, Jeremy Shearmur (2001) points out that there is no guarantee that, in attempting to remedy concrete evils, governments would not make social and economic conditions worse. As for popular agreement on this policy, Shearmur argues that, while there may be a consensus on what the social evils are, there may be no consensus on what ought to be done about them. In addition, in some contexts within a liberal democracy there may be so many 'urgent social problems' that there may be no consensus as to which should be given priority.

Nonetheless, given that no ethical framework is without its difficulties and any action may have unforeseen consequences, Popper's precepts may retain merit as a general political rule of thumb for national and international policies. His approach has strong affinities with the human rights philosophy underlying humanitarianism intervention and poverty alleviation in

---

[5] The following discussion draws on and extends arguments originally sketched in Stokes (1998). Popper's notion of piecemeal social engineering has attracted wide critical scrutiny including Ackermann (1976), p. 178, Magee (1973), p. 86, O'Hear (1980), and Parekh (1982).

developing countries. In many respects it supplies the normative foundation for non-governmental organizations such as Oxfam, Médecins Sans Frontières and Amnesty International. Certainly, there may be many unintended and unexpected outcomes, but this is no reason for deciding to do nothing in the face of severe problems such as mass starvation. Popper's proposals also share similarities with the more 'radical' views of Judith Shklar (1984, pp. 7-44) who argues for 'putting cruelty first'. That is, she recommends that we should give our highest priority to alleviating the suffering of victims of cruelty and torture. These are not arguments that can be dismissed by philosophical nitpicking.

6 Popper's democratic revisionism and realism

Popper's theory can be categorized as 'realist' on both philosophical and political grounds. Philosophically, the arguments may be understood as realist because they are based primarily upon the intellectual and political limits of our knowledge. He recognizes the futility of engaging in abstract and infinitely contestable philosophical arguments about the meaning of words such as 'rule', 'freedom', and 'reason' (Popper 1988, p. 23). It is realist *and* revisionist in the tradition of Weber and Schumpeter in that it eschews the elaboration of abstract ideals, and privileges a limited range of procedural values over substantive ones. Its realism is also evident in its preference for pluralism and elite participation over mass participation.

Popper's work is also politically 'realist' in its focus upon what he sees as concrete social evils and rejection of more utopian schemes. Because it is not realist or proceduralist in the usual senses, Popper's arguments are more significant for democratic theory than generally thought. Unlike Schumpeter and Weber, Popper's theory is founded on certain substantive values, namely, a repudiation of violence and a preference for the peaceful resolution of conflict. That is, the value of non-violence, or the avoidance of violence is a central, if not universal value priority.

In addition, Popper realizes that the pluralist requirements of instituting measures to establish 'checks and balances', protect minorities, and limit the power of government are not sufficient for creating a democratic state. Popper therefore also seeks to establish certain principles for the state intervention in society and economy. He is concerned to avoid not only the misuse of political power but also the misuse of economic power. Accordingly, he recommends that institutions be established to protect the economically weak from the economically strong. By combining an ethical proceduralism with a requirement for state social and economic intervention, Popper's theory advances well beyond democratic revisionism, towards a rudimentary social democracy. The question remains as to the practical value or application of his theory.

7 Assessment: problems and potential

One intellectual weakness of Popper's analysis is that he rarely engages with
the wider range of thinking about democracy and citizenship. His critical discussions tend to focus upon arguments of straw, and issues that are marginal
to much democratic theory. He entirely neglects a number of the most difficult problems of choosing between different democratic theories (Norman
1993, p. 262). Importantly, issues of participation and deliberation are central
to Popper's theory but he does not develop them in any detail. They are not,
for example, integrated into a theory of citizenship.

This leads him to overlook strategies that would enhance his democratic
theory in ways that would not be inconsistent with his larger epistemological
project. Given the way the original problems are posed, there is little possibility for critical renewal of his democratic theory or for conceiving of democracy
differently. In many respects, the issues of avoiding tyranny and violence are so
important, that the theory is almost inoculated against criticism. This leads
to a poverty of imagination about the possibilities for enriching liberal democracy or going beyond it, in the way that deliberative democratic theorists,
such as John Rawls, John Dryzek, Joshua Cohen, and Habermas have done.[6]

To many citizens of modern/postmodern liberal, representative democracies, Popper's theory would appear almost banal. Nonetheless, even here,
Popper's democratic theory has the advantage of making modest calls on
universal values while at the same time requiring political action in the service of social reform and progress. Given the various critiques (postmodern
and others) of universalist theories, Popper's theory allows us a minimalist
way forward that is both critical and constructive, but without all the metaphysical assumptions associated with what are characterized as 'modernist
metanarratives' about 'truth' and 'progress'.

Yet, Popper's precepts may have more applicability in some situations
than others. The parsimonious proceduralism of Schumpeterian democracy
has been rightly criticized for its neglect of socio-economic injustice (for example, Im 1996, p. 279). In many countries, the mere introduction of periodic
elections will not establish a democracy. As we have seen, however, in his
acute awareness of the other requirements of democracy, Popper's theory
is a radical advance upon Schumpeter. Indeed, Przeworski (1999, pp. 49f.)
demonstrates that democracies will survive only where there are certain levels of per capita income *and* there are elections in which governments can
be replaced. But Przeworski mistakenly criticizes Popper for neglecting such
issues. Popper may be a proceduralist and a minimalist, but he does not overlook the economic conditions under which democracy can flourish. The only
issue is whether his proposals are plausible and practical or not.

A major difficulty may be that Popper's theory is so lacking in detail for
its application that one simply cannot depend upon it for practical guidance.

---

[6]See for example the essays in Bohman & Rehg (1997), and the books by Dryzek (1990),
(2000).

What counts as suffering, or how ought we measure poverty, for example? Yet Popper would reject the idea that there could be some precise universal (essential) definition for such subjects. Given the establishment of the cluster of institutions he recommends, then democratic societies could possibly rely upon democratic debate and negotiation to determine the criteria needed, for the time being. The next issue would become that of deciding upon the appropriate means for alleviating suffering. Even here, Popper's theory provides a relevant principle by requiring that those who suffer have a say in how their suffering may be alleviated, or at least be able to vote against governments that have attempted the task and failed.

Despite its deficiencies, Popper's theory can play a crucial normative role in politics. It indicates the criteria we may use to criticize governments in those countries where democracy is not established or where it is in the process of being established. The theory's minimalism may accommodate democratic aspirations in less developed or developing countries without subscribing to wholesale modernization, westernization, or Americanization. Popper's theory recognizes the social benefits of gradualism, stability, and security. Its negative utilitarianism also defends a legitimate role for government intervention not only in society and economy, but also in cultures that may promote violence and suffering.

In many countries therefore the issues Popper raises are crucial. The problem of overcoming suffering, along with the tasks of establishing and maintaining democratic institutions, have great urgency. Certainly, the conditions of poverty and hunger are still with us. In recent years, however, the avoidance of 'concrete evils', such as genocide and ethnocide, has become a high priority. If we accept also that there are historical stages to the process of democratization, then certain kinds of normative theories may be more applicable than others. Where democracy needs to be established and maintained, Popper's theory may provide a useful method of critical analysis.

Finally, Popper's theory of democracy can make a contribution to our thinking about international issues. On Popper's account, and given his critique of nationalism, there is no reason why the primary responsibility for addressing 'urgent social problems' should remain solely within the nation state. Implicit in the arguments discussed above are the rudiments of a minimalist theory of international citizenship.[7] For example, Popper's democratic theory provides a rationale for international intervention to establish and secure democracy. His negative utilitarianism also sets out principles for humanitarian intervention beyond national borders. Given the global origins and scope of many 'concrete evils', international cooperation is often required to solve them. Indeed, Popper's brief reflections on international affairs (1945, Chapter 6, § VI), where he advocates the creation of international organizations to prevent international crime and conflict, would appear to support this possibility.[8]

---

[7] On this concept, see Stokes (2004), pp. 122f.

[8] I am indebted to Jeremy Shearmur for calling attention to this point.

8 Conclusion

Popper's theory of democracy comprises three main components. The first is an account of why democracy is important with reference to non-violence and intellectual progress. The second is a proposal about how best to argue about the nature and goals of democracy. For Popper, we should never ask 'Who should rule?', but rather 'How can we so organize political institutions that bad and incompetent rulers can be prevented from doing so much damage?' In essence, Popper is concerned with how rulers can be 'got rid of' without bloodshed and violence (1988, p. 24). The third component consists of a more substantive account of how democracies ought to operate. Central in this account are not only the familiar notions of the 'open society' and how to promote social and political criticism, but also more specific recommendations on the kinds of social and economic policies required to protect democracy, as well as the methods and principles that are to guide their implementation. By requiring state action to remedy certain kinds of 'concrete evils', Popper's theory offers more of substantive value than the usual revisionist, realist, and proceduralist forms of democratic theory. More generally, this theory allows significant critiques of governments that may lay claim to the title of 'democracy', but lie outside the main European, liberal, and social democratic traditions, as well as those governments avowedly within them. It may also offer principles for the exercise of international citizenship in global affairs.

Bibliography

Ackermann, R. J. (1976). *The Philosophy of Karl Popper*. Amherst MA: University of Massachusetts Press.

Bohman, J. & Rehg, W. editors (1997). *Deliberative Democracy: Essays on Reason and Politics*. Cambridge MA: MIT.

Dryzek, J. S. (1990). *Discursive Democracy: Politics, Policy and Political Science*. New York: Cambridge University Press.

———— (2000). *Deliberative Democracy and Beyond: Liberals, Critics, Contestations* Oxford: Oxford University Press.

Held, D. (1996). *Models of Democracy*. 2nd edition. Cambridge: Polity.

Im, H. B. (1996). 'Globalisation and Democratisation: Boon Companions or Strange Bedfellows?' *Australian Journal of International Affairs* **50**, pp. 279-291.

Magee, B. (1973). *Popper*. London: Fontana/Collins.

Marx, K. & Engels, F. (1848). *The Communist Manifesto*. Reference is to the 1888 translation of Samuel Moore, 1967. Harmondsworth: Penguin Books.

Meadaris, J. (1997). 'Schumpeter, the New Deal and Democracy'. *American Political Science Review* **91**, pp. 819-832.

Norman, W. J. (1993). 'A Democratic Theory for a Democratizing World? A Re-assessment of Popper's Political Realism'. *Political Studies* **41**, pp. 252-268.

O'Donnell, G. A. (2001). 'Democracy, Law and Comparative Politics'. *Studies in Comparative Economic Development* **36**, pp. 7-36.

O'Hear, A. (1980). *Karl Popper*. London: Routledge & Kegan Paul.

Parekh, B. C. (1982). *Contemporary Political Thinkers*. Oxford: Martin Robertson.

Popper, K. R. (1944-1945). 'The Poverty of Historicism'. *Economica* NS **XI**, 1944, pp. 86-103, 119-137; NS **XII**, 1945, pp. 69-89. Reference is made to the book edition 1957. London: Routledge & Kegan Paul.

———— (1945). *The Open Society and Its Enemies*. London: George Routledge & Sons. 5th revised edition 1966. London: Routledge & Kegan Paul.

———— (1948). 'Prediction and Prophecy and their Significance for Social Theory'. In *Proceedings of the Xth International Congress of Philosophy* (Amsterdam 1948), volume 1, pp. 82-91. Reprinted as Chapter 16 ('Prediction and Prophecy in the Social Sciences') in Popper (1963).

———— (1963). *Conjectures and Refutations: The Growth of Scientific Knowledge*. London: Routledge & Kegan Paul. 5th edition 1989.

———— (1968). 'Emancipation through Knowledge'. In A. J. Ayer, editor (1968), pp. 281-296. *The Humanist Outlook*. London: Pemberton, Barrie & Rockliff.

———— (1972a). *Objective Knowledge*. Oxford: Clarendon Press. 2nd edition 1979.

———— (1972b). 'On Reason and the Open Society: A Conversation'. *Encounter* **38**, May 1972, pp. 13-18.

———— (1988). 'The Open Society and its Enemies Revisited'. *Economist* 23.iv.1988, pp. 23-26.

Przeworski, A. (1999). 'Minimalist Conception of Democracy: A Defence'. In I. Shapiro & C. Hacker-Corden, editors (1999), pp. 23-55. *Democracy's Value*. Cambridge: Cambridge University Press.

Rousseau, J.-J. (1762). *The Social Contract*. Reference is to the translation of M. Cranston, 1968. Harmondsworth: Penguin Books.

Schumpeter, J. A. (1943). *Capitalism, Socialism, and Democracy*. 5th edition 1952. London: Unwin University Books.

Shearmur, J. F. G. (1996). *The Political Thought of Karl Popper*. London: Routledge.

———— (2001). 'Popper and Negative Consensus'. Unpublished. Italian translation 2002. 'Popper e il consenso negativo'. *Nuova Civiltà delle Macchine* **XX**, pp. 98-105. [= S. Gattei, editor, *Karl R. Popper 1902-2002: Ripensando il Razionalismo Critico*].

Shklar, J. N. (1984). *Ordinary Vices*. Cambridge MA: Belknap Press, Harvard University Press.

Stokes, G. M. (1988). *Popper: Philosophy, Politics and Scientific Method*. Cambridge: Polity.

———— (2002). 'Democracy and Citizenship'. In A. Carter & G. Stokes, editors (2002), pp. 1-23. *Democratic Theory Today*. Cambridge: Polity.

———— (2004). 'Transnational Citizenship: Problems of Definition, Culture and Democracy'. *Cambridge Review of International Affairs* **17**, pp. 119-135.

Weber, M. (1917). 'Parliament and Government in Germany under a New Political Order'. In P. Lassman & R. Speirs, editors (1994), pp. 13-271. *Political Writings*. Cambridge: Cambridge University Press.

———— (1919). 'Science as Vocation'. In H. H. Gerth & C. W. Mills, editors (1970), pp. 129-56. *From Max Weber: Essays in Sociology*. London: Routledge & Kegan Paul.

15

Popper and Communitarianism
Ethical and Political Dimensions
of Democracy

Harald Stelzer

Karl Popper never participated in the controversy between liberals and communitarians, and only rarely do they refer to his social philosophy in their debate. Nevertheless, inasmuch as Popper's political philosophy constitutes one of the main contributions to post-war liberalism, a thoughtful challenge to his social philosophy from the point of view of the communitarian critique of liberalism is in order. Popper does differ from other liberal thinkers not only with his emphasis on *political protectionism* and *economic interventionism*, but also by adding some thoughts to the liberal view that enables one to develop a better response to communitarians. These ideas can be found in Popper's concept of *negative utilitarianism*, his emphasis on the correspondence between freedom and responsibility, and his *ethos of enlightenment*. Popper also combines an institutional approach to democracy with the importance of tradition. Like other liberals Popper neglects to some degree the importance of participation, but his political thought offers a form of *critical participation*, which connects his concept of politics with the method of science. Opening with a short summary of the communitarian criticism of liberalism, this paper will focus on the correlation between freedom and responsibility, institutions and tradition, critical participation and science.

1 The communitarian criticism of liberalism

Communitarianism developed in the 1980s in the United States and Canada as a criticism of liberalism, especially in response to the political philosophy of John Rawls and his book *A Theory of Justice* (1971). Initially communitarians such as Alasdair MacIntyre, Charles Taylor, and Michael Sandel had criticized the anthropological assumptions of the liberal agenda as overly individualistic because they neglect the role of communities in constituting the identity of the individual. In consequence of the communitarians' disapproval of this liberal conception, many also reject the liberal quest for universal principles in morality. In contrast to *liberal universalism*, in which they suspect nihilism, communitarians emphasize the importance of communally shared values.

Later in the debate the communitarian perspective broadened into a political and sociological criticism of liberalism, such as can be found in the works of Michael Walzer, Christopher Lasch, Benjamin Barber, Daniel Bell, Robert Galston, Amitai Etzioni, and Robert Bellah. This line of criticism not only emphasizes the psychological and ethical importance of belonging to a community for the individual, but also postulates the conditions necessary to democracy. Here the main point of disagreement with the liberals can be found in differing assumptions about the requirements of a democratic society. For communitarians democracy depends on the realization of the common good and the voluntary subordination of individual interests. The identification of the individual with the community is brought about by the participation in communal life, its traditions and institutions. This identification is the motivational force behind *self-government*. The active participation of citizens in political and communal affairs is a main concern in regard to the communitarian revival of *republicanism*.

For communitarians, liberals fail to recognize the importance of certain traditions, virtues, and values for democracy. Liberal concepts of democracy concentrate one-sidedly on procedural and institutional aspects and do not pay enough attention to participation. Communitarians advance the criticism that for liberals, self-government and participation are merely means toward ends such as the rule of law, equality, or individual freedom. In consequence, the main activity of citizens has to be found in the enforcement of individual rights and equal treatment through the courts or the manipulation of other institutions. Participation is reduced to the election of the party that best fits the present interests. For communitarians this leads not only to an impoverishment of politics, but also to an alienation of citizens from the state and to a lack of responsibility for the political community. The liberal focus on individual freedom and autonomy brings about an individualistic society where egoistic social conflicts are reinforced at the cost of the common good.

This, in short and, of course, oversimplified, is the communitarian criticism of liberalism. As I cannot deal with it here in detail, I want to point out that most of the time the communitarian positions are much weaker in their consequences than one would expect from their harsh criticism of liberalism. In many ways communitarians weaken their own positions in an attempt to escape authoritarian and totalitarian consequences. Many of them try to find a balance between individual autonomy and social order. Still, the solutions they offer are not only very vague but sometimes constitute a threat to democratic and pluralistic societies because the strengthening of communities tends to undermine individual rights.

2 Individual freedom and responsibility

Therefore it is necessary to look for answers to questions raised by communitarians within the liberal tradition. Popper, part of this tradition, differs from other liberal thinkers especially in his emphasis on *political protectionism* and *economic interventionism.* Like other liberals, he is well aware of threats to a democratic society through the increase of tasks of the state in a modern social system and the development of technologies that allow a more extensive state control of citizens. He talks in favour of the regulative principle of a *mini-state* (Popper 1997, Chapter 8, pp. 75f.). However, this ideal of a mini-state is not be confused with the *Nozickian minimal state*. The danger of the misuse of power cannot be avoided by simply eliminating or reducing the state. The state in a modern society will always have some paternalistic aspects. Moreover, for Popper it is not enough to protect its citizens from violence, but protectionism has to extend to economic life as well. Institutions must be constructed, enforced by the power of the state, to protect the economically weak against the economically strong. The doctrine of non-intervention in the area of economy must be replaced by economic interventionism (Popper 1945, Chapter 17, § III). Popper insists that this should not lead to total planning, which he strictly opposes. Gradual reforms as demanded in his concept of *piecemeal social engineering* and the free market economy should prevent the situation in which state interventionism becomes the first step on *the road to serfdom.* But Popper's remarks on this are very vague, and economists wonder if piecemeal social engineering can avoid the slippery slope towards total planning. Here, however, I have to leave this point open for debate, for this is an important question for the liberal and libertarian critics of Popper; but it is not a major conflict with communitarian ideas as presented by Walzer, Bellah, and others.

Disagreeing with some liberals and libertarians on economic issues, Popper takes a liberal position when it comes to the importance of the defence of individual freedom in a democratic society (ibidem, Chapter 9). Here his political philosophy leans towards the liberal concept of so-called *negative freedom*, where freedom is defined as the absence of constraint by other human beings. This means that we are externally free to the degree that we are not constrained by others in the pursuit of our individual purposes. Popper goes along with Kant's ideal of 'a constitution that achieves *the greatest possible freedom of human individuals* by framing the laws in such a way that *the freedom of each can co-exist with that of all others*' (ibidem, Chapter 6, note 4).

From a liberal perspective, the state must be neutral on question of the good life. Therefore, political decisions must be, as far as possible, independent of any particular conception of what gives value to life. Indeed, the neutrality of the state is required by the diversity of interests, goals, and conceptions of the good life in a modern society. Assertions about the good life are highly personal and famously incorrigible — hence the liberal emphasis on individual choice. Conversely the foundation of a society on a special conception of the good life can lead to suppression of fringe groups and single individuals. The neutrality of the state reflects the principle of tolerance for equal rights and equal chances for differing convictions and ways of life.

The liberal commitment to individual freedom, focusing on the right to live one's life according to one's own ideas, is opposed to the communitarian emphasis on community-oriented behaviour supported by the state and controlled by the community. From a communitarian point of view the liberal focus on the neutrality of the state and individual freedom undermines the foundations of democracy because it creates an individualistic society prey to egoistic social conflicts at the expense of the common good. What is destroyed is a highly developed sense of duty, responsibility, and solidarity among the members of the political community.

In Popper's political philosophy we can find three ideas that provide a response to this communitarian critique. First he agrees about the pluralism of values described above. People should pursue their own ideas about the good. But there is a distinction between the private and the public sphere. Even though Popper strictly opposes all attempts to force one's own moral ideas on other individuals, he still gives some guidelines for social action. No positive idea of a good society should lead the agenda of public action but rather the concept of negative utilitarianism. For Popper the alleviation of suffering serves as a first principle of the public agenda. A systematic fight against the social conditions under which many are suffering is more likely to be supported by the approval of a great number of people than the fight for the establishment of some ideal (ibidem). Still, the question remains of how to transfer the resources from the private sphere to the public sector without putting at risk individual freedom and property rights. Here questions are raised concerning the correlation between individual freedom and the alleviation of suffering (Shearmur 1996, p. 48, pp. 100-106).

An answer to this can be found in the interrelation between freedom and responsibility. For Popper freedom does not mean simply to do what one wants to do. Rather, it means to take up the burden of individual responsibility for oneself, the neighbour, the community, the state, and for humankind. Individual responsibility is the foundation and, at the same time, the consequence of freedom. Popper's main difference with communitarianism in this respect is to be found in the motivation for this responsibility. For him responsibility is not the consequence of identification with a community, but rather it springs from the free will of the *enlightened* individual. If freedom is the highest value and if it is possible only in connection with responsibility, then the individual who understands this will be willing to take up responsibility. A strengthening of communal ties and values or the identification with some common good is not the crucial point for an open society but rather an insight into the importance of individual responsibility.

Here we can find one reason for Popper's emphasis on education and critical thinking. In this regard there is a third idea that Popper adds to the conventional liberal view. His political philosophy is carried by an *ethos of enlightenment* in the sense of critical thinking, education, intellectual truthfulness, and modesty. Like Socrates, Popper believed that the way to improve the political life of a democratic society is to educate the citizens — as well as the politicians — to self-criticism. The state has the responsibility 'to see that its citizens are given an education enabling them to participate in the life of the community, and to make use of any opportunity to develop their special interests and gifts . . . ' (Popper 1945, Chapter 7, §III). For Popper this responsibility is one of the protective functions of the state.

By this Popper means an education to criticism and rationality and not one that teaches values, virtues, and habits that are important for the community. The state should not look after the moral life of its citizens. Such a claim would not only oppose Popper's anti-authoritarianism but also his concern to protect the moral autonomy of the individual against all forms of external authority. The individual does not have to accept the command of an authority as the basis for ethics; rather it is the individual who has to judge if it is moral or immoral to obey a command by an authority. As Sandra Pralong puts it in her article *Minima Moralia* (1999, p. 132): 'Since liberal individuals represent self-originating sources of value, the rules, including ethical ones, are to be set by individuals, with no appeal to higher authority and coercion.'

For Popper autonomy and individual responsibility are threatened if the state intervenes in the morality of the citizens and uses its power for the control of their moral life. Such an increase of the realm of state-enforced norms would be the end of the individual's moral responsibility and thus would destroy morality. 'It would replace personal responsibility by tribalistic taboos and by the totalitarian irresponsibility of the individual' (Popper 1945, Chapter 6, § VI). It is not the business of the state to teach or enforce morality, nor can it promote a specific conception of the good life. Like other liberals Popper fears that the intervention of the state in moral questions can lead to a perfectionist state.

Nevertheless, this does not mean that the state has to remain indifferent to behaviour that threatens the foundations of a democratic society. A lack of individual responsibility can bring about state intervention. This is a main concern for Popper's late political observations, especially when he talks about the bad influence of television on children. He fears that more and more violence on television can overcome the natural resistance and aversion to violence. For Popper this undermines the rule of law, the behest of which is first of all to avoid violence. Unrestricted violence on television can lead down a slope away from civilization. What is needed are regulation and control.

Popper is not in favour of censorship, but for him freedom depends on responsibility (Popper 1997, Chapter 4.). State intervention and censorship are not in contradiction to the concept of an open society because they reflect the fundamental principle of liberalism: *that the freedom for moving my fist is limited by the position of your nose* (ibidem, Chapter 8). Popper points out that there are rules in every way of life. So it is clear that an open society cannot be built on individual responsibility alone. Rules and institutions must come into play if people do not act responsibly. And these institutions and rules will increase when individual responsibility decreases.

3   Institutions and tradition

It is characteristic of Popper's political philosophy that he shifts the focus
from personnel questions to institutions. For him all long-term politics are
institutional. All political problems are problems of the legal framework rather
than persons (Popper 1945, Chapter 9). Popper takes it as an anthropological
fact that human beings are susceptible to corruption by power. Where there
is power, there is always a danger of its misuse. So what social and political
life needs are not so much good people as good institutions. For Popper it is
madness to base all our political efforts on the faint hope that we shall be
successful in obtaining excellent rulers. Political philosophy has too long been
dominated by the question of who should rule. Popper asks for a change of
perspective leading to a new approach to the problem of politics. He wants
to replace the question of *Who should rule?* with the new question: '*How
can we so organize political institutions that bad or incompetent rulers can be
prevented from doing too much damage?* (ibidem).

Whoever rules and whatever the origins of power may be, more important than the legitimation of power is its control. This control of power, of
the dangerous accumulation of state-given power, is for Popper the basic problem of politics. This is even more important in a democratic and modern
society, where the state plays a key protective role. Popper emphasizes the
institutional control of rulers by balancing their powers against other powers.
Indeed, he favours a theory of checks and balances.

Does Popper's approach bring about an institutionalism, neglecting the importance of traditions and the role of participation of citizens for a democratic
system, as communitarians criticize in most liberal views of democracy? For
them, as stated above, liberal concepts of democracy concentrate one-sidedly
on procedural and institutional aspects. Here we can find some answers within
Popper's political thought. First, Popper does not talk in favour of a pure institutionalism, which for him is impossible. The construction of institutions
involves not only important personal decisions, but the functioning of even the
best institutions depends on the persons involved. For Popper '[i]nstitutions
are like fortresses'; they 'must be well designed *and* ...manned' (1957, § 21).

Second, Popper emphasizes the importance of social traditions, which ensure that those who are in power will not easily destroy democratic institutions. In general, traditions play an important role as intermediaries between
persons and institutions. Popper sees traditions as a link between institutions and the intentions and values of the people who run these institutions.
Traditions give the individuals, who come and go, the necessary background
and the certainty of purpose to oppose corruption (Popper 1963, p. 195). But
there is a difference between Popper and the communitarian point of view.
The communitarians focus on religious beliefs, cultural customs, and political
virtues such as patriotism. For Popper an uncritical approach to tradition can
easily lead to *traditionalism* and to authoritarian consequences. For this he
emphasizes a critical tradition and, in the case of democracy, the traditions of
a free society including a tradition of almost jealous watchfulness on the part

of its citizens, so that the state does not overstep the limits of its legitimate functions. Only this tradition can balance the power of the state by providing those checks and controls on which all freedom depends. Popper also speaks of a tradition of freedom as the traditional readiness to defend freedom, to fight for it and to make sacrifices for it (Popper 1992, p. 208). Without these traditions democracy can lead to dictatorship.

Why this emphasis on tradition, something that is rather unique among liberal thinkers? For Popper those traditions were missing in the interwar years in Central Europe. Here he sees a major factor in the development of totalitarianism. And the totalitarian experience in its form of mass support for fascism is central for Popper's thoughts on democracy. His *theory of democratic control* has to be understood as a response to the historical experience of the National Socialist take-over of Germany in 1933. Here a democratic election brought about as a consequence the destruction of democracy. Popper deals with the possibility that democratic decisions can threaten to end democracy in the so-called *paradox of democracy*. In accordance with Plato, he formulates it as the possibility that the majority may decide that a tyrant should rule (Popper 1945, Chapter 7, § I). Popper tries to avoid this paradox by shifting the focus from the election of government to the dismissal of government. He defines democracy not by the possibility of *voting for* a certain government but by the possibility of *getting rid* of a government without bloodshed. A government, regardless of whether it rests on democratic elections or not, can therefore not be called democratic if it threatens to take away a fundamental right of its citizens — namely, to dismiss the rulers.

For Popper it is important to return to the old (*Athenian*) meaning of the word democracy as the name of a constitution to prevent a dictatorship, a tyranny. In this sense he defines the principle of a democratic policy in the *Open Society* as 'the proposal to create, develop, and protect, political institutions for the avoidance of tyranny' (1945, Chapter 7, § II). He considers 'the various equalitarian methods of democratic control, such as general elections and representative government, ... as no more than well-tried and ... reasonably effective institutional safeguards against tyranny' (ibidem). Democracy turns out to be not an end in itself, but rather a means for safeguarding our freedom (Notturno 1999, p. 44).

4 Critical participation and the method of science

Does this not reduce self-government and participation to merely means toward ends such as the rule of law, equality, or individual freedom, as alleged by communitarians? Does Popper's theory of democratic control neglect the role of participation? Such a criticism of Popper's political philosophy has been raised not by communitarians but by the political theorist Geoffrey Stokes and the historian Malachi Haim Hacohen. Stokes sees Popper's procedural arguments 'within the tradition of realist and revisionist democratic theory, that gives priority to competitive elites and argues for democracy as a method of choosing governments' (Stokes 1998, p. 67). Hacohen criticizes Popper for not giving much attention to participation in political activities nor to possible restrictions thereof. For him laws, rights, and duties ought to apply equally to all citizens. But he does not, as Hacohen points out, extend this principle further and argue for equal access to political power. Instead, Popper regards arrangements for apportioning political power as pragmatic (Hacohen 2000, p. 507).

Even though Popper has not paid a lot of attention to participation in the sense of involvement in the activities of political communities, he stresses a kind of participation that I want to call *critical participation*. The freedom to criticize government, its actions and its programmes is crucial for democracy. From the citizens a certain degree of vigilance over and even distrust of the state and its officers is necessary. For Popper it is the duty of the citizen to watch and see that the state does not overstep the limits of its legitimate functions. Moreover, he focuses on freedom of thought and speech, as these freedoms are important for criticism and the exertion of public opinion. Democracy must allow individuals to criticize majority decisions and to attempt to revise them. Then, too, Popper demands for those who are affected by the action of piecemeal social engineering that they have the opportunity critically to rejoin (see also the quotation from Burke that serves as a motto at the beginning of later editions of 1945).

As is typical for the whole of his philosophy, in his political thought, too, Popper concentrates on the critical aspect. Critical participation can give another answer to problems raised by communitarians. Through participation in critical discussions individuals do not merely seek to realize personal goals. As responsible and critical citizens, they choose the most urgent social problems, search out their origins, and try to solve them. We can give up the search for a common good and concentrate on the alleviation of suffering. This is an alternative to the communitarian common good as well as to utilitarianism. Both seem in their belief in an agreement about the good to be utopian and can bring about authoritarian consequences. Popper's conception of piecemeal social engineering brings one closer to the people, who have the opportunity and should have the ability to join critically the discussion about the most urgent social problems and their possible solutions. Piecemeal engineering presupposes not only the freedom to criticize but also the willingness to learn from mistakes.

This connects politics to science. As does science, so also ought politics to centre on criticism and the method of trial and error. Indeed, Popper is concerned to transfer his method of conjectures and refutations from science and epistemology to politics. New ideas, criticism, and reason should replace force and violence as the determinants of political decision making. As in science so also in society, conflicts should be settled with peaceful means and open and critical discussion, counting on the better argument. Politicians have to learn to accept criticism just as the public has to learn that politicians can and will make mistakes. The purpose is not to avoid all mistakes, which would bring an end to all reforms because social actions will always have unintended consequences. What is important is to reform and transform our institutions step by step, and this can come about only if we are open to criticism and willing to learn from our mistakes.

But the implementation of scientific method in politics faces serious problems. The conditions for critical discussions, for the open declaration of interests, for argumentation and criticism, and for compromises, do not arise to the same extent in social practice as they do in science. Methods that can make sense in science do not automatically function in social practice, where we have to deal with very diverse interests. What is missing in Popper's political philosophy is a systematic and differentiated analysis of how to transfer his critical method to social and political practice. Such an analysis would bring us closer to the problems we face today in our liberal democracies such as low voter turnout, political apathy, and extremist parties. We have to turn to a level of problem solving that calls for a combined effort of social philosophy, the social sciences, and politics.

5 Conclusion

Even though communitarianism cannot be seen as an alternative to liberalism, it is important to take up the questions raised by this position. Popper's political philosophy offers some ideas that can enable one to develop a better response to the communitarians. But these ideas, like his political philosophy in general, are not developed to a satisfying degree. To bring out their potential fruitfulness we have to develop the moral assumption Popper often takes for granted, look for the prerequisites for critical participation, and analyse the consequences and problems of the implementation of scientific method into politics. By carrying forward Popper's political thought we should be able to overcome some of the *shortcomings* of liberalism, as they are addressed in communitarian critiques.

Bibliography

Hacohen, M. H. (2000). *Karl Popper – The Formative Years, 1902-1945. Politics and Philosophy in Pre-war Vienna*. Cambridge & elsewhere: Cambridge University Press.

Jarvie, I. C. & Pralong, S., editors (1999). *Popper's Open Society after Fifty Years. The Continuing Relevance of Karl Popper*. London: Routledge.

Notturno, M. A. (1999). 'The Open Society and Its Enemies: Authority, Community, and Bureaucracy'. In Jarvie & Pralong (1999), pp. 41-55.

Pralong, S. (1999). '*Minima Moralia*: Is There an Ethics of the Open Society?' In Jarvie & Pralong (1999), pp. 128-145.

Popper, K. R. (1945). *The Open Society and Its Enemies*. London: George Routledge & Sons. 5th edition 1966. London: Routledge & Kegan Paul.

———— (1957). *The Poverty of Historicism*. London: Routledge & Kegan Paul.

———— (1963). *Conjectures and Refutations*. London: Routledge & Kegan Paul. 5th edition 1989. London: Routledge.

———— (1992). *In Search of a Better World. Lectures and Essays from Thirty Years*. London: Routledge.

———— (1997). *The Lesson of This Century: with two Talks on Freedom and the Democratic State. Karl Popper interviewed by Giancarlo Bosetti*. London: Routledge.

Rawls, J. (1971). *A Theory of Justice*. Cambridge MA: Belknap Press of Harvard University Press.

Shearmur, J. F. G. (1996). *The Political Thought of Karl Popper*. London: Routledge.

Stokes, G. (1988). *Popper: Philosophy, Politics and Scientific Method*. Cambridge: Polity.

16

On Popper's
Concept of an Open Society

Ulrich Steinvorth

1 The ambivalent fascination of the concept

Popper's concept of an open society gives the contemporary reader trouble understanding it. On the one hand, it is difficult not to be inspired by it. Calling a society *open* or its contrary, *closed*, throws an elucidating light on an obviously important character of a society. On the other hand, it is not very clear what that character is. Nor is it clear what the status of the concept is that makes us see the character. Nor is it clear what are the consequences and commitments we are involved in by using the concept. We do not gain much when we say it is an ideal type, as did Ian Jarvie.[1] That it is, but that does not answer the question why openness of a society is so important and what its importance consists in.

It is an answer when John Hall calls the book that made the concept famous 'a paean of praise to bravery', a plea for '*Gesellschaft*' and against 'the cosy womb-like certainties of *Gemeinschaft*', and a 'rewriting of liberalism in terms of openness'.[2] Yet these descriptions lead to new questions. How aggressive is the bravery praised? How uncosy is the society to be embraced? Which liberal ideas correspond to Popper's idea of an open society? Did Popper not even defend this openness, which means insecurity and exclusion for more and more people?

Such questions are not dragged in in a desperate effort to revamp the lost appeal of ideas that looked rosy more than a half-century ago. They rather intrude on any contemporary if they read only the passages in *The Open Society and Its Enemies* that explicitly indicate or implicitly express the meaning of an open society. Their intrusion proves at the same time the strength and the weakness of Popper's concept. The concept of an open society is strong enough to direct our attention to obviously central features of modern societies and yet lacks a theory to explain or evaluate them. This is what I want to show in this paper by trying to answer the question of what is the use of Popper's concept of an open society, not without hope to instigate

---

[1] Jarvie (1999).
[2] Hall (1999), p. 83.

efforts to explicate more thoroughly or develop the concept, and a descriptive or, more probably, normative theory that might embed it.

I begin by recalling that Popper was not the first to use the concept of an open society. Rather, as he said himself, he found it in Bergson.[3] Comparing Popper's and Bergson's use of the concept will lead us to a more specific understanding of Popper's open society, but also to the first problem in using it that I want to point out, that of its capability of providing a defence of the imperialism of open societies. To better understand this problem, I shall turn to the second problem I want to recall, that of the relation of open societies to abstract societies.

2 Bergson and Popper

Like Popper, Bergson considered the open society the foundation both of democracy[4] and of a trust in one's own powers .[5] Yet we can easily recognize that Bergson's use of the concept is not that made by Popper.

Bergson distinguished, in his *Deux sources de la morale et de la religion* closed and open society. Closed society is based upon a closed morality and a closed soul; open society, upon an open morality and an open soul. The closed soul is ruled by 'that primitive instinct' that draws man to the group he has grown up in, by an instinct of self-protection and solidarity with his group and rejection of foreigners. Closed society, Bergson says, 'coats (this instinct) with so thick a varnish',[6] but it does not succeed in extinguishing or sublimating it, since it explodes in wars such as the First World War.

By contrast, open society is based on love of mankind. Bergson describes the love in both religious and philosophical terms.[7] It is a 'love which absorbs and kindles the whole soul' and extends to all nature.[8] It is a sublime experience accessible only to 'privileged men' such as 'the saints of Christianity'.[9] Hence, Bergson calls the open society a 'mystic society'.[10]

Both in Bergson and Popper the concept of open society refers to a more reflective way of life and contrasts to a more natural and spontaneous way.

---

[3]Popper (1945), note to the Introduction.

[4]Henri Bergson (1932/1935). He held democracy to be 'evangelical in essence' (p. 271; quoted from Germino 1974, p. 9. Germino's paper is illuminating in comparing Bergson and Popper (and Voegelin) although I do not agree with his judgments.

[5]Cp. Bergson (1932/1935), p. 306; quoted from Germino (1974), p. 12: 'Mankind lies groaning, half crushed beneath the weight of its own progress. Men do not sufficiently realize that their future is in their own hands. Theirs is the task of determining first of all whether they want to go on living or not. Theirs the responsibility, then, for deciding if they want merely to live, or intend to make just the extra effort required for fulfilling, even on their refractory planet, the essential function of the universe, which is a machine for the making of gods.'

[6]Bergson (1932/1935), pp. 22-24. Quoted from Germino (1974), pp. 1f.

[7]Cp. for example Bergson (1932/1935), p. 25, quoted from Germino (1974), pp. 2f.

[8]Quoted from Germino (1974), pp. 1ff.

[9]And 'the sages of Greece, the prophets of Israel, the Arahants of Buddhism' (quoted from Germino 1974, p. 3).

[10]Quoted from Germino (1974), p. 8.

Popper has recognized this when he remarked that 'in spite of a considerable difference' of his use of the term from Bergson's, 'there is a certain similarity also'. But as to the 'main difference' between Bergson and him, he said: 'My terms indicate ... a *rationalist distinction*; the closed society is characterized by the belief in magical taboos, while the open society is one in which men have learned to be to some extent critical of taboos, and to base decisions on the authority of their own intelligence (after discussion). Bergson, on the other hand, has a kind of *religious distinction* in mind.'[11]

It is certainly true and important that for Bergson the open society has a religious character and for Popper it does not. Yet Popper is wrong in describing the difference as one between a religious and a *rationalist* conception. To both, closed society is 'a concrete group of concrete individuals', 'held together by semi-biological ties — kinship, living together, sharing common efforts, common dangers, common joys and common distress'. It is a 'semi-organic unit', as Popper calls it, to which the 'so-called organic or biological theory of the state can be applied to a considerable extent',[12] and, as we may add by the way, the communitarian theory as well. This state of nature is broken up, according to Bergson, by a spiritual love of God and mankind. Yet according to Popper, it is broken up by harder and more mundane interests. The difference between Bergson's and Popper's conception of the open society is not that between a religious and a *rationalist* conception. It is that between a religious and a *prosaic* or *materialist* conception.

For Popper no less than for Bergson, the change from the closed to the open society is a 'step from tribalism to humanitarianism'. For both, it is the one great event and problem of human history, 'that great revolution which, it seems, is still in its beginning'.[13] But unlike Bergson, Popper does not infer from the sublimity of this event the sublimity of the historical steps necessary to achieve the end. Rather, not unlike Hegel and Marx, Popper thinks that human greatness is realized by hard and often selfish interests. Only because open societies are realized by hard individual interests do they show 'such an important social phenomenon as class struggle'. '[C]ompetition for status among its members', Popper stresses, is 'one of the most important characteristics of the open society'.[14] Popper's open society is based on everyone's pursuit of his *own* and often *egoistic* interests or happiness.

3 Popper's defence of imperialism

If the hard interest origin and motivation of Popper's idea of an open society are not pointed out, as is very rarely done, it becomes difficult to understand,

---

[11] Popper (1945), note to the Introduction.

[12] Ibidem, Chapter 10, § I.

[13] Ibidem.

[14] Ibidem. Popper does not say that it is class struggle or social competition that breaks up the closed society; rather, its closedness must already be somewhat slackened in order for social competition to arise. But the great revolution that realizes the open society all over the world requires social competition, and if it were to stop, that would be the end of Popper's open society.

if not outright offensive, that Popper defends ancient Athens's imperialist politics. 'I am far from defending', he said soothingly, 'everything that Athens did in building up her empire', only to start defending the principle of Athens's imperialism, saying, 'it is necessary, I believe, to see that tribalist exclusiveness and self-sufficiency could be superseded only by some form of imperialism. And it must be said that certain of the imperialist measures introduced by Athens were rather liberal.'[15]

It is not necessary for us, nor was it for Popper, to go into the details of the imperialist politics he defends. Open societies are non-tribal societies; they can arise only if individuals are ready to fight for their individual and egoistic interests and break up the bonds and ligatures of tribal societies. If the people of Athens's neighbour cities were unable to break up the bonds of their tribal societies themselves, Athens was justified, according to Popper, in military interventions that helped break up tribal societies. He seems to have considered this view a consequence of his conception of an open society. He thought he was only consistent in drawing it. Yet we may wish he had explicitly spelt it out for clarity's sake.

Popper's defence of Athenian imperialism shows us that the liberalism he rewrites in terms of openness is a militant one. From the failing of the appeasement politics of the 1930s he seems to have drawn the same consequence that the political philosopher Leo Strauss did and passed on to contemporary advisors of the American government: a democracy must be ready not only to defend itself but to attack its enemies. It must be ready to attack not only its own enemies, but also the enemies to openness in other societies. It must be ready to assist those interested in openness by military force even if they did not ask to be helped by military force.

It is interesting to see that Popper's defence of the imperialism of a democracy is not only a reason for the left to criticize Popper. It was a reason also for a conservative author such as Eric Voegelin to reject Popper's conception of the open society and prefer Bergson's.[16] Yet the question that interests

---

[15](1945), Chapter 10, § II.

[16]Cp. Germino (1974). It is little known that Erich Voegelin is the author of *Rasse und Staat* (1933), a systematic and historical description of the role of the race in political and historical theories that aims at dissolving the distrust against the 'Rassentheorie und der Rassenidee' (the theory and the idea of race) by showing that they are better founded than one might judge by the intellectual poverty of their defenders (p. 12). Voegelin talks of the contrast of 'Judentum' (judaism) and 'nordische Idee' (Nordic idea) that is made in the racist theories he describes; he reports that 'Judentum' is, compared to the 'positiv gewertete Gemeinschaft [positively valued community] . . . ein Nichts [a nothing]' (p. 207), and talks of the 'Trennung der großen kulturschöpferischen nordischen Rasse von den anderen minder begabten' (separation of the great, culture-creating, Nordic race from the other less endowed ones) and of the 'politische Gegensatz der Rassen . . . mit seiner Steigerung zu einem weltgeschichtlichen Kampf zwischen einem Prinzip des Guten und des Bösen' (political contrast of the races . . . with its enhancement into a world historical battle between principles of good and evil) (p. 158). These reports may be understood as expressing not Voegelin's own view but only that of the theories described. But since he declared the racist theories to be better founded than one might judge by the intellectual poverty of their defenders, it is difficult to decide.

us is whether or how far Popper's conception of an open society implies his defence of the imperialism of a democracy. What specifies his concept of an open society is its origin in the egoistic interests of individuals fighting for their right to break loose from the bonds of tribal societies. So the question we have to answer is: does this defence imply a defence of the imperialism of a democracy? Or, to put the question in more general terms: how much pursuit of interests will the end of realizing the open society justify? How much bravery are we to praise? Where, according to Popper, are we to draw the line between legitimate and illegitimate appeals to the idea of the open society?

There is a traditional and very important condition for an action to be legitimate. It is expressed in the Golden rule, by Hobbes's second Law of Nature[17] and by Kant's categorical imperative. It is expressed also in the 'negative golden rule' that Sandra Pralong has convincingly argued 'Popper implicitly had in mind as a rule of conduct for the open society'.[18] This legitimacy condition requires that the rule, reason, or right we presuppose in doing an action must be a rule every other one must be allowed to follow. Let us call this condition the *universality condition.*

Important though it is, the universality condition will not help us answer our questions concerning the legitimacy of imperialism. In imperialism the imperialist power typically holds that it is militarily superior to the powers it aims to subject. Imperialist powers will therefore have no problem in recognizing the universality condition. They will readily agree that any power has the same right they appeal to of enforcing their claims by the threat and use of military power. Therefore, we must look for another and more specific legitimacy condition of imperialism in Popper's ideas.

4 The abstract society

Before trying an answer, we must consider another peculiarity of Popper's open society, namely its relation to the *abstract society.*[19]

> We could conceive of a society in which men practically never meet face to face —
> in which all business is conducted by individuals in isolation who communicate
> by typed letters or by telegrams, and who go about in closed motor-cars. (Art-
> ificial insemination would allow even propagation without a personal element.)
> Such a fictitious society might be called a 'completely abstract or depersonalized
> society'. Now the interesting point is that our modern society resembles in many
> of its aspects such a completely abstract society. ... There are many people living
> in a modern society who have no, or extremely few, intimate personal contacts,
> who live in anonymity and isolation, and consequently in unhappiness.

---

[17]Hobbes (1651), Chapter 14.

[18]Pralong (1999), p. 142.

[19]Popper (1945), Chapter 10, § I.

Many critics of modern society maintain that contemporary Western societies have become nearly completely abstract societies. Their complaint is not only that so many people live in isolation but that even families or other intimate relations have become depersonalized and people have substituted the modern lures of emancipation and self-determination for the ancient virtues of community.[20]

Yet in contrast to such critics, Popper is not impressed by the dangers of an abstract society at all. True, he stresses that 'most of the social groups of a modern open society ... are poor substitutes' for closed societies, 'since they do not provide for a common life. And many of them do not have any function in the life of the society at large', that is, they do not connect people to what is important in their society. Yet he also says that '[t]here never will be or can be a completely abstract or even a predominantly abstract society' and adds:[21]

> ... there are gains. Personal relationships of a new kind can arise where they can be freely entered into, instead of being determined by the accidents of birth; and with this, a new individualism arises. Similarly, spiritual bonds can play a major rôle where the biological or physical bonds are weakened; etc. However this may be, our example, I hope, ... will have made it clear that our modern open societies function largely by way of abstract relations,

namely, by the 'division of labour and exchange of commodities'.[22] That is, we must not hope ever to get back to the concreteness of closed societies. We must rather adapt to the conditions of abstractness required by the dominant economy that is based on division of labour and exchange of commodities. Any other solution would end in disaster. 'There is no return to a harmonious state of nature. If we turn back, then we must go the whole way — we must return to the beasts.'[23]

Since Popper admits that open societies must be abstract up to a certain degree and yet must be preferred to those that the critics would prefer, the popular criticism of the abstractness or depersonalized character of modern societies can be directed against Popper. It is interesting to see that like the criticism of Popper's defence of imperialism, this one too is raised both by the right and the left.

---

[20]This criticism is the core of the many versions of communitarianism, among whose most influential contemporary representatives belong even defenders of modernity and liberalism such as Michael Walzer and Charles Taylor. For more specific communitarian criticism of the open society see Walter Berns (1996); R. Bruce Douglass (1996); and, for German critics, Joachim Fest (1993), *Die schwierige Freiheit. Über die offene Flanke der offenen Gesellschaft.* See also many of the essays in Bossle & Radnitzky (1982). For a German criticism of this conservative criticism of the open society, see Richard Herzinger (2001).

[21](1945), Chapter 10, § I.

[22]Ibidem.

[23](1945), Chapter 10, § VIII. The original has italics.

5   The appeal to the interests of the common people

Let us now look at what might be reasons for Popper's defence of both the imperialism and the abstractness of open societies. What is common to Popper's response to the symptoms of depersonalization and to his defence of Athenian imperialism is his trust in the attractions of an open society. He believes that in spite or even just because of its tendency to abstractness and imperialism it will be attractive in particular to the people who up to now have not been favoured by history, who win when they are enabled to pursue their own interests, and who are intelligent enough to see that 'rather liberal'[24] imperialist politics like that of Athens is in their own interest.

From Popper's trust in the open society we may try to infer a condition of legitimate politics in cases when we cannot decide whether the universality condition is satisfied. The condition would be simply this:

C   Politics must be attractive in particular to the less well-off people

However, if Popper accepted C, the line he would have to draw between legitimate and illegitimate imperialist measures is where the measures stop *looking* attractive or being *publicity* for the open society. Yet where we should expect Popper to draw the line is where the measures stop *being* attractive or liberal or in the interest of the masses. On the other hand, it seems, and it seems that Popper has held, that a society that does not *look* open is not open either, and that politics in favour of openness of societies, whether imperialist or not, must *look* like being in the interest of the masses, if it is to be acceptable. So to be legitimate, any politics of open societies and particularly their foreign affairs politics must both *be* in the interest of the masses and *look* like that. Therefore, we might explicate C as follows:

C1   Politics must be compatible with equal liberty of everyone.

C2   Politics must be such as to be correctly understood by the less well-off people as guaranteeing equal liberty to everyone.

By *equal liberty of everyone* I understand the liberal idea that requires of a just society that:

(1) no one is hindered in following his or her ambitions and interests unless the survival of their common society is endangered;

(2) no one is privileged in the pursuit of his or her ambitions and interests; and

(3) actions and institutions must conform to the universality condition.

With the help of C1 and C2 and our preceding reflections, we may now try to answer the question of what is the use of Popper's concept of an open society. There is more than one use of Popper's concept of open society, as

---

[24]Popper (1945), Chapter 10, § II.

there is more than one intention in his writing *The Open Society*. The uses
he is most interested in are all normative. They are:

first, to remind us that modern society is worth defending because it is
attractive to the masses in the first place, because it allows them to pursue
their own interests, and is worth defending in spite of its being less attractive
or even a deterrent to those who govern or who have much to lose;

second, to justify even militant and military actions if their militancy
promotes openness in societies;

third, to restrict politics to conditions C1 and C2.

Let me confess that I am not sure at all whether this effort of explicating
Popper's use of his concept of an open society meets all or even the most
important ideas Popper wanted to communicate in making use of the term.
It is a trial open for refutation. But the question whether my explication of
Popper's use of the term does justice to Popper is different from a question
that philosophers ought to be interested in in the first place. That is the
question whether the use I ascribe to Popper is worth making. How can we
answer that question? The best way, I think, is by applying it to contemporary
societies and see whether the application results in questions or theses worth
discussing. So, let us ask whether:

first, the value of openness of societies consists in their attraction to the
masses;

second, imperialist politics of democratic powers can be justified if they
promote openness of societies;

third, to be legitimate, politics must meet C1 and C2.

It would take books to answer these questions. I did not formulate them
to answer them but to see whether the uses Popper makes of the term *open
society* are worth making. If the questions are worth asking and even of high
urgency, perhaps today even more than sixty years ago, then we may conclude
that Popper's uses of the term are worth making, perhaps today more than
before.

I want to end by giving a short comment on the third use and its application to contemporary politics, in particular to US anti-terrorist politics and
the politics of globalization by deregulation. Applying the third use to them,
we must ask whether they meet C1 and C2. There may be much discussion
whether they meet C1 but less, I'm afraid, whether they meet C2. Neither
American anti-terrorist politics nor the politics of globalization by deregulation looks like being correctly understandable by the people in the less open
societies (nor by people in more open societies) as guaranteeing equal liberty
to everyone.[25]

Therefore, if I am right in ascribing to Popper the third one of the three
uses listed, then, in spite of his admiration for the United States and in spite

---

[25] People will never expect a country not to pursue its own interests, but they will sym-
pathize with countries that succeed in combining the pursuit of their own interests with
that of more general interests. Such a country, according to Popper, was Athens and so, I
think, was the US in the Second World War and for some time after.

of his sympathy for Athenian and no doubt also for American imperialism, he would not be able to approve consistently of American anti-terrorist politics and the politics of globalization by deregulation.

Bibliography

Bergson, H. (1932). *Deux sources de la morale et de la religion*. 12th edition. Paris: Librairie Félix Alcan. English translation 1935. *Two Sources of Morality and Religion*. New York: Holt.

Berns, W. (1996) 'Re-evaluating the Open Society'. In G. W. Carey (1996), pp. 19-34.

Bossle, L. & Radnitzky, G., editors (1982). *Selbstgefährdung der offenen Gesellschaft*. Würzburg: Naumann.

Carey, G. W., editor (1996). *Order, Freedom and the Polity. Critical Essays on the Open Society*. Lanham MD: University Press of America.

Douglass, R. B. (1996). 'The Lure and the Limits of Openness'. In G. W. Carey (1996), pp. 125-147.

Fest, J. (1993). *Die schwierige Freiheit. Über die offene Flanke der offenen Gesellschaft*. Berlin: Siedler.

Germino, D. (1974). 'Preliminary Reflections on the Open Society: Bergson, Popper, Voegelin'. In D. Germino & K. von Beyme, editors (1974). *The Open Society in Theory and Practice*. The Hague: Nijhoff.

Hall, J. A. (1999). 'The Sociological Deficit of *The Open Society*, Analysed and Remedied'. In Jarvie & Pralong (1999), pp. 83-96.

Herzinger, R. (2001). *Republik ohne Mitte*. Berlin: Siedler.

Hobbes, T. (1651). *Leviathan*. London: Andrew Crookes.

Jarvie, I. C. (1999). 'Popper's Ideal Types: Open and Closed, Abstract and Concrete Societies'. In Jarvie & Pralong (1999), pp. 71-82.

Jarvie, I. C. & Pralong, S., editors (1999). *Popper's Open Society after Fifty Years. The Continuing Relevance of Karl Popper*. London: Routledge.

Popper, K. R. (1945). *The Open Society and Its Enemies*. London: George Routledge & Sons. 5th revised edition 1966. London: Routledge & Kegan Paul.

Pralong, S. (1999). '*Minima Moralia*. Is There an Ethics of the Open Society?' In Jarvie & Pralong (1999), pp. 128-145.

Voegelin, E. (1933). *Rasse und Staat*. Tübingen: J. C. B. Mohr (Paul Siebeck).

17

Towards a New Theory
of the Closed Society

John Wettersten

Popper's interesting and widely admired explanation of the attraction of the closed society does not fit with his development of a theory of the methods of the social sciences and especially of social reform. His theory of the attraction of the closed society is an anachronism, which it may be useful explicitly to clear away in order to improve the theory of the social sciences and social reform with which it is unfortunately combined. The purpose of this essay is to explain why this theory is an anachronism, how it may be removed and how we may view closed societies as attempts to be rational gone wrong. I shall begin with a critique of Popper's theory of the attraction of closed societies.

1 Popper's theory of the attraction of the closed society leads to a Puritan approach that blocks analyses of problems

Popper's theory of the attraction of the closed society has attracted little critical attention, because it is intuitively attractive. Yet it displays a serious weakness. According to Popper's theory (1945, Chapter 10, §§ I-III) all individuals have an innate desire to live in a closed society. They have this desire, because of the way humans have evolved. For millennia humans and their forefathers lived in small tribal groups that have all the characteristics of closed societies. This tribal life gave humans a need for the emotional security that such societies offered. All individuals now living retain this emotional need, Popper says. This need leads them to be strongly attracted to the siren songs of those praising closed societies.

The theory that all individuals have an innate desire to live in a closed society poses a real problem — How can we maintain open societies? — in such a way that it has no intelligent solution. On this theory the desire to live in a closed society is the main source of the danger to open ones, and we must all deem ourselves real or potential sinners. When Popper speaks of this danger, he turns into a preacher. Instead of discussing the social and institutional problems that can lead to the decline of open societies, he moralizes. We must, he says, bear the cross of civilization. As preachers often are, he is also somewhat hypocritical. He immensely enjoyed living in the open society and would have been terribly unhappy in any closed one. Popper's theory

blocks any sensible thought about the conditions under which people succumb
to the siren songs of those calling for a closed society. It is a block toward
using social science for that purpose that Popper saw as primary in his theory
of social science, that is, the investigation of the unintended consequences of
human action, in this case, the investigation of which actions and/or institutions create favourable conditions for the return to and/or maintenance of a
closed society. There are, no doubt, many political movements that can be
superficially explained as expressions of the desire to live in closed societies.
Yet, when we view them this way, we block thinking about the specific institutional, practical, and moral dilemmas that lead people to join and support
such movements.

The core of Popper's theory contains the possibilities of building a better
theory of the causes and attraction of totalitarianism. In order to make use
of these possibilities, however, we must sort out those unfortunate aspects of
Popper's theory that merely reflect the intellectual currents of his time and
which were not systematically developed out of his theory of rationality.[1] We
may then replace them with views more conducive to the optimistic view of
science as an exciting and attractive adventure, to which his initial studies in
the logic of research have led.

2   Popper uses conflicting assumptions in philosophical anthropo-
logy to construct a theory of closed and open societies

When Popper turned to the philosophy of the social sciences, two of the tasks
he hoped to carry out were, first, to explain the attraction and influence of
totalitarian theories of society and, second, to develop a view of civilized or
rational society. The two projects are not presented as distinct. Rather, they
are woven into a seemingly unified essay on closed and open societies. The
theory of the attraction of totalitarian societies is his theory of the closed society. His theory of the open society is a new theory of civilized society, which
is based on a critical view of reason. His theory of the burden of civilization is
the attempt to unify his theories of the closed and open societies, by presenting the two alternatives as posing an all-or-nothing decision to seek one or
the other, to seek good or evil. The use of critical thinking is the path chosen
by those who seek the open society. Those who seek the closed society fall
into dogmatism and barbarism. Popper's Manichean view attributes to man
a natural tendency to avoid reason, but an intelligence that enables him to
see the evils, which flow from giving in to this natural desire for the emotional
comfort of tribal society.

Popper's theory that civilized individuals need to decide in favour of the
open society and the intensity of his moral exhortations to do so give the
appearance that *The Open Society and Its Enemies* (1945) contains a well
integrated moral appeal. It seems to pose clearly a fundamental choice facing

---

[1]I intend to show elsewhere that Popper held the core of this view long before he developed his philosophy of science.

modern man. On the one hand, we may give way to our emotions and choose the closed society at the cost of oppression and barbarism or, on the other hand, we may take the hard, moral course and choose the open society and the critical use of reason. But, when one looks at the philosophical anthropological assumptions that are so important for his philosophy of science and psychology and compare them with the same kind of presuppositions made in his theory of the closed society, the apparent unity of Popper's view breaks down.

Popper's theory of the closed society deems rationality to be contrary to man's natural inclinations. Man has to struggle steadily to become and remain rational. Popper later explained the moral intensity of his book by the fact that it was part of a war effort. The intensity of his moral exhortations, however, has another and deeper cause. In opposition to the innate desire to return to the closed society Popper had nothing more to offer than the painful decision to be rational. He had no rational moral foundation to which he could appeal. He could appeal only to human sympathy and the wish to avoid barbarism. Popper's moral exhortations are jarring. They are emotional and they come from a man who advocates the critical use of reason as an antidote to the emotional appeal of the closed society. We would expect and hope for argument and perspective in the place of passion. But his exhortations do indeed flow from the philosophical anthropological assumptions found in his theory of the tribal society and the need to overcome it.

A corollary of Popper's theory of closed and open societies is the thesis that after an open society has arisen, any attempt to recreate a closed society will lead to barbarism. Once individuals have learnt to think for themselves and to question their status in society, it is never possible to recreate the kind of highly static conditions that characterized all societies before the invention of the open society. This return to a tribal state cannot work, because any attempt to do so will encounter individuals who will not accept the terms of the closed society that some seek to impose. The dissidents will then have to be repressed. But, in a society that is moving from being open to becoming closed, this can be done only with violent means. This is an important observation. But it conflicts with his Manichean view of the attraction of the evil closed society and the burden of the open society. If we really all wanted to live in closed societies, it is hard to understand why this thesis should be true. In fact most individuals do not want to abandon the open society after they have learnt to live in it.

The moralistic stance of Popper's view of rationality and the defence of the open society may be overcome when we note that both science and rationality are supported by the natural inclination of man to want to understand his world and to enjoy thinking about it. Scientists are not merely driven by the desire to avoid evil or to achieve fame, and thus willing to pay the price of engaging in activities that are contrary to their inclinations. Such a dark and pessimistic view does not lead to enlightenment about science or rationality. When Popper speaks of the attraction of the closed society, he presumes that is not a pleasurable activity. Routine is more satisfying than facing and discovering new problems. The love of adventure is deemed foreign to man's nature. But all these alleged characteristics of scientists are foreign to them as Popper observes. Popper not only personally loved science and enjoyed it, his theory sees this love of truth as a moving force behind it. It is not a personal quirk of Popper as moral hero. In contrast to his view of scientists as lovers of the truth, his view of rationalists as moral heroes even moved in the direction of the romanticism that he so much wanted to avoid.

3   An alternative view of rationality

When Popper's students began developing new theories of rationality and new philosophical anthropological views based on them, they sought to generalize the new fallibilist theory of science. The theory of the attraction of the closed society was merely ignored. It seemed that theories of rationality did not need to take notice of it, because these theories were concerned with how humans were or should be rational and not with the inclination to avoid being rational.

If rationality is fallible, Joseph Agassi (1977) observed, it must also be partial. No individual or group can ever achieve some perfect system. We shall always have pieces of systems or various theories of this or that, which may or may not fit together. Rationality is an unending process of adjustment and not the creation of a (final) system. This view has the consequence that all individuals are rational to this or that degree. They all seek to solve problems and they all seek to bring some coherence into their thought by uniting the various elements of their intellectual baggage. But no one does this completely and no one works on the project continually. Anyone may choose or not choose to pursue this or that end or to overcome this or that difficulty. We are all critical to a degree and being critical is crucial to rationality. Those who wish to increase their degree of rationality choose to increase the quality — not necessarily the severity — of their critical methods. This is a project that all humans can and do follow to this degree or that, since all are partially rational and all can see some circumstances in which more effective thought would be advantageous.

4   If rationality is natural and satisfying, why do individuals ever choose closed societies?

When we view rationality as a natural activity that is common to all humans and when we further presume that individuals often seek to increase their level of rationality, we may ask why, in spite of this innate desire to use reason, we nevertheless regularly find movement toward closed societies and even demands for them. On an optimistic view of rationality as natural and emotionally satisfying, the desire to create closed societies is contrary to individual aims and desires shared by all humans, that is, their desire to increase their capacity.

In explaining why individuals favour social reform that decreases rather than increases their capacities, I find two significantly different kinds of mistakes. The first kind are those mistakes that are genuine, even critical, attempts to improve matters, that go awry due to misconceptions about how capacity may be improved. The second kind of mistake is pathological and corresponds closely with the behaviour of the paranoiac as described by Fried and Agassi (1976). It is characterized by the concerted attempt to rigorously impose a coherent social framework, while losing all contact with critical appraisals of the consequences of the effort. I shall discuss the first kind of case in this section and the pathological variant of it in the next.

It often appears that the more coherent a social system is, the easier it will be for individuals living in it to solve their problems. Plato envisioned the coherent social system as the ideal; and in spite of the decline of functionalism as a model for social scientific explanation, this ideal remains influential in virtually all the social sciences. When individuals think that this ideal is worth pursuing, they aim to increase their capacity to solve problems by increasing the coherence and simplicity of a social framework. But such efforts are often mistaken, because they regularly fail to take into account unintended consequences. This is a quite natural thing to do, when one believes that the coherence of a social system per se is good.

One attraction of the closed society is the hope that the institutions in such a society will raise the level of rationality that is practised in it. A closed society often appears superior to an open one due to its apparent coherence. Given traditional standards of rationality closed societies offer the hope that they will embody a very high level of rationality, that is, they will be highly coherent and systematic. They will be organized around simple principles down to the details. A society rigorously organized according to the principles of some systematic and coherent view seems to make, for example, transactions transparent, because rules will be stringently enforced. It seems to encourage trust and confidence between individuals, because cheating will be clearly defined and prohibited. It seems to enable people to understand how and why decisions are made, because they are made in accordance with quite general and quite rigid principles. When decisions are made rationally in accordance with known principles, no danger of abuse may be apparent, whereas the advantages will be clear.

An individual's desire to live in a closed society with its apparent higher degree of rationality may, then, be based in his or her desire to increase the ability of individuals to solve problems. It may appear much easier to solve problems in a simple and coherent society, because one will understand how it works and what one must do to attain the ends one pursues. It will be transparent and much less vulnerable to corruption, which often hides behind vague and shifting rules.

It is quite natural to confuse the simplicity of the framework with the simplicity of solving problems within it. When a framework is simple, stable and clear, the conditions for posing problems will remain constant. They will not have to be analysed anew every time a new problem is posed. In fact this is often the case. European businesses can solve many problems much

more efficiently and easily in a common market governed by the same laws
and regulations than in a market consisting of a number of countries with
different laws and regulations. The desirable movement in the direction of
establishing simpler and/or more comprehensive social frameworks will often
have the same characteristic, the appeal to simplicity and coherence, as the
appeal to a closed society. The latter seems to be merely an exaggeration of a
good idea, which turns it into its opposite, that is, into a hindrance to rational
rather than an aid to it. Pinochet's Chile is an example. A call for movement
in the direction of a closed society may, then, be an attempt to improve the
abilities of individuals by making the framework in which individuals seek to
solve problems simpler and clearer.

The demand for a simple framework fits traditional standards of rationality. These standards demand system, simplicity, and clarity. Most would agree
that any social organization that does not meet these standards is prima facie
poorer than one that does. Under some circumstances totalitarian theories or
simply populist demagogues can meet this standard of rationality far more
easily than any responsible politician can. The responsible politician must
look at consequences that those ideologues offering simple, clear, and coherent remedies do not have to take into account. Yet the responsible politician
will often appear not merely less rational but also more corrupt, because of
this fact. He will seem to be playing with the truth when he questions simple
principles that should govern social relations, in order to protect this or that
special interest. Conservative ideologues in America have learnt to perfect
this kind of argument to serve their own interests. But, of course, those individuals who reject oversimplifications may also use the need for responsible
accounting for undesirable consequences to do just that.

In fact we have no good standards for the desirable degree of simplicity
and/or coherence of social systems. But, whenever problems are difficult to
solve, even when a system is relatively simple and clear, changes are demanded
by some. And, any movement towards coherence and/or simplicity will have
prima facie appeal. When, for example, economic competition is too strong it
will likely be declared unfair, that is, as a violation of some simple standard
of fairness. Simple remedies may be demanded. One of these alternatives has
been racism. Racism often serves well for this purpose, since the claim that, for
example, the blacks, or the Jews, or the Turks, are responsible for problems,
is both simple and easy to apply in everyday life. The source of the problem
is relatively easy to identify. Making the system simpler — in this case more
homogeneous — may appear to offer hope to those facing difficulties. And,
even if the methods needed for doing this are drastic, they may be demanded
if the difficulties become acute enough — or appear to enough individuals
with enough influence to be acute enough. Demagogic demands for reform
often exploit the desire to increase rationality. In America many thought that
the demagogue and racist George Wallace possessed a high degree of integrity.

Attempts to improve the ability of individuals may appear both intellectually dishonest and corrupt, when they do not fit into some clear-cut

ideological view, which may serve to justify them by explaining how they will make social frameworks simpler and clearer. Attempts to help the poor with government programmes are often ad hoc when seen from the perspective of a free market. They are thus hard to defend in America, where they seem to represent a moral compromise of agreed principles. In Europe a socialist model makes the failure to provide for the poor a moral compromise of principles of fairness and so cannot be dispensed with. The actual concern that individuals have for the well-being of others does not have to differ in these differing societies to reach such widely different results about help for the poor. The differences really are intellectual. In both cases a higher level of coherence between principles and practice is demanded.

That the call for radical social change appeals to the desire to make society more rational, that is, more principled, systematic, and coherent, is made clear by the fact that the appearance of problems that are deemed acute and that call for systematic change in the direction of totalitarian systems is not the same as the appearance of poverty or oppression. They have to do with the rationality of the system and not merely with the plight of the individuals living in it. Economic problems as individuals perceive them are not merely or even primarily a matter of income, but primarily occur when change makes old techniques of dealing with problems no longer usable and the acquiring of new techniques quite difficult. An economic breakdown in an advanced society will lead more quickly to calls for radical solutions than will crushing poverty in societies that have never known prosperity; the standard techniques of solving problems in the first society break down, whereas in the second society standard techniques, in spite of their very poor results, remain at hand.

Acute problems calling for radical change are often moral problems, as was — and still is — the problem with race in America, as Gunnar Myrdal (Myrdal (with Sterner & Rose) 1944, p. xlvii) pointed out. The setting up a framework such as the American constitution combined with the practice of slavery creates for its practitioners enormous problems of justification and self-respect. Each time individuals living in a society with a blatant conflict of principles come across cases in which conflicting courses of actions are required, say practising discrimination in order to be well-integrated in the business world or not practising it to conform with principles of fairness and decency — problems will arise for individuals. In this case standards of rationality calling for system and simplicity may exert a very strong pull, because they may remove unpleasant conflicts. The call for change need not be in the direction of a closed society, but it may be. We may see this in Popper's analysis of Marx. Popper had great sympathy for Marx, because he saw that Marx did seek to create a better and a more moral society. But the attempt to remove inequities that arise due to differences in class led to a theory that could move only in the direction of closed societies: the attempt to remove classes could be carried out only with violent methods and could not be successful. Fundamentalist religious movements also seek to overcome moral conflicts in society by creating from their point of view a more rational society, that is, a more coherent society, one that rigorously follows its proclaimed principles, which are, of course, not questionable since they are known to be true. We might find much to object to in the principles of fundamentalist religious movements such as the one that Khomeini led, or the one that Pat Robertson in America has fought for. But their influence and attraction are in large part due to their claims to be working for a society that systematically applies the principles it claims to honour or that it should honour. Their opponents regularly see them as movements that reject rationality in favour of irrational belief. But they also are successful because they seem to raise the possibility that individuals can live with intellectual integrity, without violating their standards of rationality, because they not only encourage individuals to deduce the course of action they deem right from a systematic viewpoint and to follow this course of action, but they also create the social conditions under which such actions will be rewarded.

5 The attempt to construct a closed society as social pathology

In addition to the calls for movement in the direction of a closed society that are based in plausible but misguided attempts to increase abilities, there are also pathological quests to move in this direction. Such movements differ from those discussed above in that they drastically lose critical capacity to judge the success of their efforts. They attempt to impose some pure intellectual structure on society regardless of the costs of this imposition. They are characterized by fanaticism, but this fanaticism is not that of individual members of society but of groups whose individual members — beyond their involvement in such a movement — need not be mentally ill. The fact that they need not be so is puzzling but clear. After such movements die, as in the collapse of Nazi Germany, there was no massive increase in the number of mentally ill people, that there had to have been if all those who supported this social pathology were themselves mentally ill.

Examples of such pathological demands are the crusades, Nazi Germany, Mao's Cultural Revolution, Khomeini's Iran, Serbia under Milosovič and Osama bin Laden's movement. Social pathology of this sort can be generated and encouraged by the religious and political fanaticism of a few, which can then catch fire and cannot be stopped until they burn themselves out in exhaustion and/or wars with their enemies. The core of their appeal, however, still lies in their response to the fear of the loss of rationality. In the case of pathological demands, however, this does not mean so much the loss of individuals' ability to conduct their lives rationally, that is, to pose problems, to construct solutions, and to implement them with some acceptable degree of success, but the sense that the system itself must be rendered more rational, that is, more systematic and in accord with accepted principles. The chief characteristic of the pathological demand for closed societies is the demand that the system be pure without regard for the consequences. Such a social pathology has thus much of the same qualities as that of the paranoiac in that it is characterized by the demand to keep or realize some specific system at all costs.

Such a social pathology may be deliberately introduced as Mao Tze Tung's revolution in the 1960s shows. The persons who induced it did not necessarily share in it but wanted to use it for other political aims, above all to maintain power. The first communist revolution in China was a real, but misguided, attempt to create a new and better society. The second was a pathological attempt to hold on to an unsuccessful framework at all costs by making it pure. Social pathology of this sort is so unnatural that it cannot subsist without enormous effort. This exertion is similar to that labour that the individual paranoiac has to invest in his striving to protect his private system. Under normal circumstances individuals do not, however, have interest in this endeavour, which greatly limits the capacity to maintain it. For this reason pathological closed societies are quite unnatural and unstable. Khomeini introduced this kind of social pathology into Iran, but this extremism has run its course. It can no longer be maintained with the dramatic means of a pathological movement. Those who are interested in retaining their power are desperately seeking other means of maintaining a closed society.

The distinction between demands for movement in the direction of closed societies that are pathological, on the one hand, and those demands that are due to real interests in improvement but that have as unintended consequences the movement in the direction of a closed society, on the other hand, is not sharp, because pathological reactions also contain elements of rationality. The two kinds of movements share the same goal of making society systematic, simple, and clear. We may characterize the pathological attempts as those attempts that effectively block critical appraisals of alternatives and their consequences. The difference between a pathological path to a closed society and a non-pathological one is nevertheless not merely a matter of degree. Any police state can gradually increase control of the press and free speech of all sorts to this or that degree. The pathological movements use members of society to exercise self-censorship of a radical sort. The Red Guards, the Islamic virtue police, and the SS are examples. In these social situations large numbers of individuals mutually encourage each other to demand some radical and final solution without any interest among them as to whether the satisfaction of the demands made will improve the lot of individuals. The construction of a closed society in Chile is a quite different phenomenon from the Crusades or Nazi Germany or Serbia under Milosovič or Osama bin Laden. The spiralling out of control, that characterizes this social pathology, occurs when one demand for radical action leads to the next as it is recognized that purity has not yet been attained and/or established.

6 Conclusion: the quest to maintain existing open societies and to increase their number today

Although the evil of a closed society and the dangers of slipping into one are clear, it is not the case that we simply need to combat a known danger. We have to understand how individual closed societies arise and take measures to stop the development of each, before some movement gains so much momentum that it cannot be stopped. The fight against closed societies might be furthered by using the framework proposed here to pose problems about how institutions may be reformed to prevent closed societies instead of moralizing about how individuals should be autonomous. There are at least three kinds of such problems. Firstly, there are questions of how the rationality of individuals may be improved by reforming the social structures in which individuals pose and seek to solve their problems without moving in the direction of closed societies. Secondly, there are questions of how misunderstanding of the needs of problem solvers may lead to the promotion of closed societies as an unintended consequence and how this unintended consequence may be avoided. Thirdly, there are questions as to how socio-pathologies that demand closed societies arise and how they may be combated. All of these questions presume that there are rational aspects of the various appeals and paths to the construction of closed societies that may be understood, and that this understanding may be used to combat them.

Bibliography

Agassi, J. (1977). *Towards a Rational Philosophical Anthropology*. The Hague: Martinus Nijhoff.

Fried, Y. & Agassi, J. (1976). *Paranoia: A Study in Diagnosis*. Dordrecht: D. Reidel Publishing Company.

Myrdal, G., with Sterner, R. & Rose, A. (1944). *An American Dilemma: The Negro Problem in America*. London & New York: Harper & Brothers Publishers.

Popper, K. R. (1945). *The Open Society and Its Enemies*. London: George Routledge & Sons. 5th edition 1966. London: Routledge & Kegan Paul.

18

Can Popper's Ideas Enlighten Postmodern Technoscience?

Raphael Sassower

1 Preface

It would be interesting to take a poll of all the so-called postmodernists and all the technoscientists and figure out if they even know who Karl Popper was and what he wrote. Even if they know of his ideas, since some have become commonplace, like the problem of self-fulfilling prophecies, they probably would not be able to attribute them to him. So, the first quandary regarding Karl Popper and his ideas has to do with whether his ideas about epistemology, science, and methodology are to be considered part of the establishment of the twentieth century, however defined, or a radical rejection of this same establishment. This remains a mystery and a politically loaded question. His disciples, however defined, would proudly admit that his views are critical of the academic establishment and therefore his political cache has been confined to small quarters in Austria and the United Kingdom. Even the ideas of Carl Hempel, Robert Merton, and Thomas Kuhn have had a greater exposure and coverage, even popularity, than Popper's, and conferences in their honour, and academic positions for their disciples have been abundant. The same would be true for some of Popper's students, such as Paul Feyerabend, whose contributions to the philosophy of science pale by comparison to his mentor. His detractors, on the other hand, would say that Popper's ideas fit well within the establishment, and that despite his protestations to the contrary, his ideas fail to shed new light on anything significant in the history of science. Regardless of whose side you are on, you get the impression that investing in the Popper Stock Portfolio is a bad academic investment.

The second problem regarding Popper's prestige and general reputation has to do with those who would say that this is not true, as the case of George Soros illustrates. According to Soros, it was the ideas of Popper that inspired him to pursue an investment strategy in the global economy that earned him an enormous fortune. What is so tricky about Popper's ideas, whether employed by Soros or by the run of the mill academic, is that they vary greatly, cover a wide spectrum of subject matters and areas of research, and remain technical in the most European pedantic sense, that most of the world remains ignorant of their value. The richness and broadness of Popper's ideas have allowed, once again, his detractors to dismiss him as a reactionary conservative neo-liberal and his admirers to hail him as a democratic liberal visionary.

And here is a third caveat regarding Popper's ideas. While his *Open Society and Its Enemies* (1945) became a best-seller among the intelligentsia because of its indictment of central figures and texts in the history of ideas in regards to the social and political views they advocated, his other texts on science seemed devoid of any political message. Yet, to understand Popper's ideas at all, it is crucial to appreciate the political dimension of his ideas on science, the scientific community, the progress of scientific inquiry, and the quest for putative truth. To fail to make these connections is to fail to understand what contributions Popper has made in the past century.

2 Feminist critiques of science and of Popper

It is fascinating to find connections between seemingly unrelated areas of analysis in the intellectual arena, as is the case between feminist critiques of science and Popper. On the face of it Popper represents the standard, old-fashioned logocentrist view of science, as far as feminists are concerned. He is enslaved to the importance of logic and rationality, some form of reductionist analysis of the facts, and a realist commitment to what is out there. According to the standard view of twentieth-century philosophy of science, he seems to have failed to appreciate the so-called fluidity of reality (everything is in flux) and how it is socially constructed (selective modelling of reality). The social constructivists (from Marx to the Edinburgh group and some feminists) claim that those in positions of power manipulate their representations to fit their political agendas and conform to their respective self-interests and cultural indebtedness. By contrast, feminists, such as Donna Haraway (Haraway 1991), have broader concerns and a more sensitive approach to the lessons of science and the ways in which these lessons are produced, distributed, and consumed.

When I originally drew attention to some affinity between Haraway's 'situated knowledge' and Popper's 'situational logic' (Sassower 1995, Chapter 5), I was hoping to bridge the intellectual and political gaps that run between them, so as to illustrate how they can benefit from each other. When I considered the similarity between their concerns, their views, and their proposals, I offered three hypotheses against which to test my conjecture. First, epistemology is politicized so that in both cases an engagement with methodological issues, such as objectivity, empiricism, rationality, and criticism, illustrates a certain political commitment responding to the dominant ideology of the scientific community, such as the self-policing functions of the community. In short, there is a certain radical and critical element in the approach both demonstrate regarding the sacred cows of the scientific enterprise. Perhaps a significant disclaimer is in place at this juncture. Different people slaughter different sacred cows, and even when they slaughter the same cows they may do so for different reasons. My interest in looking for similarities between some Popperians and some feminists need not be construed as an attempt to obliterate their differences or their ultimate agendas.

My second hypothesis had to do with transcending situatedness in both cases, so that in their respective ways (in their senses of situational analysis) they attempt to set up more appropriate methods of inquiry and a better conceptual framework for science. In their own ways they try to do the same thing: overcome the limitations of Baconian inductivism and the strictures of logical positivism in order to account more fully for the involvement of humans in the scientific enterprise. It is not that induction as a method of inquiry and a means for collecting data and postulating conclusions is fully mistaken and useless. Rather, this method needs revisions (as it has received over the years), and ultimately it still remains inadequate, as Hume already noted, for anything but a guideline for one's customs and habits. The data collected in the name of science or within the scientific enterprise remain, therefore, imperfect, incomplete, sometimes inconsistent, and always open for new conjectures, different tests, and multiple interpretations. Likewise, and even though one is a liberal and the other a socialist, they expect their contributions to provide a more equitable political environment where human rights are protected and human aspirations are respected.

The third hypothesis had to do with the different ways in which Popper and Haraway must remain true to their ideological commitments and therefore are bound to situate their versions of transcendence, of a successor science, if you wish. In this context, then, they are both politicizing epistemology — they have an agenda, a clear set of values they refuse to ignore. As such, they have both given up, if only marginally, a strong claim for objectivity and value-neutrality in the classical sense of disembodied inquirers who are in their laboratory islands with moats that keep their cultures out of sight and out of mind.

Instead of rehearsing the details of both Popper's view of situated rationality and Haraway's situated epistemology, it should be noted that their quest for achieving a more accurate picture of the world is a quest in the long tradition of the Enlightenment's zeal for progress and individual liberation. These, in turn, are values that need a set of political conditions and guarantees to ensure eventual fulfillment. Furthermore, as Ian Jarvie (1967) so aptly comments, in order to contextualize the logic of a situation, whether perceived by the participant or an observer (or both) an appeal must be made to a culture. The culture itself is open to multiple interpretations, so that one layer of interpretive scheme is layered on top of an another, preventing a simple, straightforward reductionist move that would lead to an unambiguous set of answers.

But by now we have moved a long way from the confines of the logical positivists with their protocol sentences and their correspondence theory of meaning and truth. By now we are at the gates of the social sciences, having jumped the fence of the radical demarcation between science and pseudo-science. We already allowed Popper's metaphysics to play a role in scientific investigations, and allowed the concept of scientific progress to guide our methodological choices. We even admitted along the way that values (moral principles) do play a role in how we conduct our research and how we disseminate it to others. In short, we are in the camp of critics, all of whom seem to use logic and rationality, despite some forgivable lapses of intellectual indiscrimination. So, before I move into postmodernism, let me recapitulate and explain the gist of my interest here.

Many support criticism as a method of inquiry and as a tool to avoid foolhardy orthodoxy. If it is not considered a means to uncover the truths of the world, it is at least a means to uncover deceit and misguided beliefs. Popper's innovation in this arena was the use of criticism to combat the problems of induction — to push the intellectual community to appreciate how selective confirmation (from the historical records or from observation reports) is inherently misleading and mistaken. Haraway and other feminists understand, along Popperian lines (Popper 1959), how useful criticism is to fight against the scientific establishment as well as to further their own political concerns. Lyotard and other postmodernists similarly understand, along Popperian lines (Popper 1963), how useful criticism remains when they unravel orthodox views or hierarchies. In their respective and divergent ways they remain true to the Socratic method, now in its refined Popperian version and applied to scientific questions, that is, questions of ontology, metaphysics, and epistemology.

3 Popper the postmodern technoscientist

To describe postmodern technoscience we must describe technoscience first and then postmodernism and in both cases find the ways in which Popper could fit these definitions or classifications. Technoscience is a late twentieth-century term used by Jean-François Lyotard (1979) as well as Stephen Toulmin as early as the 1970s to describe the inter-relatedness and mutual dependence of science and technology. Rather than understand technology as applied science and science as the theoretical foundation of technological developments (as Popper 1957 has), there has been an appreciation of the rich historical record (as in the case of Pierre Duhem 1908) in which technological innovation led to scientific breakthrough, and in which scientific theories can be tested and reformulated only because of engineering insights (as shown by Agassi 1971, especially Chapter 3). I shall come back to this issue in a minute.

Postmodernism can be characterized as incorporating the following three elements. First, it denies any privileging whatsoever, so that any claim or principle or idea or theory is on par with any other claim. No matter their origins and current credibility, they ought to have their day in the intellectual courts. Second, it insists on the fluidity of adherence to tradition, so that pre-modern, modern, a-modern, and postmodern methods of inquiry should all be consulted and incorporated into the knowledge framework on which decisions are based. This means, for example, that romantic ideals are not contrasted with those of the Enlightenment rationalists but are interwoven with them. And third, it refuses to reduce all ideas and observations, all claims and theories, to one set of foundations, one set of principles. In this sense, then, postmodernists insist on contextualizing judgments to particular frameworks and settings so that the appropriateness of the criteria by which something is judged will be examined as well.

This brief summary does injustice to the many variants of postmodernism and to the many variations on the themes mentioned above. Nor does it account for the artistic and architectural antecedents of the movement, whether Robert Ventura is mentioned or others (for more on this see Hoesterey 1991). The French and the American prototypes differ in many respects, and it would not further our discussion here to discern their differences. Likewise, there are those who still insist that there is no such thing as postmodernism: either it is a reincarnation of some forms of romanticism or it is a faddish misconception whose fashionable acceptance is politically irresponsible and epistemologically misguided. Even among its most familiar advocates, postmodernism has been mocked, derided, and critically presented. Here is Lyotard (1983, p. 136):

> Is postmodernity the pastime of an old man who scrounges in the garbage-heap of finality looking for leftovers. . . . and who turns this into the glory of his novelty, into his promise of change?

Yet, despite this line of questioning and self-doubt, I wish to plead for some sensitivity to the salient points one can glean from this way of doing business. Furthermore, I wish to argue that Popper the conservative empiricist, the realist with an approximation of the Truth, and the strict rationalist, does exhibit postmodernist symptoms in every chapter of every book he has ever written. Likewise, postmodernists deploy Popper's insights and are influenced by his contributions without giving him credit. Having said this, I do not mean it in the trite sense that anyone's words and ideas might contain in them the seeds of postmodern gestures or critical rationalism. Rather, I mean it in a more profound sense that to be postmodern in relation to anything scientific, for example, is to be a critical rationalist in the Popperian tradition of Agassi and Jarvie. That is, to be critical of the scientific establishment is a social, political, economic, and moral posture that lowers the threshold for debate and dismisses the gatekeepers.

For example, think of his landmark recommendation to provide conjectures and falsify them: is not this a way to disallow privileging? Is he not advocating the egalitarian principle of listening to every conjecture, however foolish, and allowing anyone, however meek, to refute it? Is he not a liberal champion of equal opportunity to conjecture and falsify? Amidst the rich history of the aristocratic engagement with and subsidy of the sciences in the United Kingdom, attention was paid to outsiders and to foreigners, even to Jews, as possible contributors to the advancement of the sciences. Likewise, it was Popper who reminded us to go back to the pre-Socratic thinkers to bolster his methodological proposals. Juxtaposing ancient Greek ideas to the context of twentieth-century philosophy of science was adventurous and bold. It was a journey similar to the one he took when examining the history of political ideas in order to formulate his principles of an open society. Old ideas were treated with the same care as the new; re-examining their currency against a tradition that accepted them as if no reinterpretations were ever warranted was a novel and fruitful approach. And finally, though one could find a reductionist and heavy-handed rationalist foundation in all of his works, Popper is still the one speaking of putative truths and not of an absolute Truth. He is still claiming that the process of approximating the truths we might never fully know is itself a worthwhile and epistemologically significant process in the progress of the sciences.

Of course some would argue against everything said so far about the affinity of Popper to the postmodern way of thinking. For some, Popperian rationalism is anathema to postmodern irrationalism; to others it would be the way in which for Popper there are clear criteria by which to choose among competing theories while the postmodernists seem to let anything be equal in meaning and importance to anything else. But before we continue on this line of fruitless comparison, it might be more fruitful to tease out those elements that do have some similarity and some affinity between the two ways of thinking so as to translate and bridge between intellectual gaps. The reason for doing so is more political than epistemological for two reasons. First, it would underscore the fact that every epistemological conviction and choice belies a political or ideological commitment of sorts, and second, it would create alliances and provide a more fertile critical landscape in which to cultivate new ideas. So, even if we agree that postmodernists such as Lyotard have an affinity with Popper and his ideas to the extent that they use rational means to make their points and that they all believe in the value of critique, there is a contested issue at hand: relativism. It is this issue that brings Popper's ideas to the brink of my stretched comparison.

If relativism is traditionally contrasted with objectivity and absolutism, and if relativism is associated with postmodernism, and if relativists are accused of being irrational in choices of criteria of demarcation and decision making, then how can anyone in his right mind bring Popper close to this way of thinking? Perhaps the answer has more to do with the kind of relativism associated with postmodernism as opposed to recasting Popper's ideas in a relativist framework. Perhaps Lyotard's questions about the Holocaust can help highlight some of these concerns.

4 Lyotard, the Holocaust, and Popper

If one were to adhere to the postmodern injunction to judge, as Lyotard suggests, everything case by case, that is, to contextualize every set of conditions and provide the criteria according to which they ought to be assessed, then one would be unable to appeal to some overarching principles or foundations. In short, one could be in the position of being unable to condemn the Holocaust. But the Holocaust must be condemned — but according to what principles?

What objective and universal principles could be agreed upon? And what about the facts of the matter, namely, the horrible reality of Auschwitz? As Lyotard says (1988, p. 58):

> But, with Auschwitz, something new has happened in history. ... the facts, the testimonies. ... the documents ... and the names, finally the possibility of various kinds of phrases whose conjunction makes reality, all this has been destroyed as much as possible.

Following Fackenheim, Lyotard admits that 'Auschwitz is the most real of realities in this respect' (ibidem). As a label to a whole discourse of the Holocaust, Auschwitz suspends and empties the speculative elements of language and its interpretive ambiguities (ibidem, p. 88). The facts and testimonies, the observational reports scientists worry about and continue to contest, take on a new meaning in the case of the Holocaust. Can the fact of the termination of six million Jews be challenged? Of course it is. Can it be substantiated? By what methods? Are the criteria themselves universal or subjective? What status and legitimacy should we give to survivors? Should we apply the criteria of the Royal Society, those of Bacon, or those of the Vienna Circle?

Before we know it, we slip from the esoteric debates of the academic community to the front-page news and popularity of Spielberg's film *Shindler's List*. Where do facts end and the fictions begin? If a movie-maker could set a stage with gas chambers — a fictionalized rendition of unimaginable acts of human humiliation and destruction, why not claim that the whole affair was nothing but a Jewish fiction to solicit sympathy and destroy the good reputation of National Socialism? Besides, if relativism should determine everything from ontology to epistemology and metaphysics, then why not listen only to the narratives of the Nazis and accept their right of national eugenics? As with any kind of representation, as Lyotard reminds us, 'representing "Auschwitz" in images and words. ... must remain unrepresentable' (1988, p. 26).

In order to answer these questions, and in order to modify his general endorsement of the view of contextualizing decisions and assessing the criteria by which they are made, Lyotard comes up with his view of Auschwitz. For him the Holocaust is the litmus test for the cavalier reinterpretation of language, facts, and the reality they attempt to describe. For him, the downfall of a postmodern critique would be its inability to condemn the Holocaust, to show that no matter what context or what language game one were to use, the ethical dimension of such a reality would become clear no matter who observed or when it was observed. And here Popper and Lyotard (Lyotard & Thebaud 1979) could come closer to each other's views. But do they?

Some would say that if Lyotard is a relativist, then he fails his own test for he must either uphold standards, foundations, or a set of moral principles, or relinquish any such appeal. If he is not a relativist after all, then he is already in the rationalist, Popperian camp, and then obviously their views are close. So, perhaps the more precise phrasing of the relationship between these thinkers' ideas should be: though their starting points and convictions

seem diametrically opposed on the face of it, once they examine some difficult
situations and pieces of reality, they find themselves making metaphysical
compromises that brings them closer together. Popper moves towards con-
textualization without relinquishing his adherence to rationality and critique,
and Lyotard moves toward a rational assessment of the criteria by which the
context or situation are judged without relinquishing his case-by-case epistemology.

Though Popper doesn't address the Holocaust directly in his philosophical
discussions of science and its progress, and though Popper allows a great deal
of latitude to the veracity and ultimate credibility of any claim, his method
remains critical and rational — it probes while remaining skeptical; it conjectures while inviting falsification; it suggests examining the logic of the situation (as we have seen in the comparison with Haraway's situated knowledge
above). It is in this sense of openness that it informs the postmodern turn.
Lyotard relies on reality and refuses to deny it (unlike some more radical social
constructivists in the British Isles or their French counterparts). He worries
that without the testimonies of survivors and the truths associated with their
memories of sufferings, the very facts of the Holocaust would be challenged. In
short, Lyotard worries about the political and ethical consequences of poorly
or inappropriately applying the postmodern insights.

The moral of the story, then, is threefold. First, epistemological pronounce-
ments are political in the sense that they belie antecedent ideological commitments and have political consequences. Put differently, there is a short
distance between the philosophy of science and the Holocaust (whether we
speak of eugenics, or of facts and observations, reality, meaning, and truth).
Second, to refuse an appeal to ultimate principles or reduce all knowledge
claims to one static foundation is not to refuse making any reasonable appeal to guidelines and criteria of judgment. As long as any appeal remains
open-ended and invites ongoing criticism and revision, then there is hope that
some progress in improving the human condition will take place (because the
discourse or debate itself will be rational). And third, to be a philosopher
(whether of science or of history) without appreciating the ethical dimension
of every intellectual choice one makes is to do injustice to the very notion of
being a philosopher. Popper's open society was not limited to the political
arena, but extends to the scientific community. I wish at times he would have
extended it to the academic community so as to test the applicability and
efficacy of his ideas. Are we willing to invite criticism and change our views in
every arena? Do we assume that rationality of some sort could be the common
ground on which to hold our debates? Are we interested in applying insights
from one arena to another? Do we welcome junior faculty and students to
falsify our statements and opinions? Probably not enough for either Popper
or Lyotard.

Bibliography

Agassi, J. (1971). *Faraday as Natural Philosopher*. Chicago & London: University of Chicago Press.

Haraway, D. J. (1991). *Simians, Cyborgs, and Women: The Reinvention of Nature*. London: Routledge.

Duhem, P. M. M. (1908). *To Save the Phenomena: An Essay on the Idea of Physical Theory from Plato to Galileo*. English translation, 1969. Chicago: University of Chicago Press.

Hoesterey, I., editor (1991). *Zeitgeist in Babel: The Postmodernist Controversy*. Bloomington: Indiana University Press.

Jarvie, I. C. (1967). 'The Objectivity of Criticism in the Arts'. *Ratio* **9**, pp. 67-83. Reprinted in J. Agassi & I. C. Jarvie, editors (1987), pp. 201-216. *Rationality: The Critical View*. The Hague: Martinus Nijhoff.

Lyotard, J.-F. (1979). *The Postmodern Condition: A Report on Knowledge*. English translation, 1984. Minneapolis: University of Minnesota Press.

—— (1988). *Heidegger and 'the Jews'*. English translation, 1990. Minneapolis: University of Minnesota Press.

—— (1983). *The Differend: Phrases in Dispute*. English translation, 1988. Minneapolis: University of Minnesota Press.

Lyotard, J.-F. & Thebaud, J.-L. (1979). *Just Gaming*. English translation, 1985. Minneapolis: University of Minnesota Press.

Popper, K. R. (1945). *The Open Society and Its Enemies*. London: George Routledge & Sons. 5th edition 1966. London: Routledge & Kegan Paul.

—— (1957). *The Poverty of Historicism*. London: Routledge & Kegan Paul.

—— (1959). *The Logic of Scientific Discovery*. London: Hutchinson.

—— (1963). *Conjectures and Refutations: The Growth of Scientific Knowledge*. London: Routledge & Kegan Paul. 5th edition 1989. London: Routledge.

Sassower, R. (1995). *Cultural Collisions: Postmodern Technoscience*. London: Routledge.

19

Karl Popper's 'Third Way'
Public Policies for Europe and the West

Marcello Pera

1 Introduction

As far as I see them, the fundamental principles of Popper's philosophy lie in two main ideas: the freedom of human beings and the value of critical discussion.

Popper thought that individuals are free from any complete determination, be it physical, biological, genetic, or historical. Thanks to the objective World 3 — which is an intellectual artefact autonomous from World 1's material conditions and interactive with World 2's psychological states — individuals transcend the matter they are made of.

Popper believed also that the 'critical rational method must not be mistaken for a method of proof ...; nor is it a method which always secures agreement. Its value lies, rather, in the fact that participants in a discussion will, to some extent, change their mind, and part as wiser men'.[1] And this, in its turn, presupposes and fosters the autonomy and freedom of individuals.

Popper worked out his two simple ideas in an extraordinarily creative way, and applied them to almost every field of culture. One of his most outstanding philosophical achievements — the methodology of falsificationism — is no more than an 'application' of the Socratic method of critical discussion, as Popper himself writes in *The Logic of Scientific Discovery*.[2] And the same holds true for his social and political philosophy. This provides his intellectual contribution with a systematic character, which makes him a giant in the contemporary philosophical setting, which too often is devoted to sterile specialization.

Popper wrote his major works in a cultural atmosphere very far from ours. The main targets of his criticisms were essentialism and totalitarianism. Today, essentialism has been replaced by relativism and totalitarianisms have been definitely defeated, at least in the versions that Popper could analyse. In his 'Intellectual Autobiography', Popper wrote that *The Poverty of Historicism* and *The Open Society* were his 'war effort'.[3] Popper won his war, and

---

[1] Popper (1954), p. 352.
[2] Cp. Popper (1959), § 8, note *1, and § 11, note 3.
[3] Popper (1974), p. 91.

we all must be grateful to him for his contribution in defence of liberty and democracy. However, in today's radically changed cultural setting, the open society nowadays faces new challenges. Can Popper's work help us to cope with them? I believe that his thoughts are still a source of inspiration. I believe also that in his works we can find a useful method to approach, and possibly to solve, some of contemporary societies' main problems.

I shall try to substantiate this claim through a close examination of two issues that, in my view, are among the most relevant for Europe and the West.

The first issue concerns the relationships between state intervention and market economy in the light of the current welfare state crisis. This issue is related to the much debated question as to whether Popper was a democratic socialist, as many maintain, or a new rightist, as others claim. I shall try to argue that he was neither of them. In my view he was a *liberal conservative.*

The second issue concerns the relationship between the West and other cultures in the light of such phenomena as immigration and religious fundamentalism. This issue is related to the question of pluralism and to its degeneration — which unfortunately is rather widespread in the West —, that is relativism. Here, too, I shall argue that Popper's position is original and much more suitable than the socialist and new rightist ones.

Since the fall of the Berlin Wall, there have been political leaders and intellectuals especially in Europe who are looking for a 'third way' between communism and capitalism, socialism and democracy, state intervention and free market economy. To the best of my knowledge, the paths that have been explored are conceptually verbal and politically disappointing. Popper had already found his 'third way'. He had put forward and elaborated upon a solution before the events. Since, in my view, his solution is satisfactory and promising for Europe, I shall try to explore and recommend it.

2 A new agenda for public policy

Let me then start with my first issue, the relationship between state intervention and market economy. Everybody knows how crucial this problem is for most states of the European Union.

Popper defends state interventionism in the economy on the grounds of what he calls the 'paradox of freedom'. This paradox shows the necessity of a legal system of (negative) rights. Without a legal system, freedom is a value that defeats itself, since the stronger could easily deprive the weaker of his or her freedom.

Popper applies this very same line of reasoning to the economic realm. He writes:[4]

> I believe that [the paradox of freedom], originally meant to apply to the realm of brute-force, ... must be applied to the economic realm also. Even if the state protects its citizens from being bullied by physical violence (as it does, in principle,

---

[4]Popper (1945), Chapter 17, § III.

under the system of unrestrained capitalism), it may defeat our ends by its failure to protect them from the misuse of economic power. In such a state, the economically strong is still free to bully one who is economically weak, and to rob him of his freedom. Under these circumstances, unlimited economic freedom can be just as self-defeating as unlimited physical freedom, and economic power may be nearly as dangerous as physical violence.

This is where Popper's state interventionism comes from: the need to defend and preserve freedom. But as soon as the state intervention is justified this way, it seems there is no strong reason to prevent the state from intervening on a more general scale: 'Pain, suffering, injustice, and their prevention, these are the eternal problems of public morals, the "agenda" of public policy'.[5]

If this is the state's agenda, we should conclude that the author of *The Open Society* was a democratic socialist. I actually agree with Bryan Magee when he claims that 'the *young* Popper worked out, as no one else has ever done, what the philosophical foundations of democratic socialism should be'.[6] However, Popper's writings, like any great scholar's, allow a variety of interpretations. We should not be intimidated by what he claimed or believed, since what matters is the content of his claims, which belongs to the Popperian World 3. As he used to say, 'I do not believe in belief'. In the same way, I do not believe in Magee's, and perhaps the young Popper's, view that he was committed to democratic socialism.

By opposing this interpretation, I am not interested in offering the would-be 'orthodox' or 'correct' interpretation of Popper. Although I shall argue that considering Popper a liberal conservative is much more coherent with his writings and the evolution of his thinking, I do not want to embark on an exegetic work. I would rather like to outline the main characteristics of, and suggest a possible consensus on, a new view, a really viable 'third way', between, on the one hand, state intervention policies, which are maintained by socialists, and, on the other hand, the pre-eminence of individuals, which is advocated by the New Right followers.

3 Popper's conservatism

To set out Popper's 'third way', it is first necessary to reflect upon the role he ascribed to state intervention.

---

[5] Popper (1945), Chapter 24, § III.

[6] Magee (1974), p. 84; italics mine. In this regard, see also Hacohen (2000). Hacohen distinguishes between the 'committed young socialist' Popper and the 'old, more conservative' Popper. However, following his historical reconstruction it is unclear why Popper changed his mind about an issue of such an importance. Along with a 'negative' influence of Hayek on Popper, Hacohen seems to believe that Popper's conservatism is mainly due to personal or psychological factors, foreign to the main thrust of his philosophy. I maintain that it is more sensible to see a conceptual (that is, strictly theoretical) continuity in the evolution of Popper's thought.

As is well known, Popper distinguishes two kinds of interventionism. He says:[7]

> the first is that of designing a 'legal framework' of protective institutions (laws restricting the powers of the owner of an animal, or of a landowner, are examples). The second is that of empowering organs of the state to act — within certain limits — as they consider necessary for achieving the ends laid down by the rulers for the time being. We may describe the first procedure as 'institutional' or 'indirect' intervention, and the second as 'personal' or 'direct' intervention.

Popper adds that the first interventionism is much better than the second, since '[i]t alone makes it possible to apply the method of trial and error to our political actions' (ibidem). Therefore piecemeal social engineering is basically conceived in terms of long-term institutional policies. 'Personal' interventionism is potentially much more dangerous than its institutional counterpart because it directly leads to an increase in the state power and bureaucracy. As he writes, 'state power must always remain a dangerous though necessary evil'.[8]

These ideas provide Popper with the theoretical background that allows him to oppose both the minimal state view and the socialist doctrine. Let us see why.

The minimal state or New Right doctrine leaves *no* room for state intervention and public policies. In this view, the political game has only two players, the state, whose only function is to secure people's safety, and the individual, who is allowed to be free to do whatever he or she wishes (including, for example, not going to school, if he or she wants, or taking drugs, if he or she likes). Think of the way Robert Nozick characterizes the minimal state in the last chapter of *Anarchy, State, and Utopia* (1974). There is no need for a critical debate either *about* the minimal state, because it is derived from a general theory of property rights, or *within* the minimal state, because people are busy joining and leaving specific communities, according to their own tastes, values, and wishes, and every issue reduces to such questions as 'if you like this, you may join our community' or 'if you do not like this, you may leave'.[9]

On the other hand, the socialist doctrine leaves *much* room for state intervention. Here, too, the players of the game are two, the state and the individual, but the view is different. Since individuals, once left alone, get poor, unequal, hurt, sad, and so on, the state is given the function of balancing the situation and public policies are devised in order to make people, equal, wealthy, happy, and so on.

Popper's view was different. As I have said, his position can be depicted as that of a liberal conservative. And this is so because of the role that, according to him, is played by traditions in society. Let me expand this point.

---

[7]Popper (1945), American edition (1950), and 2nd UK edition (1952), Chapter 17, § VII.
[8]Popper (1945), Chapter 17, § VI.
[9]Cp. Nozick (1974), Chapter 10.

Popper was a rationalist, and rationalists do not generally trust traditions, since, as Popper himself noted, they want to judge the merits and demerits of institutions with their own brains. However, Popper realized that such attitude is naïve and even dangerous because it transforms rationalism into what Hayek called 'constructivism', that is to say, the idea that institutions and social formations are the result of human design.[10]

This kind of rationalism must be rejected for at least two good reasons. First, it does not recognize that social institutions are very often unintended results of intentional human actions. Second, human beings, rationalists included, are always immersed in a tradition. We can free ourselves from a tradition, or more likely from part of it, but whenever we do this we end up accepting a different, or modified, tradition.

By themselves, these arguments do not make Popper a conservative, but in his paper 'Towards a Rational Theory of Tradition' he adds a new element that gives a strong conservative flavour to his philosophy.[11]

Popper claims that no institution can work properly without an underlying tradition that supports it. Furthermore, he notes that the beginning of a new tradition is a rather complex matter. A new tradition cannot be created by the mere will of a legislator, as traditions concern people's attitudes and their ways of behaviour.[12] It is then exceedingly naïve to believe that specific traditions, born and evolved in a certain social environment, can be easily transplanted into another. (Incidentally, this explains why Popper harshly criticized Gorbachov's over-hasty attempt to introduce the market economy into the former Soviet Union.)

This view of Popper's leads to a drastic reduction in the scope of state intervention. As he, implicitly but clearly, notices, institutional piecemeal engineering cannot be effective without the relevant tradition that supports the institutional change. Since the beginning of new traditions is outside the scope of social engineering, what is left is the betterment of the *existing* institutions together with the protection of the *living* traditions supporting the existing institutions.

This is Popper's conservatism. Popper is a conservative because of the favour, the privilege, the pre-eminence, he accords to existing traditions. And this is Popper's 'third way'. Like democratic socialists, Popper admits state intervention, but, unlike them, he limits it to those public policies that are directed to the betterment of those existing institutions — such as schools, universities, churches, hospitals, unions, professional organizations, and so on — that promote individual well-being. In the same way, like the new rightists, Popper emphasizes individual freedom, but, unlike them, he leaves room for public policies.

---

[10]See, for instance, Hayek (1970).

[11]Cp. Popper (1949).

[12]The role played by traditions in Popper's thought has been deeply explored by Shearmur (1996). However, Shearmur tries to associate Popper with Nozick and the New Right (see especially Chapter 5). As I have already claimed, I have a different view on this point.

4 Popper's paternalism

There is another reason why Popper can be taken as a conservative, namely his paternalism, which, again, is linked to his state interventionism.

The word 'paternalism' sounds shocking for classical liberalism. For different reasons, Locke, Kant, and Tocqueville condemned the paternalistic state as morally illegitimate and dangerous for liberty. Of course, Popper was aware of this tradition. If, in spite of it, he decided to employ a term historically laden with negative values it was because he provocatively wished to question an ethical principle that is at the heart of the New Right libertarianism, namely Mill's principle, so-called: we should always give adults the liberty to act even when their acts are openly harmful to themselves.[13]

To be more precise, what Popper really rejects is not the principle as such, but the idea that it provides us with a general and clear-cut theory for public policy. For instance, he argues that paternalism is sensible in such cases as personal accident insurances, the sale of drugs, the possessions of arms, the use of safety belts, and the broadcasting of TV programmes.[14] Although Popper is very careful to add that paternalism can be as dangerous as any state intervention, what really matters is understanding that Popperian protectionism does not concern only traditions and institutions, but also, more directly, individuals' well-being.

With this, I hope I have substantiated the first part of my claim. If I am right, Popper has given us the theoretical background for defining a common agenda — the agenda of a 'third way' — in the realm of public policy.

5 The 'paradox of multi-ethnic societies'

I now move to my second issue, the relationship between the West and other cultures, which is another hot problem in Europe.

'What does the West believe in?', asked Popper in a minor but illuminating paper. His answer was: in the pluralism of its ideas, values, and traditions.[15]

If we carefully scrutinize this answer we soon realize that it is less trivial than it may appear at first glance. Popper is not simply suggesting that in Western societies individuals are accustomed to tolerating traditions different from their own, a claim that is true but disputable, since we know how much pain and suffering intolerance did cause in Europe. What Popper is suggesting is something more radical: We should encourage differences in tradition, for the West progresses only through the clash of different cultures. As he writes:[16]

> The population of Europe ... is the result of mass migrations. From time immemorial wave after wave of people have surged from the steppes of Central Asia and encountered earlier immigrants on the southern, south-eastern and particularly on the fissured western peninsulas of Asia, which we call Europe,

---

[13]Cp. Mill (1859).

[14]Cp. Popper (1992a).

[15]Cp. Popper (1958).

[16]Popper (1981), p. 121.

and disperse. The result is a linguistic, ethnic and cultural mosaic: a chaotic jumble, which cannot possibly be disentangled.

According to Popper, this chaos proved to be beneficial from several angles, since 'the value of a discussion depends largely upon the variety of the competing views. Had there been no Tower of Babel, we should invent it.'[17] Indeed, Greek civilization, together with scientific tradition, could have arisen only thanks to the conflict between different cultures and world views.

If we take this view seriously, we should look on immigration from extra-European countries without fear. Leaving aside economic factors, which I do not want to discuss here, immigration from countries with different cultural traditions may enrich the pluralistic tradition of Europe, and therefore we should be interested in fostering the development and growth of the immigrants' traditions. To give an actual example, together with state primary schools, we should allow the birth and growth of voluntary primary schools run by Jewish and Muslim communities, provided they are in accordance with the national rules of education and respect fundamental human rights.

Undoubtedly these proposals will give rise to a host of objections. Why should conservatives adopt policies that resemble those proposed by radical democrats? Don't we have our own traditions to foster and defend?

These objections misunderstand Popperian pluralism. They assume that pluralism presupposes a very thin moral framework, within which almost everything goes. On the contrary, pluralism requires a *thick* or *strong* morality, namely the morality of the tradition of critical discussion that characterizes science, which Popper takes as a model for the open society. This is the moral tradition that encourages tolerance and requires open-minded individuals. This is also the moral tradition that believes in critical debates as means to get nearer to truth and justice. This, simply, is the moral tradition of the West, within which we should integrate immigrants' traditions.

We are now in a position to understand the sort of relationship between the West and other cultures that Popper had in mind. Different cultural communities should be fostered through policies aiming to strengthen, not weaken, pluralism. To go back to our previous example, voluntary school students must be aware of different cultures. They must be open to dialogue and tolerant. Dogmatic or intolerant attitudes should be discouraged through appropriate curricula under public control.

Today, in our society pluralism is too often confused with relativism, which is in actual fact a degeneration of pluralism. Popper criticizes relativism not only on epistemological grounds but also because, according to him, it is immoral. Relativism makes truth and justice relative to a given conceptual framework or age or culture, and consequently it makes the search for truth and justice impossible, dialogue useless, discussion merely verbal or ornamental or rhetorical. Therefore the spread of relativism would disarm the

---

[17]Popper (1954), p. 352.

open society in the face of its enemies, such as totalitarians and fundament-
alists.[18]

Pluralism, however, is *not* relativism. Unlike relativism, the morality of
pluralism is full of positive contents and has limits. The open society cannot
be open without reservation. As Popper used to say, 'the West must defend
itself even with arms'. Here we find a paradox very close to the paradoxes of
freedom and tolerance. Unrestrained pluralism is self-defeating, since it would
accept and even foster traditions that are enemies of pluralism. We might call
it 'the paradox of pluralistic societies'.

I believe that this Popperian view is sensible. European inheritance lies
in its cultural diversity. This is also the case if we focus on the nationalities
that make up Europe. Everywhere in Europe the ideal of a single and organic
community is a mere fancy that should not be taken seriously, unless it offers
a pretext for reactionary policies in the name of an alleged common national
inheritance. It would be misleading, and even dangerous, to defend the West
on the grounds of a common hierarchy of values that nowhere exists in our
countries.

If the distinction between pluralism and relativism is clearly understood,
problems arising in multi-ethnic societies do not lie in their lack of a strong
common morality, but in the balanced institutional policies we need to cope
with the 'paradox of pluralistic societies'. If we allow an unrestrained immigration of communities hostile to pluralism we are doomed to lose *our* tradition.
If we block immigration of other communities we lose *their* traditions. What
we should do is to allow immigrants and make them accept the *culture of
pluralism.*

It is time to close. Popper was a tenacious optimist. He was convinced
that there is no historical necessity and the destiny of mankind depends on
us. He was convinced also that the West has sufficient moral and intellectual
resources to solve all of its major problems. Sometimes Popper appears to
be too optimistic. I am not sure we shall be up to dealing with the problems
Europe and the West must face. Yet if we succeed in this difficult task Popper's
intellectual legacy will no doubt prove to be valuable and possibly vital. This
is the greatest tribute we may pay to a scholar.

---

[18]On contemporary fundamentalism, see Popper (1992c).

Bibliography

Hacohen, M. H. (2000). *Karl Popper – The Formative Years, 1902-1945. Politics and Philosophy in Interwar Vienna*. Cambridge & elsewhere: Cambridge University Press.

Hayek F. A. (1970). 'The Errors of Constructivism'. Reprinted in F. A. Hayek (1978), pp. 3-22. *New Studies in Philosophy, Politics, Economics and the History of Ideas*. London: Routledge & Kegan Paul.

Magee B. (1974). *Popper*, London: Fontana/Collins.

Mill J. S. (1859). *On Liberty*. References are to D. Bronwich & G. Kateb, editors (2003). New Haven: Yale University Press.

Nozick R. (1974). *Anarchy, State, and Utopia*. New York: Basic Books.

Popper K. R. (1945). *The Open Society and Its Enemies*. London: George Routledge & Sons. 1st American edition 1950. Princeton NJ: Princeton University Press. 2nd UK edition 1952. London: Routledge & Kegan Paul. 5th edition 1966.

——— (1949). 'Towards a Rational Theory of Tradition'. In F. Watts, editor (1949), pp. 36-55. *The Rationalist Annual 1949*. London: Watts & Co. Reprinted as Chapter 4 of Popper (1963).

——— (1954). 'Public Opinion and Liberal Principles'. In Popper (1963), Chapter 17. Reprinted as Chapter 11 of Popper (1992b).

——— (1958). 'What does the West Believe in?'. In Popper (1992b), Chapter 15.

——— (1959). *The Logic of Scientific Discovery*. London: Hutchinson.

——— (1963). *Conjectures and Refutations*. London: Routledge & Kegan Paul. 5th edition 1989. London: Routledge.

——— (1974). 'Intellectual Autobiography'. In P. A. Schilpp (1974). pp. 1-181. *The Philosophy of Karl Popper*. La Salle, IL: Open Court. Reprinted as *Unended Quest*. 1976. London & Glasgow: Fontana/Collins.

——— (1981). 'On Culture Clash'. In Popper (1992b), Chapter 8.

——— (1992a). 'La lezione di questo secolo'. Edited by G. Bosetti. Venezia: Marsilio. English translation, 1997. *The Lesson of This Century: with Two Talks on Freedom and the Democratic State. Karl Popper Interviewed by Giancarlo Bosetti*. London: Routledge.

——— (1992b). *In Search of a Better World. Lectures and Essays from Thirty Years*. London: Routledge.

——— (1992c). 'Io, il Papa e Gorbaciov'. Interview with B. Spinelli. *La Stampa* (Turin). 9.iv.1992, 'Società e Cultura', p. 17.

Shearmur J. F. G. (1996). *The Political Thought of Karl Popper*. London: Routledge.

Index